BODIAN'S PUBLISHING DESK REFERENCE

*A Comprehensive Dictionary of
Practices and Techniques for Book and
Journal Marketing and Bookselling*

by Nat G. Bodian

Phoenix ● New York
ORYX PRESS
1988

The rare Arabian Oryx is believed to have inspired the myth of the unicorn. This desert antelope became virtually extinct in the early 1960s. At that time several groups of international conservationists arranged to have 9 animals sent to the Phoenix Zoo to be the nucleus of a captive breeding herd. Today the Oryx population is nearly 800, and over 400 have been returned to reserves in the Middle East.

Copyright © 1988 by Nat G. Bodian
Published by The Oryx Press
2214 North Central at Encanto
Phoenix, Arizona 85004-1483

Published simultaneously in Canada

Printed and Bound in the United States of America

♾ The paper used in this publication meets the minimum requirements of American National Standard for Information Science—Permanence of Paper for Printed Library Materials, ANSI Z39.48, 1984.

Library of Congress Cataloging-in-Publication Data

Bodian, Nat G., 1921–
  [Publishing desk reference]
  Bodian's publishing desk reference : a comprehensive dictionary of practices and techniques for book and journal marketing and bookselling / by Nat G. Bodian.
    p. cm.
  Includes index.
  ISBN 0-89774-454-3
    1. Publishers and publishing—Dictionaries. 2. Book industries and trade—Dictionaries. 3. Booksellers and bookselling—Dictionaries. 4. Books—Marketing—Dictionaries. 5. Periodicals, Publishing of —Dictionaries. I. Title.
  Z282.5.B63 1988
  070.5'0321—dc19   87-26130

Contents

Contents

Preface

Today, as never before, the bottom line in all publishing activity is tied to these three words: "Will it sell?" Without acceptance and resulting sale in the marketplace, no publishing activity can succeed. Consequently, all individuals involved in publishing—whether actively engaged in a marketing activity or in a related area leading up to marketing and selling—must be able to communicate on a timely and effective basis with one another if the marketing process is to work effectively. At the same time, those entering or active in marketing-related activities must not only be cognizant of the tools and state-of-the-art techniques that produce the best results, but must also know how to interpret and use them to greatest advantage.

Bodian's Publishing Desk Reference aims to serve this double purpose. On the one hand, it presents a broad overview of all the terms, jargon, tools, and techniques one is likely to encounter in book marketing and bookselling. On the other hand, it provides a sound, reliable, and succinct source of reference for those who may work or have interest in adjunct areas to book marketing and bookselling and need to know the terminology.

Almost 4,000 entries provide a comprehensive overview of facts, ideas, techniques, and approaches for workers at all levels of book and journal marketing and bookselling, as well as for the many others who make up the complex publishing industry. Together, the entries consititute a convenient resource, useful either as a stand-alone desk reference or as a complement to any other volume or collection on book marketing, bookselling, or book or journal publishing.

Coverage is comprehensive, encompassing knowledge and information drawn from all aspects and levels of book and journal marketing and bookselling. Here is the language of book and periodical marketers, advertisers, copywriters, publishers and editors, field sales representatives, booksellers and jobbers, librarians and information professionals, scholars and researchers, mail-order entrepreneurs and their suppliers and resources, promotion printers and compositors, mailing houses and lettershops, mailing list sources, and computer experts.

In today's publishing environment, the marketer must be familiar with a myriad of techniques and practices related to space advertising, such as budgeting, planning, placement, and response tracking. He or she must be familiar with publicity techniques such as news release formats and preparation, book reviewers' practices and major review media, key book trade and library review publications, and, generally what works and what doesn't and why. This publishing desk reference answers these questions and covers all important terms in these areas. In addition, it illustrates the definitions with guidelines and examples.

Today's publishing marketer must also have a working knowledge of all aspects of direct mail, including formats, copy, production, mailing lists and sources, testing, tracking, and evaluation of results, as well as knowledge of catalog types and formats, of the various direct-mail markets for books, and of the vehicles, offers, and timing for achieving best results. In many houses, marketers must also know about the various aspects of journal publishing, circulation efforts, and promotion practices. All the essential terminology for these areas of publishing marketing, illustrated with suggestions, examples, and techniques, are included in this book.

To be fully effective, publishing marketers need to understand the terminology of the trade—the special argot spoken within the channels of distribution for books and journals. How, for instance, does the U.K. differ from the U.S. in journals distribution? Publishing marketers must also be familiar with the language of typesetting, printing, and binding. This comprehensive information source gives all essential terms related to these elements of publishing as well as numerous practical usage guidelines and tips.

This volume fills numerous other informational needs for the publishing marketer, bookseller, or sales rep. The marketer must know the important tools and key information sources essential for planning, conducting, or supervising various types of promotions; the important book and library convention exhibits and all the accompanying terminology involved in arranging, opening, and participating in exhibits; the approaches, procedures, and special language involved in setting up, operating, and dealing with special sales accounts; the channels for identifying and reaching a book's prime markets and for identifying the subgroups within these markets; the types of booksellers; how the various approval jobbers operate and who they are; and the different types of libraries, how they differ from one another, what and when they buy, how they view a publisher's promotional efforts, and what formats they favor.

Bodian's Publishing Desk Reference differs in one important aspect from past books and glossaries that have dealt with publishing-related terms. The content of this book draws substantially on the author's considerable experience of nearly 30 years as book marketer and bookseller with large and small publishing establishments and as a former head of sales for the nation's oldest and largest wholesale bookseller. This comprehensive publishing dictionary also draws upon and benefits from the author's industry-wide research and investigations, in both the U.S. and abroad, performed in the writing of six publishing-marketing related books, and over a score of published articles on book marketing and bookselling, as well as his extensive contacts industrywide with leading book marketers and booksellers in North America and abroad.

Prior to publication, the manuscript was reviewed by a panel of U.S. and U.K. publishing professionals with long experience in all of the areas covered to ensure the accuracy, currentness, and comprehensiveness of its presentation. This work was also reviewed by selected specialists with professional library experience to ensure accuracy of library-related entries.

A series of appendices enhances the dictionary portion of this work. They include checklists, ideas, techniques, guidelines, and useful information on a wide range of book and journal marketing topics, assembled by the author over a period of years, and not included in any of his previously published works.

In summary, the almost 4,000 entries and the 18 appendices that make up this dictionary of publishing practices and techniques represent a unique, state-of-the-art contribution to the literature of publishing and marketing, and a compendium of information destined to provide a useful, needed, and enduring reference tool for all who labor in the publishing industry or its related services, and all who seek a better understanding of the various aspects involved in the making and selling of books and journals.

Nat Bodian
Cranford, New Jersey

A

A & I publisher   A publisher of abstracting and indexing services.

AAP (abbreviations)   American Academy of Pediatrics; American Academy of Periodontology; American Academy of Psychoanalysis; American Academy of Psychotherapists; Association for the Advancement of Psychoanalysis; Association for the Advancement of Psychotherapy; Association of American Physicians; Association of American Publishers; Association of Applied Psychoanalysis.

AAP (publishing)   See *Association of American Publishers.*

AAP Exhibits Directory   An annual directory compiled by the Association of American Publishers. Lists meetings of over 350 educational, library, scientific, and technical associations at which publishers can exhibit books and related materials. See also *Association of American Publishers.*

AAP-NACS Monthly Microfiche Service   Since 1980, this joint effort of the Association of American Publishers and the National Association of College Stores has provided subscribing stores with monthly updated listings on microfiche of all the college textbooks available from each participating publisher. The 42X microfiche lists author, title, ISBN, list price, and inventory status.

AAP Newsletter   A newsletter issued approximately every six weeks discussing matters of interest to the publishing industry. Address: Association of American Publishers, 2005 Massachusetts Avenue, NW, Washington, DC 20036. See also *Association of American Publishers.*

AAs   See *author's alterations.*

1

AAUP   See *Association of American University Presses.*

ABA (book industry)   See *American Booksellers Association; ABA Convention.*

ABA Book Buyer's Handbook   A manual issued in a loose-leaf binder by the American Booksellers Association which is updated annually. It provides an alphabetical listing of book publishers with full details of their terms for booksellers. Included are Single Title Order Plan policies, and lists of publishers offering cash discounts and those with 800 numbers or who accept collect calls from booksellers. See also *American Booksellers Association.*

ABA Convention   The annual meeting of the American Booksellers Association features the largest exhibit of book publishers in North America. Usually held in late May (often over the Memorial Day weekend), the convention draws as many as 17,000 booksellers, publishers, and guests. Previews of the fall's "big books," receptions with celebrity authors, press conferences, autographing sessions, and often lavish entertainments mark this as the biggest single annual event on most booksellers' and publishers' calendars. See also *American Booksellers Association.*

ABA Newswire   A weekly newsletter, published by the American Booksellers Association for subscribing booksellers. Lists forthcoming publicity about trade books and authors, information about TV and radio appearances, lectures, articles, and book reviews, and provides a listing of major publisher advertising and promotion offers. See also *American Booksellers Association.*

AB Bookman's Weekly   A weekly publication used mainly by antiquarian book dealers to locate out-of-print, rare, or difficult-to-obtain books. Also contains topical review coverage of nonfiction books. Started in 1948 as a separate periodical called *Antiquarian Bookman* by R.R. Bowker. Prior to 1948, it had been a section of *Publishers Weekly* with the same title. Address: AB Bookman Publications, Box AB, Clifton, NJ 07015. Phone: 201-772-0020. See also *antiquarian book dealer.*

AB Bookman's Yearbook   An annual publication listing dealers of used, out-of-print, and rare books. Address: AB Bookman Publications, Box AB, Clifton, NJ 07015. Phone: 201-772-0020.

ABC   See *Audit Bureau of Circulation.*

Abel Company (Richard Abel & Company)   The Richard Abel Company, a library supplier based in Portland, Oregon, pioneered and refined library approval plans. Great success, mainly with academic libraries, led to overexpansion, and the firm was forced into bankruptcy in 1974. Its assets and premises were acquired by Blackwell-North America. See also *approval plan, origin of; Blackwell North America.*

ABI forms   These forms from the R.R. Bowker Company enable publishers to provide data about forthcoming books for the *Books in Print* database from which the directory of the same name and the related books-in-print products are derived. The ABI provides concise information about a book's content, author, intended readership, planned promotion, ISBN, pages, price, and format. Copies of the form can also be sent to wholesalers, jobbers, and other major customers to facilitate prepublication orders and inclusion in library approval plans. Forms are available from the Department of Bibliography, R.R. Bowker Co., 245 W. 17th Street, New York, NY 10010.

ABPA   See *American Book Producers Association.*

abridged edition/abridgement   Elimination of sections of a book, or the rewriting of the text in condensed form so as to make the text desirable to a different audience, or to broaden the market for an expensive library work to individuals by price reduction.

abstracting and indexing services   These services analyze and, in some cases, summarize the information content of recorded knowledge and provide systematic access to published materials, making their work invaluable to librarians and researchers in all fields. They are useful to book publishers as an auxiliary book review medium since they often provide summaries of a book's content and full bibliographic data. See also *Abstracting & Indexing Services Directory.*

Abstracting & Indexing Services Directory   A useful reference that lists and describes over 2,200 current and continuing publications, including abstracts, indexes, digests, bibliographies, catalogs, and similar works in all fields. Also included are abstracts and bibliographic compilations that are parts of standard journals. Provides full name and address information, year first published, description and scope, subject coverage, arrangement, and other details. A useful aid for journal publishers seeking information on abstracting sources for new journals. Address: Gale Research Co., Book Tower, Detroit, MI 48226. Phone: 313-961-2242.

ABT   See *Association of Book Travelers.*

academic library   A library at a college or university. See also *college library collection; university library collection.*

academic library jobber   See *jobber, academic library.*

academic library subject area specialists   Those bibliographers at larger libraries who specialize in the selection of books in a specific subject. See also *college library lists, CMG Information Services.*

academic library subscription decisions   At smaller academic libraries, final journal subscription decisions are usually made by the director. In larger institutions, the decision may be made by the head of serials or the subject selector (bibliographer), often with faculty input.

academic list (compiled)   See *compiled list (academic).*

academic mailing list broker   A mailing list broker who specializes in academic mailing lists and serves mainly that part of the publishing community that deals with textbooks. See also *Thor Information Services, Inc.*

Academic Mailing Lists, Inc.   A compiler of college faculty lists focusing on such areas as business, data processing and computer science, economics, mathematics and statistics, psychology, and the sciences. All lists are derived from the most recent class schedules or directly from departmental secretaries. Founded in 1987 by Howard Smith, marketing manager for over 20 years with several major college publishers. Address: 3659 India Street, Suite 105, San Diego, CA 92103. Phone: 619-260-8590.

academic mailing lists, U.K. and Western Europe   See *IBIS Information Services.*

academic mailing lists, U.S.   A number of compilers specialize in academic mailing lists in the United States. The major sources are CMG Information Services, the Educational Directory segment of Market Data Retrieval, and Academic Mailing Lists, Inc. See separate entries for each of these firms for addresses.

academic mailing lists, Western Europe   See *IBIS Information Services.*

academic rep   See *college rep.*

academics' sources of book information   See *book information sources for academics.*

academic trade book   A book written by a scholar for the academic market, but for which the publisher sees a far wider market and plans the pressrun, pricing, and promotion accordingly. See also *academic trade discount.*

academic trade discount   1. A trade discount of at least 40% given to bookstores and wholesalers to encourage stocking of scholarly books that might otherwise not be carried in stock because of their short discounts. Occasionally used by university presses for selected titles believed to have appeal to a wider audience. 2. A short discount book on which a publisher applies a 40% (trade) discount on initial bookstore (or wholesaler) orders either in advance of publication or during the first season of publication, with the regular short discount applying on all reorders. See also *academic trade book.*

accordion fold   Method of folding paper in which each fold is parallel to, and in the opposite direction from, the previous one. Also called fanfold, z-fold, and zig-zag fold. In the U.K. called accordion pleat or concertina fold.

account management, sales   See *sales call (retail accounts).*

acetate overlay   A sheet of clear or transparent plastic superimposed in register on an art mechanical for a color separation, or other modification, of the base mechanical. See also *overlay (artwork).*

acid free paper/non acidic paper [∞]   Paper that meets certain levels of pH and alkaline reserve and contains no groundwood and should therefore last for centuries.

ACP   See *Association of Canadian Publishers.*

acquisitions librarian   Usually a technical services professional on a library staff who often makes decisions on what and how to buy and who handles the paperwork for book orders after a decision to buy has been made.

action device   1. An enclosure with a mailing that requires the recipient to do something, such as to affix a stamp or return label. 2. Any device or technique used in a mailing which will stimulate the recipient to respond.

active account   Any account in which transactions take place on a regular basis, or with which there is a large volume of sales activity. See also *agency account*.

active life   The period during which a book is available for sale, or is worth keeping in print.

active list/active titles   Books on a publisher's list, both old and new, that are stocked, sell, and are deemed profitable to keep in print.

actives   Those names on a customer mailing list of people who have made a purchase within a recent period and are paid up.

ad   Used interchangeably with advertisement. See also *service ad*.

ad, co-op   See *co-op ad; 100% co-op ad*.

ad, t.f.   See *till forbid (advertisement)*.

ad card   A listing in the front of a book of other published books by the author.

add-on sales   Sales of related titles recommended at the time a telephone order is received for a particular book or publication.

address area   Area on a mailing piece in which the address or mailing label should appear.

address change rate of college faculty   See *mobility of college faculty*.

address change rate of professionals   See *mobility of professionals*.

address correction requested   A line added to a mailing piece requesting the Postal Service, for a fee, to supply correct address when addressee is no longer at address on the mailing piece. See also *return postage guaranteed*.

address file   A collection of individual addresses.

addressing, cheshire label   See *cheshire label addressing*.

addressing by job function   See *job function.*

addressing by job title   See *job title (direct mail).*

address labels, pressure-sensitive   See *pressure-sensitive label.*

address line, USPS regulation for   The United States Postal Service delivers only to the address on the line immediately above the city/state line. When address contains both a street address and a P.O. box number, delivery will be made to the location on the lower line.

address size, cheshire label   See *cheshire label maximum address size.*

adhesive binding   See *perfect binding.*

ad mat/ad slick   An advertisement in ready-to-use form supplied by a publisher to a bookseller, usually for a cooperative advertisement. Such ads are usually for a particular book and are complete except for insertion of bookseller's name and address. Also referred to as a "Velox." See also *co-op ad.*

adoption   1. Selection of a book as a textbook by a state, district, or school, an academic institution, or an individual course of study. 2. Selection of a book by a book club for a member offering. See also *college textbook adoption considerations.*

adoption letter   1. Any letter to college faculty not designed to sell, but rather to elicit a request for an examination copy leading to a possible adoption. 2. A letter sent to a college professor to reinforce a sales rep's textbook presentation. 3. A letter sent to a college professor whom a college rep missed on a call at the school. 4. A letter sent to a college professor who is a potential adopter and listing for the professor other schools where the book has been adopted and is being used.

adoption list   A listing of schools that have adopted a textbook for classroom use.

ad slick   See *ad mat/ad slick.*

advance/advance orders   Orders received by the publisher prior to a book's publication date. In trade publishing, the advance is often used as a guide in determining the size of the initial printing. See also *prepublication orders/prepub orders.*

Advance Book Information forms   See *ABI forms.*

advance copies   Copies of a new book sent to reviewers in advance of the announced publication date. See *publication date/pub date.*

advanced-level text   See *graduate-level text.*

advance galleys   Copies of advance uncorrected proofs of a book—bound or unbound—sent by book publishers well in advance of publication to book reviewers, to prominent individuals for advance quotes, and to book clubs and other subsidiary rights prospects. See also *advance copies.*

advance information sheet   An advance information sheet or AI is sent by publishers in the U.K. to library suppliers three to six months in advance of a book's publication date. It provides detailed information about the book, its contents, the author, readership, planned promotion, ISBN, pages, and price. Similar in content and purpose to the ABI in the U.S.

advance orders   See *advance/advance orders.*

advances (serial publication title)   Critical review articles by specialists in the field, usually published in annual volumes on broad topics, as in *Advances in Chemistry.*

advertisement, camera-ready   A typeset advertisement suitable for reproduction as submitted. The most widely used format in which advertising is submitted to publications for insertion. See *camera-ready copy.*

advertisement, consumer (for trade books)   A book advertisement designed to stimulate bookstore sales. Consumer ads by publishers for trade books are usually timed to begin on a book's publication date.

advertisement, coupon   See *coupon advertising.*

advertisement, institutional   See *institutional advertisement.*

advertisement, list   See *list advertisement/list ad.*

advertisement, online   An advertisement transmitted electronically to computer terminals.

advertisement, product   See *product advertisement.*

advertisement, sale catalog   See *sale catalog advertisement.*

advertisement, two-step   One in which the reader must go through two steps in order to complete a purchase. For example, an ad offering a catalog, from which the reader may subsequently place an order; or an ad offering a prospectus on a major reference work, on the basis of which an order will subsequently be placed.

advertisement heading   See *headline (advertising).*

advertising, announcement   See *announcement advertising.*

advertising, collaborative   See *collaborative advertising programs.*

advertising, consumer   See *consumer advertising.*

advertising, co-op   See *co-op ad.*

advertising, coupon   See *book coupons; coupon advertising; coupons, use of.*

advertising, direct-response   See *direct-response mailing.*

advertising, editorial approach in   See *editorial approach (in advertising).*

advertising, exhibit and convention   See *convention issue.*

advertising, image   See *image advertising.*

advertising, P.I. or P.O.   See *P.I. deal.*

advertising, publishers imprint in   See *publisher's imprint (in advertising).*

advertising, RSC   See *reader-service-card book ad.*

advertising, scholarly book   Scholarly books are best advertised in specialized periodicals that focus on their target or primary audiences. Such advertising frequently places emphasis on the publisher's imprint, rather than headline "sell" copy, as many scholarly works are sold on the strength of the publisher's reputation in the field.

advertising, space   See *space advertising.*

advertising, trade   See *trade advertising.*

advertising, USP in   See *unique selling proposition (USP).*

advertising allowance (bookseller)   Funds for advertising offered to all booksellers by publishers, usually based on a percentage of sales over a prescribed period. See also *co-op ad; cooperative advertising policy (bookseller).*

advertising appeals (to engineers)   See *engineers, copy approach to.*

advertising appeals (to scientists and scholars)   See *scientific and technical book copy approach.*

advertising benefit   See *benefit (in book advertising).*

advertising budget (book)   1. Funds allocated for advertising in the launch of a book. 2. Funds allocated for an advertising campaign for a single book or for a line or series of books. 3. The allocation of advertising funds within a specific period of time such as a season or a fiscal year. 4. An allocation of advertising funds for various publication purposes such as those outlined above.

advertising call-in   An individual who telephones in response to an advertisement or promotion.

advertising combination rate   See *combination rate (advertising).*

advertising containing coupons   See *coupon, in advertising.*

advertising containing prices   See *price, in advertising.*

advertising contract   A agreement between an advertiser and the entity controlling the medium in which the advertiser intends to place an advertisement. The contract specifies such matters as the amount of advertising space or time that will be taken, the rate at which the advertiser will pay for the ad or ads, and the applicable discounts and terms of payment. See also *contract year (advertising); earned rate; frequency discount.*

advertising copy using "you" approach.   See *you approach (in advertising copy).*

advertising drop-off   See *drop-off (in advertising).*

advertising exchange program   1. A vehicle through which many periodical publishers conduct circulation promotion programs. Advertising is exchanged with compatible publications on a space-for-space basis. Exchange can also be based on circulation; repeat insertions can be offered to compensate for lower circulation. 2. Exchange of advertising space for either space in another publication or for mailing list names or some other consideration, with no money changing hands.

advertising feature   See *feature (n.) (book advertising)*.

advertising format response speed   The format in which space advertising appears often determines the speed with which readers respond. For example, a tabloid format is usually read and discarded and therefore readers tend to act quickly on advertising before discarding. A weekly periodical is likely to be looked at more quickly than a monthly. An annual directory is generally considered not for immediate reading and is therefore likely to be referred to on the basis of need and to produce a slower advertising response

advertising headline   See *headline (advertising)*.

advertising income, journals   See *journal advertising income*.

advertising insertion order   See *insertion order (advertising)*.

advertising job number   See *job number (advertising)*.

advertising key   A code or identifier inserted in an advertisement that will enable the advertiser to trace the source from which the responses are derived, and also to gauge the effectiveness of the advertisement.

advertising media, primary trade   See *trade advertising media, primary*.

advertising negative   A format favored by many publications for submission of advertising. The most popular is "right-reading, emulsion side down."

advertising order, firm   See *firm order (advertising)*.

advertising policy, retail cooperative   See *retail cooperative advertising policy*.

advertising positioning   Advertising is positioned in a publication at the discretion of the publisher. While the words "Would appreciate" in an insertion order may suggest a desired position by an advertiser, only a firm request committing the advertiser to a premium payment will guarantee a particular position, and then subject to approval of the publisher and availability.

advertising positioning (scientific book)   See *book review readership*.

advertising rate card   A printed card issued by the publisher of a print advertising medium providing full details of advertising costs, sizes, mechanical requirements, and other information useful to potential advertisers or their agencies. U.K.: advertisement rate card. See also *media kit*.

advertising rates for business publications   See *SRDS Business Publication Rates and Data*.

advertising rebate   A refund by an advertising medium to an advertiser as a result of a discount earned for volume of space or number of insertions beyond that anticipated.

affiliated relationship   A contractual arrangement between a small publisher (affiliate) and a (usually) larger publisher who agrees to handle all details of warehousing, shipping, and billing for an agreed upon percentage of the net billing. See also *distribution deal*.

affinity, mailing list   See *list affinity (direct mail)*.

AFIPS   American Federation of Information Processing Societies.

against the grain (paper)   Folding paper at right angles to the grain of the paper. Paper folds easily with the grain, but may crack when folded against the grain. See also *grain (paper)*.

agate   A size of type measuring approximately 5½ points in the American point system. See also *point (typography)*.

agate line   A unit of measurement used to sell advertising space, particularly in newspapers. The cost per agate line is usually for space occupying the depth of one agate line (5½ points) by the width of one column. There are 14 agate lines to the column inch. An advertisement 100 agate lines by 2 columns would be billed at 200 agate lines. An advertisement 2 columns x 10 inches would be billed as 280 agate lines.

agate type   Type measuring 5½ points or ¼₄ inch. Used as a unit of measurement of newspaper column depths.

agency (subscription)   See *subscription agent/agency.*

agency account   A bookseller who has agreed to stock and offer for sale the books of a publisher under the publisher's bookseller agency plan. U.K.: standing order customer. See also *bookseller agency plan.*

agency agreement   See *agency account; bookseller agency plan.*

agency discount   A special discount given to a bookseller or wholesaler for subscribing to a publisher's agency plan. See also *bookseller agency plan.*

agency plan   See *bookseller agency plan.*

agency plan network   All of the booksellers that participate in a particular publisher's agency plan.

agency system, Canadian   See *Canadian agency system/Canadian agency.*

agent   See *European agent; literary agent; rep; repping group; sales rep/sales representative; subscription agent/agency.*

agent, authors'   See *literary agent.*

agent, European   See *European agent.*

agent, journal subscription   See *subscription agent/agency.*

AI   See *Advance Information Sheet.*

AIDA formula (in advertising)   Attention (advertisement must attract); Interest (advertisement must arouse); Desire (advertisement must create); Action (advertisement must stimulate).

AIM   1. Abbreviation for Association of Information Managers, an organization with many special librarians as members. 2. Abbreviation for Automatic Inventory Management, a periodicals program for bookstores by Ingram Periodicals Inc., under which bookstores are supplied with magazines based on demographic information and space availability supplied by the bookseller. Ingram's periodicals division resulted from Ingram's acquisition of the Chicago-based Prairie Distribution Company.

airmail, U.S.   Airmail envelopes are not required for mailings within the U.S. All first-class mail travels by air as a normal procedure.

air service charge (journals)   An optional charge applied to international journal subscriptions for those who wish to receive their copies by airmail instead of normal surface post.

air speeded   The practice of periodical publishers in sending their European subscriptions by air cargo to a European destination from where they continue by surface mail to individual subscribers. Many European periodical publishers do the same with American subscribers.

ALA   See *American Library Association.*

ALA Booklist   See *Booklist/Reference Books Bulletin.*

ALA Conference/Meeting   The main annual convention of the American Library Association, usually held in late June. An important showcase for publishers to the library market and an opportunity for publishers to meet with librarians from all the important libraries and library systems and to make contact with the various library jobbers who also participate in the exhibits. Total attendance averages 12,000 to 15,000 librarians, exhibitors, and guests. ALA also holds a smaller annual midwinter meeting with exhibits, usually in January, with an average total attendance of 5,000 (although the 1989 meeting has a February date). Upcoming sites for the June meeting are: 1989, Dallas; 1990, Chicago; 1991, Atlanta; and for the midwinter meeting: 1989, Washington; 1990 and 1991, Chicago. See also *American Library Association (ALA).*

all caps   Type composition set all in capital letters.

alphabet length (typography)   Length of the 26 lowercase letters in any typeface and size. Usually stated in points. Alphabet length may also be indicated by characters per pica.

alterations   Changes in composition already set or any modification of a piece of printed matter after the job is in progress. Such changes result in additional charges called "alteration charges." See also *author's alterations (AAs)*.

alternate delivery   Delivery of books, periodicals, newspapers, and other advertising matter by means other than the U.S. Postal Service. While the USPS has a monopoly on first-class mail, other forms are not included and may be delivered by private carriers. See also *UPS*.

alternate selection (book club)   A second-choice offer of a book club to its membership during one of its cyclical offering periods. See also *main selection (book club)*.

AMA Masterfile   A database containing detailed information on all 550,000 U.S. physicians. This file can provide mailing lists segmented in numerous ways, including specialty, whether based in an office or hospital, and more. It is available through a number of authorized agents.

American Book Council (ABC)   An organization formed in 1986 by 11 book industry associations, "to promote professionalism and education in the book field." John Dessauer of the University of Scranton Center for Book Research chairs the advisory board. Address: Room 102, The Gallery, University of Scranton, Scranton, PA 18510. Phone: 717-961-7724.

American Book Producers Association (ABPA)   An association of individuals who "package" or create ready-to-publish books for publishers. Organized in New York City in 1980. Address: 4th Fl., 319 E. 52nd Street, New York, NY 10022. See also *packager*.

American Bookseller   Monthly publication of the American Booksellers Association with information on bookstore operations, industry problems, meetings, and exhibits. Nearly 5,000 of the approximately 7,500 subscribers are member bookstores.

American Booksellers Association (ABA)   A national organization, founded in 1900, of individuals and firms engaged in the retail sale of books in the United States. Its annual convention is the scene of the largest trade book fair in the U.S., with most major trade publishers displaying their forthcoming titles to the attending booksellers. Publications of ABA include *American Bookseller*, published monthly, and *ABA Newswire*, a weekly newsletter for booksellers. Address: 137 W. 25th Street, New York, NY 10001. See also *ABA Convention.*

American Book Trade Directory   Directory of more than 20,000 bookstores and book outlets in the U.S. and Canada. Includes wholesalers, booktrade associations, and exporters/importers. Bookstore listings are detailed and include types of books stocked, owner or manager, and telephone number. Appears annually in August from R.R. Bowker Co., 245 W. 17th Street, New York, NY 10010.

American Library Association (ALA)   The oldest and largest library association in the world. Founded in 1876, ALA has 40,000 members including librarians, library educators, researchers, and publishers. The member publication is *American Libraries,* a monthly. Most ALA divisions publish a journal and many publish newsletters as well. Address: 50 E. Huron Street, Chicago, IL 60611. Phone: 312-944-6780. U.K.: Library Association (LA); also ASLIB which is more oriented towards information science. See also *ALA Conference/Meeting; Booklist/Reference Books Bulletin.*

American Library Directory   Directory of about 30,000 U.S. and more than 3,000 Canadian academic, public, county, provincial, regional, medical, law, and other special libraries and library systems. Also includes a section for library networks and consortia. Entries include department heads, budget, special collections, automated functions, and type of catalog. Update service available at extra cost. Appears annually in fall from R.R. Bowker Co., 245 W. 17th Street, New York, NY 10010. Phone: 212-645-9700.

American Medical Association Masterfile   See *AMA Masterfile.*

American Medical Publishers Association (AMPA)   An association of 42 medical publishers for information exchange and improvement of the creation, distribution, and sale of medical books and journals. Address: P.O. Box 944, Crystal Lake, IL 60014.

American National Standards Institute (ANSI)   A clearinghouse for nationally coordinated voluntary standards, some relating to libraries, publishing, and the book trade. See also *National Information Standards Organization.*

American point system, American-British point system The typographic measurement system invented by American printer Nelson C. Hawks and in use in the United States since 1886. Uses the point as the basic unit of type measurement, with the pica as a secondary unit measuring 12 points. See also *pica (typography); point (typography)*.

American Society for Information Science (ASIS) *See ASIS.*

American Wholesale Booksellers Association (AWBA) An association of wholesale booksellers whose annual sales are at least 75% books. Formed in 1984, AWBA meets annually on Memorial Day weekend in conjunction with the American Booksellers Association annual convention/meeting.

AMPA See *American Medical Publishers Association.*

announcement advertising 1. Advertising concerned with presenting such information as a publisher's entire list of titles for a particular season in the announcement issue of *PW*. It may or may not call for an immediate response from the reader. 2. Advertising designed to announce a book's availability to a particular market. See also *announcement mailing; direct-response mailing.*

announcement catalog A catalog describing books for a forthcoming season. See also *catalog; seasonal catalog.*

announcement mailing A mailing intended primarily to announce or make known certain information rather than to elicit direct orders. Library mailings and promotions to academics often fall into this category. See also *direct-response mailing.*

annual A publication, in any format, issued once a year.

annual catalog A yearly catalog—usually calendar year—listing all of a press's books in print and including titles to be published during the coming season, or all of those in production. Listings may or may not be annotated, depending on the size of the list. Such catalogs are often organized by subject and indexed by title, author, and subject. See also *seasonal catalog.*

annual marketing plan See *marketing plan, annual; marketing plan, annual, key elements.*

annual mobility of professionals See *mobility of professionals.*

annual rate of journal subscription renewals   See *renewal rate (subscription product)*.

ANSI   See *American National Standards Institute*.

antiquarian book dealer   A bookseller who deals in rare and out-of-print books, often servicing primarily librarians seeking out-of-print works needed for collections, research, or to replace a missing or stolen item in a collection. See also *Antiquarian Booksellers Association of America, Inc. (ABAA)*.

Antiquarian Booksellers Association of America, Inc. (ABAA)   The national trade association for professional antiquarian book dealers. Their search publication is *AB Bookman's Weekly*. Address: 50 Rockefeller Plaza, New York, NY 10020. See also *AB Bookman's Weekly*.

antiquarian bookselling terms   See separate entries under *association copy; bumped; chipped; cracked hinge; ex-lib; fair; fine; foxing; good; mint; poor; sunned; very fine*.

antique paper   Paper with a surface of relatively rough texture.

approach test (direct mail)   An approach direct-mail test is one tied to the recipient's reaction to a specific component, such as format, price, or presentation (e.g., one headline vs. another). See also *test, tactical (direct mail)*.

approval copy   A book shipped with an invoice requiring payment or return of the book within a specified period, depending on whether or not the book is recommended for purchase by students or adopted for a course of instruction. See also *complimentary copy; desk copy; examination copy/exam copy; free examination offer*.

approval plan   A library collection development plan whereby a wholesaler or jobber selects and orders books that match the selection profile chosen by a library. The profile may be comprehensive for any given library, or it may be only for particular subjects or types of books. The supplier sends copies of all books that match the profile to the library which, in turn, reviews the books and keeps those it wants and returns unwanted items to the jobber. See also *blanket order; book lease plan; forms only library awareness plan; standing order*.

approval plan, origin of   The concept of the library approval plan was introduced by Richard Abel and Company in the 1960s. Before its demise in 1974, the Abel organization had hundreds of libraries, primarily academic, as subscribers. The efficiency of the Abel approval plan was such, that some libraries substituted it for an acquisitions staff. Presently, at least 10 approval plan vendors, some of them employing former Abel staff members, serve many of the libraries that formerly dealt with Abel.

approval plan dealer   See *approval plan jobber/dealer.*

approval plan exclusions   Publishers seeking to furnish books to library jobbers for inclusion in approval plans should be aware of the types of books many libraries exclude from approval plans. These may include trade and juvenile titles, government documents, foreign books, mass market paperbacks, hobby books, poetry, nonmonographic serials, laboratory manuals, subscription books, very expensive books, reprints, textbooks, dissertations, books in spiral or loose-leaf binding, and popular fiction.

approval plan jobber/dealer   A library jobber who offers an approval plan to libraries. See also *approval plan;* "Appendix 9: Directory of Major General Library Approval-Plan Jobbers."

approval plan profile   A systemized formulation of a library's wants in terms of subjects, publishers, and other book description terms. The profile is usually drafted according to a format provided by the jobber (or publisher). In academic libraries the profile is closely related to the curriculum and research needs of the faculty and students.

approval vendor   An alternative term for approval plan jobbers or library jobbers with library approval plans. See *approval plan.*

approved copy   Advertising copy requiring prior approval by the author, the author's employer, or some outside source before it can be used by the publisher for promotion of the author's book. Such a requirement is unconventional and does not appear in most publishing contracts.

approved mailing piece   See *sample mailing piece requirement.*

AQ   See *author questionnaire/marketing questionnaire.*

arbitrary pricing   See *pricing what the traffic will bear; value pricing.*

archival journal   A journal that is published mainly for library archives and not for individual purchase or subscription. It is priced for the library market and virtually no effort is directed toward personal subscriptions.

ARL   Association of Research Libraries, based in Washington, DC and founded in 1937. ARL meets semiannually in May and October and is concerned with solving problems fundamental to large research libraries. Membership includes 118 of the nation's largest and most prestigious libraries, most of which are university libraries, but private research libraries and several public libraries are also members. Address: 1527 New Hampshire Avenue, NW, Washington, DC 20036. Phone: 202-232-2466.

ARL library   A library, usually a large research library, that is a member of the Association of Research Libraries, a group that includes university, public, private, and government libraries.

art/art work   An all-inclusive term used by advertisers, artists, and printers to describe such matter as photographs, line illustrations, hand lettering, or other creative work.

art director   An individual in an advertising agency or publishing establishment responsible for the general design and supervision of final artwork and typography of advertisements and other creative works.

art work   See *art/art work.*

ascender (typography)   That part of a lower case letter extending above the body, as in "h," or "b," or "d." See also *descender (typography).*

ASIS   American Society for Information Science. A 4,000-member organization of individuals interested in the use, organization, storage, retrieval, evaluation, and dissemination of recorded specialized information. Address: 1424 16th Street, NW, Washington, DC 20036. Phone: 202-659-3644. See also *ASLIB.*

ASLIB   The Association for Information Management, the British counterpart to ASIS. Formerly the Association of Special Libraries and Information Bureaux. Address: Information House, 26-27 Boswell Street, London WC1N 3JZ. Telephone: (01) 430-2671.

ASLIB Book List   The British equivalent of *New Technical Books*. Each monthly issue from U.K. and European publishers contains 50-75 reviews of scientific and technical books from U.K. and European publishers, critically reviewed with indication of audience level. See also *New Technical Books*.

assembly date (direct mail)   See *direct-mail promotion assembly date*.

assigned account (sales rep)   While commission reps usually cover a geographic territory, they are usually not credited with all sales within the assigned region. Often they will have specific accounts assigned for which they receive sales credit, although they may also receive credit for new accounts that they open. See also *sales rep/sales representative*.

assigned mailing date   The date or dates assigned or authorized by a mailing list owner for a list to be used for mailing. Any other date(s) must have prior approval of the list owner. See also *protected mailing date*.

association and society book characteristics   See *professional association book publishing*.

association copy (antiquarian bookselling)   A copy of a book bearing some connection with its author and identifiable because it is signed, or inscribed with a message, or bears a personal note that the book is a gift to the indicated recipient. See also *antiquarian bookselling* terms for the list of such terms with separate entries.

association list (direct mail)   A mailing list of the membership of a professional or trade association or a society. Many societies and professional associations have different classes of membership and may rent by member classification or by division. Rental of lists may also be segmented by domestic only, or foreign only, or a combination.

Association of American Publishers (AAP)   The trade association of the U.S. book publishing industry, founded in 1970, and composed of the following divisions: Direct Marketing/Book Club; General Publishing; Higher Education; International; Paperback Publishing; Professional and Scholarly; and School. Annual meeting always held in March. Address: 220 E. 23rd Street, New York, NY 10010. Phone: 212-689-8920.

Association of American Publishers, origin of   In 1970, the American Book Publishers Council (ABPC) merged with the American Educational Publishers Institute (AEPI) to form the Association of American Publishers. W. Bradford Wiley, head of John Wiley & Sons, was its first board chairman, and Sanford Cobb headed the paid executive staff as president.

Association of American University Presses (AAUP)   A trade association of scholarly publishing divisions of colleges and universities in the United States and Canada. AAUP presently consists of 94 member and associate presses. Formally organized in 1937; annual meeting in June. Address: One Park Avenue, New York, NY 10016. Phone: 212-889-6040.

Association of Book Travelers (ABT)   An association of 500 publishers' representatives selling to the retail and wholesale book trade. Founded in 1884, ABT holds its annual luncheon in New York City in December. Address: ABT, c/o Vicki Brooks, The Serberus Group, P.O. Box 470, Frenchtown, NJ 08825.

Association of Canadian Publishers (ACP)   A national trade association representing Canadian-owned book publishers. Founded in 1971 with 17 members, the organization now has over 130 members. Its main objective is to encourage the writing, publishing, distribution, and promotion of books written by Canadian authors in particular, and the reading and study of all books in general. Address: 70 The Espanade, Toronto, Ontario M5E 1A7. Phone: 416-361-1408. See also *Canadian Book Information Centre (CBIC); Canadian Book Publishers Council (CBPC); Canadian Booksellers Association (CBA).*

Associations Directory/Encyclopedia   See *Encyclopedia of Associations.*

AT&T 800 Service   A telephone service designed to allow inward calling telecommunications service with reverse billing characteristics as part of the basic service. Formerly called Inward-WATS. For equivalent U.K. service, see *Linkline 0800*.

AT&T 800 Service-Canada   A telephone service that allows a customer in the adjoining United States to subscribe to dedicated access lines in order to receive calls from a subscriber area composed only of certain Canadian areas.

AT&T Toll-Free 800 Business Directory   An annual AT&T directory listing business firms with 800 toll-free numbers. It has a white-page alphabetical listing and a yellow-page Business Products and Services section. Because many businesses provide toll-free numbers for nonpublic purposes only, those numbers are listed that have been authorized. Hundreds of publisher and wholesale bookseller names are included.

attached mail   First-class mail that can be enclosed with lower-class mail without paying the full first-class rate. Such mail must be closely related to the package with which it is traveling.

attendance (convention)   The anticipated or actual registration at an exhibit or convention, often an important criterion in whether exhibit participation is warranted. A convention with small attendance often will not warrant the investment in both money and personnel time, while a large attendance provides increased opportunities for book exposure. Some show-registration figures include exhibitors and often inflate the actual attendance figures. One should be wary of first-time shows that may inflate expected attendance or shows in remote and hard-to-reach locations where attendance may be only a small fraction of what it would be in a popular convention city such as San Francisco or New York.

attention line   Job title or function, usually printed on an envelope when a mailing label has only the name of a company or institution. Also sometimes made part of address label.

auction   1. A simultaneous offering by a publisher of certain publication rights to all interested parties, the highest bidder winning the rights. 2. An offering by an author's agent of publication rights to the author's book to potential buyers through a bidding process.

auction, book club   See *book club auction.*

audience (book)   See *market.*

audit (periodical)   Examination of circulation figures. See also *Audit Bureau of Circulation (ABC); Business Publications Audit of Circulation, Inc. (BPA).*

Audit Bureau of Circulation (ABC)   A not-for-profit organization of publishers, advertisers, and agencies to standardize and check the correctness of the circulation of publisher-members, including magazines, newspapers, farm publications, and business publications (both paid and controlled circulation). See also *Business Publications Audit of Circulation, Inc. (BPA).*

author affiliation   That part of biographical information about an author that indicates his or her current professional position. An important ingredient in all promotions of scientific and scholarly publications to both individuals and libraries. The affiliation provides sufficient authority for a purchase decision, especially if the author is affiliated with a company or institution prominent in a field related to the subject of the book.

author credibility (library market)   The reliability of an author's works in a library will often trigger purchase of one of his or her new publications if the librarian feels the prior works provided useful information in a needed area.

author discount   A discount given an author by a publisher on purchase of copies of the author's own work beyond the number given as part of his or her publishing contract. A number of publishers also allow authors the same discount on all of their other published works. This is a beneficial policy since authors as a rule are substantial book buyers and tend to favor the presses that publish for them.

author questionnaire/marketing questionnaire   A multipage form that an author is asked to complete and return to the publisher, usually after the manuscript has been put into production. The answers provide guidance on where to market and promote the book and are also used in the preparation of jacket copy.

author questionnaire for special sales   See *special sales questionnaire.*

author's alterations (AAs)   Changes made by the author after the work has been typeset. Author's alterations beyond a certain dollar amount or percentage of the cost of typesetting are often borne by the author. The term is also used in conjunction with advertising composition for other than normal and reasonable changes in copy.

author's editor   An editor, often employed in a scholarly institution, to assist members of that institution in preparing their writing for publication. More prevalent in the sciences, where many researchers do not speak English as their first or native language.

author's track record   A record of sales of the author's previous books. While not always reliable, it provides some indication of the type of selling potential the author may have. Both booksellers and jobbers use this method for estimating purchases of the author's new book.

author tour   A trip by an author, usually arranged by the publisher of his or her book, for the purpose of promoting the book through autographing parties, media appearances, and so on. Such tours are essentially for trade books and cover travel and related expenses, but no payment to the author for time spent. See also *autographing party*.

autographing party   An author visit to a bookstore or book dealer to inscribe copies of his or her book and to otherwise help publicize it by his or her presence.

Automatic Inventory Management   See *AIM*.

automatic shipment   A procedure in book clubs whereby the club ships each new selection automatically until requested to stop (in contrast to negative or positive option book club shipments whereby the customer is informed of each shipment). Also known as "till-forbid" offer. See also *negative option; positive option*.

availability date   Date on which books are ready for release from publisher's shipping facility. See also *bound book date; publication date/pub date*.

awareness sources for college texts   See *college textbook awareness sources*.

AWBA   See *American Wholesale Booksellers Association*.

Ayer Directory of Publications   The Ayer Directory, first published in 1869, became in its 115th edition the *IMS Directory of Publications*, and in its 119th edition in 1987 became the *Gale Directory of Publications*. See also *Gale Directory of Publications*.

B

B.A.   See *Booksellers Association of Great Britain and Ireland.*

backboard (exhibits and conventions)   1. A vertical board attached to a table riser to enhance the appearance of a display, as well as to keep books or other displayed materials from falling off the back. 2. A term referring to the back of the jacket where a listing of related titles often appears on scientific and scholarly books.

back end (direct mail)   A mail-order term related to all aspects of the process, including fulfillment, evaluation of buyer performance, and pay-up, which occur after the order has been received. See also *front end (direct mail).*

back end results   The final results of a mailing, including both paid and unpaid orders. Essentially the back end indicates the profitability or lack of profitability of a mailing effort. See also *front end results.*

backlist   1. All books on a publisher's active list that were published prior to the current publishing season. 2. Books more than one year old. 3. "Books that unlike current titles, have stood the test of time and sell steadily year-in, year-out...require little promotion or advertising and provide publishers with their highest profit margins." —Ivan Obolensky, publishing analyst, in *The New York Times,* March 10, 1987. See also *backlist incentive programs (bookseller); frontlist; working the backlist.*

backlist catalog   See *catalog.*

backlist discount   See *backlist incentive programs (bookseller).*

backlist incentive programs (bookseller)   Publisher programs designed to encourage booksellers to stock assortments of backlist titles. The two most popular means are expanded discounts on backlist assortments and delayed billing. Such programs almost always have a minimum order quantity.

backlist order form   A listing of books on a publisher's active backlist.

backlist publisher   A publisher whose sales come mainly from backlist titles, rather than from those of the current season. The backlist publisher depends on books that sell steadily and well over a long term. See also *backlist; frontlist publisher.*

backlist stock plan   A publisher plan whereby a bookseller will receive an advantageous discount on selected backlist titles on which the bookseller agrees to stock a minimum number of each, and to maintain a fixed inventory level.

backlist title, solid   A title that enjoys a steady sales performance.

back order   An order for a book not yet published or currently out of stock, to be shipped when the book becomes available. U.K.: dues.

backwall (exhibits and conventions)   An arrangement of panels installed against the back wall of an exhibit booth for display purposes.

Bacon's Computerized Media Bank (publicity)   A bank of over 100,000 editorial contacts, available on pressure-sensitive mailing labels. Includes business, industrial, trade, farm, and consumer magazines, as well as daily and weekly newspapers, news services, and radio and television stations. Labels are computer generated on a custom basis as ordered. Address: Bacon's Publishing Company, 14 E. Jackson Boulevard, Chicago, IL 60604. Phone: 800-621-0561.

Bacon's International Publicity Checker   A guide to 7,500 business, trade, and industrial publications plus over 600 national and regional daily and Sunday newspapers in 15 countries. Every magazine is classified by country, then by market, and provides full details plus types of publicity material accepted. See also *Bacon's Publicity Checker.*

Bacon's Publicity Checker An invaluable resource for book publicists. Includes over 4,000 trade and consumer magazines, 1,700 daily newspapers, and 8,000 weekly newspapers in the U.S. and Canada. Furnishes full details for each publication, giving names for about 20 editorial departments, including book review editor. Published annually in October in two volumes with quarterly updates. See also *Bacon's Computerized Media Bank (publicity)*; *Bacon's International Publicity Checker.*

bad break (typography) Incorrect hyphenation at the end of a typeset line, or a page that breaks, leaving a widow. See also *widow (typography).*

bad copy Copy that is either illegible or so difficult for the compositor to read that it requires extra effort to be set, and, therefore, involves extra charge.

bad debt prevention See *"eyeball" credit checking.*

bag stuffer A flier or printed advertising piece inserted into a bag by the bookseller as an accompaniment to a customer purchase. See *envelope stuffer; flier/flyer; insert; statement stuffer.*

The Baker & Taylor Company A supplier of books to libraries and bookstores. America's oldest and largest wholesale bookseller has its headquarters at 652 E. Main Street, Bridgewater, New Jersey 08807-0920, with divisions located at Somerville, New Jersey; Momence, Illinois; and Reno, Nevada. It was founded in 1828 and has been exclusively in book wholesaling since 1912. Prior to that year, Baker and Taylor was a book publisher as well as a distributor.

Baker & Taylor publications *Book Alert* (monthly): General adult titles. *Directions* (monthly): Listings of scholarly titles for academic libraries. *Forecast* (monthly): Annotated listings of forthcoming general adult and juvenile titles.

bank, copy See *copy bank.*

bank card A credit card issued by a bank.

bar code 1. A series of parallel bars on a mailing piece to facilitate automatic letter sorting by the U.S. Postal Service. 2. A code designed for machine readable scanning used on the cover or jacket of a book to designate it as a book product, and to give its ISBN and, sometimes, its price. See *Bookland EAN; International Standard Book Number (ISBN)*.

bargain books   A term used by booksellers that includes both promotional books and remainders. See also *promotional book; remainder*.

barter arrangement   See *advertising exchange program; card pack exchanges; list exchange (direct mail)*.

baseline (typography)   1. The bottom of x-height. 2. An imaginary horizontal reference line on which all typeface and size variations align. See also *x-height (typography)*.

basic rate   See *one-time rate*.

basic size (paper)   Specific standard sheet size from which weight of a given grade of paper is determined. See also *paper sizes*.

basic stock list   A seasonal, sometimes annual list carried by publisher sales representatives and used as an order form.

basis weight (paper)   Weight of a ream (500 sheets) of paper in the standard (basic) size for that class of paper. The metric equivalent of basis weight is grammage, the number of grams per square meter. See also *grammage*.

BCO   Blank check order or open check order. See *open check/open draft*.

benday (or Ben Day)   A "screen" or pattern of lines or dots, applied to an area of reproduced art by the printing-platemaker, to fill in areas that would normally reproduce in a solid color or as pure white.

benefit (in book advertising)   What's in it for the prospective reader; what will it do for the reader in specific terms? A benefit is not to be confused with a feature; the book's feature yields the benefit. If a book's feature is that it contains "Over 5,000 literature references," the benefit would then be that it "Enables you to investigate in greater depth any topic touched upon." See also *feature (n.) (book advertising)*.

bestseller   1. When applied to trade books, the term is generally based on sales rank over a given period on one of the national indexes, such as *The New York Times* bestseller list. 2. When applied to sci-tech, professional, or scholarly books, it is generally used for a title that has gone through several printings and/or editions and has enjoyed a steady sales pattern over a protracted period, or, if published serially, by the number of standing orders or subscriptions for the series.

bestseller indexes, trade   Indexes of best-selling trade books, compiled by newspapers, trade periodicals, or book suppliers, and based on contacts with retail booksellers. The major bestseller indexes are those of *The New York Times*, *Publishers Weekly*, *The Washington Post*, and Ingram Book Company (*Ingram Index*).

b.f.   See *boldface type (b.f.)*.

bible paper   A thin, opaque printing paper for use when low bulk is important, for example, in the printing of bibles, dictionaries, and encyclopedias. See also *bulking paper*.

bibliographer   The common designation for book selection specialists in large academic libraries. See also *collection development librarian*.

bibliographic database   An index or bibliography, with or without annotations, stored on a computer for online access and designed to help users find citations to published material about specific subjects. See also *source database*.

bid   See *contract bid*.

bidder, qualified   See *qualified bidder*.

bids, government   See *government bids*.

big book   A book by name authors who traditionally sell in the 100,000-plus to 500,000-plus range in hard cover. (Definition by Bill Hammond, former sales manager at Little Brown, in *Publishers Weekly*, July 31, 1987.)

big ticket   A term used in publishing to indicate a book or series being offered at a high price, or at a higher price than usual for a comparable item. Term interchangeable with *high ticket*.

bill stuffer   See *envelope stuffer; statement stuffer*.

binders (loose-leaf publishing)   1. *Ring binder:* Usually three metal rings that open and shut simultaneously. Sometimes with opening and closing boosters that make opening and closing the rings easier. 2. *Compression binder:* A form of post binder that allows the posts to be compressed after the pages are placed over the posts so that the covers will hold the pages together tightly for compactness.

binder's board   See *board (paper).*

bind-in card   A detachable reply card usually bound into a periodical. If sold to an advertiser, it usually supports an accompanying advertisement. Some periodical publishers restrict bind-in cards to "in-house" promotions only. See also *blow-in cards; onsert.*

bind-in envelope   An envelope stapled into a catalog or mailing piece that can be removed and used as a response vehicle.

binding, comb   See *comb binding.*

binding, library   See *library binding.*

binding, mechanical   See *mechanical binding.*

binding, perfect   See *otabind; perfect binding.*

binding, spiral   See *spiral-bound edition.*

binding operation (printing)   The final touches applied to a printed piece. It encompasses any additional work beyond the printing process that is necessary to prepare the piece for the reader.

bingo card   See *reader service card.*

BIP   See *Books in Print.*

BIP **price**   The price shown for a published work in *Books in Print.* Under the ABA's Single Title Order Plan (STOP), many of the participating publishers will honor bookseller orders at the price listed in the current edition of either *Books in Print* or *Publishers' Trade List Annual.* See also *Books in Print; Single Title Order Plan (STOP).*

BISAC   See *Book Industry Systems Advisory Committee (BISAC).*

BISG   See *Book Industry Study Group (BISG).*

black and white (B/W)   Printed sheets or photographic prints in one color, usually black, on white paper. See also *one-color printing*.

Blackwell North America   Second largest library wholesaler (after Baker & Taylor) of professional and scholarly books in North America. Blackwell's of Oxford, England started its U.S. affiliate in 1974 when it acquired the assets, premises, and records of the bankrupt Richard Abel Company. Blackwell has a facility serving accounts west of the Rockies and in western Canada at 6024 SW Jean Road, Building G, Lake Oswego, OR. Phone: 800-547-6426. All other accounts are serviced by the facility at 1001 Fries Mills Road, Blackwood, NJ 08012. Phone: 800-257-7341. See also *Abel Company (Richard Abel & Company); The Baker & Taylor Company; Blackwell's.*

Blackwell's   A group of bookstores headquartered in Oxford, England with a reputation as one of the best known and largest sellers of scientific and scholarly books in the world. Blackwell North America (see separate entry) is an affiliate of this group.

BLAISE   British Library Automated Information Service.

blank check order (BCO)   See *open check/open draft.*

blanket order   An order from a library authorizing a publisher or jobber to send one or more copies of every title published according to certain agreed upon criteria—for example, in a specific subject area. See also *approval plan.*

blanket order plan, origin of   The idea was originated by Emerson Greenaway of the Free Library of Philadelphia in 1958.

blanket standing order   See *blanket order.*

bleed   Any printed matter (most often an illustration) that extends to the full limit of the trimmed size in any print job. It "bleeds off" the edge of the paper.

bleed charge (advertising)   A charge, usually a flat added dollar amount, added to the cost of advertising space for oversized units or "bleed" ads. Usually 5% to 15%.

bleed size   See *size indications in printed matter.*

blind bidding   A type of rights auction in which the bidders do not know what their competitors are bidding. Sometimes used by a publisher in the first round of an auction in hopes of raising the basic bidding price quickly.

blind corner   An envelope or card in which no return address appears in the upper left-hand corner.

blow-in card   A single, loose card inserted into a periodical to solicit subscriptions. Term derived from the fact that the cards are "blown in" by machine between the periodical pages by air pressure. Blow-ins are said to be less expensive and more effective than bind-in cards. See also *bind-in card; insert; onsert.*

blow-up   A photographic enlargement of any copy.

blue (blueprint or blueline)   A same-size contact print made from a film negative or positive for final check and proofreading purposes before making the printing plate, and usually blue in color.

blueprint   See *blue (blueprint or blueline).*

blurb   A short sales pitch or review of a book usually printed on the jacket or in an advertisement. For paperbacks, the blurb usually appears on the back cover. The word was coined by Gelett Burgess and first used in his *Burgess Unabridged* (1914).

board (paper)   Heavy and fairly rigid paper used for binding hardcover books. The type used for books is mainly binder's board. U.K.: millboard.

board artist/mechanical artist   The artist who assembles and pastes up the mechanical. Also called mechanical artist or paste-up artist. See also *mechanical/mechanical paste-up.*

board book   A children's picture book in which the pages are made of board, usually the thickness of most hardback covers.

body (typography)   Formerly used, for foundry type, to describe the size of the metal on which a type character was cast, measured in points; e.g., 10-point characters were set on a 10-point body. See also *leading (typography).*

body copy/body matter   Textual material.

body height   See *x-height (typography)*.

body type   The type, usually from 6 to 14 points, used to set textual matter, as contrasted with display or headline type.

boldface type (b.f.)   A heavier weight of typeface, usually used for emphasis. Instructions to compositors to set in bold face may be made by marking such copy "b.f." or by placing a wavy underline under the typewritten copy. See also *italic/italics*.

Bologna Children's Book Fair   World's largest fair for sale of foreign rights to children's books, held annually in Bologna, Italy. Contact: Children's Book Fair, Bologna Piazza della Constituzione 6, 40128, Bologna, Italy.

bond paper   A grade of writing or printing paper for which strength, durability, and permanence are essential requirements. See also *basic size (paper)*.

bonus distribution (periodicals)   Extra distribution, above and beyond normal circulation, of a periodical, usually at a meeting or convention in a subject-related area. For example, *Science* magazine distributed its annual instrumentation issue (February 27, 1987) at conventions in six different scientific areas over the four months following publication.

book   See *encyclopedia; handbook; loose-leaf publication; standard; textbook; yearbook*.

book (ANSI Standard)   A nonperiodical of at least 49 pages, exclusive of cover pages. See also *American National Standards Institute*.

book (as magazine)   The popular advertising trade term used to refer to any magazine for advertising purposes. "If a periodical publisher refers to the publication as a 'book,' then you know they publish a magazine."—Bill Begell in *Book Marketing Handbook, Volume 2*. See also *magazine*.

book (UNESCO definition)   A nonperiodical literary publication containing 49 or more pages, not counting covers.

book (USPS description for Special Fourth Class Rate)   A publication of 24 pages or more, at least 22 of which are printed, consisting wholly of reading matter or scholarly bibliography or reading matter with incidental announcements of books. See also *book post.*

book, big   See *big book.*

book, board   See *board book.*

book, coffee table   See *coffee table book.*

book, gift   See *gift book.*

book, homage   See *festchrift.*

book, hurt   See *hurt book.*

book, instant   See *instant book.*

book, lead   See *lead book.*

book, managed   See *managed book.*

book, marginal   See *marginal book.*

book, missionary   See *missionary book.*

book, modeled   See *modeled book.*

book, new age   See *new age books.*

book, packaged   See *packaged book.*

book, photography   See *photography book.*

book, pop-up   See *pop-up book.*

book, safe   See *safe book.*

book, TSM   See *TSM book.*

book, up-market   See *up-market book.*

book advertisements with coupon   See *coupon, in advertising.*

Book Alert   A bibliographic publication of The Baker & Taylor Company.

Bookbank   The new name, since January 1988, for *Whitaker's British Books in Print* on CD-ROM. Currently a monthly service, Whitaker has under consideration a plan to offer an every-other-month subscription at a reduced rate for users who do not need a monthly service.

book benefit (in advertising copy)   See *benefit (in book advertising)*.

bookbuyer lists   Lists of individuals who have purchased books by mail. Most publishers maintain lists of their bookbuyers and find them the most responsive type of list in mail promotion. College Marketing Group has a database of some 3.5 million bookbuyer names of over 40 different publishers, by subject category and other breakdowns. See also *College Marketing Group.*

Book Buyer's Guide   A monthly library and bookstore publication published by The Baker & Taylor Company until the mid-1960s. It served both the library and retail book trade markets and was competitive with the two R.R. Bowker publications—*Publishers Weekly* and *Library Journal. Book Buyer's Guide* had been in continuous publication for over 65 years.

Book Buyer's Handbook   An annual loose-leaf directory published by the American Booksellers Association and issued to its bookseller members. Lists terms and buying arrangements of publishers. U.K. equivalent: *A Directory of British Publishers and Their Terms: Including Agents for Overseas Publishers.* See also *American Booksellers Association.*

book card   A page in the front of a book, often facing the title page, listing either other books by the same author, or, if the book is part of a series, other books in the series.

book characteristics, professional association   See *professional association book publishing.*

book characteristics, scholarly   See *scholarly book characteristics.*

Book Chat   A 5½" by 8½" monthly catalog listing new trade titles of all publishers. Bookstores can use the catalog as handouts or self-mailers with their imprint. The Christmas issue in November is published in a larger-size format. Produced bimonthly by Booksellers Catalog Service, 29 South Wabash Avenue, Chicago, IL 60603.

book club   1. A membership arrangement for the purchase of books by mail from main, alternate, or special selections, at discounted prices from the original publisher's list price. An introductory offer is usually combined with a minimum-purchase commitment over a given period—usually a year. 2. A term sometimes used by special sales accounts such as associations, professional societies, or magazines for book offerings to members, constituents, or subscribers. See also *alternate selection (book club); continuity program; main selection (book club); professional book club; special interest book club.*

book club, pilot   See *pilot book club.*

book club, professional   See *professional book club.*

book club, religious   See *religious book club.*

book club, special interest   See *special interest book club.*

book club adoption   See *adoption.*

book club alternate selection   See *alternate selection (book club)*

book club auction   The practice by a publisher, after receiving an initial book club offer, of contacting other book clubs and soliciting higher bids. The rights will then generally be awarded to the club making the highest up-front offer. See also *book club up-front offer.*

book club contract   An agreement between a publisher and a book club granting book club rights under terms agreed upon in the contract. See also *book club rights; book club rights, first use; exclusive book club rights; nonexclusive book club rights.*

book club direct mail seasonality   January is considered the best month for book club mail promotions. September (late August to early October) is second best.

book club discount (to members)   Typically, the book club discount is about 20% off the publisher's price.

book club edition   An edition of a book produced specifically for use by a book club, either as a member selection or alternate selection, or as a premium to attract new members. Such editions may be a press overrun of a publisher's printing, or a separate printing from the publisher's plates or negatives. As a rule, the book club edition is identical to the publisher's edition; however, a club may sometimes use cheaper materials to turn out a less expensive (to manufacture) edition.

book club edition, sources of supply 1. Direct purchase from existing inventory of the original publisher. 2. Joining original publisher's press run. 3. Book club manufacture, with or without original publisher's needs added.

book club exclusive rights See *exclusive book club rights*.

book club main selection See *main selection (book club)*.

book club member-get-member promotion See *member-get-member*.

book club premium offer A "bribe" offered as an incentive to attract new members. Premium offers tend to age and decline in effectiveness and must be replaced when effectiveness begins to subside. On rare occasions, a particular premium may maintain its effectiveness for many years without change as with *The Compact Edition of The Oxford English Dictionary* by Book-of-the-Month Club.

book club rights The issuing to book clubs by book publishers of the rights to issue the publishers' books to their members. As a rule of thumb, club rights are shared 50-50 with the author. See also *book club contract; exclusive book club rights; nonexclusive book club rights*.

book club rights, first use Granting a book club first use of a book as an offering to its members with the provision that the publisher may offer it to another publisher after a specified period of time, such as three months or six months.

book club sale benefits (publisher) (1) Increased income; (2) reduced unit costs on pressruns; (3) added promotional exposure; (4) increased author satisfaction; (5) enhanced prestige for small or little-known publishers.

book club selection A title selected by a book club as its main selection. See also *alternate selection (book club)*.

book club selection criteria (1) How well the club has done with a book by the same author in the past; (2) how well the club has done with other books in the same subject area; (3) how much promotional effort the book is currently being given by the publisher; (4) how closely the book fits the membership interests of a special-interest book club; (5) timeliness of the subject matter; (6) price of the book compared with other offerings; (7) how well the club did with other recent books from the publisher.

book club types   (1) General book clubs; (2) special interest book clubs; (3) professional book clubs; (4) religious book clubs; (5) children's book clubs.

book club up-front offer   The amount of money a book club guarantees to pay a publisher as an advance against royalties on the club's income from a particular offer involving the publisher's book. See also *book club auction*.

book coupons   Coupons used in conjunction with a book offer. The term "book coupon" signifies a *format*, namely a block of copy framed by a dash line or broken line framing or border bearing some offer, discount, or vehicle to make an order possible. See also *coupon advertising; coupons, use of; discount coupon; dollars-off coupon*.

book dealer, antiquarian   See *antiquarian book dealer*.

book distribution jargon (bookstores)   Typically, a sales representative reports distribution of a particular new book among his or her trade accounts in a number of ways. He or she might report the book has a "nice spread" or a "good laydown," meaning nearly every account has taken the book. He or she may also report only a "few skips," meaning nearly every account has ordered the book, or "coverage is very spotty," meaning distribution has been difficult and only a few accounts have ordered. If overall sales have been generally good, he or she may also say the book "has advanced well," or "the spread has been good."

book dividend   A book offered as a premium, usually by a book club, after a certain membership or buying activity has been complied with.

book exhibit   A display of books at a meeting, convention, or trade fair. Publishers frequently use such exhibits to display their specialized books before the professional or scholarly audiences for whom they are intended. Publishers sometimes actively solicit orders at book exhibits. In the case of college textbooks, they fulfill requests for examination copies at exhibits. Librarians order books displayed at library meetings from their normal supply sources. See also *convention discount; cooperative book exhibit; exhibits, convention; trade show.*

book exhibits, cooperative   See *cooperative book exhibit.*

book feature (in advertising copy)   See *feature (n.) (book advertising).*

book has advanced well   Sales rep language for a book that has had a good advance sale in the bookstores the rep calls on.

book industry (ANSI definition)   The American National Standards Institute defines the book industry as including book publishers, wholesalers, distributors, and retailers; college bookstores, libraries, library binders, and serial vendors; schools, school systems, technical institutes, colleges and universities. (Source: ANSI Z 39.43-1980). See also *American National Standards Institute.*

Book Industry Study Group (BISG)   A voluntary, nonprofit research organization working since 1976 to promote and support research in and about the book industry. Membership includes representatives of publishers, manufacturers, suppliers, wholesalers, retailers, librarians, and others with book-related interests. Publishes *Book Industry Study Trends* annually. Managing agent: SKP Associates, 160 Fifth Avenue, New York, NY 10010. Phone: 212-929-1393.

Book Industry Systems Advisory Committee (BISAC)   An organization founded to promote systems standardization and development of computer-to-computer book ordering and distribution. Address: 160 Fifth Avenue, New York, NY 10010. Phone: 212-929-1393.

Book Industry Trends   An annual compilation of book industry statistics published by the Book Industry Study Group (BISG) and broken down by type of book and ultimate consumer. It includes a ten-year summary of unit and dollar sales.

book information sources for academics   In various studies, academics reported learning about new books from these sources and in this order: published reviews and articles, publisher space advertising, publisher direct mail, booksellers, publisher college representatives.

book insert   1. An advertising piece inserted with an outgoing book shipment. Some publishers use insert advertisements of related books or journals in all copies of a book printing, or as a stuffer in outgoing shipments or invoices. 2. A separately printed section of a book, usually illustrations, inserted in the book at binding stage.

book jacket   See *jacket*.

book jobber   See *jobber, library; wholesale bookseller*.

Bookland EAN   A bar code symbol that permits electronic scanners in bookstores to "read" an identification on books. The "EAN" is the International Article Number (formerly called the European Article Number). In November 1985, BISAC voted to recommend that book publishers print the Bookland EAN in the lower right-hand corner of the back cover of the dust jacket of all of their publications. In 1987, the National Association of College Stores (NACS) formally recommended use of Bookland EAN on books sold in college stores to facilitate inventory control. This represented the first market-specific use for the system in the United States. See also *bar code; Book Industry Systems Advisory Committee (BISAC)*.

book lease plan   A plan offered by some library jobbers. Under the plan, a library, for a fixed monthly payment, can lease currently popular fiction, mysteries, and biographies that are in high demand. When patron demand levels off, the library can return the books for credit toward other titles. Sometimes called a rental plan. See also *McNaughton Plan*.

booklet   A series of printed pages usually bound together by saddle stitching, but sometimes glued. Sizes usually vary from 6″ x 9″ to 8½″ x 11″, and may be either vertical or horizontal. When covered with the same paper as the inside pages, it is a self-cover booklet. When a heavier paper is used on the outside, it is called a covered booklet.

book life   See *life cycle; sales life (of a book)*.

Booklist/Reference Books Bulletin   A review publication of the American Library Association, published on the 1st and 15th of each month (once in July and August) and covering materials recommended for purchase by public libraries. *Reference Books Bulletin* is a separate publication within *Booklist* and reviews such works as encyclopedias, dictionaries, directories, and other reference sources. The 22 issues per year are delivered to over 32,000 public, academic, school, and corporate libraries. See also *American Library Association.*

book market, nontraditional   See *nontraditional market (books).*

book market, traditional   See *traditional market (books).*

Book Marketing Handbook: Tips and Techniques,   A classic two-volume guide on book marketing by Nat Bodian offering a wealth of practical approaches to marketing and promotion, advertising and publicity of scientific, technical, professional, and scholarly books and journals. The first volume was published in 1980 and the second in 1983 by R. R. Bowker Co. Available separately or as a two-volume set.

Book Marketing Update   An interesting and informative bimonthly newsletter by John Kremer of Ad-Lib Publications. Each issue contains numerous useful marketing tips and information for the small press, with emphasis on improving sales to bookstores. Address: Ad-Lib Publications, 51 N. Fifth St., P.O. Box 1102, Fairfield, IA 52556-1102. Phone: 800-624-5893.

bookmobile   Essentially a library on wheels, staffed by a librarian-driver. Such vehicles serve rural areas as well as aged and handicapped inner city residents who cannot get to a library easily. Nearly 2,000 bookmobiles operate throughout the United States, while others are active in Canada. The National Center for Education Statistics estimates that of 70,000 library outlets in the United States, approximately 70% are bookmobile stops.

Book News   Monthly publication of Bro-Dart, Inc., a major library vendor. Contains reviews, notes, and editorial notes about books. Distributed free to librarians. From: Bro-Dart, Inc., 1236 S. Hatcher St., City of Industry, CA 91748.

Booknotes   A bimonthly newsletter of marketing and business advice for the small and self publisher. From: Interpub, P.O. Box 42265, Portland, OR 97202.

Book of Books   A mail-order catalog containing the books of 12 publishers in the sciences and engineering offered by Omega Engineering Corp., Stamford, CT. First produced in 1987 and widely distributed to scientists and professionals.

book packager (producer)   See *American Book Producers Association (ABPA); packager.*

book packaging   See *boxed edition/boxed set; shrink-wrapping; slipcased edition.*

book packaging in journal format   see *packaging, journal format.*

book paper   Any kind of paper suitable for printing, except for newsprint, used for books, periodicals, leaflets, and folders. Available in a variety of finishes and in a wide range of thicknesses. See also *basic size (paper).*

book post   See *book rate.*

book premium   See *premium book.*

Book Previews   A slide presentation given annually at the (spring) meeting of the National Association of College Stores previewing titles of various publishers expected to be big sellers on college campuses during the year ahead. Sponsored by the paperback publishing division of the Association of American Publishers. See also *Association of American Publishers; National Association of College Stores (NACS).*

Book Promotion House   An independent U.K. organization relying on funds from publishers for trade marketing and to increase public interest in books. The idea originated in 1972 and has been under consideration since then.

book promotion sweepstakes   See *sweepstakes.*

Book Publishers Representatives' Association   An association of sales representatives for the British book publishing industry. Address: 3 Carolina Way, Tiptree, Essex C05 0DW.

Book Publishing Career Directory   An annual paperbound volume in which leading book industry pros offer advice on entering and succeeding in publishing. Good description of various types of advertising and marketing jobs in different types of publishing establishments. From: Career Press, P.O. Box 34, Hawthorne, NJ 07507. Phone: 201-427-0229.

book rate (postage) A term often used to describe the special fourth-class mail rate applicable to books which consist entirely of reading matter. The U.S. Postal Service term is *special fourth-class rate.* See also *library rate (postage).*

book review A critical evaluation of a published work. Reviews are an important factor for library selection and acquisition of new books. They also strongly influence purchase by academics and by bookstores, and help create traffic for bookstores. See other entries under *review.*

book review media, major scientific See *scientific book review media, major.*

book review media, requirements Different types of book review media have differing requirements for review copies of books. Those catering to public libraries prefer galley proofs well in advance of publication so reviews can aid librarians in ordering books likely to be in heavy demand. Newspapers and other trade book media prefer books in whatever form available sufficiently in advance of publication so that reviews can be prepared to appear at or about the time of publication. Scholarly review media are likely to favor the printed book since, in most instances, the book is the reviewer's "payment" for the review, which may appear a year or more after publication.

book review readership In scientific and scholarly periodicals, readership of book reviews is often as high or higher than other editorial content. Consequently, advertising in the book review section will enjoy higher readership than in many other positions considered as premium locations.

book reviews See *abstracting & indexing services; publicity (book); reviews, book.*

book reviews, engineering Many types of engineering books are not likely to be reviewed if sent directly to the publications for which they are intended. Most of the 12 engineering societies housed in the United Engineering Societies building in New York City depend on the staff of the Engineering Societies Library for book reviews for their journals. Review copies are best sent directly to the Engineering Societies Library, unless the periodical is known to have its own book review editor. Write: Engineering Societies Library, 345 E. 47th Street, New York, NY 10017.

book review syndicate   A reviewing service that writes and distributes reviews to a number of clients in the print and broadcast media. A listing of book review syndicates may be found in *Literary Market Place (LMP)*, published by R.R. Bowker Co.

book rush   The start of a new semester at an academic institution when college store personnel are fully occupied and mailings to college stores should be avoided. On the other hand, it is courteous and customary during this period for publisher's college reps to call on stores and offer their services as unpaid sales assistants.

books, new age   See *new age books*.

books, twig   See *twig books*.

book selection specialist, library   See *bibliographer*.

bookseller   1. Anyone engaged in the sale of books. 2. A term used by smaller academic library jobbers to distinguish themselves from wholesalers. 3. Generally applies to those engaged in the sale of books retail, whether in a retail establishment or by mail. See also *antiquarian book dealer; college store; medical book distributor; religious bookstore; technical bookstore; wholesaler (book)/jobber*.

The Bookseller   The weekly organ of the U.K. book trade. The U.K. equivalent of *Publishers Weekly*. A highly informative and well-edited publication. Published by J. Whitaker & Sons, Ltd., 12 Dyott Street, London WC1A 1DF, England. Phone: (01) 836-8911.

bookseller, antiquarian   See *antiquarian book dealer; out-of-print dealer; rare book dealer; used book dealer*.

bookseller, mail-order   See *mail-order bookseller*.

bookseller, specialty   See *specialty bookseller*.

bookseller, wholesale   See *wholesaler (book)/jobber*.

bookseller agency plan   A publisher plan for booksellers whereby a bookseller places an initial stock order and, often, a standing order for automatic shipment of one or more copies of each new book published within specific subject categories. In return, the bookseller receives a preferential discount on all books from that publisher. See also *selective order plan (bookseller)*.

bookseller discount categories   1. Trade discount for current popular fiction and nonfiction. 2. Short discount for professional, reference, and encyclopedic works. 3. Textbook discount for books used for classroom courses.

bookseller distributors, U.K. and Europe   See *distributing booksellers, international; European agent.*

bookseller mailing lists, major sources   (1) Ad-Lib Publications, 51 N. 5th Street, Fairfield, IA 52556. Phone: 800-624-5893. Approximately 2,000 specialty booksellers, by subject; (2) R.R. Bowker Co., 245 W. 17th Street, New York, NY 10011. Phone: 212-916-1699. Approximately 20,500 booksellers; (3) Christian Booksellers Association, 2620 Venetucci Boulevard, Colorado Springs, CO 80901. Phone: 303-576-7880. 7,000 Christian booksellers; (4) American Booksellers Association, 137 W. 25th Street, New York, NY 10001. Approximately 4,500 independent booksellers; (5) Dustbooks Mailing Lists, P.O. Box 100, Paradise, CA 95969. Phone: 916-877-6110. Approximately 2,000 booksellers who order from small presses; (6) National Association of College Stores, 528 E. Lorain Street, Oberlin, OH 44074. Phone: 216-775-7777. 2,700 college bookstores in directory form. *See also Canadian bookseller mailing lists, major sources.*

Booksellers Association of Great Britain and Ireland   The trade association for over 3,000 member bookshops selling new books in the U.K. and Ireland. The U.K. equivalent of the American Booksellers Association. Address: 154 Buckingham Palace Road, London SW1W 9TZ, England. See also *American Booksellers Association.*

Booksellers Order Service (BOS)   An electronic ordering and group buying program introduced by the American Booksellers Association in the first half of 1984 and discontinued on November 30, 1986. See also *FirstCall; One Touch; PUBNET.*

bookselling, religious   See *religious bookstore.*

book shelf   1. A term often used by commercial magazines that offer books of various publishers for sale on a special page as a revenue enhancement activity. 2. A term used by a special sales account for its book offerings.

bookshop   Term of reference for bookstores in the United Kingdom. See also *bookstore.*

Books in Print   A six-volume reference published annually in October by R.R. Bowker that lists by author and title the books of over 17,000 publishers and distributors. A supplement update is issued in April. From: R.R. Bowker Co., 245 W. 17th Street, New York, NY 10011. Also available in microfiche, online, and CD-ROM. See also *ABI forms; Books in Print Plus; Subject Guide to Books in Print.*   Books-in-Print (U.K.)   See *British Books in Print (BBIP)/Whitaker's Books in Print.*

Books in Print Plus   The CD-ROM version of *Books in Print.* A single disc less than 4¾″ in diameter incorporates *Books in Print, Subject Guide to BIP, BIP Supplement, Forthcoming Books,* and *Subject Guide to Forthcoming Books,* and is now also available with reviews from *Library Journal, Publishers Weekly, Booklist,* etc. Updated quarterly. From: R.R. Bowker, 245 W. 17th Street, New York, NY 10011.

Books-in-Print products   R.R. Bowker Company regularly publishes a number of different cumulative indexes of various types of books in bound books, online, and on microfiche. These include *Books in Print, Subject Guide to Books in Print, Medical and Health Care Books and Serials in Print, Paperbound Books in Print, Scientific and Technical Books and Serials in Print,* and *El-Hi Textbooks in Print.* Details from R.R. Bowker Co., 245 W. 17th Street, New York, NY 10011. See also *ABI forms.*

book society   See *book club.*

"Books Received"   A listing in many scientific and scholarly journals that provides complete bibliographic details, and sometimes a short descriptive sentence as well, on all new books received for review. The actual review may appear a year or more later. However, for many scholars, the listing is a notice of publication and availability and often provides sufficient information to prompt an order.

bookstall   See *exhibit booth.*

books that move (bookstores)   Books with strong sales, or with steady sales turnover.

bookstore   1. A retail establishment in which the primary product line is books. 2. A retail establishment that identifies itself as a bookstore even though it carries a diverse range of merchandise such as stationery and greeting cards along with books. 3. A term used by some associations or societies in their publications to describe book offerings offered for sale as a member benefit as well as a means of revenue enhancement. U.K.: bookshop.

bookstore, independent   See *independent/independent bookstore/ independent bookseller.*

bookstore, stand-alone   See *stand-alone store/bookstore.*

Bookstore, World's Largest   Slogan of Foyle's bookshop in London. See also *Foyles.*

bookstore chain   A group of bookstores owned and operated by the same company. The two largest are B. Dalton Bookseller, owned by Barnes & Noble, and Waldenbooks, owned by K-Mart Corporation. These two chains claim over 1,800 branches. The next ten largest bookstore chains claim another 500 branches.

bookstore market, retail outlets (Canadian)   Approximately 2,185 bookstores in Canada.

bookstore market, retail outlets (U.S.)   Approximately 19,000 stores in the United States.

bookstore turnover   See *turnover (bookstore).*

bookstore videotape   See *promotional video.*

book telemarketing rule   See *50-50-50 rule (in book telemarketing).*

book that travels well, easily   A book that will sell well in other countries. Medical books, for example, "travel well," according to one AAP study which showed that for one particular year, nearly 13% of all medical book sales of U.S. publishers were outside the United States and Canada. Scientific and technical books also sell well in international markets. *Infrequent usage:* A book that can sell well in various market channels.

book trade advertising media   See *trade advertising media, primary.*

The Book Trade in Canada A directory published annually every spring that covers about 450 Canadian publishers and distributors of books, about 400 non-Canadian publishers who sell direct, and 2,000 booksellers, wholesalers, and sales agents. Also lists government departments, associations, and organizations related to book publishing and book industry services. From: Ampersand Communications Services, Inc., R.R. 1, Caledon, Ontario LON 1CO, Canada.

book trade publications *American Bookseller, Booklist, Bookstore Journal, Choice, Christian Retailing, College Store Journal, Magazine & Bookseller, Publishers Weekly, Small Press. Canada: Canadian Bookseller, Quill & Quire. U.K.: Booknews, The Bookseller, Bookselling News, British Book News.* See also *publishing newsletters.*

book traveler See *college rep; sales rep/sales representative; trade rep; traveler.*

Book Travelers Association See *Association of Book Travelers.*

Book Traveller A fascinating volume by Bruce Bliven that describes the life of a commission sales rep selling trade books. Published in 1973 by Dodd, Mead, the book is based on interviews with George Scheer. See also *trade rep; traveler.*

book wholesaler/jobber See *Wholesaler (book)/jobber.*

booth See *exhibit booth.*

booth area (exhibits and conventions) The floor area occupied by an exhibit booth, usually in two dimensions, such as 8' x 10', or 10' x 10'. Many exhibit sponsors charge for booth area by the number of square feet occupied by the booth.

booth number (exhibits and conventions) The number assigned by the booth management to a particular booth to be shown both on the exhibit floor plan and in the convention program.

border box See *box/border box/boxed in.*

BOS See *Booksellers Order Service (BOS).*

bottom line An accounting term that in publishers' marketing refers to the net result of an activity or promotion.

bounceback (direct mail) Sales literature sent to a customer as an enclosure with an order shipment, or with an invoice or statement after fulfillment of an order. On the premise that the best customer is one who has already bought, the bounceback is a highly effective selling vehicle. See also *envelope stuffer; package insert campaign; statement stuffer.*

bounceback sales See *package insert campaign; package insert program.*

bound book date The date bound copies of a book are available in a publisher's warehouse or shipping center. For trade books, publication dates are set one to two months after bound book dates so there is time to get books into bookstores nationwide, as well as to give major publications sufficient time to schedule and publish reviews. See also *availability date; publication date/pub date.*

bound deck (direct mail) A card deck in which the deck of cards is issued in the form of a wire-stitched bound booklet. This format is rarely used since direct mail testing by various users of the loose deck format often outpulled the bound deck by 100% or more. (MarketPlace Publications is one of the last remaining major users of this format). The bound deck was first introduced by Cahners Publishing Co. in 1960 and enjoyed a brief period of popularity during the late 1970s in bound formats with one, two, and three cards on a bound page. See also *card deck; loose deck (direct mail).*

bound galleys Proofs of an unpublished book, cut and bound and distributed to generate early publicity, reviews, or comments.

Bowker ABI forms See *ABI forms.*

box/border box/boxed in Use of a box is a good method for making one part of text matter stand out from accompanying text, i.e., have a line or plain ruled border placed around the text. Most common box thickness used is a 1-pt. rule.

boxed edition/boxed set A book or set of books packed in a box specifically designed for the publication itself and usually containing printed identification on the outside of the box. Such boxing is usually done as part of the binding process. See also *slipcased edition.*

BPA See *Business Publications Audit of Circulation, Inc. (BPA).*

BPRA See *Book Publishers Representatives' Association.*

BPRA Handbook A directory giving names, addresses, and telephone numbers of all members of the (U.K.) Book Publishers Representatives' Association and the firms they represent. Alphabetical listings of publishers and their reps are also included. From: Booksellers Association Service House Ltd., 154 Buckingham Palace Road, London SW1W 9TZ, England. Phone: (01) 730-9258.

BP Report A weekly newsletter on the business of publishing that deals mainly with publishing management and industry trends. From: Knowledge Industry Publications, Inc., 701 Westchester Avenue, White Plains, NY 10604. Phone: 914-328-9157.

BRAD (British Rate and Data) United Kingdom equivalent of the U.S. advertising rate reference *Standard Rate and Data.* Issued monthly and sold on a yearly subscription basis.

BRC See *business reply mail.*

BRE See *business reply mail.*

breakdown (mailing list) See *list segmentation.*

break-even 1. An advertising or promotion effort that recoups its cost in sales. 2. The point at which a sufficient number of copies of a book have been sold to recoup its printing and production costs.

brightness (paper) A characteristic of paper that affects the contrast or sparkle of the printed subject. Artificial brighteners are sometimes added, such as fluorescent additives.

Bristol board Any of a variety of stiff, moderately heavy papers used for booklets, postcards, index cards, display cards, etc. Various types include: Plain Bristol, Index Bristol, Coated Bristol, Cardboard. The term "Bristol" is derived from the fact that the first cardboard was made in Bristol, England.

British Book News A monthly book review journal published by The British Council, a government agency established to promote the export of British books and information to other countries. It is similar in terms of content and scope to the U.S.

publication, *Choice*, issued by a division of the American Library Association. Each issue contains approximately 200 reviews by subject specialists of books that are appropriate for academic libraries; all reviews are subject classified with full bibliographic details. Distributed by: Journals Department, Basil Blackwell, 108 Cowley Road, Oxford OX4 1JF, England. See also *Choice*.

British Books in Print (BBIP)/Whitaker's Books in Print An annual multivolume directory listing over 420,000 titles from 11,500 publishers. Also available as a monthly microfiche service—an important resource for those who need up-to-date information on new titles and price changes. Now also available on CD-ROM. From: J. Whitaker & Sons Ltd., 12 Dyott Street, London, WC1A 1DF, England (R.R. Bowker is the U.S. distributor.) (Note: Beginning in 1988, BPIP has been renamed *Whitaker's Books in Print*. The reason, according to a statement by Sally Whitaker in the May 8, 1987 *Bookseller* is that "the title has become increasingly inaccurate. About 30% of listings are American and the title change reflects the intention to expand the coverage of European publishers' output in the English language.")

British Rate and Data See BRAD.

BRM See *business reply mail*.

broadside A single sheet of advertising, usually large in size and in most publishing promotions printed on two sides. A useful device when a publishing project has a large story to tell, as with an encyclopedia. Usually folded down several times and distributed as a self-mailer.

brochure A pamphlet, folder, or booklet containing advertising matter usually including headlines, text, and graphics. Special attention is given to design, and a variety of production materials and techniques may enhance the effectiveness of brochures. Brochures vary widely in size and format and may be either folded or stitched.

broker See *list broker*.

Brotherhood of Associated Travelers Original name for Association of Book Travelers. Used until 1975. See *Association of Book Travelers (ABT)*.

Brotherhood of Book Travelers   Name used by Association of Book Travelers from 1975 until adoption of the current name in 1979. See also *Association of Book Travelers (ABT)*.

browser-copy discount   A substantial discount on a high-ticket book, used by publishers to encourage booksellers to stock a display copy. Used mainly by publishers of illustrated gift books.

bulk   The thickness of printing paper, expressed in pages-per-inch. See also *bulking paper; caliper; ppi*.

Bulk Business Mail   A name designation given to second- and third-class mail by the U.S. Postal Service in 1983.

bulking paper   Book papers are available in a wide variety of thicknesses. A thin book can be made to look much thicker, or a thick book thinner, through the use of high- or low-bulking paper. In the 50-pound weight alone, book papers are available that bulk from as many as 800 pages per inch to as few as 334 pages per inch. High-bulking papers are highly porous and do not lend themselves to quality illustrations. See also *bible paper; bulk; caliper; ppi*.

bulk mailing   The mailing of third-class matter at special bulk rates that are lower than the established rate for regular third-class mail.

bulk sales   1. Sales of multiple copies of a book or periodical to a single purchaser, usually at a preferential or bulk sales discount. 2. A term used by some publishers to identify special sales activity. See also *special sales*.

bulk subscription (periodical or newsletter)   A subscription to a periodical or newsletter sold in a bulk quantity to a sponsor, sometimes with sponsor imprint added. Such subscriptions are usually distributed by the sponsor, which may be a professional society, company, organization, or government agency. Copies usually go to clients, customers, prospects, employees, or others.

bullet (typography)   A bold or heavy dot used to draw attention to a part of the text. Bullet size is usually stated in points. Specification of bullet point size should equal point size of x-height, rather than adjacent typeface. Also called dot. See also *typography; x-height (typography)*.

bulleted copy (typography) Features in an advertisement or printed promotion, each preceded by a black dot or bullet. Bullets are usually vertically aligned. See also *bullet (typography)*.

bumped (antiquarian bookselling) A book with damaged cover corners. See also *antiquarian bookselling terms*.

business, technical, and special library market See *special library market, including business and technical libraries*.

business book Generally applies to titles on real estate, financial planning, management, tax planning, and development of business skills. See also *professional business book (PBB)*.

business book, professional See *professional business book (PBB)*.

business books, advertising Advertising in media designed to reach mainly individuals engaged in commerce, finance, or business. The primary media for reaching business management or relating to business practice are *The Wall Street Journal* and *Harvard Business Review*. See separate entries for each. In the U.K. the equivalent media are *The Financial Times* (daily) and *Investor's Chronicle*.

business directory of toll-free 800 numbers See *AT&T Toll-Free 800 Business Directory*.

business directory renewal campaign See *renewal campaign, business directory*.

business paper/publication A periodical serving a particular business area and editorially positioned to give news of the field covered, rather than the results of research—the main focus of scientific and scholarly journals. Business publications are also referred to as trade publications or trade magazines.

Business Publications Audit of Circulation, Inc. (BPA) A not-for-profit, independent organization that provides independent verification of all paid and controlled circulations for nearly 800 business publications and professional journals. See also *Audit Bureau of Circulation (ABC)*.

business reply mail A term now used in the U.S. for all permissible postage-paid response devices enclosed in mailings to encourage replies. Under current U.S. Postal Service regulations, all business reply cards (BRCs) and business reply envelopes

(BREs) must be identified under the single classification "business reply mail." All business reply mail is printed with a permit number issued by the U.S. Postal Service. Postage is paid after business reply mail is received by the permit holder. To comply with regulations, BRCs must be at least 3½" high and 5" long, and at least seven-thousandths (.007) of an inch thick. BREs must conform to a standardized design and be no smaller than 3½" × 5" and no larger than 6⅛" × 11½". Mailers are advised to consult U.S. Postal Service Publication 25, *A Guide to Business Mail Preparation*, for the requirements of the latest regulations. Business reply mail is valid only for the United States and its possessions and cannot be used for mail originating from a foreign destination. See *Freepost; return envelope*.

buy (n.)   Sales rep lingo for a bookstore order for a particular title. "The buy is small because this type of title has not sold well in the past."

buyer (bookselling)   The bookstore individual responsible for selecting and ordering books from publishers. Also a specialist employed by a chain or wholesale bookseller charged with buying responsibility for specific categories of books.

buyer/distributor system (bookstore chain)   A buying and control system used by the B. Dalton book chain. Under the system, bookbuying responsibility is allocated to a group of MMDs (manager of merchandising stores or "merchant"). Each "merchant" is responsible for the stock problems of a group of stores in a particular part of the country. See also *category buying system (bookstore chain); open-to-buy system (bookstore chain)*.

buyer's signature   See *signature line*.

buying around   Legally bypassing an exclusive distributorship arrangement by buying books published abroad from a distributor in the country of origin to avoid an importer's price markup.

B/W   See *black and white (B/W)*.

B/W plus One   A printed job done in black ink plus one other ink color.

C

calendar-year basis (journals)   Subscriptions for most scientific and other scholarly journals are on a calendar-year basis. Therefore, subscriptions placed between January and December will include all back issues for that year.

calendar-year starts   A term used by periodical subscription agents for professional and scholarly journals, since, typically, they have subscription cycles that run the calendar year.

caliper   Thickness of a sheet of paper. See also *basis weight (paper); bulking paper.*

call, follow-up   See *follow-up call (telemarketing).*

call back (sales rep)   The practice of a sales rep coming back to make a second sales presentation because on the first selling call it was not possible to close the order. It could be that the bookbuyer was too busy, or the rep did not have the information needed, or some other reason.

call-in, advertising   See *advertising call-in.*

call report   A written report by a publisher's sales rep summarizing the results of a visit to a bookseller. Generally, they are used only by salaried reps.

camera-ready copy   Copy ready to be photographed for reproduction without further alteration. Also called repro copy or camera-ready art.

CAMEX Show   See *Campus Market Expo (CAMEX).*

campaign   A promotion effort aimed at a specific objective, over a given period of time, such as launching a new edition of a best-selling reference book, handbook, etc.

campaign, direct-mail   See *direct-mail campaign*.

campaign, package insert   See *package insert campaign*.

campaign, saturation   See *saturation campaign*.

campaign evaluation period   See *campaign length (direct mail)*.

campaign length (direct mail)   The time or period over which responses are tallied from a publisher mailing. Various publishers use different criteria. However, the most common is nine weeks after the first week in which sizable response is recorded from a mailing or ten weeks from mailing date. It should be noted that if not-yet-published books are included in a mail offering, the tracking period should be extended. Also known as *mailing life cycle*.

Campus Market Expo (CAMEX)   The renamed annual April meeting and trade show of the National Association of College Stores. The new name became effective in 1987. Upcoming Meetings: 1988, Cincinnati (11-15); 1989, Baltimore (10-14); 1990, San Diego (2-6); 1991, Indianapolis (8-12).

Canadian agency system/Canadian agency   The method by which foreign publishers have their books represented in Canada. A publishing firm already established and operating in Canada will become the agent and distributor for a foreign publisher. Canadian bookbuyers who bypass the authorized Canadian agent are said to be "buying around." See also *buying around*.

Canadian Book Information Centre (CBIC)   A project of the Association of Canadian Publishers that promotes Canadian books and provides regional, national, and international promotion and marketing services to ACP members. CBIC attends over 100 book displays a year, sponsors workshops and seminars about Canadian books, publishes catalogs, and maintains permanent book displays in Toronto, Vancouver, Halifax, and Winnipeg.

Canadian Book Publishers Council (CBPC)   A Canadian trade book association. Its main strength is foreign-owned subsidiaries. See also *Association of Canadian Publishers (ACP)*.

The Canadian Bookseller   A monthly publication for the Canadian retail book trade and the official publication of the Canadian Booksellers Association. Coverage includes technology and change, terms of trade, economics, and professional development. Address: 301 Donlands Avenue, Toronto, Ontario M4J 3R8. See *Canadian Booksellers Association (CBA)*.

Canadian bookseller mailing lists, major sources   (1) Chilton Direct Marketing and List Management Co., Chilton Way, Radnor, PA 19089. Phone: 800-345-1214. Approximately 3,000 bookstores. (2) R.R. Bowker Co., 245 W. 17th Street, New York, NY 10011. Phone: 212-916-1699. Approximately 2,100 bookstores.

Canadian Booksellers Association (CBA)   A national organization of approximately 600 retail booksellers in Canada; the Canadian equivalent of the American Booksellers Association. Annual convention held the last week in June. Official publication is *The Canadian Bookseller*. Address: 301 Donlands Avenue, Toronto, Ontario M4J 3R8. See also *Canadian Bookseller*.

Canadian Books in Print   A reference and guide to all English-language Canadian books in print. Issued in January with quarterly revisions by University of Toronto Press, it contains over 25,000 titles and nearly 1,900 publishers with addresses and ISBN prefixes. Indexed under 600 subject categories. Address: University of Toronto Press, Toronto M5S 1A6, Canada.

Canadian Library Association (CLA)   A national organization in Canada representing approximately 5,000 personal and institutional members devoted to improving the quality of library and information service in Canada and working toward higher standards of librarianship. Address: 151 Sparks Street, Ottawa, Ontario K1P 5E3, Canada. Phone: 613-232-9625.

Canadian Library Yearbook   A directory listing 5,000 libraries, library associations, library systems, library schools, library science periodicals, and suppliers to libraries in Canada. Published annually in June in both English and French. From: Micromedia Ltd., 158 Pearl Street, Toronto, Ontario M5H, 1L3, Canada.

Canadian Publishers Directory   An annual directory of Canadian book publishers issued by *Quill & Quire*, Key Publishers Co. Ltd., 59 Front Street E., Toronto, Ontario M5E 1BE, Canada.

Canadian rights exclusion   See NCR.

Canadian Telebook Agency   A database and electronic ordering system used by Canadian booksellers.

c & lc (typography)   Capitals and lower case letters. (Also u & lc, for upper and lower case). See also *lower case (typography); upper case, all caps (typography).*

c & sc (typography)   Capitals and small capitals. See also *caps (typography); small caps (typography); upper case, all caps (typography).*

caps (typography)   Capital letters of a typeface. Indicated in proofreaders' marks by three straight lines under all letters to be capitalized. See also *lower case (typography); upper case, all caps (typography).*

caption   Descriptive matter accompanying an illustration.

card deck   The card deck is a collection of business reply cards, usually in loose deck format, each containing an advertisement that recipient can complete and mail back (usually postage-paid) to an advertiser to receive a product, service, or additional information. Widely used for selling professional books. First use of the card deck for book promotion was in the early 1970s by John Stockwell in the McGraw-Hill professional and reference book division. See also *card pack.*

card deck, accordion fold   A card deck in which the cards are continuous and accordion folded and must be detached along perforated lines. Rarely used. See also *accordion fold.*

card deck, bound   See *bound deck (direct mail).*

card deck, sponsored   See *cooperative card deck/co-op deck/co-op pack.*

card deck bestseller (evaluation formula)   A card is considered a "bestseller" in a publisher's multibook deck mailing when it produces sales equal to the production cost of the card. New-book offerings must be considered bestsellers until tried since they still have their full market potential and, as a rule, have their greatest percentage of sales during the period immediately after publication.

card deck envelope formats   These formats include paper envelope, polybag, and silverfoil.

card deck formats See *bound deck (direct mail); loose deck (direct mail).*

card deck house offering A publisher deck mailing in which all of the cards in the deck are offers of the issuing publisher only. See also *card deck mixed/syndicated offering; card pack exchanges; cooperative card deck/co-op deck/co-op pack.*

card deck mailings, medical See *Publishers' Row card deck program.*

card deck mixed/syndicated offering A card deck mailing by a publisher that contains a mix of the publisher's own offerings and cards of outside advertisers. A number of publishers favor mixed offerings as a means of earning back part or all of the mailing production cost. See also *card deck house offerings; card pack exchanges; cooperative card deck/co-op deck/co-op pack.*

card deck stock The standard paper used for most card decks is uncoated .007 white high-bulk stock.

card deck syndicated offering See *card deck mixed/syndicated offering.*

card deck terminology (1) *Advertising side:* The side of a card in a deck carrying the advertising; (2) *Business reply side:* The side of a card containing the return address; (3) *Cost per card:* Although listed as an overall figure, such as $1,250 for a single-card participation in a cooperative deck, most deck advertisers view card costs in terms of cost-per-name reached; (4) *Cost per name:* Cost per name reached for a participation in a cooperative deck will vary. For large, general circulation co-op decks, the cost may be between 1¢ and 2¢ per name. As the quality of the audience increases, the cost-per-name increases to many times that amount; (5) *Card size:* The length and width of the card. Most are 3½" × 5½". All must be at least .007" thick and at least 3" × 5" to meet postal requirements. Also called "trim size"; (6) *Postage option:* Most card deck advertisers pay return postage. When respondent pays postage, response is diminished, but quality of response improved.

card pack A widely popular alternate name for the card deck. Seasoned mailers use "deck" and "pack" interchangeably. A few users and suppliers favor "pac" instead of "pack." The term "pack" is likely to prevail ultimately since it more aptly describes the loose pack of cards comprising a card deck and is favored by card deck producers. See also *card deck*.

card pack exchanges Sponsors of card packs will sometimes insert a card in the pack of a competitor in exchange for a like privilege in the competitor's pack. See also *card deck mixed/syndicated offering; cooperative card deck/co-op deck/co-op pack*.

card page See *book card*.

card rate The cost of advertising space quoted on the publication's rate card. See also *advertising rate card; one-time rate*.

caret (proofreading) A mark, similar in appearance to an upside down "v" used in proofreading or writing to show that something is to be added (from the Latin, "it is without, is wanting"). See also *proofreading*.

carriage paid U.K. term for free freight, i.e., where publisher absorbs shipping costs for a shipment to a bookseller.

carrier envelope The separate outer envelope in a classic direct mail package. Also called *outer envelope* or *outside envelope*.

carrier presort/carrier route presort third-class mail A subclass of third-class mail whereby mailers who sort bulk third class by individual carrier routes earn a discount off the bulk third-class rate. See also *first class voluntary presort*.

carry away bags (exhibits and conventions) Bags handed out at a convention display to aid attendees in carrying away literature and samples from the various exhibitors. Also known as *tote bags*.

case bound See *clothbound; hardcover*.

cash discount (booksellers) A price discount given booksellers by publishers to encourage prompt payment. According to the *ABA Book Buyers Handbook*, between 150 and 200 publishers offer a cash discount to booksellers. Most offer 2% for bills paid within 10 days of the end of the month billed. Other publishers offer 1%.

cash discount offer (direct mail) An offer of a discount for prepayment on a direct-mail book offer. The greater the discount, the better its chances. A professional society offered a 20% cash discount for prepayment versus a free examination offer and a prepayment requirement with no discount. The discount offer was by far the more responsive. This test was to the society's membership list.

cash up front   See *cash with order (CWO)*.

cash with order (CWO)   A requirement that payment in full accompany an order. Publishers who have such a requirement will often consider credit card payment as cash, although a few who absorb shipping and handling charges for prepaid orders often will not treat a credit card payment as a prepaid order.

casting off   Estimating the number of pages or amount of space that typewritten copy will occupy when it is set in a specific size and measure of a given typeface.

catalog   A bound publication, usually issued annually or biannually, listing all of a publisher's titles currently in print. Many professional and reference publishers include contents of titles published in recent years. See also *announcement catalog; annual catalog; seasonal catalog; short-title catalog*.

catalog, announcement   See *announcement catalog; seasonal catalog*.

catalog, integrated   See *integrated catalog*.

catalog, international   See *international catalog*.

catalog, journal   See *journal catalog*.

catalog, mail order   See *mail-order catalogs, publisher*.

catalog, mini   see *mini catalog*.

catalog, online   See *online catalog*.

catalog, sale   See *sale catalog*.

catalog, seasonal   See *seasonal catalog*.

catalog, self-cover   Catalog in which all pages, including the cover, are printed on the same paper.

catalog, specialized   See *specialized catalog*.

catalog, subject   See *subject catalog*.

catalog, thematic See *thematic catalog.*

catalog company See *catalog house.*

catalog copy A full description of a book intended for inclusion in a catalog. For specialized and reference books, contents may also be included or may be used in place of copy. Scientists and scholars often prefer contents to publisher-prepared copy. Catalog copy is often the starting point for all other promotional copy on a book—advertising, jacket, etc. Trade catalog copy tries to sell. General catalog copy tends to be factual and objective.

catalog format See *booklet.*

catalog house A business seeking to serve a specialized audience through mail order catalogs. Catalog houses are prime prospects for many types of specialized books, and in most large publishing establishments such accounts are serviced by the special sales department.

catalog house book requirements Books with high dollar value and with high appeal to the audiences reached. Stress is not so much on new books, but rather on books with proven sales records and good discounts.

Cataloging-in-Publication (CIP) Program See *Library of Congress CIP Program.*

catalog insert An insert added to a catalog with late breaking or supplemental information, or with corrections or amendments to the printed text.

catalog price See *list price/retail price.*

catalog publisher See *catalog house.*

category buying system (bookstore chain) A system of book buying utilized by the two largest book chains—Waldenbooks and B. Dalton. Buyers for the bookseller select titles by subject or category from the publishers assigned to them. The publisher's sales rep must deal with several different buyers, but each buyer for the bookseller in effect becomes a specialist in the subject area in which he or she is buying and, therefore, better able to spot trends. See also *buyer/distributor system (bookstore chain); open-to-buy system (bookstore chain).*

cathode ray tube (CRT)   A high-resolution "TV" tube that is used in phototypesetting to form characters under computer control for exposure to photographic paper or film. See also *CRT composition*.

Catholic Library Association (CLA)   A 3,100-member association of librarians, teachers, and booksellers founded in 1921 and concerned with Catholic libraries and their specialized requirements. Annual meeting and convention usually held in April. Address: 461 W. Lancaster Avenue, Haverford, PA 19041. Phone: 215-649-5250.

CBA   Canadian Booksellers Association; Christian Booksellers Association.

CBIL   *Chinese Book Information Letter* is a monthly newsletter published out of Hong Kong by Adrienne Lam, a publishing consultant specializing in the Chinese market, for publishers seeking sales to mainland China. Address: CBIL/China Book Information Letter, 4/f Fu House, 7 Ice Street Central, Hong Kong.

CBPC   See *Canadian Book Publishers Council (CBPC)*.

C.C.C.   See *Copyright Clearance Center (C.C.C.)*.

CD-I   Compact Disc Interactive.

CD-ROM   Compact Disc Read Only Memory. An information storage and retrieval medium that utilizes compact discs to provide access to large volumes of data that are recorded digitally. Once stored, the data cannot be edited or erased on the disc but can be searched and displayed on a terminal. CD-ROM can, on a single disc, store still or moving images, sound tracks, computer programs, and text files. A single 4.72" platter can contain 550 million characters of text, the equivalent of 275,000 manuscript pages, or more than 1,000 books. Among the first commercially available CD-ROM publications are R.R. Bowker's *Books in Print*, the Wilson Company's *Reader's Guide to Periodical Literature*, and Grolier's *Academic American Encyclopedia*. Wholesalers such as The Baker & Taylor Company and Ingram Distribution Group, and subscription agencies such as Ebsco and Faxon are using CD-ROM to publish large catalogs.

CD-ROM publishing   The publication of any data via CD-ROM technology, including, by themselves or in combination on a single disc, text, sound, still or moving pictures, or computer software programs. Today, most CD-ROM publishing involves large, relatively stable databases that are updated periodically, often quarterly, and sold on a subscription basis. Freed from online telecommunications charges, users can search CD-ROM files without fear of running up costs. See also *CD-ROM*.

CD-ROM: The New Papyrus   A book published by Microsoft Corporation providing a detailed explanation of the CD-ROM industry. Available from Microsoft Press, 6011 E. 36 Way, Redmond, WA 98073-9717.

center spread (advertising)   An advertisement on facing center pages of a publication. See also *spread (advertising)*.

cents-per-name (card deck)   A rule-of-thumb measuring factor when comparing card cost of comparative cooperative card decks. Usually, for comparable decks, the cents-per-name cost will be about the same, although cost-per-card may vary greatly. See also *card deck; cooperative card deck/co-op deck/co-op pack; card deck terminology*.

certificate of liability insurance   Some mail order catalog houses, as a prerequisite to listing a publisher's products, request from the publisher a certificate of liability insurance. They do this so that if information in one of their catalog offerings causes harm or damage and they are sued, they will be covered.

certified mail   First-class mail of no intrinsic value sent with a receipt, which recipient must sign. The receipt is returned to the sender.

chain   A group of two or more bookstores centrally owned and operated. See also *bookstore chain; college chain bookstores*.

character, copy unit   An element that is typeset, such as a letter, numeral, punctuation mark, or symbol.

character count (typography)   A count of all characters and spaces (using line averages) to be used in determining the area that text copy will occupy when set in type. See also *casting off; copy fitting*.

characters-per-pica (typography)   The number of characters in a particular typeface and point size that will fit in one pica (⅙ of an inch). See also *alphabet length (typography); typeface; typography.*

charging what the market will bear   See *differential pricing, (journals); pricing, charging what the market will bear.*

chase (letterpress printing)   The steel frame in which metal type is locked into position for placing on the press. An unfamiliar term to those who have grown up with offset printing. See also *letterpress printing.*

checking copy   1. A copy of a specific issue of a publication in which an advertisement has been inserted. 2. A duplicate copy or sheet listing of a rented mailing list, used to check response to a mailing or telemarketing campaign. See also *tear sheet.*

check names (direct mail)   Names added to a mailing list at the place of mailing for checking purposes, especially when it has not been possible to seed rented mailing lists. See also *seeds.*

Cheshire   A labeling machine. Also refers to type of label used. See also *cheshire label.*

cheshire (adj.)   A term applied to machine affixable labels prepared by a computer or word processor.

cheshire (v.)   To machine affix computer-prepared address labels.

cheshire label   A type of mailing label involving the use of fanfolded continuous forms. These are machine cut to various sizes, depending on the addressing format used. The most common format is 4 across and 11 deep, permitting 44 names per page. See also *cheshire label format (mailing list); label types.*

cheshire label addressing   Uses a mailing list in cheshire-label format. This requires special equipment and, unless such label affixing equipment is available, list-rental orders should specify a format other than cheshire label addressing, such as self-adhesive labels. See also *pressure-sensitive label.*

cheshire label depth   Cheshire labels produced in the United States generally have a standard depth of 1″. However, in the United Kingdom and in Europe, because addresses tend to run much longer, label depths may run 1¼″ or 1½″ in depth although 1″ labels are also used.

cheshire label format (mailing list)   Standard cheshire label format, in which most mailing lists are supplied to renters, is 4-across, east-west, produced on continuous forms—44 to a page. These labels are ungummed and unperforated, and they must be applied to mailing pieces by special high-speed machines that cut paper stock into individual labels and apply glue. Each label measures 2.5″ by 1″. See also *label types*.

cheshire label maximum address size   Most rental lists are supplied in 4-across cheshire labels. In the U.S. such labels will accommodate eight 30-character lines.

The Chicago Manual of Style, 13th Ed.   The "bible" of style books for authors and publishers. It serves as a comprehensive set of work rules for all in publishing who come in contact with the manufacturing aspects of the industry. The first edition, in 1906, was compiled from the jottings of copy editors and proofreaders. Called *A Manual of Style* through the first 12 editions. Available from University of Chicago Press, 5801 Ellis Avenue, Chicago, IL 60637.

Children's Book Fair—Bologna   See *Bologna Children's Book Fair*.

children's book publisher   A publisher of books designed for children and that are often substantially illustrated. See also *children's books*.

children's books   Books aimed at the juvenile market. The U.S. Department of Commerce breaks the classification into two parts: (1) juvenile books and (2) children's picture books. Books are usually either board, i.e., paper over board, paperbacks, or hardcover. Children's book sales are fairly evenly divided between bookstores and libraries, although the retail market continues to grow.

Children's Books in Print   An author, title, and illustrator index to more than 45,000 children's books in print, fiction, and nonfiction. Annually from R. R. Bowker, 245 W. 17th Street, New York, NY 10011.

children's trade book   A book created for a young person's voluntary, recreational reading.

chipboard   A low-density board, used as a stiffener and protective covering for mailing photos, and also as an easel for counter cards.

chipped (antiquarian bookselling)   A book in which tiny fragments are missing from the dust jacket. See also *antiquarian bookselling terms.*

Choice   A major review medium for books appropriate for academic library collections. Reviews 6,000–7,000 books per year, all prepared by academic reviewers, from completed books. A monthly publication of the College and Research Libraries division of the American Library Association. Address: 100 Riverview Center, Middletown, CT 06457. Phone: 203-347-6933.

Christian Bookseller   See *Christian Retailing.*

Christian Booksellers Association (CBA)   A national association of retail stores that sell religious books. The annual CBA convention is a major display opportunity for publishers of books of religious and inspirational interest. CBA publications: *Bookstore Journal* (monthly); *CBA* (monthly); *Suppliers Directory* (annual); *Current Christian Books* (annual). Address: P.O. Box 200, Colorado Springs, CO 80901.

Christian Retailing   A tabloid monthly with 20,000 paid circulation for Christian bookstores published by Strang Communications Co., 190 N. Westmonte Drive, Altamount Springs, FL 32714. Phone: 305-869-5005. Before switching to tabloid format in December 1986, it was known as *Christian Bookseller.*

CIP Program   See *Library of Congress CIP Program.*

circular   See *flier/flyer.*

circulation   The number of copies of a publication that are distributed. See also *Audit Bureau of Circulation (ABC); readership.*

circulation, net paid   See *total net paid.*

circulation, total   Full distribution of a publication, including subscribers, single-copy sales, in-house use, and complimentary copy distribution.

CLA Canadian Library Association; Catholic Library Association; Connecticut Library Association; Copyright Licensing Agency (UK).

claims (library) Term for problems or complaints relative to books or periodicals supplied to a library.

class A library binding See *library binding*.

classic direct-mail package See *direct-mail package, classic*.

clean copy Copy sent to a printer or compositor to be set into type, according to printing trade customs, should be clearly typed, double-spaced with 2″-3″ minimum margins on one side, on 8½″ × 11″ paper, uncoated, and typed on one side only. Copy in any other form and difficult to read may lead to additional charges.

clean proof A proof of typeset material that coincides exactly with originating copy and is free from marks by proofreader, editor, or author.

clinical book A book directed to medical practitioners and containing more advanced information than a textbook.

clipping bureau/clipping service See *press clipping service/bureau*.

closed draping (exhibits and conventions) Draping over risers and tables at an exhibit or conference display. When stapled into position, it is called closed draping. See also *open draping (exhibits and conventions)*.

closed-face envelope A regular envelope with no window. Closed-face envelopes are less expensive than window envelopes and easier to use since an address bearing enclosure does not have to be positioned in the envelope to show through. See also *window envelope*.

closed job (advertising) Job in which all activities have been completed, all billing accounted for, and a final job cost determined.

closing date The last date on which a publication will accept an advertisement for a specific issue.

cloth (book format)   A term commonly used in publisher catalogs and advertising to differentiate a clothbound or hardcover edition of a book from the same book in a paperbound edition. See also *clothbound/cloth*; *hardcover*; *paperback/paperbound*.

clothbound/cloth   A book bound in stiff boards (called binder's board) covered with cloth. See also *board (paper)*; *hardcover*; *paperback/paperbound*.

cluster promotion   The advertising or direct-mail promotion of related books in groups or clusters. See also *list advertisement/ list ad*; *list affinity (direct mail)*.

CME   See *continuing medical education*.

CMG Data Base   A database containing over 2,600,000 current mail order buyer names of over 40 publishers and available by subject for publisher promotions. See also *CMG Information Services, Inc.*; *College Marketing Group*.

CMG Information Services, Inc. (CMG)   A multidivision operation in Winchester, Massachusetts. Divisions include College Marketing Group (for college mailing lists); CMG Data Bases (for publisher book buyer lists); CMG Mailing List Services (computer service bureau); and CMG Information Publishing (faculty directories and other publications). Address: 50 Cross Street, Winchester, MA 01890. Phone: 617-729-7865. See also *college library lists, CMG Information Services*; *College Marketing Group*; *CMG Data Base*.

CMG Medical Book Buyers   A list of approximately 122,000 mail order buyers of professional-level books in various medical specialties. Most are practicing MDs. Available by subject from CMG Information Services.

C/NS   See *cost-to-net-sales ratio*.

coarse screen   See *fine screen*; *halftone screen*; *screen*.

coated stock (paper)   Paper with a coating applied to the surface to provide a smooth, hard finish. Screened illustrations reproduce best on coated stock. Some varieties of coated stock are cast coated, glossy, dull or semidull coated, machine coated, coated one-side, and coated two-sides. See also *finish (paper)*.

code (direct mail)   An identifying key used to verify the source of a mailing or an individual segment of a mailing. Also known as *key code*. See also *bar code*.

code (print publication)   See *standards (print publication)*.

Code of Ethics, AAP College Representative   See Appendix 14.

co-edition   An edition shared by two or more publishers. See also *co-publishing (book); joint publication*.

coffee table book   A large, lavishly produced and illustrated book designed more for scanning and show than for reading. Often excluded in approval plans established by academic libraries.

cold list   An untried mailing list. Also known as *prospect list*.

cold-type composition/cold composition   Composition in which no molten metal is involved. Usually created by either "strike-on," photographic, or laser methods. See also *hot type*.

collaborative advertising programs   Joint advertising ventures conducted by regional bookseller associations on behalf of their independent retailer members.

collection development (library)   The selection of materials for a library collection. Involves authority for selection, criteria to be used in selecting materials, fields of emphasis (including such things as levels of collection intensity, chronological and geographic areas covered, etc.), policies on foreign materials, formats of collection—books, periodicals, microfiche, etc., whether part of interlibrary group, etc. See also *bibliographer; collection development librarian*.

collection development librarian   The subject librarian (or head of such subject librarians or bibliographers) who usually makes selection decisions in large academic libraries (with collections over one million volumes). See also *bibliographer*.

college and university libraries   See *academic library; college library collection; university library collection*.

college and university library market   Approximately 1,900 libraries. See also *junior college library market*.

college bookstore market Approximately 3,700 bookstores classify themselves as college stores.

college chain bookstore A college store belonging to a chain. Barnes and Noble owns or licenses approximately 140 college bookstores in the United States and is the largest college chain. See also *leased bookstores.*

college course lists See *college faculty lists.*

college course offering A specific course of study in a college or university. CMG Information Services offers lists of faculty for over 4,600 course offerings. Textbooks for such course offerings are usually written by an instructor with extensive experience in that particular offering. By contrast, elhi course texts are often written by editors within the publisher's establishment, or by free-lance writers aided by teachers.

college faculty lists Lists of college faculties, usually by subjects or courses taught. A major supplier is CMG Information Services. It offers more than 600,000 faculty, administrator, and college librarian names, segmented into 4,600 course categories. Another source is the Educational Directory segment of the Market Data Retrieval database. A third reliable source is Academic Mailing Lists, with lists in the growth areas of business, data processing and computer science, economics, math/stat and the sciences. See also *Academic Mailing Lists, Inc; CMG Information Services, Inc.; Market Data Retrieval.*

college libraries by book budget (2- and 4-year and graduate) Over $100,000: 633; over $50,000: 877; over $25,000: 1,261; over $10,000: 1,511. Consolidated total: 1,887. Source: R.R. Bowker *1987–88 List Directory.*

college library collection A book collection designed to support the curriculum needs of the college. Acquisitions tend to include materials that are timely, relevant, and readily accessible. See also *academic library; university library collection.*

college library lists, CMG Information Services The CMG college and library lists include colleges by two- and four-year institutions, by college enrollment size, and by choice of any or all of the following: (1) departmental library representatives; (2) subject area specialists; (3) subject area generalists. See also *CMG Information Services, Inc.; college library representatives, depart-*

mental; college library subject area generalists; college library subject area specialists.

college library representatives, departmental   Professors on college faculty who represent their departments in dealing with library staff in collection development, channeling acquisition requests from other professors within their department, and administering the department library budget. See also *CMG Information Services, Inc.; college library lists.*

college library subject area generalists   Those bibliographers at smaller libraries who buy books in all subject areas. See also *college library lists, CMG Information Services.*

college library subject area specialists   See *academic library subject area specialists.*

college mailing objectives (book promotion)   (1) To reach influential educators; (2) to inspire requests for examination copies that may subsequently lead to textbook adoption orders; (3) to encourage direct orders for the faculty member's personal library; (4) to encourage the faculty member to recommend acquisition for his or her institutional library; (5) to encourage the faculty member to recommend outside purchases by those for whom he or she serves as a consultant.

college mailing objectives (journals promotion)   To sell subscriptions to individuals or encourage a recommendation for library acquisition, and to solicit submission of manuscripts for publication by a journal.

College Marketing Group   The college and university mailing list division of CMG Information Services. College Marketing Group holds over 600,000 college faculty names representing 4,600 course offerings in its database. It will merge-purge any groupings into a single list to eliminate duplication without added charge. See also *CMG Information Services, Inc.*

college rep   A textbook publisher's representative who calls on college faculty in an assigned territory to encourage textbook adoptions and generally promote the use of the company's new and current textbooks. The rep also solicits manuscripts that may be suitable for publication. Leads for new manuscripts are forwarded to appropriate editors. U.K.: *academic rep.* See also *sales rep/sales representative.*

college sales manual   A selling tool used by a college traveler or representative. It is carried by the representative for interviews with college faculty. Among its purposes: (1) indicate course offerings available in each discipline; (2) indicate what new course offerings are available; (3) offer comparisons of the rep's offerings with the competition; (4) orient the rep to selected courses and disciplines; (5) identify the rep's best sellers; (6) present product information to the professors.

college sales representative   The approved description by the AAP Higher Education Division for individuals who call on college faculty representing various presses. See also Appendix 14; *college rep; sales rep/sales representative.*

college store   A bookstore organized to serve the students and faculty of a college or university. College stores may be operated by the institutions they serve, or independents operating under contract to the institution, or as consumer cooperatives. Numerous others are privately owned or branches of retail chains.

College Store Journal   A bimonthly publication of the National Association of College Stores (NACS). Issued to all members and contains news, articles, and advertising of interest to the college store industry. See also *National Association of College Stores.*

college stores (U.K.)   There are two types: Small stores that serve schools with modest enrollments and stock only texts that have been recommended by faculty; also very large stores such as Dillon's, Foyle's, or Blackwell's, which serve the university market and carry wide-ranging inventories of virtually everything available. U.K. college stores, as a rule, are not owned by the school. In the U.K., college stores are called university bookshops.

college stores, leased   See *leased bookstores.*

college store textbook department   The textbook department serves as a depository and liaison between the professor and the publisher and will order and have in stock textbooks required for classroom use on a timely basis. See also *book rush.*

college text, graduate-level   See *graduate-level text.*

college text, intermediate-level   See *intermediate-level text.*

college text, introductory   See *introductory-level text.*

college text, textbook   One designed primarily for the college classroom, but sometimes also with sales potential as a professional reference or trade title.

college textbook adoption considerations   In diminishing order of importance, professors have indicated these reasons why they consider textbooks for adoption: (1) recommendations from other faculty members; (2) examination of an unsolicited copy received for review; (3) positive comments from students who have used the text; (4) reputation of the author; (5) literature received from the publisher; (6) prior adoption by a leading school in the subject area of the book; (7) publisher advertising in an academic journal; (8) recommendation of publisher's college traveler.

college textbook awareness sources   In diminishing order of importance, professors learn of newly published textbooks from these sources: (1) publishers' advertising and promotion; (2) reviews in professional journals; (3) college travelers; (4) conversations with colleagues; (5) own research or initiative; (6) departmental or institutional sources; (7) libraries; (8) displays in bookstores.

college textbook decision-making months   The time of the year when a college professor selects the textbook his or her students will be using during the upcoming semester. For the fall semester, approximately 95% of adoption decisions are made in the second quarter, May being heaviest, followed by June and then April. For junior colleges, the decision pattern is exactly one month earlier. Textbook promotion and sampling should be timed to reach instructors prior to the decision-making periods. See also *textbook decision month.*

college textbook publisher   One who publishes college texts. See also *graduate-level text; intermediate-level text; introductory-level text.*

college text "we-the-people" approach   The practice of selecting members of a faculty from five or six "name" colleges to coauthor a book. It is hoped that each faculty member will generate adoption sales within his or her own college. Another practice is to select two or three college faculty members within a specific region as coauthors. It is assumed that this will influence the adoption of the book throughout the region.

college traveler See *college rep; sales rep/sales representative.*

colophon Trademark or device used in some books or on promotional matter to identify a particular publishing house or imprint. Also, a description of how the book was designed or manufactured. (Originally, printer's statement at the end of a book.)

color, optical illusions in See *optical illusions in color.*

color coding Use of different colored paper stocks to aid in identification. Some directories may have color-coded indexes. Sometimes color coding is done in different ink colors or with different tinting on white stock.

color matching system (printing) See *PMS colors.*

color printing A reference to any type of printing other than black ink on white paper. See also *black and white (B/W); four-color process printing (4/C); one-color printing; process printing; two-color printing.*

colors in mechanical preparation (1) *Black*: Anything to appear in print; (2) *Red*: Thin lines indicate size, shape, and position of halftone and benday (screened) areas; also outlines of reverse panels that have not been filled in; (3) *Light Blue*: Instructions for sizing, screen percentages, screen size, either on mechanical or tissue overlay. Also to indicate shapes and positioning to aid artist in assembling mechanical and for the printer to produce blue lines (proofs).

color test (direct mail) A test in which different segments of a mailing to the same audience use different colors of paper, different colors of ink, or both.

column inch Advertising space equal to a publication's column width by one inch of depth. Sometimes the smallest unit of advertising space sold by a publication. Column widths will vary from one publication to another. In the U.K. and Europe, the comparable unit of advertising measurement is the single column centimeter or scc. Three scc's are roughly equal to one column inch.

column width rule (typography)   The narrower the column, the more quickly it can be read. Ideal column width for readability is 1.5 to 2 alphabets. Newspaper columns are set narrow for fast reading. Multiple narrow columns are preferable to one wide column. See also *typography.*

comb binding   A loose-leaf binding in which a row of flat, curled plastic teeth are inserted through slots along the sides of the pages to hold them together. The spine can bear printing. Favored for lab manuals, workbooks, and many types of industrial catalogs because the comb binding permits books to open flat on desks or tables. Also called *plastic comb binding.*

combination plate   A photoengraving or offset plate made from copy combining both line and halftone.

combination rate (advertising)   An advertising rate based on insertions in more than one periodical, and earning the frequency rate for the combined number of advertising insertions in all of the periodicals concerned. For example, any advertising in the various journals of the American Chemical Society are counted toward a combination rate applicable to all. See also *co-op ad.*

combined book exhibit   A fairly common reference for any cooperative book exhibit. Cooperative book exhibitors also favor use of term "combined" in place of "cooperative." See also *cooperative book exhibit.*

Combined Book Exhibit   A book exhibiting organization that established the concept of cooperative book exhibits at conventions in 1933 and continued business until June 30, 1985, when it ceased operations. The concept of cooperative book exhibits is still referred to as "combined book exhibits" by seasoned exhibitors. See also *cooperative book exhibit.*

comic book (trade paperback)   See *graphic novel.*

commercial journal   Typically a reference by a librarian to a journal published by a commercial or for-profit publisher, as contrasted with a journal published by a nonprofit organization such as a learned society or university press.

commercial publisher A publisher operating for profit. Books are viewed as products and publishing decisions are more often than not dependent on profit potential or sales suitability rather than the presentation of books as ideas. See also *professional association book publishing; university press.*

commission group See *repping group.*

commission rep A book salesperson covering a specific territory for one or more publishers, receiving a commission from each publisher he or she represents, based on either all sales or sales from specific accounts assigned to him or her within a designated geographic territory. A commissioned rep is considered to be self-employed, or a member of a sales group, rather than an employee of the publisher(s) he or she represents. Though arrangements may vary, commission reps usually receive 10% of net on bookstores, and 5% on wholesalers, with selected large bookstores and wholesalers more often than not retained by the publisher as "house" accounts. See also *house rep; repping group; sales rep/sales representative.*

commission salespeople, medical Sales representatives for medical publishers who call on institutions as well as on physicians, dentists, veterinarians, and associated allied health professionals. They mainly work on a straight commission basis, getting a percentage of the list price of products sold. Any discounting to customers, as a rule, comes out of their commission. Commission percentages may vary, but one of the largest medical publishers pays 30%, with the salespersons covering their own expenses.

commission stringer See *commission rep.*

common carrier convention shipments One of two ways to ship convention books and display materials. The term is interchangeable with "motor freight," and this means of shipment does not guarantee delivery of materials shipped on any particular date. The alternate shipping means is padded van.

community college A two-year college.

community college library market See *junior college library market.*

comp (n.)   1. Abbreviation for complimentary copy. 2. A comprehensive sketch of art or design. 3. A compositor (typesetter). See also *complimentary copy; compositor; layout.*

comp (v.)   The prhase "comp it" is used to indicate a complimentary or free copy will be given. See also *complimentary copy.*

Compact Disc Read Only Memory   See *CD-ROM.*

comp and colleague letter   A method used by some publishers of texts, mainly in medical publishing, to provide complimentary copies of new texts for faculty review. It works this way: (1) Prior to publication, a letter is mailed to appropriate department heads describing book and promising a complimentary copy on publication. The letter asks for names of appropriate individuals within the department who might use the book in specific courses and the names of these courses; (2) On publication, books are sent to the named individuals along with a letter indicating mailing is at the suggestion of their department chair (who is mentioned by name).

competitive use (mailing list)   Learning whether a mailing list broker's list recommendation has been used by a competitor and, if so, with what results. See also *mailing.*

competitor mailing list, rules-of-thumb for   (1) A list of bookbuyer names from a competitor will usually produce a higher rate of response than a compiled list; (2) a list of paid subscribers from a comparable but not competitive periodical will usually produce a higher rate of response than a compiled list.

compilation date (mailing list)   The date on which a mailing list was compiled. May also refer to the cover date on a directory from which a mailing list was derived. Compiled lists go out of date rapidly. When renting a compiled list, the renter should check the compilation date; the compilation date is important. See also *compiled list; deterioration index; mailing list deterioration.*

compiled list   A mailing list compiled from a directory, catalog, or other information source. See also *compilation date; compiled list (academic); database (mailing list); response list.*

compiled list (academic)   An academic compiled list is usually the most comprehensive list of names available in a specialized area and is most suited in mailings to academics who influence library acquisitions. However, in terms of measurable direct response, an academic response (bookbuyer) list will usually produce better results. See also *compiled list; response list.*

compiler   See *mailing list compiler.*

compiler, mailing list   See *mailing list compiler.*

complimentary copy   A book sent free to a faculty member for evaluation as a required or supplemental text in a course. Also any copy of a book given away to promote the sale of the book. See also *approval copy; desk copy.*

comp list   A periodical's list of complimentary subscribers. Many include contract advertisers.

composition   The setting and arrangement of original manuscript text into type in a form suitable for platemaking and printing.

compositor   1. A typesetter. 2. Anyone who performs any operations incidental to preparing forms for the press.

comprehensive layout   See *layout.*

CompuServe   An electronic utility serving personal computer owners. Subscribers receive information via special subject bulletin boards. Subscribers receive software and electronic mail as well as access to encyclopedias, news wire services, stock quotations, and other services. Address: 126 E. 56th Street, New York, NY 10022. Phone: 212-486-2440.

computer book market (breakdown of sales)   According to a 1986 study, sales of computer books in the U.S. totalled nearly a third of a billion dollars. Breakdown of the market: Trade books: 47%; College texts: 33%; Professional books: 20%.

computer letter   See *word processor letter.*

computer match, mailing list   See *duplication rate (mailing list); hit rate; merge-purge (mailing list).*

computer program A coding system consisting of a series of instructions or statements in a form acceptable to a computer, prepared in order to accomplish a certain result.

computer service bureau A company that maintains a publisher's (or any other company's) customer list on a computer, updates the list, and provides various other data processing services.

computer terminal See *cathode ray tube (CRT)*; *terminal*.

computer typesetting See *electronic composition*.

concept How an offering is to be made to its market. See *marketing plan*.

concept meeting See *launch meeting*.

concertina fold See *accordian fold*.

condensed type A narrower version of a typeface which has the appearance of the face, but permits a greater number of characters to fit in the same space. See also *expanded type*; *typeface*.

conference, mini sales See *mini sales conference*.

conference discount U.K. equivalent for "convention discount." See *convention discount*.

conference proceedings A book consisting of all or some of the papers given at a scientific or scholarly meeting or conference, edited for printed presentation and with related statements made. Such works generally appear long after the event. Most sales occur within a year of publication, with an additional small percentage during the 18 months following.

conference proceedings markets The primary markets for published proceedings are (1) libraries with a special interest in the field of the conference or symposium; (2) participants; (3) the membership of the sponsoring organization.

conference proceedings publishing criteria (1) Originality; (2) currentness; (3) reputation of contributors; (4) clear and readable manuscript; (5) information not readily available elsewhere and needed.

connectors (in direct-mail copy)   Devices at the end of a paragraph or the beginning of the next that give direct-mail copy a sense of movement. Example: "Even more important..."

consignment   See *on consignment*.

consolidated air or sea freight   A combined freight service favored by many publishers when shipping quantities of books across the Atlantic to or from the U.K. or Europe.

consolidated billing   See *journals, consolidated billing*.

consolidated edition   Two or more volumes joined into one book in a single binding.

consolidated shipment   The practice by publishers of combining back orders with new releases in a single shipment to reduce freight and postage cost to booksellers.

consortia, journals   See *journals consortia*.

consumer advertising   Advertising to the general public that is intended to generate bookstore traffic for a trade book and, in effect, to help move the book out of the bookstore.

consumer mail timing   See *mail responsive month, best*.

contingency planning   An accompanying factor to a long-term marketing plan to accommodate unforetold situations that may affect the plan. It is an emergency plan to account for the unexpected and take appropriate actions.

continuation mailing   See *rollout*.

continuation order (book)   See *standing order*.

continuation order (mailing list)   An instruction sent with a mailing list order to a computer service bureau to indicate that portions of a list have been used in a previous mailing and that previously mailed names should not be included in the upcoming order.

continuing education markets   (1) Professionals interested in vocational or retraining courses; (2) degree-seeking individuals employed during regular school hours; (3) students seeking extra credits for more rapid advancement; (4) professionals pursuing government-mandated programs for licensing purposes; (5) individuals interested in recreational courses.

Continuing Medical Education (CME) State-mandated programs requiring physicians to devote a prescribed amount of time annually to updating their medical knowledge. CME in some states is required for license renewal.

continuity program Arrangement whereby customer asks publisher to ship a series of similar or related books in a previously announced program at certain intervals with provision that customer may discontinue program without penalty at any time. Unlike book club, no membership is required. See also *book club*.

continuous tone A photograph or illustration with continuously differing black-and-white (or color) tone values. See also *halftone screen*.

contract bid A bid by a publisher or book supplier to an institution, school, library, or government to supply books under the terms of the contract for a specified period and at pre-agreed-upon discounts by category. See also *discount categories*.

contract jobber See *jobber, contract*.

contract rate A special discounted rate given a periodical advertiser for advertising placed within a specified period, usually a year. See also *contract year; frequency discount; one-time rate; short rate*.

contractual promotion commitment Contractual promotion commitments are publisher commitments to authors that certain types of promotion will be done in marketing their books. Because publication dates may be indefinite, it is useful to set aside the amount of the commitment as a separate budget item so that it will not disrupt normal promotional operations if a book is delayed or published out of sequence or in a different year than originally planned.

contract year (advertising) A 12-month period that starts on the date of the first advertising insertion, and guarantees the special contract advertising rate for all insertions placed during that period. See also *advertising contract; frequency discount; one-time rate*.

control (testing)　1. The standard in any test against which variables are measured. 2. Any promotion package that has performed satisfactorily in mailings and is used as the basis for comparison against test packages.

controlled circulation　A business publication containing at least 25% editorial matter, issued on a regular basis, and circulated free or mainly free to individuals within a particular profession, business, or industry. Income is generated mainly from advertising revenue rather than from the sale of subscriptions. See also *direct response circulation; qualified readership; unqualified reader.*

convention discount　Most publishers offer a discount for orders placed at the booth during the period of the display at a convention. Scientists and scholars often will compile lists of desired books prior to a major meeting and place orders at the meeting to benefit by the convention discounts offered by the various publishers. Convention or "show" discounts usually range from 10% to 20%, with 15% being the average. See also *conference discount; convention price list.*

convention discount, extended　The practice of some exhibiting publishers of permitting a convention discount to extend for a period after the convention, usually 30 days, if an order is submitted to the publisher on the publisher's convention order form.

convention displays　See *exhibits, convention.*

convention exhibit drayage contractor　See *exhibit drayage contractor.*

convention exhibits　See *exhibits, convention.*

convention exhibit service kit　See *exhibitor's kit.*

convention issue　An issue of a periodical dedicated to an upcoming meeting or convention and listing exhibitors, program, and full details of the meeting or convention. For many book publishers who exhibit, the convention issue of the core periodical in the field of the exhibit is a good advertising medium. It not only reaches the full readership, but also helps build traffic and orders for the publisher's exhibit booth.

convention kit   A kit of materials handed to registrants at many meetings and conventions. The kit usually includes a program, a floor plan, and a list of exhibitors. Exhibitors sometimes can arrange for a piece of advertising literature to be included in such kits.

convention press room   A special room set aside at a meeting or convention for contact with the working press. This is an ideal place to leave news releases or press kits if such are available in conjunction with an ongoing exhibit.

convention price list   A handout at an exhibit or convention with a detailed listing of all books on exhibit, usually arranged alphabetically by author with full title, publication date, and list price. If there is a convention discount, publishers often show list price and show price. Many have an order form or coupon attached at the bottom or at the bottom of the last sheet if on multiple pages. A few publishers add a notation to convention price lists that orders placed on the order form will be honored at the convention discount up to 30 days after the close of the exhibit. See also *convention discount*.

convention television   A closed-circuit television advertising medium through which convention exhibitors may reach television sets in all participating hotels where convention registrants are housed.

conversion rate   1. The percentage of inquirers or responders to a promotional effort who are converted to customers or subscribers. 2. Term used for first year renewal rate on periodical subscriptions. This is the most important year since the initial offer may have been a result of a premium or special offer—an incentive lacking for the second year. See also *projected conversion rate*.

conversions   1. Inquiries that subsequently are converted into sales. When such inquiries involve college textbooks and a sale results, it is called an *adoption*. See also *adoption*. 2. In periodicals publishing, the term is used to describe those subscribers up for first-year renewals. Conversions usually renew a subscription at a lower percentage rate than longer-term subscribers.

co-op (direct mail)   Slang term for a cooperative mailing.

co-op ad   1. An advertisement supplied by a publisher to a bookseller account for which the publisher agrees to pay part of the cost of the advertisement. The publisher sometimes pays the entire cost. 2. A book advertisement run by a bookseller for which the publisher is expected to pay some part of the cost, sometimes based either on the amount of space occupied by the publisher's book or books and/or a percentage of the bookseller's net purchases from the publisher during the previous year.

co-op customer rebate (bookseller)   The practice of some cooperative bookstores (Harvard Coop and Yale Co-op are two examples) declaring an annual dividend based on profits and dividing it among their charge customers. This is a practice of cooperative stores run by academic institutions on a nonprofit basis.

co-op deck   See *cooperative card deck.*

cooperative advertisement   See *co-op ad.*

cooperative advertising allowance   See *cooperative advertisement; cooperative advertising policy; previous year's net billing.*

cooperative advertising benefits   (1) Book ad is placed by the retailer at the local retail rate; (2) bookseller will not usually place the ad until there is an ample inventory of the book on hand; (3) other book outlets in the territory of the advertising medium also benefit from the advertisement.

cooperative advertising policy (bookseller)   1. The general terms of a publishing establishment relative to types of books and conditions under which a bookseller account can obtain a cooperative advertising allowance. 2. The terms of a publisher to a bookseller for a cooperative advertising allowance for a specific title. These terms and conditions may be tailored to that title only and will not be applicable to other books ordered from the same publisher.

cooperative advertising request (bookseller)   A form issued by publishers for a cooperative allowance. Bookseller completes and submits the form to the publisher for approval, and it is returned after being validated, usually by either the rep or the trade sales manager.

cooperative book exhibit A display, representing the books, journals, and related materials of various publishers at a professional meeting, conference, or trade show. Usually an adjunct to other individually sponsored exhibits. Affords publishers an opportunity to have exhibit representation at a modest fee per item exhibited. See entries under *convention*; see also *book exhibit*. Three well-known cooperative exhibit companies are: (1) Academia Book Exhibits, 4036 Poplar Street, Fairfax, VA 22030 (703-691-1109); (2) Conference Book Service, 80 S. Early Street, Alexandria, VA 22304 (703-823-6966); (3) Publishers Book Exhibit Inc. (the successor to Combined Book Exhibit), 86 Millwood Road, Millwood, NY 10546 (914-762-2422).

cooperative card deck/co-op deck/co-op pack A card deck mailing in which individual cards represent different advertisers. The deck publisher sells the cards to advertisers and handles all details of printing, mailing, and distribution.

cooperative card deck cost-per-thousand The cost-per-thousand for a cooperative card deck participation, as a rule, is closely tied to circulation. A 1986 survey showed decks over 100,000 circulation costing in the $15-$20/M range. At 60-75,000 circulation, costs averaged $20/M; 35-40,000 averaged $29/M; 10-15,000 averaged $53/M. Cost may also be much higher for very specialized audiences.

cooperative mailing/co-op mailing A mailing shared by a number of participants or advertisers. Usually arranged by a single sponsor who sells participation to outside advertisers. Cooperative card decks are a form of cooperative mailing. See also *cooperative card deck*; *Direct Mail Promotions, Inc., IBIS Information Services*.

cooperative mailings, international IBIS Information Services periodically mails to libraries worldwide on a cooperative basis, by subject. Mailings fall into two categories: (1) U.K., Western Europe, and Israel; (2) other major markets. Mailers may participate in two ways: (1) include their own promotional material; (2) have their information printed by IBIS on 3″ × 5″ "Publishers Information Cards." See *IBIS Information Services*.

cooperative marketing 1. Cooperative sales agreements as defined below. 2. Cooperative mailing as defined above. See *cooperative mailing*; *cooperative sales agreement*.

cooperative sales agreement   Sales agreement between publisher and a society, association, periodical, or other nontrade bookselling medium that agrees to advertise and/or promote and sell, at its own expense, a publisher's books. The discount may be the same as that given the publisher's bookstore accounts.

cooperative sales arrangement   See *cooperative sales agreement.*

co-op mailing   See *cooperative mailing.*

co-op money   A trade publisher's budgeted allocation to support bookseller cooperative advertising programs.

co-op pack   See *cooperative card deck.*

co-publishing (book)   The sharing of an edition of a book between an originating publisher and one or more other publishers, each having exclusive marketing and distribution rights within a territory or publishing category. The book may carry the title-page imprint of the originating publisher only, the joint imprint of the co-publishers, or the imprint only of the publisher taking the book for a specific territory. The originating publisher may arrange for the simultaneous (initial) printing of the co-edition. Subsequent printings may be done jointly or independently.

co-publishing (journal)   An arrangement whereby a publisher of a scientific or scholarly journal in one country will work out a cooperative venture with a publisher in another country to do either separate editions for each country, or a bilingual edition that each will market in its own territory.

copy   Text that is to be converted into printed matter.

copy (origin of term)   The term "copy" is derived from the practice of requesting compositors to "copy" in type the material submitted in handwritten or typewritten form.

copy, approved   See *approved copy.*

copy, book jacket flap   See *flap copy/jacket flap copy/jacket copy.*

copy, clean (printing trade customs)   See *clean copy.*

copy, effective (direct mail)   Copy that is clear and readable. It provides sufficient information and incentive to make ordering both desirable and relatively simple.

copy, envelope teaser   See *envelope teaser copy.*

copy, jacket   See *flap copy; jacket copy, scientific and technical.*

copy, negative   For effective copywriting, negative thoughts or phrases should be eliminated.

copy, sell   See *sell copy.*

copy, targeted   See *targeted copy.*

copy, typewritten   Copy produced on a typewriter. See also *keyboarding.*

copy, underlined   See *underlined copy.*

copy appeal   Copy written to appeal to the special interests of a specific audience. See also *copy approach.*

copy approach   1. Written matter intended to create contact and establish rapport with the reader. 2. The basic idea or direction around which an advertisement is developed.

copy approaches using "you"   See *you approach (in advertising copy); you (in sales letter copy).*

copy approach for journals   See *journals copy approach.*

copy approach for scientific and technical audiences   See *scientific and technical book copy approach.*

copy approach for self-help books to consumer audience   Tell the consumer what is in the book. Spell out the benefits and give specific examples.

copy approach to engineers   See *engineers, copy approach to.*

copy approach to law libraries   See *direct-mail to law libraries.*

copy approach to lawyers   See *lawyers, copy approach to.*

copy approach to school librarians   See *school library, copy approach.*

copy approach to special sale accounts   See *special sale accounts, copy approach.*

copy bank   A place where appropriate copy has been prepared and stored to be extracted and used as needed for a particular promotion.

copy chief   The supervisor of one or more copywriters in a department, agency, or service. The copy chief has responsibility for setting and maintaining copy quality, and for planning and organizing the work.

copy fitting   Adjusting type size and line width to fit a piece of typed copy into a prescribed space.

copy fitting, square-inch method   A formula for estimating the approximate number of words that must be written to fill a given area. It is based on locating a block of copy set in the same typeface and size as the ad to be set and counting the number of words in one square inch. This is then applied to the number of square inches of type area in the ad for which copy is to be written.

copy oversell   See *oversell*.

copyright   Protection of an "intellectual work" reserving to the author or other owner the right of publication. A copyright protects the work as a whole, but not the concept, idea, or theme if expressed another way. Definitions and information about fees and other services are available from: Copyright Office, Library of Congress, Washington, DC 20559. Ask for Circular R4, *Copyright Fees Effective January 1, 1979*.

copyright, U.K. registration   One copy to The British Library, plus up to five via the copyright agent to the libraries of the Oxford University and the University of Cambridge, The National Library of Scotland, the Library of Trinity College, Dublin, and The National Library of Wales.

Copyright Clearance Center (C.C.C.)   A payment center created in 1978 to collect and make payments to publishers for the right of photocopying. Over 800 photocopy users are registered. Address: 21 Congress Street, Salem, MA 01970.

copy test (direct mail)   Determination of relative effectiveness of an advertisement or some element of it in comparison with an alternate choice or choices. The purpose of the test is to determine the successful elements of the advertisement. To ensure maximum success, these elements can be applied to a future promotional effort. Test may be of any aspect of copy: headline, body copy, price, etc. See also *split-run test*.

copywriter   A writer of advertising matter for print advertising as well as direct mail. A staff copywriter may also do catalog copy, sales letters, and varied other writing assignments. Nonstaff copywriters may be employed in advertising agencies or work for various publishers and other clients on a freelance basis, one job at a time.

Copywriter's Handbook: A Practical Guide for Advertising and Promotion of Specialized and Scholarly Books and Journals   A useful resource by Nat Bodian for the writing of all types of copy from space ads and promotion letters to jacket copy writing. Published in cloth and paper by ISI Press, 3501 Market Street, Philadelphia, PA 19104.

copywriting, "you" in   See *you (in sales letter copy)*.

core journal   A journal in a discipline or research area in which the most significant work is published. Sometimes called primary journal. See also *primary scientific journal*.

core market   The primary market for a book or journal.

corner card   The imprint in the upper left-hand corner of an envelope or mailing piece usually bearing the mailer's name and address and presented in compliance with postal requirements. Initially conceived to satisfy postal requirements for a return address. See also *blind corner*.

corner card copy   Text placed on the left-hand side of the face of an envelope, postcard, or self-mailer. Such copy may be the start of the main message, or may be designed to stimulate interest in the subject matter or to arouse sufficient curiosity for the recipient to read the mailing.

corner marks   See *crop marks*.

corporate library   A special library in a business organization with collection needs based on ongoing research within the organization or on the immediate needs of the users. See also *special library*.

COSMEP: The International Association of Independent Publishers
An association of small publishers that provides a monthly newsletter, annual meeting, and numerous aids for small and individual self-publishers, including cooperative book exhibit at the annual American Booksellers Association Convention. Address: P.O. Box 703, San Francisco, CA 94101. Phone: 415-922-9490.

COSMEP Newsletter   A monthly letter of news of small presses and publishing news of interest to small presses, including marketing tips and trade show opportunities. Price included in membership. See also *COSMEP*.

cost of field sales   The ratio between keeping a sales rep (total costs, salary, benefits, etc.) in the field and total net sales generated.

cost of sales   The combined total of manufacturing costs and royalties. Also called "cost of goods sold." See also *gross margin on sales*.

cost-per-card   1. The cost to purchase a single-card participation in a cooperative card deck. 2. For a self-sponsored card deck, the overall or gross cost of the deck divided by the number of cards in it. See also *cents-per-name (card deck)*.

cost-per-inquiry   Total cost of a mailing or advertisement divided by the number of inquiries or orders received. See also *cost-per-order (direct mail)*.

cost-per-name (card decks)   A method used by many in evaluating the value of a single-card participation in a cooperative card deck. Cooperative deck sponsors feature cost-per-name in advertising and mail offers to potential participants.

cost-per-order (direct mail)   The cost to obtain one order from a mailing. If your mailing cost you $400 per thousand pieces mailed and you get 20 orders per thousand pieces, the cost per order is $20. See also *cost-per-inquiry*.

cost-per-return   See *cost-per-inquiry*.

cost-per-thousand (CPM)   1. The cost per thousand circulation for a full-page advertisement in an advertising medium. 2. The cost per thousand pieces to produce and mail a promotion. 3. The cost per thousand names, sometimes a criterion in mailing list rentals.

cost-to-net-sales ratio   The relation between the cost of a promotion and the net sales realized from it, usually expressed as a percentage. Used by many as a yardstick to measure results of mail-order campaigns, book sales, etc. See also *cost-to-sales*.

cost-to-sales   What it costs to produce a dollar of list price sales by direct mail. See also *cost-to-net-sales ratio*.

counter card   See *easel*.

counter display   See *easel*.

coupon, discount   See *discount coupon*.

coupon, dollars off   See *dollars off coupon*.

coupon, in advertising   The use of a coupon in advertising increases awareness of such advertising according to a 1986 study by Cahners Publishing Company. While the study indicated 13% more readers remembered seeing coupon bearing advertising, the author's own studies have indicated that direct orders from book advertising bearing coupons often did not pay the cost of the advertising space occupied by the coupon, particularly for books that are also available in stores; also that the rate of direct ordering for the same or similar books did not drop off materially when the coupons were omitted.

coupon, use of   (1) As ordering vehicle in advertisement; (2) as an incentive to get buyers started with a series or set; (3) in a regional or geographic edition of a newspaper or periodical either to generate orders for booksellers in that area or to test a book's regional appeal through coupon response; (4) as an insert in a publisher's catalog with a special offer to help improve ordering of a high-priced, slow-moving, or surplus-inventory title; (5) as a handout at a meeting or convention as an ordering incentive; (6) for a prepublication offer, to help build advance sales; (7) to test responsiveness of an advertising medium. See also *book coupons; coupon advertising; discount coupon; dollars-off coupon*.

coupon advertising   Mail-order advertisements bearing a coupon and designed solely to produce coupon orders. The most successful effort in publishing history was for a book produced by American Heritage on the assassination of President John F. Kennedy. The book, titled *Four Days*, is said to have sold 2.5 million copies, with one newspaper ad drawing 25,000 orders in a single day.

couponless advertising   Advertising that solicits orders may often omit a coupon and use an 800 telephone number instead. See also *800 number (telephone)*; *800 numbers in advertising*.

coupon program   A promotion in which special offers are made in coupon form, enabling the respondent to obtain special consideration—a discount, free book, premium, or subscription extension, etc., in exchange for returning one or more coupons within a given time period, or before a specified cut-off date. Such coupons may be loose inserts with other mail offerings or independent offerings. See also *special offer*.

courtesy discount   A nominal discount, given as a courtesy to a buyer because of the buyer's special status. An example might be a 10% discount to a school or college faculty member ordering a personal book on school or institutional stationery.

cover   Any of the outer four pages of a periodical, book, booklet, or catalog. The outside front cover is called the first cover (or cover 1); the inside front cover is called the second cover (cover 2); the inside back cover is called the third cover (cover 3); the outside back cover is called the fourth cover (cover 4). See also *cover position*.

coverage (review or publicity)   1. The extent of distribution of either review copies or publicity regarding any book or publicity effort. 2. The amount of publicity exposure resulting from a specific effort or release. 3. Publicity resulting from a press conference. 4. Term used in printing to indicate percentage of ink being used on a job.

covered booklet   See *booklet*.

cover paper   Specially made heavier weight papers suitable for covers of catalogs and booklets. They are made in a variety of colors and finishes. The basic size on which cover paper substances are figured is 20″ × 26″. This size is slightly larger than one-half standard book paper size (19″ × 25″) as covers sometimes are a slightly larger size than text pages. See also *paper sizes.*

cover position   Placement of advertising on one of the covers of a publication. Ads thus placed have a much greater chance for reader exposure, but usually require payment of a premium over the regular one-page cost. The single most noted advertising position is the fourth, or outside back cover.

cover price   See *list price.*

cover quotes   Quotations by experts, well-known individuals, or reviewers that appear on a book jacket.

cover rate (advertising)   Advertising rates for covers in periodicals are generally billed at a premium over the advertising rate for inside pages.

CPM   See *cost-per-thousand.*

cracked hinge (antiquarian bookselling)   A book with a break or tear along the seam that connects the pages to the book's covers. See also *antiquarian bookselling terms.*

crash printing   1. Impressing an image through surface pressure to other parts of a set, as in a three-part memo or invoice form. The surface pressure carries the image through to the second and third copies through carbon or carbonless materials. 2. A method used for embossing book covers.

crease   See *score.*

credit allowed (bookseller)   Credit allowed to a bookseller against future purchases.

credit card option   An optional method of payment on an order form, coupon, or other promotional offering. Useful on high-priced offers, where prepayment is required, or for offers directed to a specific market.

credit card response dropoff   The tendency of response to be suppressed in a direct-mail free examination book offer when a credit card payment option is added to the response vehicle.

credit hold   Withholding of credit to an account pending receipt of payment for previous shipments. Book trade credit holds are usually not threatened or applied until after 45 to 90 days.

credit line   A group of words or line accompanying a photograph, illustration, or quotation identifying the photographer, source from which the illustration was derived, or author and published source of the quotation.

crop marks   Corner marks on a piece of artwork or printed area indicating the precise area to be reproduced. They are indicated by ruled black lines placed outside the area to be reproduced and usually not less than ³⁄₁₆″ from the corner so as not to interfere with bleed lines.

cropping   Using crop marks to show where to trim an illustration in order to permit it to fit into a specific space. Usually done to change proportions of an illustration to a desired length and width. Also may be done to eliminate nonessential background.

cross-marketing   Selling a book in various markets other than its primary market.

crossover book (religious)   A book essentially written for Christian readers that subsequently finds a wider market among the general reading public.

Crouse Library   The William H. and Gwynne K. Crouse Library for Publishing Arts has the most extensive collection of books and reference materials on book publishing in America. Dedicated in 1983, it was initially funded by an endowment from William Crouse, a former editor at McGraw-Hill. Closed summer 1987 at its New York City location for lack of funds and quarters. With a search underway for new operating funds, the library at presstime was hoping for a 1988 or 1989 reopening in New York City.

CRT   See *cathode ray tube; CRT composition.*

CRT composition   Computer-controlled type composition produced by photographically exposing images in a series of vertical strokes (vectors) on a cathode ray tube. See also *cathode ray tube (CRT).*

ctr   Designer instruction to compositor or platemaker to center type or illustration copy between understood limits.

cumulative index   An index that combines in a single source the entries of earlier volumes of a particular book or periodical.

cumulative supplement approach (loose-leaf publishing)   After the main volume has been sold, loose-leaf publishers supply customers with all subsequent data in supplements. The cumulative supplement is usually issued on an annual basis by subscription. See also *loose-leaf publishing*.

customer file   Another name for customer mailing list or house list. See *customer mailing list*.

customer mailing list, rule-of-thumb for   Your own house list of book buyers will generally produce a greater direct mail response than any rented mailing list.

cut   A printing plate, usually metal and usually for an illustration, used in letterpress printing. Sometimes loosely used to signify any illustration, copy, or reproduction.

CWO   See *cash with order*.

D

damp-test mailing A prepublication merchandise in which the customer is guaranteed delivery of the merchandise when available. The process is used to identify segments of a mailing list or lists that will be effective for future promotional mailings when the product is available. See also *dry-test mailing*.

dash (typography) The short horizontal line used in typography. Can be specified in four sizes: (1) *hyphen* or *short dash*: used for breaking words on syllables or in hyphenated words; (2) *en dash*: used between numbers to denote "to" or "through," for example—"Index on pages 270–279"; (3) ¾ *em dash*: used to replace full em dash when a condensed typeface is used and full em dash would not look right; (4) *em dash*: used to indicate missing material, as a rest in reading, or to separate two thoughts. See also *em dash (typography)*; *en dash (typography)*.

data A generic term for anything processed by a computer.

database (computer) A collection of interrelated information stored in a computer that can be added to, cross-referenced, deleted, and retrieved in desired formats.

database, customer profile Basic information about bookbuyers stored in a computer file to facilitate its retrieval for maximum marketing effectiveness. Should include such things as: (1) what do they buy and how often; (2) when do they buy; (3) payment record; (4) types of purchases; (5) payment method.

database, source See *source database*.

database mailing list A mailing list compiled from data stored in a database and selected according to criteria specified by the person planning the mailing.

database publishing Creation and dissemination of publications or other information-based products and services from information stored in a computer database.

database publishing formats (1) Print publications, including books or periodicals, derived from the database; (2) magnetic database formats such as floppy disks or removable hard disks that are distributed to the end user; (3) online publication, often through a third-party vendor that permits users to search the database via telecommunications; (4) optical disc formats such as CD-ROM that permit large, relatively stable databases to be distributed to end users.

database publishing product characteristics Typically large reference works, directories, or indexes the usefulness of which is facilitated and enhanced through electronic information retrieval techniques.

data file A collection of related information that can be called up by a computer.

data overlay The transfer of specific types of information to a mailing list from another list to improve its segmentation capability.

dating See *extended credit.*

dating plan An arrangement whereby a bookseller can get immediate shipment of books and pay at a later date. See also *extended credit.*

dead back self-mailer See *self-mailer, dead back.*

deal A special offer made by a publisher to a bookseller as a stock ordering incentive. See also *special deal.*

December dating Special offers to booksellers as a buying incentive with orders taken at the May ABA Convention or during summer calls by trade reps. These orders are filled in summer or early fall, but with invoices dated December 1, and, therefore, payable in December or after the Christmas selling season. See also *special deal.*

decision months for college texts See *college textbook decision-making months.*

deck, bound See *bound deck (direct mail)*.

deck card A card in a card deck.

deck card direct mail effort See *card deck*.

decoy A name, usually fictitious, inserted in a mailing list to monitor list usage. Also referred to as seeding or salting a list. U.K.: Sleeper. See also *salting; seeds*.

decoy, specific order (mailing list) A decoy name inserted into a mailing list for a specific rental, and used one time only.

dedicated system A system totally independent of any other system in the publishing organization, e.g., a subscription-fulfillment system.

de-dupe See *merge-purge (mailing list)*.

delayed billing Incentives offered to booksellers for getting backlist stock into stores on a delayed payment basis. These incentives include: shipment spring or summer with no payment due until the first of the following year and quarterly and semiannual delayed billing programs. See also *extended credit*.

delete To remove.

deliverability A term used to attest to the quality of the names and addresses on a rented mailing—i.e., mail sent with such lists will be delivered to the person or place to which it is addressed. See also *deliverability guarantee*.

deliverability guarantee A guarantee by many mailing list compilers that a certain percentage (93% or 95%) of the names they rent will be delivered as addressed. When the number of undeliverable labels (nixies) exceeds the permitted level, the list owner pays the list renter a predetermined amount for each bad name. Envelopes bearing undeliverable names must be returned to list owner, often within 30 days, to collect the guarantee. See also *nixie*.

delivery, alternate See *alternate delivery*.

Delta Limited An expert wholesaler based in Surrey, England whose operation is geared to supplying books of all British publishers to overseas booksellers on an expedited basis and invoicing with a choice of payment in either sterling or local currency. On volume ordering, shipments are consolidated. Address: 43 Elmgrove Road, Weybridge, Surrey KT13 8PB, England. Phone: 0932 54776.

demographic edition   An edition of a publication permitting advertising to a segment of the total circulation identified by job title or function, by type of industry, by type of equipment used, etc.

demographics/demographic characteristics   The social, economic, and geographic characteristics of a group. See also *psychographics*.

demographic screen   Computerized elimination of potentially nonresponsive names from a mailing list prior to mailing.

demographic selection   Placing an advertisement in a medium where the advertiser can select which segment of the circulation will receive the advertising. For example, advertisers in *Science*, through the Clinical Demographic Edition, will reach only PhDs and MDs in research related to human health care. See also *geographic selection*.

denominational store   See *religious bookstore*.

departmental library   A library serving the immediate reference needs of faculty members within a particular department in an academic institution. Book acquisitions for the department library depend on funding sources. If funded by the library, purchases are library controlled. If funded by the department, acquisitions may be made by faculty members who usually order direct from the publisher, which is especially true in Europe.

departmental library representative   A professor in a college department responsible for liason with the library staff, recommending acquisitions, channeling acquisition requests from others in the department, and sometimes administering the departmental library budget. Lists of department library representatives are available from CMG Information Services. See also *CMG Information Services*.

descender (typography) That part of a lowercase letter that extends below the body of the letter as in "g," "j," "p," "q," and "y." See also *ascender (typography)*.

deselection The discontinuing of a journal subscription by a library. The action may be based on a user study or on a faculty committee recommendation.

desk copy A book furnished free to serve as the instructor's copy when copies have been ordered for students' use in a specific course. A complimentary copy may be considered a desk copy upon the instructor's decision to use it as a required supplemental text. See also *approval copy; complimentary copy; examination copy/exam copy*.

desktop publishing Typesetting, page make-up, and production of camera-ready copy on microcomputer-based systems comprised of desktop publishing software and small laser printers. Quality is considered acceptable for many advertising applications and even some small book projects. See also *word processing*.

desktop publishing, professional The systematic use of PCs (personal computers) by publishing professionals to prepare electronically and process text and graphics to produce typeset publications and documents. (Definition by Armond J. Irwin, Publication System Associates, Inc., Schenectady, NY).

deterioration index A term and concept for the annual rate at which a mailing list deteriorates or becomes ineffective, expressed as a percentage. See also *mailing list deterioration*.

die cut 1. The cutting of paper or other materials on a press or die-cutting machine by means of a raised steel die shaped in the form of the area to be cut (or perforated). 2. A cutout used for design impact, such as a hole cut in the cover of a booklet to reveal an inside portion, or in an envelope to reveal partial inside contents (or an address). In a printed promotion, die-cutting is done after printing and before folding and binding.

differential pricing (journals) 1. A two-tiered pricing schedule of some journal publishers under which individual subscribers pay at one rate and libraries or institutions pay at a higher rate. The logic used is that individual subscriptions serve a single person whereas library subscriptions serve many. 2. The practice of some European publishers of charging North American subscribers disproportionately high rates compared with those charged to subscribers at home.

digital press printing   See *ink jet printing.*

digital typesetter   A type composing machine that produces its letters by drawing them out of a computer memory instead of photographing them through a lens. The method is extremely fast and flexible.

dimensional printing/dimensional insert   See *pop-up.*

direct advertising (direct mail).   Advertising in any printed form, reproduced in quantity and distributed to prospects, usually by mail.

direct-impression composition   See *cold-type composition/cold composition; strike-on composition/direct impression composition.*

Directions   A publication of The Baker & Taylor Company, a wholesale bookseller, which includes selected subject bibliographies and complete bibliographic information on recently published titles of interest to academic libraries. Data are derived from books included in the Baker & Taylor approval plan. See also *The Baker & Taylor Company; Forecast.*

direct mail, classical   Mailing efforts oriented toward a single direct response, essentially toward influencing a purchase. See also *direct mail, modern.*

direct mail, inquiry-response   See *inquiry-response mailing/promotion.*

direct mail, institutional   See *library mailings.*

direct mail, mail order   See *mail order (direct mail).*

direct mail, modern   Modern direct mail is oriented toward an ongoing response from the same customer. See also *direct mail, classical.*

direct mail, retail   A program designed to sell books to retail stores by mail. An essential ingredient of retail direct mail is that it spell out discount terms and sales policies. Most publishers selling to stores by mail require cash with order, at least with the first order.

direct mail, solo   See *solo mailing.*

direct mail, supportive   Direct mail designed to support a publishing program, rather than to elicit orders. For example, a college division mailing providing information on a new edition of a textbook to faculty. The purpose, in this instance, would be to generate requests for examination copies.

direct-mail advertising   Advertising sent through the mails or other direct delivery service. Its function is to place advertising about a publisher's offerings in the hands of a targeted audience, with direct response not necessarily the primary consideration. See also *direct-response mailing.*

Direct Mail and Mail Order Handbook, 3rd Ed.   A comprehensive and useful reference by Richard Hodgson, although much of the material is outdated. Published 1980 by Dartnell Corp., 4660 Ravenswood Avenue, Chicago, IL 60640.

direct-mail bookbuyers lists   See *bookbuyer lists.*

direct-mail campaign   A single mailing or a series of mailings designed to achieve a specific objective for a specific book or group of books over a stated period of time. See also *campaign length (direct mail).*

direct-mail campaign length   See *campaign length (direct mail).*

direct-mail envelope eye flow   See *envelope eye flow.*

direct-mail eye flow studies   See *mailing package eye flow studies.*

Direct Mail List Rates and Data   See *SRDS Direct Mail List Rates and Data.*

direct-mail package   1. Typically the mailing piece as placed in the mail. 2. All of the elements involved in any particular direct-mail effort. See also *direct-mail package, classic.*

direct-mail package, classic   The classic direct-mail package consists of these four elements: outer or mailing envelope, letter, reply form, and return card or envelope.

direct-mail package test   A test of part or all of the elements of one mailing piece or package against another. See also *direct-mail package; direct-mail testing.*

direct-mail promotion assembly date   The date on which all of the components of a mailing and all of the mailing lists to be used must be on hand in the mailing house or lettershop. This date should be early enough to permit ample time for collating, addressing, inserting, and, when applicable, sorting, tieing, and bagging. See also *printing completion date (direct mail)*.

Direct Mail Promotions, Inc.   A sponsor of cooperative mailings to schools, libraries, and bookstores. Mailings are made in 9″ × 12″ envelopes to selected lists, and publishers may participate either by supplying a preprinted mailing piece up to 8½″ × 11″ in size, or by buying a fractional page in inserts printed by the sponsor. A low cost and useful mailing vehicle, in operation since 1966. Address: 342 Madison Avenue, New York, NY 10017. Phone: 212-687-1910.

direct-mail quality of response   See *quality of response (direct mail)*.

direct-mail response, inquiry qualifying   The purpose of some mailings is to elicit inquiries from qualified buyers. Such mailings may offer a kit, an expensive prospectus, or examination copy to those who respond. Requiring the respondent to pay postage also tends to elicit responses only from serious prospects. Also called *inquiry-response mailing/promotion*.

direct-mail telegram format   See *gram format*.

direct-mail testing   Measuring the potential success of a campaign through controlled tests of direct-mail variables within a small segment of a market. Test elements may include: format (package vs. self-mailer), copy, price offers, single-book offering vs. list offering, reply devices, ink color, paper, postage, etc. See also *list testing; list test size rules; market testing; rollout/roll out/rollout mailing; mailing list test sample*.

direct mail to law libraries, key ingredients   (1) Subject; (2) contents; (3) price; (4) author credentials; (5) publisher credentials.

direct mail to libraries, rule for   Direct mail to libraries has its best chance for success when the offering is closely tied to the mission of the library, whether college, business, or other type of institution.

direct mail to school libraries See *school library direct mail approach.*

direct mail to top management, rule for Direct mail to people in top management is most effective when the offer is limited to a single item and without distractions. At lower management levels, an assortment offering may work better.

direct marketing The selling of any goods or services directly to the consumer. See also *direct-response advertising.*

Direct Marketing Association (DMA) Oldest and largest international trade association representing users, creators, and suppliers of direct-mail advertising and other direct-marketing techniques. Headquarters: 6 E. 43rd Street, New York, NY 10017; Washington, DC office: 1730 K Street NW 20006.

Direct Marketing: Strategy, Planning, Execution, 2nd Ed. A clear and well-written guide by Ed Nash on many aspects of direct marketing. Published in 1986 by McGraw-Hill, 22 W. 19th Street, New York, NY 10011.

direct marketing to schools See *Direct Response Marketing to Schools Newsletter.*

direct ordering, library When librarians place orders for publications directly with publishers, rather than through subscription agents, jobbers, or wholesalers, they are practicing "direct ordering." This practice has declined in recent years as acquisition librarians have taken advantage of the various economies and services offered by wholesalers and subscription agents. See also *jobber, library; library wholesaler; subscription agent/agency.*

directories of periodicals See *Bacon's International Publicity Checker; Gale Directory of Publications; MLA Directory of Periodicals; Standard Periodical Directory; SRDS Business Publication Rates and Data; SRDS Consumer Magazine and Agri-Media Rates and Data; Ulrich's International Periodicals Directory.*

directory A systematically-arranged reference, usually alphabetical, or alphabetical within classification or subject, listing names and addresses, and/or other detailed information. The subject of the directory is usually part of its title accompanied by the word "Directory."

directory list A mailing list compiled from entries in a directory. Such lists are partially out of date by the time the directory is published. Therefore, attention must be given to the date of publication when renting or using a directory list. See also *directory list recompilation; mailing list cleaning.*

directory list recompilation The practice of some mailing list compilers to recompile an entirely new list from each new edition of a directory, rather than to correct undeliverable addresses from a current one. As a consequence, all list rentals from a current compilation will have at least the same number of nondeliverables as the preceding rental, until a new list is compiled from a future edition of the directory.

directory of associations See *Encyclopedia of Associations.*

***Directory of Book Publishers and Wholesalers* (United Kingdom)** A directory of nearly 5,000 book publishers and nearly 100 book wholesalers in the U.K. and Ireland. For publishers, lists full details, including types of books published and terms offered. Published annually in April. Available only to booksellers and publishers. See also *Booksellers Association of Great Britain and Ireland.*

Directory of British Publishers and Their Terms: Including Agents for Overseas Publishers. An annual publication of the Booksellers Association of Great Britain and Ireland (see separate entry).

The Directory of Directories A directory providing extensive and detailed information on over 10,000 business and industrial directories, professional and scientific rosters, directory databases, and other lists and guides of all kinds. Beginning with the 1987 edition, published in two parts, the first part being mainly business, science, engineering, law, and government. The second part consists of information sciences, social sciences, humanities, arts and entertainment, public affairs, health and medicine, religious and ethnic affairs, and more. Beginning in 1988 it will be titled *Directories in Print.* Published annually in October by Gale Research Company, Book Tower, Detroit, MI 48226.

Directory of Federal Libraries A directory edited by William Evinger that identifies more than 2,400 libraries serving the Federal Government throughout the United States and overseas. Includes all libraries serving any agency of the Federal Government, including boards, commissions, committees, and/or quasi-official agencies such as the Smithsonian Institution and the National Gallery of Art Library. Includes type-of-library index and subject index. Published in 1987 by the Oryx Press. Address: 2214 N. Central at Encanto, Phoenix, AZ 85004-1483. Phone: 800-457-6799.

Directory of Publishers (college textbooks)   A listing of over 400 publishers of college textbooks that provide faculty with desk copies. Published annually in April by National Association of College Stores. See also *National Association of College Stores.*

Directory of Regional, State and Local Organizations   See *Encyclopedia of Associations: Regional, State, and Local Organizations.*

Directory of Special Libraries and Information Centers   Covers over 17,000 special libraries, information centers, documentation centers, etc., in the United States and Canada. Published by Gale Research Company.

directory of toll-free business numbers   See *AT&T Toll-Free 800 Business Directory.*

directory renewal mail campaign   A mail campaign designed to elicit orders for a new edition of a directory from previous buyers. Emphasis in such campaigns should be on number of changes in new edition as well as on new material added and benefits offered from this material. A key ingredient should always be a postpaid response vehicle. See also *renewal campaign, business directory.*

direct positive (DP)   A photographic positive reproduction made by a single contact exposure with the artwork or object photographed.

direct-request circulation   Term used in controlled circulation publishing whereby recipient of publication has filled out a form requesting the periodical and also given pertinent employment and title code information. Important for auditing by Business Publications Audit of Circulation (BPA) and Audit Bureau of Circulation (ABC).

direct-response advertising   Advertising through any medium designed to generate a measurable response (TV, radio, newspapers, periodicals, telephone, etc.). See also *direct marketing.*

direct-response card deck   See *card deck*.

direct-response cards   The classification given to cooperative card decks in *SRDS Direct Mail List Rates and Data*, and in *SRDS Business Publication Rates and Data*. See also *card deck; card pack*.

direct-response mailing   A mailing aimed solely at generating direct responses from those to whom it is mailed. It asks the recipient to mail or phone the order in at once. See also *direct-mail advertising*.

direct-response marketing   Any promotional effort aimed at obtaining direct orders. See also *direct marketing; inquiry response mailing/promotion*.

Direct Response Marketing to Schools Newsletter   A monthly publication with ideas, case studies, and interviews on ways to improve direct marketing to schools. Published by School Market Research Institute, P.O. Box 10, Haddam, CT 06438.

direct subscriber   A subscriber to a subscription publication who orders directly from the publisher.

discipline promotion   A mailing to individuals within a specific branch of knowledge or learning.

discount, agency   See *agency discount*.

discount, author   See *author discount*.

discount, backlist   See *backlist incentive programs (bookseller)*.

discount, browser copy   See *browser copy discount*.

discount, convention   See *conference discount; convention discount*.

discount, courtesy   See *courtesy discount*.

discount, educational   See *educational discount*.

discount, library   See *library discount*.

discount, membership   See *membership discount*.

discount, nonreturnable   See *nonreturnable discount*.

discount, prepayment See *prepayment discount.*

discount, prepublication See *prepublication discount.*

discount, professional See *professional discount.*

discount, quantity See *quantity discount.*

discount, reference See *reference discount.*

discount, sale See *sale discount.*

discount, set See *set discount.*

discount, short See *short discount.*

discount, standing order See *standing order discount.*

discount, subscription See *subscription discount (book); subscription discount (periodical).*

discount, textbook See *textbook discount.*

discount, trade See *trade discount (bookseller); trade discount (periodical).*

discount categories/classes (contract bidding) In many types of bidding, there are sometimes three distinct discount classes: trade, textbook, and reference. However, library wholesalers and others also recognize as discount classes such categories as library editions (especially juveniles), binding types, and technical books (as separate from textbooks). See also *contract bid.*

discount coupon A coupon or printed form offering a discount off the selling price if the buyer returns coupon with order. Usual usage is in publisher direct-mail offers. Also used occasionally at conventions or other types of book exhibits. See also *dollars-off coupon.*

discounted book offer See *sale, inventory reduction.*

discount from list price A percentage off the list price. The traditional billing formula of most publishers used to determine the selling price to booksellers, or, in some instances, to libraries and nonprofit institutions. See also *cash discount (bookseller); library discount; list price/retail price; net price; short discount; trade discount (bookseller).*

discounts, general bookseller   See *bookseller discount categories.*

discount schedule, graduated   A range of bookseller discounts based on the number of copies of single or assorted titles on an order, usually with a low discount for single-copy purchases and increasing discounts as volume of order increases.

discounts on special sales   See *special sales discount; special sales, industrial training; special sales, premium.*

discretionary book   A book that may have limited appeal, but is not considered essential. Price is often a significant factor in purchase of such books.

display, dump   See *dump display, dump bin.*

display, unstaffed   See *unstaffed display (conventions).*

display advertising   See *space advertising.*

display copy   A book, usually high priced, that the bookseller will show for examination, while copies to be sold are untouched in storage or are ordered on demand. Also called *browser's copy.* See *browser-copy discount.*

display type   Type that is usually 14 points or larger, used for headings, as distinguished from body type. See also *body type.*

display unit, free standing   See *free standing display unit.*

display unit, island   See *island display unit.*

disposals   A term used at Harper & Row to reflect inventory reduction through sales or other means—comp copies, etc.

distributing booksellers, international   Booksellers may often serve as distributors for U.S. or other foreign publishers—either on an exclusive or nonexclusive basis. As distributors, they may perform many of the functions done by publisher marketing personnel in the U.S. For example, they maintain their own customer lists for mailing purposes, issue subject catalogs, set up displays at conventions and congresses, and employ field sales agents to call on other bookshops. See also *distributing booksellers, international advantages; European agent.*

distributing booksellers, international advantages (1) Intimate knowledge of book markets; (2) customer delivery and service from a local source; (3) localized promotion with the distributing bookseller's other ongoing promotions and displays; (4) elimination of currency-exchange problems for buyers in international markets. Books are sold in local currency. See also *distributing booksellers, international; European agent.*

distribution arrangement, exclusive An arrangement whereby a publisher, for certain considerations, agrees to name a bookseller or other selling or distributing organization as the sole or exclusive distributor within a given geographic territory, for example, only in Japan, or only in the United Kingdom. Other arrangements may be for certain markets. For example, a publishing society may give an exclusive distribution arrangement for all outlets and territories worldwide, exclusive of its membership— for which it retains sole sales rights.

distribution arrangement, nonexclusive An arrangement whereby a bookseller agrees to stock and sell the books of a publisher and, sometimes, perform other marketing services on a nonexclusive basis, i.e., other agents in the same territory may also be permitted to stock and sell the same books. See related entries under *distributing booksellers.*

distribution arrangement, U.K. exclusive In the U.K., only an exclusive distributor is allowed to enter imported titles in *Whitaker's Books in Print* (formerly British Books in Print) and Teleordering. Without inclusion in this database, the distributor has no guarantee that orders will be sent directly to him or her, so this system prevents orders bypassing the distributor and going directly to the (U.S.) publisher.

distribution arrangement, U.S. exclusive In the U.S., only an exclusive distributor of a foreign publisher may list that publisher's books in *Books in Print*. However, because many importing publishers mark up the prices of import titles, academics and others sometimes get around the "exclusive" by ordering from a bookseller in the publisher's home country. See *buying around.*

distribution deal An arrangement between two publishers under which one, usually the larger, agrees to warehouse, distribute, and handle billing for the books published by the other. Sales may be generated by the larger publisher's sales force. See also *affiliated relationship*.

DMA Direct Marketing Association.

DMLRD See SRDS *Direct Mail List Rates and Data*.

doctors, medical See *medical bookbuyer lists; medical book exhibits, cooperative; medical book market; Publishers Row card deck program*.

documentation 1. Systematic collection, classification, storage, and dissemination of specialized information 2. A description for evidential reference materials. 3. In computer systems, a written record of records used to hold information about the software of a computer system.

dollars-off coupon A coupon enclosure within a direct mail package that offers a fixed number of dollars off a purchase if enclosed with an order. See also *discount coupon*.

double column Typeset pages with two vertical columns rather than type extending across the entire page.

double-ordering The practice of some college stores of ordering the same textbooks simultaneously from their publishers and from used book dealers. They sell the used books first, and use the new stock only as needed, resulting in high returns.

double-page spread See *spread (advertising)*.

double spread See *spread (advertising)*.

double truck See *spread (advertising)*.

down-market book A book appealing to unsophisticated tastes. See also *up-market book*.

DPO (British) Direct Purchasing Organizations. Refers to library consortia who group orders and buy directly from publishers at more favorable quantity prices, and in turn are able to offer greater discounts to their members.

drayage (exhibits and conventions) Those activities involving the movement of exhibit materials into and out of the convention or exhibit booth.

drayage contractor (exhibits and conventions) See *exhibit drayage contractor.*

drop Delivery of a mailing to a post office facility. See also *drop day/date.*

drop day/date The day the mailing is to be taken to the post office. See also *drop.*

drop-head A smaller or secondary headline directly underneath a main headline. Sometimes called a *deck.*

drop-off (in advertising) Reduction in response for a book advertisement when it has been repeatedly run in the same publication.

dropout See *reverse out.*

dropout halftone Halftone with no dots in the highlight areas.

drop ship (v.) An instruction by the buyer to ship an ordered book to an address other than the one on the invoice. See also *drop shipment; drop shipment (in special sales).*

drop shipment Order placed by bookseller with publisher whereby book is sent directly to the customer, but billed to the bookseller.

drop shipment (in special sales) In the area of special or cooperative sales, associations and societies dealing with publishers like to have book orders drop shipped to their members. By contrast, mail order catalog houses, as a rule, do not drop ship to their customers.

drop shipment, STOP order When a bookseller uses a single-title order form and wishes the book drop shipped, it can be accomplished by including a shipping label and these specific instructions: "USE ATTACHED SHIPPING LABEL: RETURN THIS COPY TO BOOKSELLER." See also *Single Title Order Plan (STOP); STOP order.*

drop shopping The reverse of shoplifting, i.e., individuals leaving books behind in a bookshop that are not part of its inventory. A London bookshop manager reported in *The Bookseller* (March 20, 1987) that it was a frequent practice in his Great Russell Street shop. He listed 17 books that had been left with the suggestion they might be missing from other nearby bookshops.

dry-test mailing   A prepublication offer in which customer is offered an opportunity to buy a product usually with a "bill-me" option and no guarantee of final delivery of product. Usually used by publishers to test market before making a commitment to produce the product offered.

DTP   See *desktop publishing.*

Dualabel   A two-way pressure-sensitive address label that can be removed and reused on the reply device. See also *pressure-sensitive label.*

dual addressing   The use on business reply mail of a return address that includes the street address on one line and P.O. box number on another. So long as the P.O. box number is directly above the city/state/ZIP code line, the mail will be delivered to the P.O. box.

dual edition   Simultaneous hardcover and softcover printings.

dual imprint   See *joint imprint.*

dual rep   A publisher's sales rep who calls on both bookstores and libraries.

dues   U.K. term for back orders, i.e., books on order not immediately available, but which will be shipped when they are in stock.

dummy   A preliminary layout of a planned printed work showing the position of headlines, text, illustrations, and other elements of the job as a guide for the artist, printer, or others concerned with the job. See also *rough layout.*

dummy name   See *decoy; salting.*

dump display, dump bin   A freestanding display holding a quantity of books. See also *easel display poster.*

duotone   A two-color reproduction made from one black-and-white original and printed from two halftone plates (one in black and one in color), designed to achieve a unique tinted effect.

dupe (mailing lists) See *dupe elimination; duplicate (mailing list).*

dupe elimination The elimination of duplicate names when two or more lists are to be used for a mailing. See also *merge-purge (mailing list).*

duplicate (mailing list) 1. A name appearing more than once on the same mailing list is called an intralist dupe. 2. A name appearing on more than one list when multiple mailing lists are merged and purged to form a single composite list. See also *dupe elimination; duplication rate (mailing list); merge-purge (mailing list).*

duplicate copy, mailing list See *mailing list duplicate copies.*

duplicate mailing pieces, effectiveness Mailing duplicate pieces to the same name does not increase response. Where two lists are suspected of having a high rate of duplication, effectiveness can be increased by staggering the mailing dates.

duplicate order form An extra order form added to a mailing with a suggestion that the mailing be passed along to a friend or colleague. See also *routing instructions.*

duplication rate (mailing list) The percentage of names on a rented mailing that already exist on the publisher's house list. See also *hit rate; merge-purge (mailing list).*

dust cover See *jacket.*

dust jacket See *jacket.*

dust wrapper See *jacket.*

DVI Digital Video Interactive. Based on a technology developed at RCA's David Sarnoff Laboratories in Princeton, New Jersey, it has the ability to display one hour of motion video from compressed digital data stored on a single standard CD-ROM disc.

E

EAN bar code   A machine readable bar code printed on some book covers that identifies the book by ISBN. See also *International Standard Book Number (ISBN)*.

early look   See *first look*.

early selling/early release   Release of a book prior to its designated release date or scheduled publication date by a wholesaler or bookseller.

earned net local rate (advertising)   The publisher basis for all cooperative advertising allowances to booksellers. Permissions always state that cooperative advertising allowance is based on lowest earned net local rate charged to retailer. It may not reflect any advertising agency fees. (The *local rate* is the advertising rate charged by a local communications medium—newspaper, radio, etc.—to a local advertiser. This rate is usually lower than the rate charged to national advertisers.)

earned rate   An advertising rate "earned" in a publication by the use of a number of insertions within a period of one year. An advertiser billed at the one-time rate would receive a rebate to the earned three-time rate by placing three insertions within a year. See also *contract year (advertising); frequency discount; one-time rate*.

easel   A rack or stand used to hold a book for face-out display at book exhibits or in store windows. See also *slanted shelving*.

easel display poster   An advertising poster, attached to an easel and usually used either for display on a bookstore counter or an exhibit table. Noneasel posters are usually wall mounted.

easy reader   A children's book category with few words and heavily illustrated. Designed for the beginning reader with low vocabulary skills, generally K-2.

echo effect (of direct-mail promotion)   The "spillover" or indirect sales effect from a publisher's direct-mail (or space) advertising campaign. Various studies have shown that in addition to the keyed or directly traceable returns, publisher's direct-mail promotions produce indirect and untraceable sales, called *echo*, through all of the other outlets where books are normally sold. See also *echo studies*.

echo effect, reverse   See *reverse echo effect*.

echo studies   1. Research into the beneficial side effect of direct-mail promotion, usually by measurement of sales or orders generated by but not traceable to a promotion. 2. Studies designed to measure specific indirect sales from a publisher advertisement or direct-mail promotion. Details of publisher echo studies appear in Volume 1 of *Book Marketing Handbook* (R.R. Bowker, 1980), and in *Publisher's Direct Mail Handbook* (ISI Press, 1987), both by Nat Bodian.

echo test   A test to establish the spillover or indirect ordering resulting from a promotion effort. Virtually all promotions aimed at direct response produce an echo sales effect which may be anywhere from 1 to 20 times as great as the traceable direct response, depending on product, price, audience, and timing. The author has used a conservative estimate of 1.5 echo orders for each direct order of a book as a rule-of-thumb, although in one echo study, a mailing that brought in no direct responses resulted in total sales 17 times greater in the period following the mailing compared with a similar period prior to the mailing.

edition   1. All the copies of a book printed from substantially the same setting of type and in the same format. 2. A form in which a literary work is published, for example, original, revised, reprint, textbook, paperbound, library, etc. 3. A literary work designed and produced for a specific purpose or market.

edition, abridged   See *abridged edition/abridgement*.

edition, annual   See *annual*.

edition, book club   See *book club edition*.

edition, boxed See *boxed edition/boxed set.*

edition, consolidated See *consolidated edition.*

edition, demographic See *demographic edition.*

edition, expanded See *expanded edition.*

edition, export See *export edition.*

edition, first See *first edition.*

edition, geographic See *geographic edition.*

edition, international student See *international student edition.*

edition, limited See *limited edition.*

edition, loose-leaf See *loose-leaf edition.*

edition, multilingual See *multilingual edition.*

edition, on-demand See *on-demand edition.*

edition, paperback See *paperback edition/paper edition.*

edition, pirated See *pirated edition.*

edition, reprint See *reprint edition.*

edition, retitled See *retitled edition.*

edition, slipcased See *slipcased edition.*

edition, special See *special edition.*

edition, spiral-bound See *spiral-bound edition.*

edition, sponsored See *sponsored edition.*

edition, textbook See *text edition.*

edition, trade See *trade edition.*

edition, xerographic See *on-demand edition.*

editorial approach (in advertising) A copy approach in which advertising matter is designed (or disguised) to look like editorial or news matter.

editorial matter   That part of a periodical prepared by the staff as contrasted with advertising in the same edition, the space for which is paid for by the advertiser. See also *space advertising*.

Educational Directory   The college faculty list segment of the Market Data Retrieval educational database. See also *library lists, Market Data Retrieval*.

educational discount   A discount given by some publishers for orders from academics or teachers that are placed on institutional stationery.

eggshell finish   A paper with a smooth, pitted-effect finish not unlike that of an eggshell.

800 number (telephone)   A toll-free telephone service. The owner of an 800 number agrees to pay for incoming calls. This service was first introduced by AT&T in 1967. The 1986-87 *AT&T Toll-Free 800 Business Directory* listed approximately 500 publishers. See also *AT&T 800 Service*.

800 numbers in advertising   Inclusion of an 800 telephone number in advertising improves advertising awareness by 20% according to a 1986 study by Cahners Publishing Company. Earlier publisher studies have indicated that such numbers, when "buried" in coupons or order forms, have little effect.

800 telephone numbers, book publisher   Several hundred publishers have 800 toll-free numbers for bookseller ordering. A few have some restrictions for 800 orders such as "minimum of 10 books." Others have larger minimums such as 12 or 25, or a minimum price order, for example over $15.

800 telephone numbers, periodical publisher   Periodical publishers also use 800 numbers for order taking. Magazine publishers do not require prepayment; however, they usually prefer credit card orders or confirming purchase orders.

800 telephone service   See *AT&T 800 Service; AT&T 800 Service-Canada; 800 telephone service (U.K.)*

800 telephone service (U.K.)   A service parallel to the AT&T service that is available in the U.K. is called Linkline 0800 and has a variation called Linkline 0345. See separate entries for each. See also *Freefone service*.

800 toll-free number in mail promotion An 800 number in the main body of a mail offer will usually improve response, but will not be effective if it appears only on the response vehicle—BRC or BRE. Most such numbers in promotion are for ordering only—not for customer service.

electronic composition/typesetting A form of type composition that utilizes a computer for input, editing, formatting, and producing finished galleys. Copy is processed before it goes to the typographer, minimizing the time required by the typographer and reducing cost.

electronic publishing 1. A computer-aided publishing system utilizing a video terminal that combines the basics of word processing—an ability to write, edit, proofread and transmit documents or ready-to-print pages of composed matter—with a graphics capability that allows integration of headlines, drawings, illustrations, or charts and tables into the pages. Composed matter can then be sent electronically to a typesetter or an office printer. 2. The use of electronic media to disseminate information to end users. The formats and technology employed include the following: online access to a computer via telecommunications, magnetic disks (either floppy or removable hard disks), or optical discs such as CD-ROM.

electronic publishing applications Some typical applications of electronic publishing include: directories (names, addresses, and related data); bibliographic databases (references to articles in various periodicals and journals); periodicals or journals (full text); financial databases (full details on individual companies for investment decisionmaking); collections of scientific data; consumer databases (such as for amusement events, airline and hotel accommodations, and a wide range of general interest information); collections of data from printed reference works.

electrostatic printing See electrostatic reprography.

electrostatic reprography A process of printing or copying in which an image is bonded to an electrically charged sheet using carbon particles. See also xerography.

elementary school library buying pattern The elementary school library builds its collection with picture books, easy-to-read books, and concept books for the lower grades. It provides books that support the school's English, science, and history curriculums. The elementary school library also acquires classics and current books for recreational reading, as well as reference and research books.

elementary school library market (public) Approximately 51,000 libraries.

elementary school market Includes kindergarten through 8th grade and usually referred to as the K-8 market.

elhi/el-hi market The elementary and high school market, grades K–12.

elhi text A textbook produced for use in elementary schools and high schools. Most elhi texts are repeatedly revised and updated so as to retain their market share.

ELT publisher A publisher of books on English language teaching.

em (typography) The square of any type size. An 8-point em measures 8 points by 8 points.

em dash (typography) A horizontal printed line the width of an em, sometimes used to indicate a rest in reading or to separate two thoughts. See also *em (typography)*.

em space (typography) A space the width of an em in any typeface. See also *em (typography)*.

en (typography) A printer's unit of measurement half the width of an em. See also *em (typography)*.

enclosures, mailing package See *letter enclosure readership study; mailing package enclosure instructions*.

encyclopedia According to Kenneth Kister in *Best Encyclopedias*, (Address: The Oryx Press, 2214 North Central at Encanto, Phoenix, AZ 85004), an encyclopedia "is a reference source in either print or electronic form that summarizes basic knowledge and information on all important subjects or, in the case of a specialized encyclopedia, a particular subject. An encyclopedia is an attempt to encompass, or encircle, that knowledge and information deemed essential or universally worth knowing . . . . Encyclopedias are always arranged in a systematic manner, usually alphabetically but sometimes by subject in a classified, or topical, sequence." Encyclopedias are purchased primarily by libraries and schools as well as by individuals for home use. Specialized encyclopedias are sold to libraries and to professionals in the fields covered by each work. See also *handbook.*

Encyclopedia of Associations: A Guide to Over 23,000 National and International Organizations   An invaluable annual reference from Gale Research Co. (Book Tower, Detroit, MI 48226) for book marketers. Volume 1 covers over 20,000 national and international nonprofit trade and professional associations; social welfare and public affairs organizations; and religious, sport, and hobby groups. Includes complete contact details, activities, publications, and convention schedules. Entries are arranged by subject, and accessed by alphabetical and keyword indexes. (Volume 2, Geographic and Executive Indexes; Volume 3, New Associations and Projects; Volume 4, International Organizations.

Encyclopedia of Associations: Regional, State, and Local Organizations   A new seven-volume work from Gale Research providing information on organizations active in local business and politics, the arts, education, medicine, community service, recreation, and other categories by geographic region of the U.S. Volumes include: Great Lakes States, Northeastern States, Middle Atlantic States, Western States, Southeastern States, Southwest and South Central States, and Northwest and Great Plains States. Available in single volumes or as a set.

encyclopedia of journal publishers   See *Standard Periodical Directory; Ulrich's International Periodicals Directory.*

Encyclopedia of Mailing List Terminology and Techniques   A guide to virtually everything one needs to know about mailing lists, their rental, selection, and use, in A to Z format. Written by Nat Bodian and published 1986 by Bret Scot Press, the book division of CMG. See also *CMG Information Services, Inc.*

encyclopedia pricing   Encyclopedias are viewed primarily as library reference tools, and, depending on size and scope, and may be priced beyond the reach of individual purchasers. This distinction diminishes as encyclopedias get smaller, as with a one-volume work. See also *encyclopedia; handbook pricing.*

en dash (typography)   A horizontal printed line the width of one en in any typeface. Frequently used to indicate "to" as in 1987–1988. See also *em (typography); en (typography).*

end leaves See *endpapers.*

end marks (news/press releases) Some marking must be inserted at the end of a news release to indicate to those handling or typesetting the release that there is no additional copy following. The request coupon at the end of a release asking for a review copy of a book will suffice if the release is to elicit a review request only. However, typical news release end marks, in order of preference, are "###" or "-30-" or "-o-." The end marks are double-spaced and usually centered under the last line of the release. See also *more line; news release.*

end-of-edition price increases See *price increases, end of edition.*

endpapers Four pages, two at the beginning and two at the end, of a casebound book. One at each end is pasted to the inside of the cover board. Endpaper stock is stronger and heavier than text stock and may be white or colored, printed or plain. Also called *endsheets, endleaves,* or *lining paper.*

endsheets See *endpapers.*

end user (database) 1. The individual (user) for whom a librarian conducts a literature search. 2. The receiver of transmitted data or information.

Engineering Societies Library This library is sponsored by a dozen engineering societies. The library serves the book review needs of 13 journals published by these societies. The societies are headquartered at United Engineering Center, 345 East 47th Street, New York, NY 10017.

engineers, copy approach to Copy to engineering audiences should stress newness and completeness of the work and the competence of the author to write the work. Specific features within the book should be clearly outlined. A single feature often can provide a buying incentive. Copy should indicate how the book will solve specific problems, help the reader to update professional skills or knowledge, advance himself or herself in a present job, or provide information that may be needed in the future.

English language in international promotion See *translations in international promotion.*

en space (typography)   A space the width of an en in any typeface. See also *em (typography); en (typography).*

entrapment   During processing, smaller pieces of mail can be picked up within catalogs or periodicals that are not mailed in envelopes or wrappings. This is called "entrapment." To prevent this problem, many countries outside the U.S. have entrapment postal regulations that require that catalogs and periodicals be enveloped. See also *trap envelope; U.K. mailing entrapment rule.*

envelope   1. A container, usually made of paper, used to mail written or printed matter. Basic parts of an envelope are (a) the seal flap; (b) the seal gum on the flap; (c) the shoulders (the flaps to which the envelope back is pasted); (d) the throat (the open area under the flap which provides clearance for inserting; (e) the front or face; (f) the side flaps; and (g) the bottom flap. 2. One of the basic components in a direct-mail package. See also *business reply mail; envelope ordering requirements; mail size surcharge, USPS; return envelope; wallet flap envelope; window envelope.*

envelope, bind-in   See *bind-in envelope.*

envelope, carrier/outer/outside   See *carrier envelope.*

envelope, closed-face   See *closed-face envelope.*

envelope, mailing   The outer envelope used in a direct mailing.

envelope, manila   See *manila envelope.*

envelope, open-end   See *open-end (catalog) envelope.*

envelope, open-side   See *open-side (booklet) envelope.*

envelope, reply   An envelope enclosed with a mailing to enable the recipient to respond. See also *business reply mail.*

envelope, open-window   See *open-window envelope.*

envelope, Tyvek®   See *Tyvek® envelope.*

envelope, wallet-flap   See *wallet-flap envelope.*

envelope window   See *window envelope.*

envelope, wove   See *wove envelope.*

envelope clearance   For mass mailings that will be machine inserted, the inserts should be at least one-half inch narrower than envelope length and at least one-quarter inch shorter than the envelope height.

envelope corner card   The name and address imprint of a mailer in the upper left-hand corner of an envelope. See also *blind corner; corner card; envelope eye flow.*

envelope eye flow   The common pattern of eye flow by the recipient of an envelope mailing before opening. The pattern is usually from (1) name of recipient and address, to (2) any teaser copy adjacent to name and address, to (3) corner card return address, to (4) stamps, postal indicia, or meter impression (Source: Clark-O'Neill *Indicia,* January 1987). See also *letter eye flow, personalized.*

envelope headline   See *teaser copy.*

envelope ordering requirements   When ordering envelopes for a promotion, discussion with an envelope manufacturer's representative is often helpful. Be prepared to discuss (1) when the envelopes will be needed; (2) the size or bulk of the contents; (3) how contents will be inserted—by machine or hand; (4) the type of postage being used—a paper grade, substance weight, or size may produce savings; (5) whether a window envelope will help; (6) what type of closure—regular gum or pressure sensitive; (7) what color— you may want the outside to tie in with the theme of the mailing.

envelope package   A mailing with the contents encased in an envelope as contrasted with a self-mailer. See also *direct-mail package.*

envelope requirements, international   1. All forms of international mailings, whether a promotional flier, catalog, or periodical, must be enclosed in a sealed envelope before being mailed. Self-mailers are illegal in most foreign countries. See also *entrapment.* 2. Envelopes bearing a window must have a cellophane covering over the window, rather than an open window. 3. Airmail envelopes should be true "airmail"—not air speeded international mail. See also *air speeded; ISAL.*

envelope sizes

Commercial and Window

No. 6¼	3½″ × 6″
No. 6¾	3⅝″ × 6½″
No. 7	3¾″ × 6¾″
No. 8 (Monarch)	3⅞″ × 7½″
No. 9	3⅞″ × 8⅞″
No. 10 (Official)	4⅛″ × 9½″
No. 11	4½″ × 10⅜″
No. 12	4¾″ × 11″
No. 14	5″ × 11½″

Booklet Envelopes

No. 3	4¾″ × 6½″
No. 5	5½″ × 8⅛″
No. 6	5¾″ × 8⅞″
No. 6½	6″ × 9″
No. 7	6¼″ × 9⅝″
No. 9	8¾″ × 11½″
No. 9½	9″ × 12″
No. 10	9½″ × 12⅝″
No. 13	10″ × 13″

envelope stuffer   1. Advertising enclosed with statements, bills, or correspondence. 2. Promotional material enclosed in an envelope with outgoing business mail, invoices, statements, etc. U.K.: free-ride. See also *bag stuffer; flier/flyer; statement stuffer.*

envelope teaser copy   Copy on the mailing face of an envelope designed to entice the recipient to look inside the envelope. See also *envelope eye flow; teaser copy.*

envelope test   A test mailing in which different types or colors of envelopes are used, or in which some segments of the mailing may be with a reply envelope and others without.

EOM   End of Month. Books billed to the book trade prior to the 25th of the month are payable or subject to discount up to the 10th of the following month. If billed on the 25th or later, payment and discount date is figured as the 10th day of the second following month.

EPOS systems Electronic Point of Sale Products. Systems that involve the reading of data by electronic means, such as scanning of bar codes, at point of sale.

ESL English as a Second Language. See also *ESL market.*

ESL market The market or markets for books aimed at audiences in which English is a second language.

ESL publisher A publisher that produces books specifically designed for the ESL market.

estimate, printing See various entries under printing.

estimated mailing quantity The figure on which a mailing house may invoice its customer for postage prior to the mailing.

Ethics Code, AAP for College Sales Representatives See Appendix 14.

European agent A firm already established and operating in the U.K. or on the European continent that offers an American publisher marketing, warehousing, and distributing facilities in Europe. The agent may itself be a publisher or a subsidiary of an American publisher.

European distribution sources See *European agent; U.K. and European distribution sources.*

European subscription agent Periodical subscription agents based in Europe. The European agent may be a bookseller as well, since most European libraries tend to order journal subscriptions through their bookseller, rather than direct from the publisher. See also *distributing booksellers, international.*

examination copy/exam copy Book sent to an educator for examination and consideration as a possible classroom text. Examination periods of many publishers are 30 to 60 days. Exam copy invoices for professional- and graduate-level books should state terms, period of examination, and that invoice will be canceled on adoption or return of book. See also *approval copy; desk copy.*

excerpt See *review excerpt/book review excerpt.*

exchange ads   Advertising exchanged between periodicals in the same or related subject areas without payment but based on equity in circulation. Such ads are generally aimed at attracting subscribers from the circulation of the periodical in which the advertisement appears. See also *advertising exchange program*.

exchange advertising program   See *advertising exchange program*.

exchange agreement/program   See *advertising exchange program; card pack exchanges; list exchange (direct mail)*.

exclusion slip   See *forms only library awareness plan; notification slip*.

exclusive book club rights   Rights sold to a book club are said to be exclusive when the agreement precludes the sale of the same book to any other book club during the term of the contract. See also *book club rights; book club rights, first use; nonexclusive book club rights*.

exclusive distribution arrangement (bookselling)   See *distribution arrangement, exclusive; distribution arrangement, nonexclusive*.

exclusive first look   The practice of trade publishers of giving one potential buyer of reprint rights an opportunity to examine a manuscript before it is officially available for bid. If interested, the bidder may make a "preemptive bid" or at least negotiate a "floor" for the future auction. See also *floor (reprint rights auction)*.

exclusive to (publicity)   A heading used on a news release written exclusively for one publication. The sender is obliged to issue no other publicity on the subject until the "exclusive" release has appeared, or the recipient publication has indicated the release will not be used. See also *special to (publicity)*.

exhibit, book   See *book exhibit; exhibits, convention; trade show*.

exhibit and convention advertising   See *convention issue*.

exhibit booth   A display space at a convention or meeting where publishers and other interested exhibitors display books or other products and services for the duration of the event—usually referred to as a "show." Spaces are preselected by exhibitors in advance of show from an exhibit floor plan showing sizes and prices of various exhibit spaces. U.K.: bookstall. See also *exhibits, convention; exhibit booth location.*

exhibit booth location   Publishers frequently exhibit books at meetings of professional associations and societies. Some meetings have a "Publisher's Row" in which all book exhibitors are grouped. Such locations ensure good traffic, no matter the location. However, when selection must be made from a full floor plan, booths at ends of aisles are usually best. Front end better than back end. Smaller publishers sometimes seek locations adjacent to the larger houses to ensure good booth traffic. See also *exhibit location selection.*

exhibit drayage contractor   A service company that contracts to receive and store, over a period prior to a convention or exhibit, all displays and exhibit material and to deliver such materials directly to the exhibitor's booth; the contractor also removes and stores empty crates and cartons during the display, returns empties at the conclusion of the show, and removes repacked material and ships as directed after the show.

exhibit floor   The area at a trade show or convention where the exhibits are.

exhibit floor plan   A printed sheet showing the numbered booth locations for an exhibit or convention. Such plans are sent to potential exhibitors in advance to solicit participation. Usually, several choices are requested, and the exhibit sponsor assigns exhibit spaces based on various criteria, including (a) previous exhibitors; (b) first come, first served basis; (c) a lottery or drawing for spaces. Often such plans will have a marked-off area for publisher exhibits usually called "Publishers' Row."

exhibit lighting   Since publishers set up exhibits to display published works, a bright, well lighted booth not only tends to make the booth more inviting but also makes it easier for browsers to examine books.

exhibit location selection   Experienced exhibitors return exhibit forms with their booth selections immediately upon receipt to ensure prime locations. It is best to plan exhibit participations far in advance and to make prompt booth selections to ensure good booth location. See also *exhibit booth location.*

exhibitor's kit   A package of materials prepared by exhibit sponsors and sent to potential exhibitors or those who have reserved exhibit space with forms to be completed and submitted to the various contractors for show services such as booth furnishings, carpeting, lighting, drayage, cleaning, etc. Also called *show kit.*

exhibit risers   Platforms or benches placed atop tables at an exhibit to provide greater elevation for the products displayed. Most exhibit tables are 30″ high. Most risers are 10″ or 12″ high and thus provide greater visibility. Risers are generally 10″ or 12″ across and, therefore, occupy less than half the table width, permitting two display levels on an exhibit table. Tables are usually 18″ or 24″ wide.

exhibits, convention   Displays of products or services at a meeting of an association or society, usually in preassigned exhibit spaces in a central exhibit hall. See also *book exhibit; cooperative book exhibit; exhibit booth; exhibit floor.*

exhibits, cooperative book   See *cooperative book exhibit.*

Exhibits Directory   See *AAP Exhibits Directory; Trade Show and Professional Exhibits Directory.*

exhibit success criteria   (1) Number of authors present; (2) number of editorial leads obtained; (3) number of literature and catalog requests; (4) dollar volume of orders taken; (5) ratio of attendance to total membership of sponsoring organization; (6) volume of exhibit booth traffic; (7) number of textbook exam copy requests; (8) number of subsriptions obtained.

exhibit tables   Most decorators at exhibits rent tables 30″ high. However, when requested to do so, they may furnish tables 36″ high. For shows where the publisher wants to stop people as they go by with a specific item, it is best to use a 36″ high table on the aisle where it is likely to be at or closer to eye level. Inside the booth, if added appeal is desired, risers can be placed atop tables which raise displayed materials 10″ or 12″ above table height. See also *exhibit risers.*

ex-lib (antiquarian bookselling)   A book discarded from a library and bearing all the usual library markings. See also *antiquarian bookselling terms.*

expanded edition   The enlargement of a published work by the addition of important new information. Sometimes this is done by the addition of supplements or appendixes, with no revision of the original text.

expanded type   Type in any particular typeface in which the letters are wider than usual. Expanded typefaces are usually used for headlines and subheadlines, or in small blocks of ad copy where extra emphasis is desired. The term serves as a synonym for typefaces that come in semiexpanded, expanded, extraexpanded, and ultraexpanded. Other terms used for expanded type include *extended type* and *wide type*. See also *condensed type; typeface.*

expertise audience   See *target audience.*

expiration date/cutoff date   A date included in print or mail advertising in association with an offering. Generally, prices or special discounts in the offering are good until the cutoff date. Examples: A prepublication offer; a sale catalog with sharply discounted book prices; a mail promotion—catalog or deck, guaranteeing prices up to the expiration date.

expires (n.)   Former subscribers to a periodical or newsletter.

expires list   A mailing list of former subscribers to a publication. Many tend to be a number of years out of date and have a high rate of undeliverables.

export edition   An edition prepared for sale outside its country of origin, or in another specific country.

export representative   An individual or organization under contract to handle promotion and sale of a publisher's books outside the country of origin or publisher's sales territory.

export sales agent/agency   A U.S. based organization that calls on major book trade accounts in foreign countries on behalf of American publishers. Most operate with exclusive sales rights in certain overseas areas. Such agents handle all overseas marketing, distribution, and fulfillment activities for their client publishers.

exposure   The number of individuals in a given market who have seen and read an advertisement or received and read a mailing. See also *impression (advertising).*

Express Mail (EM)   The highest priority of mail offered by the USPS. Delivery is promised on time or postage is refunded upon application by the mailer. Four types of Express Mail are: (1) Same Day Airport Service; (2) Custom Designed Service; (3) Next Day Service; (4) International Service.

extended cover   A pamphlet or brochure cover that extends beyond the trim of the enclosed pages. See also *flush cover.*

extended credit   1. A book offering, usually to booksellers, with billing at a later specified date, or with a specified future date on the invoice. Some publishers of trade books may offer books late summer or early fall with December 1 billing, so that payment is not due until January 1—after the Christmas buying season. 2. A form of credit applied to export sales. Credit terms are sometimes 90 days, 180 days, or more, providing time for receipt and sale by the export account before payment becomes due. See also *December dating; delayed billing; net 90 days (wholesale booksellers); special deal.*

extended offer   An offer continued beyond its originally announced expiration date. Used by some publishers for prepublication and introductory price offers when high promotional response warrants continued promotion of the offer. Also sometimes used by publishers for reissue of sale catalogs for an extended period beyond original expiration date.

extended type   See *expanded type.*

external mailing list   A mailing list from a source other then the publishers own in-house files. Also called *outside mailing list.*

extra dating   See *delayed billing; extended credit.*

"eyeball" credit checking   According to Arthur Winston, a New York attorney, certain signs in orders are sometimes considered debits in evaluating credit worthiness. Among these are a P.O. box or general delivery address; illegible handwriting; lack of a telephone number where one is called for; lack of a first name; or omission of street, avenue, road, or ZIP code (in *DMA Release 750.1,* August 1982).

eye flow studies (direct mail)   See *envelope eye flow; letter eye flow, personalized.*

F

face   1. In letterpress printing, the raised portion of type that receives the ink and produces printing. See also *typeface*. 2. Typeface. 3. The cover of an envelope or self-mailer (mailing face). 4. The front cover of a book.

face out   Display of a book with front cover showing. The most desirable way of displaying a book at point of sale or in an exhibit. See also *spine out*.

face out display   See *easel; slanted shelving*.

facing editorial matter   A position request for advertising placed in a periodical that asks for an advertisement to be opposite editorial matter, rather than facing another advertisement.

facing identification mark (FIM)   A bar code pattern required to be printed near the upper right-hand corner of business reply mail and certain other bar coded mail that allows U.S. Postal Service equipment to mechanically face, sort, and cancel mail. See also *FIM*.

fact sheet   A sheet containing essential facts, usually in non-narrative form, on a forthcoming book. Useful in disseminating information on publishing projects for publicity purposes before any other form of printed promotion is available. Also used to provide advance information to in-house and field sales staff.

faculty committee   In the context of library acquisitions, individuals within a college or university who assist in or make recommendations for the development of the library collection.

Faculty Directory of Higher Education   A 12-volume reference published in 1988 by Gale Research Co. (Book Tower, Detroit, MI 48226) and listing 60,000 faculty members from over 3,300 U.S. and Canadian colleges and universities. Consists of 11 subject volumes plus an index volume. Derived from CMG Information Services database.

faculty editorial committee   University faculty members designated to advise on the publishing program of a university press.

faculty lists, graduate level   See *graduate-level faculty list.*

fair (antiquarian bookselling)   A copy of a book that appears to have been well read with faded and fraying binding and with dust jacket, if any, badly torn or incomplete. See also *antiquarian bookselling* terms.

fall list (publishers)   Books scheduled to be published August through February.

fall season (trade bookselling)   Usually Labor Day to Christmas. Many trade publishers try to publish their strongest titles during this period since three-fourths of the year's sales generally occur within this season.

family (typography)   The entire range of styles available in a given typeface. This could include different forms, weights, and proportions. Variations might include regular, italic, light, semi-bold, bold, condensed, bold condensed, bold italic, etc. See also *boldface type (b.f.); expanded type; condensed type; series (typography); typeface; typography.*

f & g's   See *folded and gathered sheets.*

fan fold   Zig-zag or accordian-folded continuous forms. This is the method by which computer-prepared mailing lists are usually supplied. See also *accordian fold.*

FASEB meeting   An annual meeting in April of research biologists in areas embracing physiology, biochemistry, pharmacology, pathology, nutrition, or immunology. The more than 25,000 attendees are highly book oriented. Publishers in these areas consider FASEB their primary exhibit opportunity of the year. FASEB is an acronym for Federation of American Societies for

Experimental Biology, an umbrella organization for six member societies involved in the various branches of research biology.

feature (n.) (book advertising)   A special attribute or strong part of a book—a specific sales strength or special characteristic. Writers of advertising copy often confuse features with benefits. The rule is that the feature yields the benefit. If the feature of the book is "complete up-to-date coverage of the field," the derived benefit is "enables you to be current on latest developments." See also *benefit (in book advertising)*.

feature (v.)   1. To give special display emphasis to a book in a bookselling establishment or at a trade show or convention. 2. To emphasize one aspect or strength of a book in an advertising or promotion effort.

feature mailing   See *solo mailing*.

Federal Libraries Directory   See Directory *of Federal Libraries*.

Federation of American Societies for Experimental Biology (FASEB)   See *FASEB meeting*.

Feffer & Simons Inc.   A U.S. export sales agent, founded in 1955, that markets books for approximately 200 U.S. publishers throughout the world and receives a commission based on sales made. A subsidiary of Baker & Taylor.

festschrift   The practice of paying homage to a scholar with a volume of essays by former students, friends, and colleagues, upon the scholar's retirement or on special occasions (e.g., his or her 70th birthday).

few skips   See *book distribution jargon (bookstores)*.

FGI   Focus group interview.   Used to obtain consumer reactions. See also *focus group*.

field reps, field staff   A field sales force. The salespeople may be salaried, on commission, or a combination of both. See also *commission rep; library rep; repping group; sales rep/sales representative*.

field testing, elhi market   A technique used by elhi textbook publishers prior to publication of a text. Page proofs are sent to practicing teachers who read and criticize them and sometimes test them in the classroom, usually for a fee. Desired changes or needed corrections may then be made.

50-50-50 rule (in book telemarketing) "If you reach 50% of the people called, and you sell 50% of those reached and you get a 50% returns on books sent." (This is a 12½% response)—Peter Hodges, given at Professional Publishers Marketing Group Seminar, New York, May 14, 1986.

fill-in letter A letter in which the body is printed, and the address and salutation are typed in manually. Most are hand signed, or have the appearance of being hand signed, and are usually sent by first-class mail.

fill rate The percentage of books that a book wholesaler is able to supply from stock in filling an order.

film lamination Bonding plastic film, by adhesives or heat and pressure, to a sheet of paper to protect it and improve its appearance. An alternative coating to varnish and uv coating. See also *uv coating; varnish.*

FIM Facing Identification Mark, a requirement on all Business Reply Mail. See also *facing identification mark.*

***Financial Times* (U.K.)** The U.K. equivalent to *The Wall Street Journal* for business book advertising. *The Financial Times* runs a "Business Books Feature" on the first Saturday of every month. Publishers may insert a book description of approximately 40 words plus title, author name, publisher name, and address at an extremely modest cost. Address: The Financial Times Ltd., Bracken House, 10 Cannon Street, London EC4P 4BY, England.

fine (antiquarian bookselling) A copy that is clean and crisp and bears no serious indications of wear. See also *antiquarian bookselling* terms.

fine screen See *coarse screen; halftone screen; screen.*

finish (paper) The texture, or surface contour, of paper. Typical finishes in order of smoothness are antique, eggshell, vellum, and machine finish. See also *antique paper; eggshell finish; machine coated; vellum paper.*

finishing (printing) The various operations done to complete a printed job after it comes off the press.

firm order (advertising)   A positive order that cannot be cancelled for advertising space on a specific date or in a specific issue of a publication.

firm order (bookstore)   A nonreturnable order. UK: firm sale.

firm order (library jobber terminology)   Among library jobbers, "firm order" refers to an order for a book as opposed to an approval plan shipment or a continuation or standing order. Firm orders placed by libraries with jobbers are ordinarily returnable.

FIRSTcall   An electronic ordering service available to booksellers from The Baker & Taylor Company. Working through the store's personal computer, orders are keyed in by ISBN during the day and transmitted to B&T over toll-free telephone lines. Within five minutes, the bookstore is able to receive on its computer a report on the status of the order. The report can be seen on the screen or in a printout. Shipment is made within 24 hours.

first-class mail, forwarding of   See *mail forwarding (USPS regulations)*.

first-class voluntary presort   First class mail can be separated into eight different categories, depending on volume and distribution pattern: (1) local and out-of-town; (2) state; (3) three-digit zip code; (4) five-digit zip code; (5) ZIP plus 4 code; (6) carrier route number; (7) carrier delivery sequence; and (8) direct to a single address. To qualify, a mailing must consist of at least 500 pieces.

first edition   All of the copies of a published work first printed from the same type and made available for sale at the same time.

first look   The opportunity for a potential buyer of reprint rights to examine the manuscript before any of the competition sees the manuscript.

first renewal (periodical)   The first time a new subscriber renews a paid subscription. Many in periodical fulfillment feel that after a first renewal is received, the subscriber is likely to renew again and again. A concentrated effort should be made toward all first renewals.

first serial rights   The selling of an excerpt from a book to another print medium to appear shortly before publication of the book. Such rights tend to whet the appetite for the book and help bookstore sales when the book is subsequently published. See also *second serial rights.*

flap copy/jacket flap copy/jacket copy   1. The printed matter on book jacket flaps. 2. Flap copy should motivate the reader to open the book. Usually, the fron flap describes the book; the back flap tells the prospective buyer about the author and his or her credentials for writing the book. 3. Many publishers give special care to this copy since it serves as the "meat" for some book reviewers who may not read a book beyond its flaps when writing a review. It is also a strong selling feature at the point of sale. See also *jacket copy, scientific and technical; trade book jacket functions.*

flat   1. A specification to a printer with a print order indicating the trimmed size of the finished (flat) piece before folding. See also *folded.* 2. A press negative (film negatives or positives in a signature, ready to be exposed to a plate).

flat rate (mailing list)   A price for a mailing list as a whole, irrespective of number of names included. Available for rental only as a complete unit.

flat rate (space advertising)   An advertising rate not subject to frequency or other types of discounts.

flexible binding   See *limp binding.*

flier/flyer   A small, inexpensively produced advertising piece, usually on a single sheet of paper, which may be distributed flat or folded for mailing in an envelope. In publishing promotion, fliers are often letterhead size, and may use a letterhead format. In U.K. and Europe, the term "leaflet" is used instead of "flier." See also *bag stuffer; envelope stuffer; insert; statement stuffer.*

flip chart   An easel-mounted pad used for presentations.

floor (reprint rights auction)   An amount of money established by the publisher and the first bidder together. Any other bidder wishing to compete, must offer more than the "floor." See also *exclusive first look; first look; preemptive bid; topping privileges.*

floor plan, exhibit See *exhibit floor plan.*

floppy disk A flexible plastic disk used for magnetic storage of computer data. A single disk of the usual size (5¼" diameter) can store up to 60 pages of text. Its entire contents may often be effectively accessible without the need for sequential search to reach a particular location, as is required with computer tape.

flush (in type composition) Type lined up vertically so that all lines are even on the left (flush left), or so that they are all even on the right (flush right), or so that type is even both on the left and right (flush left and right). See also *flush left; flush right; justification.*

flush cover Cover of a booklet, brochure, or publication trimmed even with its pages. See also *extended cover.*

flush left Type composition set so left-hand margin aligns vertically. Right-hand margin may be allowed to terminate normally with no attempt at vertical alignment. See also *flush (in type composition).*

flush paragraphs Paragraphs having no indentation.

flush right Type composition set so as to align vertically along the right-hand margin. See also *flush (in type composition).*

flyer See *flier/flyer.*

focus group A form of market research in which a group of individuals, representative of a market is assembled in a room with a research person trained in the subject area (group leader). A dialogue is created to bring out opinions related to the products or services discussed. The opinions expressed generally are believed to be typical of the market as a whole.

focus panel See *focus group.*

fog index A formula for measuring the clarity of writing. It is based on the length of sentences and the number of words of three syllables or more—the lower the index number, the clearer the writing. For additional information, see *The Technique of Clear Writing, Revised Edition* by Robert Gunning, McGraw-Hill, 1968, or *Copywriter's Handbook* by Nat Bodian, ISI Press, 1984.

fog indexed   Tested for readability or clarity, usually expressed as a number.

fold, four-panel   See *four-panel fold.*

fold, French   See *French fold*

folded   A specification to a printer with a print order indicating the finished size of the piece after trimming and folding. See also *flat.*

folded & gathered sheets/f & g's   All the signatures (folded printed sheets forming the various sections of a book) assembled in the sequence in which they are to be bound into a book. Also called f & g's, folded and gathered sheets are often sent to reviewers, book clubs, and exhibits to meet deadlines when bound books are not yet available. See also *signature (in bound publication).*

folder   A printed sheet of paper, unstitched or bound, and folded one or more times.

folding (paper)   When planning a printed and folded promotion piece, you should bear in mind that parallel folds should run the same way as the grain of the paper. If this is not done, folding may be more difficult and a final folded job may pop open.

folding dummy   A properly folded sample of a proposed mailing piece to illustrate written folding instructions to the printer or lettershop. See also *sample package (lettershop).*

folding rule (for paper)   When planning printed promotions, you should make sure the first fold and subsequent parallel folds are with the grain. On any stock, paper folds more easily with the grain. See also *grain (paper); score.*

fold marks   1. Broken lines added in the margins of mechanical artwork to indicate where the finished piece is to be folded. 2. Marks added to a negative flat, along the margins of a press sheet, as a guide for subsequent folding.

foldout   See *gatefold.*

folio publishing   Print on paper. See also *telepublishing.*

follow-up call (telemarketing)   A call made to an individual on a mailing list as a follow-up to a direct-mail campaign. These calls are generally much more successful than cold calls since the person called is considered to have been informed of the offer in advance of the call. See also *telemarketing/telephone marketing*.

follow-up mailing   A second mailing to a specific audience within a reasonable time after a first mailing. Multibook mailings to professional audiences two to four weeks after an earlier mailing sometimes do almost as well in the follow-up. However, most book professionals gap their mailings to the same list by at least two to three months. See also *remailing; rollout.*

font   The complete assortment of type (one size and face) including cap and lower case, small caps, punctuation marks, and commonly used symbols. See also *typeface; wrong font (wf).*

Forecast   A monthly publication of Baker & Taylor, wholesale booksellers, for the public library market. Includes annotations and bibliographic information on forthcoming trade titles of all publishers. See also *The Baker & Taylor Company; Directions.*

foreign distribution   See *distributing booksellers, international; U.K. and European distribution sources.*

foreign publication rights   Rights granted to a publisher in another country to publish a book in the language of original publication (including, for example, rights granted to a publishing house in Great Britain to be the British publisher of an American book). See also *reprint rights; translation rights.*

foreign subscriber price (journal)   The price charged by a journal publisher for a subscription from a foreign country. The price may be higher than the price to a comparable domestic subscriber and may have been increased to include added postage cost to the foreign destination.

foreign subscriptions (journals)   See *journals, foreign subscriptions.*

foreign subsidiary   A publishing operation that is partially or totally owned by a publisher located in a different country than the subsidiary.

for immediate release (publicity)   See *release date (news releases).*

form (printing) The assembly of all the pages to be printed on one side of a sheet at one time usually in a multiple of eight pages. U.K.: Forme. See also *signature (in bound publication)*.

format (book) The page size, quality of paper, binding style, typeface, margins, printing requirements, and any other characteristics related to the appearance of a book.

format (book promotion) The size, shape, style, and general appearance of a promotional effort.

format, booklet See *booklet*.

format, broadside See *broadside*.

format, brochure See *brochure*.

format, flier See *flier/flyer*.

format, folder See *folder*.

format, gram See *gram format (printed promotion)*.

format, letter, See *letter format*.

format, mailing card See *mailing card*.

format, self-mailer See *self-mailer*.

format, telegram See *gram format (printed promotion)*.

format as response-speed indicator See *advertising format response speed*.

format-change rule When an established format is working well, it should not be changed without a compelling reason. This rule applies to promotion formats and not necessarily to journals, which alter formats frequently.

formats, card deck See *bound deck (direct mail)*; *loose deck (direct mail)*.

formats, card deck envelope See *card deck envelope formats*.

format test (direct mail)   A test mailing in which different formats are used to different segments of the same audience and then compared for responsiveness. Such tests may be self-mailer vs. package, or card deck vs. catalog.

forms only library awareness plan   An adjunct to some jobber library approval plans for libraries that do not wish to receive books automatically. Instead, printed forms are sent in all or selected subject areas. The library may order the book by returning a portion of the form or transferring the information into its ordering system. In a recent year, Coutts Library Services received 20% of its sales on such forms. Librarians also call these *exclusion slips, notification slips,* or *title announcement forms.* See also *approval plan.*

Form 3602   See *proof of mailing.*

Forthcoming Books   A bimonthly index by author and title of books to be published in the U.S. during the five months following, as well as books published since the previous edition of *Books in Print.* Listings include price, publisher, publication date, and Library of Congress catalog number. By yearly subscription from R.R. Bowker Co., 245 W. 17th Street, New York, NY 10011. See also *Books in Print.*

foundation publishing   Publishing programs conducted by institutions founded and supported by endowments, usually in research, education, or in furtherance of some public cause.

four-color process printing (4/C)   By overprinting with plates using three specific colors (yellow, red, and blue) combined with a fourth color (black), it is possible to produce practically any other color, yielding a "full-color" look.

four-panel fold   A sheet folded in half to create four panels. See also *French fold.*

fourth cover   The outside back cover of a periodical, catalog, booklet, or book. This is the most desirable position for an advertisement because of the high potential for readership. It is therefore usually sold at a premium over the page rate for advertising. See also *cover position; cover rate (advertising); second cover; third cover.*

four-up   See *two-up/three up/four up (printing).*

four-up labels   See *cheshire label format (mailing list)*.

foxing (antiquarian bookselling)   A book with pages that have a spotty appearance due to chemical reactions in paper. See also *antiquarian bookselling terms*.

Foyle's   The largest bookshop in London, located at the corner of Charing Cross Road and Manette Street, with books on five floor levels. A favorite hunting place for those seeking specialized books. In addition to serving academic customers, it attracts an international clientele. Foyle's claims to be the "World's Largest Bookstore."

FPT price   A price carried on the jacket or cover of a book (sometimes accompanied by the letters "FPT") that is actually higher than base price against which the bookseller is billed. The higher price, or freight pass through, enables the bookseller to sell at the higher price to recoup freight costs from the consumer. For example: The FPT price shown on a book might be $14.95, but the publisher will bill the bookstore from a base of $14.00. The $.95 helps offset shipping charges from publisher to bookstore.

fractional page space (advertising)   Sizes of advertising, less than page size, that a periodical will accept. When a fractional page unit of advertising is planned, it is a good idea to check the rate card or contact the publication to verify in advance that that size and shape will be accepted. Some *Time*-size periodicals with 2-column pages will only accept vertical half pages; some with 3-column pages will only accept horizontal half pages. See also *agate line; column inch*.

Frankfurt Book Fair   World's largest book exhibit and book trade event held annually in October in Frankfurt, Germany, mainly for the purpose of contracting sales rights or arranging for co-editions. Potential exhibitors should bear in mind that exhibit forms are issued in February of each year and must be returned by March 31. See also *Lufthansa*.

free controlled subscriber, periodical   See *periodical mailing list, free-controlled-subscriber*.

free examination offer   An offer to send a book with invoice for examination for a given period, usually 30 days. Recipient has option of either returning book or remitting payment. Or, if an adoption order for a specified number of copies is placed, recipient may keep the book as a desk copy. See also *examination copy/exam copy.*

Freefone service   A U.K. telephone service similar to 800 telephone service in the U.S., although via the operator. See also *Linkline 0345; Linkline 0800.*

free freight, publisher   Shipping charges paid by the publisher. For example, free freight sometimes is applied to orders placed at the American Booksellers Convention or for new accounts placed at that meeting. Free freight also is granted on orders beyond a minimum number of copies. U.K.: carriage paid.

free freight, wholesaler/jobber   Shipment free of shipping charges is a frequently applied term of sale between wholesaler/jobbers and libraries, particularly the school and public library markets.

freelance book sales representative   See *commission rep; sales rep/sales representative.*

freelance copywriter   A self-employed writer who is an independent contractor working on a per-project basis. See also *copywriter; freelancer.*

freelancer   A writer or illustrator who sells services as an independent contractor, usually by the project. Many publishers use freelance copywriters, artists, publicists, and copy editors. See also *in-house.*

Freepost   The U.K. equivalent of Business Reply Mail in the U.S.

Freepost address   Under the U.K. business reply mail system, a volume mailer obtains from the Post Office a unique Freepost address with a different postcode (similar to ZIP code). Post Office traces mail using this code, tallies cost at second-class postage rate, and charges such costs to the mailer on a monthly basis. Freepost can be used only for U.K. mail and does not apply to international mail.

freestanding display unit   A display unit that is self-supporting, i.e., it does not require attachment to a back wall or other support.

freestanding insert   A loose advertising insert enclosed in a particular issue of a newspaper or periodical. It may go to full circulation or a selected segment. See also *blow-in card; insert.*

freight   In the book trade, typically refers to shipping charges. U.K.: carriage.

freight pass through (FPT)   See *FPT price.*

French fold   A single sheet of paper printed on one side only and folded first across its length, and then again at a right angle to the first fold, so that the unprinted side is folded in and the printed side constitutes four pages. Most greeting cards printed on paper stock utilize this fold.

frequency   1. An advertising term meaning number of times an advertising message is inserted in a publication within a specified time period. See also *contract year.* 2. A mail-order term meaning the number of times a customer has made a purchase. 3. A direct-mail term meaning two to four times a specific market is contacted with a promotional offer. 4. A publishing term meaning number of issues per year a periodical is produced (i.e., weekly, monthly, bimonthly, quarterly, etc.).

frequency, for new editions   See *new edition frequency.*

frequency discount   A discounted advertising rate given by a publication to an advertiser for a given number of insertions stipulated by the publisher within a contract year. See also *advertising contract; contract year (advertising); earned rate; one-time rate.*

freshen a mailing   The practice of adding new or different titles to a repeat mailing to give it a different look from its predecessor.

front end (direct mail)   A mail-order term for all necessary activities that occur prior to receipt of a promotion order. See also *back end (direct mail).*

front end results   The returns or response received from a mailing. See also *back end results.*

frontlist   1. Books published during the current season or year. 2. Current and best-selling titles. See also *backlist.*

frontlist publisher A publisher heavily dependent on new titles for the bulk of sales, e.g., a paperback house that aims for a few bestsellers each season. See also *backlist publisher*.

FSI See *freestanding insert*.

fulfillment year The period in which all issues pertinent to an annual subscription are sent to subscribers.

full package direct-mail effort See *direct-mail package*.

fully protected (list) See *protected*.

G

Gale Directory of Publications An annual two-volume directory of nearly 25,000 newspapers, magazines, journals, and related publications with detailed information for advertising and publicity purposes. Includes information about circulation, advertising rates, and more. Added sections give names of newspaper feature editors, college publications, Black publications, newsletters, nondaily newspapers, and more. Published as *IMS Directory of Publications* to 1983, and before that since 1869 as *Ayer Directory of Publications*. Address: Gale Research Co., Book Tower, Detroit, MI 48226.

Gale's Directory of Research Centers See Research Centers Directory.

Gale's Encyclopedia of Associations See *Encyclopedia of Associations*.

Gale's Newsletters Directory See Newsletters Directory.

galley/galley proof (typography) Typeset material from a compositor, often in long, unbroken sheets, used for proofreading before page make-up. Originally referred to the metal tray that held lines of freshly set type, or the tray on which type composition was held until made up into pages in the form or chase (metal frame holding type for printing).

galley proof See *galley, galley proof (typography)*.

galleys, split See *split galleys*.

Gallup survey of book buying An ongoing monthly telephone survey by the Gallup Organization, Princeton, New Jersey, on book buying. Over 1,000 adults 18 and older are called, representing a national sample. Both basic and special questions are asked in each interview relative to book buying habits and preferences. Articles based on the survey are prepared by Gallup and appear periodically in *Publishers Weekly.*

gang run   Two or more jobs "ganged up" or printed simultaneously on the same press for reasons of economy.

gatefold   A page in a publication or promotional piece that is wider than the other pages and must be folded to fit. The folded portion of the page swings out like a gate. In many mail promotions, a gatefold is used for the perforated, removable reply card or order form. Also called a *foldout,* or *shortfold.*

gatekeepers of information (for books)   A term referring to two general groups whose influence can help a book reach its market: 1. Decision makers in and allied with the publishing industry who control media attention given to books. 2. Decision makers who control the media or affect the thinking of individuals and groups that comprise the market for a book. Definition based on article "A Business School Master Plan for Marketing Books" by Leonard Felder in *Publishers Weekly,* January 29, 1979. Acquisitions editors are sometimes called gatekeepers of knowledge within the university press and scholarly-scientific publishing worlds.

gatekeeper title   Title of someone in a company or organization with the power to influence purchasing decisions by others. For example: A training gatekeeper title might be *Director of Training.*

general catalog   See *catalog*

general interest book   A book intended for a general audience. See also *special interest book; trade book/trade title.*

geographic edition   An edition of a publication permitting advertising to a segment of the total circulation within a specific geographic region.

geographic selection   Placing an advertisement in a medium where the advertiser can select in advance the specific geographic areas in which the advertising is to appear. Advertisers in the *Wall Street Journal,* for example, can advertise in either the Eastern, Midwest, Western, or Southern editions, as well as the National or International Editions. See also *demographic selection.*

gift book   A book bought to be used as a gift, rather than for personal reading. See also *coffee table book.*

glossy print/glossy   A photograph with a smooth, shiny surface. This is the most suitable form of photograph for reproduction purposes. Always use glossies when submitting publicity photos with a news release.

going online   Providing or seeking electronic access to information stored in a computer.

good (antiquarian bookselling)   A book that shows average use, i.e., the usual soiling, fraying, or page discoloration typical of a used book. See also *antiquarian bookselling terms*.

good laydown (bookstore)   Sales rep language for a book that has had a good advance sale in bookstores that he or she regularly services.

good press/excellent press (book reviews)   The manner in which a book is dealt with by reviewers. A book that generally gets good reviews is said to have a good press, or if reviews are highly laudatory, an excellent press. In the U.K. and in countries where direct mail may not be a major factor, book sales are often heavily dependent on a good press, since this is a primary factor in building bookstore demand. See also *book review*.

government, federal, and armed forces library market   Approximately 2,400 libraries. See also *Directory of Federal Libraries*.

government bids   Many government agencies invite bids on book purchases and may include both publishers and jobbers. Once a bid is accepted, all books furnished under the accompanying contract must be at the discount agreed upon. Some government agencies will not pay until an order under a bid is completed, or missing titles are reported and accounted for as unavailable. A missing report or single copy unfilled on a bid can hold up payment on the entire contract.

Government Printing Office   See *Publication Reference File; U.S. Government Printing Office (GPO)*.

Government Printing Office (U.K.)   Her Majesty's Stationery Office, or just H.M.S.O. See also *Her Majesty's Stationery Office (HMSO)*.

GPO   See *U.S. Government Printing Office (GPO)*.

graduated schedule of discounts   See *discount schedule, graduated*.

graduate-level faculty list Lists of college and university professors teaching courses at the graduate level. Lists of professors who teach graduate-level courses by discipline are available from CMG Information Services, 50 Cross Street, Winchester, MA 01890. Counts can be obtained by telephone at 617-729-7865.

graduate-level text A textbook used for graduate-level courses. Graduate-level college courses tend to have small enrollments and, therefore, often are unlikely to attract authors willing to write textbooks specifically at that level. Consequently, many graduate-level courses adopt professional references as textbooks. Conversely, where a graduate-level text is written, it usually is designed also to serve as a reference for professionals in the field.

grain (paper) The direction in which the fibers in paper lie. Grain is an important factor in paper folding. Paper folds more easily and tears more cleanly with the grain than against the grain. To test for grain, moisten one side of a piece of offset paper so that the sheet will curl. The grain will run the long way on the curled sheet.

grain, short See *short-grained paper*.

gram format (printed promotion) A printed message with a heading designed to appear similar to a telegram and to impart a sense of urgency.

grammage Grams per square meter. The means by which paper weights are expressed in the metric system. The term is used in this manner: If one sheet, one square meter in size, weighs 104 grams, the grammage of that paper is 104. This would be the equivalent of 70-pound paper. Some metric equivalents of basis weights for a 25″ × 38″ sheet are:

Basis Weight	Grams per Square Meter
30	44
45	67
50	74
60	89
70	104
80	118
90	133
100	148

graphic novel   A short novel that tells its story through comic artwork, typically in trade paperback format (7″ × 10″ or 8½″ × 11″), usually in full color, and priced from $6.95 to $12.95. A comic novel combines prose and the visual excitement of artwork. Usually a minimum of 64 pages, but can extend to over 100 pages depending on the story. (Adapted from *Publishers Weekly* article by George Beahm of Donning Company, November 6, 1987).

graphics   The illustrative material on a printed page, intended to support the copy aspects or message.

Greenaway Plan   See *blanket order plan, origin of.*

gripper edge (printing)   The leading edge of a sheet of paper that the grippers take hold of to carry it through the printing press. See also *gripper margin (printing); grippers.*

gripper margin (printing)   A blank allowance on the leading edge of a printed piece that makes it possible for the metal grippers to control the printed sheet as it passes through the press. Because of the gripper allowance, paper sizes must be larger than the actual print area.

grippers   A printing term for the mechanical fingers that grip the leading edge of a sheet of paper as it passes through the press. See also *gripper edge; gripper margin.*

gross margin on sales   The difference between net sales and cost of sales. See also *cost of sales; net sales.*

gross orders per hour (telemarketing)   The number of orders obtained per hour from a telemarketing sales effort. Orders are often only an agreement to sample or to examine and are not considered true orders. See also *net orders per hour (telemarketing).*

gross sales   All sales billed in dollars and units, exclusive of shipping charges and with discounts deducted.

guaranteed position   See *position charge; position guarantee.*

Guide to Special Issues and Indexes of Periodicals   An infrequent publication of the Special Libraries Association that lists over 1,300 U.S. and Canadian periodicals that publish special issues and gives details about each issue. Address: Special Libraries

Association, 1700 18th Street, NW, Washington, DC 20009. Phone: 202-234-4700.

gutter   The inside margin of a bound page from the printed area to the binding edge.

gutter bleed   Printed or illustrative matter that extends to the center of binding edge of a publication, book, or booklet. See also *bleed*; *gutter*.

gutter position (advertising)   Advertising placed adjacent to the gutter on the page of a publication.

H

hairline   The narrowest or thinnest line used in printed matter.

hair spacing (typography)   Extra spacing between lines of less than one point thickness.

half-life formula   A formula used by some mailers for projecting the total anticipated response from a mailing during the early weeks of the mailing. It is based on previous experience with the same mailing lists, which, when charted on a 9-, 10-, or 12-week campaign period, show that about half the total response usually comes in at a certain point in the campaign, typically about 3 to 4 weeks after the mailing date. The formula is predicated on bulk third-class mailing.

half-page spread (advertising)   A half-page advertisement across two facing pages.

halftone   A reproduction of a continuous tone image, such as a photograph, by use of a screen formed by very small dots of various sizes. See also *continuous tone; halftone dot; halftone screen; line copy.*

halftone dot   One of a series of small dots in varying sizes which when mixed with white space gives the perception of a gray tone. The darkness or lightness of the tone is dependent on the ratio of black dots to the white space between them. See also *halftone; halftone screen; screen.*

halftone enlargement   With a Velox or screened print, where every dot is clear, it is possible to enlarge a halftone. However, in the enlarging process, the screen becomes more coarse. Halftone screen reduction is not recommended. See also *Velox.*

halftone screen   Usually a cross-line mesh engraved on glass, the lines being black and the spaces between them transparent. By photographing a continuous tone image through this screen, the original is converted into a series of very small dot patterns which, when printed, recreate the original subject photographed. See also *screen*.

handbook   Generally, single-volume reference works that provide a concise, accessible overview of a subject or field of knowledge. Handbooks are designed primarily for purchase by individuals for ready reference or for solutions to problems in the subject area. See also *encyclopedia*.

handbook pricing   Because handbooks are usually aimed at the specialist for everyday desk use, they must be priced to be affordable to the individual buyer, rather than as a library purchase. See also *handbook*.

handle/sales handle   A concise summary of selling features of a book used by a rep in sales calls on booksellers and, subsequently, by the bookseller to describe why someone should want to buy a book, what it offers, and its potential benefit to the reader.

hardback   See *hardcover*.

hardbound   See *hardcover*.

hard copy   Copy printed on paper, as opposed to electronically stored or displayed copy. See also *soft copy*.

hardcover   A book bound in stiff paperboards that may be covered in cloth, plastic, paper, or leather. U.K.: hardback. See also *clothbound/cloth*; *paperback/paperbound*.

hard sell   See *"nice to know" (book pricing and promotion)*.

Harvard Business Review   A key book review and advertising medium for reaching those in business management. Circulation in excess of 240,000. Published alternate months by Harvard Graduate School of Business Administration. For advertising, contact Ellen Jarvis or James P. Quinn, Room 2600, 50 E. 42nd Street, New York, NY 10017. Phone: 212-972-0740.

head   See *headline (advertising)*; *headline/head (in sales letter)*.

head, drop   See *drop-head*.

headband   Decorative band of cotton or silk filling the gap between the spine and the cover of a hardcover book.

headline (advertising)   The large-type heading over an advertisement or block of advertising copy has a twofold purpose: (1) to attract the reader's attention; and (2) to entice the reader into reading the copy following. The headline is a vital ingredient of book offerings to professional and scholarly audiences. In many cases, a book's title makes an excellent headline, for example, Herschell Lewis's *More Than You Ever Wanted to Know About Mail Order Advertising*.

headline/head (in sales letter)   A heading, usually featuring a benefit and designed to entice the reader to read the remainder of the letter. A headline is favored by many promotion writers as a substitute for a salutation in a printed sales letter.

headline, requirements of   (1) Attract attention; (2) lead reader into copy; (3) be clear; (4) be reasonably short.

head margin   Distance from the top edge of a printed page to the top of the first type appearing on the page, usually the running head. See also *running head*.

head of house   The chief executive officer; the individual who directs the editorial direction of a publishing establishment and who reports to the board of directors on the activities and profits of the firm.

Her Majesty's Stationery Office (HMSO)   The United Kingdom equivalent of the U.S. Government Printing Office. Printer of all U.K. government official publications. See also *HMSO Books*.

hickey   Print industry term used to describe spots on a finished printed piece which may have been caused by dust on the press negative or lint on the offset blanket.

high bulk (paper)   See *bulking paper*.

highlight halftone   See *dropout halftone*.

high opacity paper   Paper with little show-through of printing from the opposite side of the sheet.

high school library collection development   This level of school library devotes the major portion of its budget to adult and reference books designed to serve student needs, both for course requirements and for personal enrichment. High school libraries also buy current and topical books aimed at the general reader, as well as software, audio tapes, periodicals, and more.

high school library market (private and Catholic)   Approximately 2,500 libraries.

high school library market (public)   Approximately 15,500 libraries.

high school lists, international   Mailing lists of high schools in almost any country of the world are available from IBIS Information Services (for which see separate entry).

high school lists, U.K.   Mailing lists of high schools in the U.K. are available by enrollment size, subjects taught, or facilities from IBIS Information Services (for which see separate entry).

high school market   Covers grades from 9 through 12.

high-ticket book   High-priced book. See also *big ticket*.

hit   An impression from a stamping die.

hit rate   The percentage of identical names appearing on both lists when two mailing lists are matched by computer. See also *duplication rate (mailing list)*; *merge-purge (mailing list)*.

HMSO   See *Her Majesty's Stationery Office*.

HMSO Books   Books published by the official printing agency for the United Kingdom and distributed in the United States by HMSO Books/Bernan Associates, 4611 Assembly Drive, Lanham, MD 20706-4391. The U.K. HMSO bookshop is located at 71-73 Lothian Road, Edinburgh EH3 9AZ Scotland. Telephone: 031-228-4181. See also *Her Majesty's Stationery Office*.

home-address mailing option   The capability of some mailing list owners of offering names of professionals or educators either at their place of employment or at their home address. Market Data Retrieval is one source that gives this choice for elementary school educators. See also *Market Data Retrieval*.

horizontal half page   Periodical half-page advertisement in which the longer dimension of the ad is horizontal.

horizontal mailing list   A list that includes individuals spread across many different classifications of business. See also *vertical mailing list*.

horizontal publication   A publication targeted to persons holding similar positions or having a common interest, or operating at a particular job level in different types of businesses. Horizontal publications would include *Journal of Accountancy, Office Management*, and *Industrial Hygiene News*. See also *vertical publication*.

hospitality suite (conventions)   A room or suite of rooms taken at a convention as an add-on to an exhibit in the main exhibit area or in place of it. The hospitality suite has the advantage of being away from competitive exhibits. However, there must be a means of generating traffic to the suite. Also used for author negotiations, special meetings, and social receptions.

hotline list (direct mail)   A list of recently acquired names, usually related to a buying activity. Most such lists contain names acquired within a recent three to six month period. In direct-mail promotion, the more recent the activity of a name, the greater the chances for a repeat mail-order sale.

hotlines (book trade)   Extra-fast order fulfillment service by publishers or wholesalers on orders received from booksellers by telephone or over telephone lines. Many are set up only during high-volume selling periods such as Christmas when fast order turnaround is critical.

hot type   Type cast from molten metal. The various forms of metal composition—Monotype, Linotype, Ludlow, and foundry—are rarely used now. See also *cold-type composition/cold composition*.

house   General reference to a publishing house or establishment.

house ad   An advertisement for a publisher's books or journals in a publication or promotion of that publisher.

house agency   An advertising agency on the premises of or controlled by the advertiser.

house bookbuyer list rule   The best mailing list for any type of offering is the house bookbuyer list.

house list (direct mail)   A company-owned mailing list.

house list suppression   The omission of names on a rented mailing list that already exist on the mailer's house list. See also *list suppression, database.*

house rep   A book salesperson who is employed by and represents only a certain publisher, and who is usually on salary and bonus. See also *commission rep; repping group; sales rep/sales representative.*

how-to-do-it book   A practical manual, often elementary in content, that provides information on a particular topic in a step-by-step manner.

Hudson's Newsletter Directory   An annual publication of Newsletter Clearinghouse that lists over 3,000 newsletters available by subscription, including field or subjects, circulation, name, address, and phone number of publisher. Address: 44 W. Market Street, P.O. Box 311, Rhinebeck, NY 12572.

hurt books/hurts   Books that are soiled or damaged and, therefore, considered unsaleable. The major source of hurt books is returns from free examination shipments or from booksellers or wholesalers. Such books, when accumulated, are sold to remainder dealers. In some houses, when a review inquiry is received from a doubtful or questionable source, hurt books will be sent rather than to ignore the request.

hybrid journal   A periodical that combines the features of both a journal and a magazine, e.g., *Analytical Chemistry* and *Environmental Science and Technology*, both published by the American Chemical Society. Each functions as the journal of its field, but also has a magazine section in the front.

hype   Abbreviation for hyperbole. Exaggeration in copy not meant to be taken literally.

I

IBIS Information Services   A major supplier of international mailing lists and other international mailing services including international cooperative mailings to special libraries outside the United States. Address: IBIS Information Services, 152 Madison Avenue, Suite 803, New York, NY 10016-5424. Phone: 212-779-1344. See also *cooperative mailings, international.*

ID   See *independent distributor (ID).*

IIA *See Information Industry Association.*

image (in promotion)   The perception a press wishes to project to those reading its advertising or promotion. When a press already enjoys a favorable image in the markets it reaches, the advertising and promotion should be reflective of that image. Publisher "image" is often a factor in library book acquisition.

image advertising   Advertising with the purpose of building a publisher or product image rather than offering specific ordering information to generate a direct sale.

image area (printing)   Actual area on which printed matter will appear; the printable area of a page. See also *live area (advertising).*

import book   A book brought into a country for sale after being produced and published in another country.

imported book, same, from different sources   See *parallel importation.*

imposition (printing)   The arrangement of pages in a press form so that they will fall in correct order when the printed sheet is folded. For types of imposition, see *sheetwise imposition*; *work-and-tumble*; *work-and-turn*.

impressing (printing)   The pressure of type, plate, or blanket as it makes contact with the paper.

impression (advertising)   The number of individuals who may read an advertising message in a magazine or journal, including both subscribers and pass-along readers.

impression (book)   All copies of a book printed at one time. See also *edition*.

imprint   1. The name of the publisher on the title page of a book. 2. A subdivision within a publishing company bearing its own name and run by a particular editor or publishing certain types or subjects of books. 3. The name and address of an advertiser on its advertising material. Many publishers offer advertising material to booksellers with imprint omitted. The bookstore may then add its own imprint and use the material for promotion to its own customers and prospects.

imprint, publisher's (in advertising)   See *publisher's imprint (in advertising)*.

imprint loyalty   The tendency of bookbuyers to favor books issued by a particular publishing source.

impulse purchase   A spur-of-the-moment or unplanned purchase. Designers of mass-market paperbacks place great emphasis on cover design because of the high degree of impulse buying of such books.

IMS Directory of Publications   Beginning with the 1987 (119th Edition), the IMS Directory became the *Gale Directory of Publications*. See also *Gale Directory of Publications*.

inactives   Names of individuals on a publisher's customer mailing list who have not made a purchase over a specified period of time.

inbound telemarketing   See *telemarketing, inbound*.

incentive   A device used to increase response from a promotion. For example, a discount or a premium.

income-to-cost ratio   A method of evaluating a mail-order promotion, especially in a multibook mailing. Some professional-book publishers consider a mailing effective if the cost does not exceed 33¢ to 42¢ of each sales dollar. See also *echo effect (of direct-mail promotion)*.

indention   Any line in a block of type composition less than the full measure in width. The simplest indent is for a paragraph signifying the beginning of a text block. Paragraphs are easier to read when indented.

independent/independent bookstore/independent bookseller   1. An individual bookselling establishment not owned or controlled by any other organization. 2. A proprietor-operated bookstore. See also *bookstore; bookstore chain; mom and pop store*.

independent distributor (ID)   A wholesaler of magazines and paperback books to newsstands and nonbookstore accounts. See also *rack jobbing*.

independent magazine wholesaler   See *independent distributor (ID)*.

independent rep   See *commission rep*.

indexing services   See *abstracting and indexing services*.

index paper   A stiff, inexpensive, ink-receptive paper frequently used for postcard mailings and reply cards. Available in smooth or antique finish.

India paper   A very thin, tough, and opaque printing paper, originally from Asia, that is used for printing bibles. Now used as a term of reference for bible paper. See also *bible paper*.

indicia   The postal permit imprint on a mailing used in place of a stamp or cancellation.

Indicia   A monthly newsletter of Clark-O'Neill/Fisher-Stevens, produced for mail marketers in the medical and health care fields. Free if you use medical mailing lists. Address: Clark-O'Neill/Fisher-Stevens, One Broad Avenue, Fairview, NJ 07022-1570.

individual negative letterspacing See *kerning (typography)*.

individual subscription price (journal) See *personal subscription price (journal)*.

industrial sales A term used by some publishers to describe special sales activity. See *special sales*.

industry magazine One that provides news of a particular field or industry. See also *business paper/publication*.

inertia selling See *negative option*.

inferior characters (typography) Small letters or figures set slightly below the baseline of other type on the same line as in some chemical formulas. See also *baseline (typography); superior characters/superior letters/superior figures/superscript (typography)*.

inflationary price increases See *price increases for inflation*.

in-flight publication One found only on an airline and designed to be read by passengers in flight. A good medium for advertising certain types of business books.

influencers Individuals who do not actually buy, but who influence others to buy. An example might be a college professor who recommends a textbook or adjunct reading for a college course. See also *influentials*.

influentials 1. Authorities. 2. Individuals known to wield influence over others within a profession or occupational specialty. 3. Individuals known to be prominent in some sphere of activity. Mailing lists of influentials may be found in *SRDS Direct Mail List Rates and Data* (for which see separate entry).

information center See *special library*.

Information Industry Association Trade association of companies and organizations involved in the creation, dissemination, and use of information, especially business-related information that is published electronically or with the aid of computers. Comprised of some 500 corporations and organizations represented by approximately 4,500 individuals active in the association. Address: 555 New Jersey Avenue, NW, Washington, DC 20001. Phone: 202-639-8262.

Ingram Advance/Ingram Paperback Advance   Two monthly publications of the Ingram Distribution Group designed to alert book retailers and others to new titles of interest to the general public.

Ingram Book Company   A leading supplier to trade bookstores and public libraries headquartered in Nashville, Tennessee (Box 17266, 347 Reedwood Dr., Nashville, TN 37217), and with additional shipping centers in City of Industry, California, and Jessup, Maryland. Booksellers may use a toll-free number before 10:30 A.M. and get same-day shipment on stock orders. Phone: 800-251-5902 (Tennessee: 800-468-9464).

Ingram Library Services   A division of Ingram Distribution Group selling Ingram products to libraries. In addition to books, other Ingram library products include videocassettes, software, compact discs, spoken word audiocassettes, and special interest periodicals.

in-house   Work performed by staff inside a publishing establishment, rather than by outside vendors or freelancers.

in-house composition   Typesetting for books or journals done on the premises of the publisher.

ink, opaque   Ink that conceals all color beneath it.

ink color matching (printing)   See *PMS colors.*

ink jet printing   A plateless printing process that reproduces a computer generated image on paper using fine jets of ink.

inline type   A typestyle in which a thin "white" line appears within the contour of the stroke of each character, making it appear as if the letter were drawn with a heavy outline. Rarely used. See also *outline letters/open-faced letters (typography).*

in play   Term used to describe a publishing company being bid on by prospective buyers. Once the bid is made publicly, it often attracts other bidders even if the initial purchase attempt is successfully thwarted. The company is then said to be "in play."

in press   A work in production. When such works are advertised and as yet unpriced, book advertisements may use the words "In Press" in lieu of book price. See also *price, in advertising.*

in-print   A book currently available from the publisher's stock. See also *out-of-print (OP)*.

inquiry list   A list of individuals who, at a meeting or convention, have requested catalogs and literature or book information. They have asked that their names be added to the publisher's mailing list, but have not yet made a purchase. See also *house list (direct mail)*.

inquiry-qualifying response   See *direct-mail response, inquiry qualifying*.

inquiry-response mailing/promotion   See *direct-mail response, inquiry qualifying*.

insert   A separate printed piece, usually bearing advertising matter, inserted in a book, periodical, mailing envelope, or outgoing shipment. In some trade houses, mailing inserts supplied to booksellers are referred to as "enclosures." See also *bag stuffer; envelope stuffer; statement stuffer*.

insert, book   See *book insert*.

insert, catalog   See *catalog insert*.

insert, magazine   See   *magazine insert*.

insert, package   See *package insert*.

insert, shrink-wrap   See *shrink-wrap insert*.

insertion   A single advertisement in a publication.

insertion order (advertising)   A set of instructions issued to a periodical or print medium authorizing publication of an advertisement on a particular date or in a particular issue in accordance with the specifications stated on the order. These may include size of ad, date or issue of insertion, position desired, applicable discounts or contract rates if any, and whether advertisement accompanies or will follow separately. Additional instructions may request proofs, tearsheets, and/or checking copy. If the order goes separately from the ad, a copy of the order must accompany ad.

inspection copy   Books sent to a librarian for inspection and possible ordering. Some booksellers, especially in Europe, will send inspection copies of new books they think will be of interest to the library. See also *approval plan*.

installation (exhibits and conventions)   Setting up an exhibit booth display according to preliminary planning. See also *set-up (exhibits and conventions)*.

installment buyer   One who orders a publication or a set and pays in two or more periodic payments after delivery.

installment sale   A sale in which buyer pays for purchased item in two or more payments.

instant book   A book released immediately after a major news event with details of the happening. The leader in this field is Bantam Books, which has released over 70 such works in paperback.

instant printing   See *quick printing*.

instant publishing   See *on-demand publishing*.

institutional advertisement   An advertisement designed to build goodwill, establish corporate image, or deliver a message, rather than to sell.

institutional store   A store owned and controlled by a college or university. See also *college store; leased bookstores*.

institutional subscription price (journal)   The price charged by a journal publisher for a subscription placed by a library or other institution. Some publishers charge more for institutional subscriptions than for subscriptions placed by individuals for their own personal use. See also *personal subscription price (journal)*.

insurance   See *certificate of liability insurance*.

integrated catalog   A catalog in which various product lines and products are presented by subject.

interline spacing   See *leading (typography)*.

intermediate-level text   A college textbook at a junior year to first year of graduate school level. Also called junior-level text. See also *graduate-level text*; *introductory-level text.*

internal list   See *house list (direct mail).*

International Book Information Service   See *IBIS Information Services.*

international catalog   A catalog specially prepared for use in the international market. Domestic prices may be eliminated or increased, and the catalog will be produced on a lighter stock of paper to reduce mailing costs.

international co-edition   A book, usually heavily illustrated, issued in various countries and languages by publishers cooperating to share the costs. See also *co-publishing (book).*

international cooperative mailings   See *cooperative mailings, international*; *IBIS Information Services.*

international envelope requirements   See *envelope requirements, international.*

international envelope sizes   The international envelope size range has been developed from the A series of paper sizes (see *international paper sizes*), allowing extra space to insert A size sheets into an envelope. The range of envelope sizes, designated as the "C" sizes, follows:
Size C3 (324 × 458mm/12¾″ × 18″)
   Used for computer printouts, brochures, calendars, showcards. Takes A3 paper size (297 × 420mm) unfolded.
Size C4 (229 × 324mm/9″ × 12¾″)
   Used for brochures, booklets, and general printed matter. Takes A4 paper size (210 × 297mm) unfolded, or A3 paper size (297 × 420mm) folded once.
Size C5 (162 × 229mm / 6⅜″ × 9″)
   Used for small brochures and letterheads A4 folded in half. Takes A4 paper size (210 × 297mm) folded once, or A5 paper size (148 × 210mm) unfolded.
Size C6 (114 × 162mm/ 4½″ × 6⅜″)
   Used for general correspondence, invoices, etc. Takes A4 paper size (210 × 297mm) folded twice, or A5 paper size (148 × 210mm) folded once.
DL size (110 × 220mm/4⅜″ × 8⅝″)

Is a development of the "C" sizes to allow an A4 sheet (210 × 297mm) to be folded twice or an A5 sheet (148 × 210mm) to be folded once. See also *envelope sizes.*

International Group of Scientific, Technical and Medical Publishers (*STM*) See *STM.*

international lists, high school See *high school lists, international.*

International Literary Market Place (ILMP) A companion volume to *Literary Market Place* that provides a comprehensive guide to the book trade in 160 countries outside the United States and Canada. Includes full addresses and key personnel for 9,000 publishers and 3,500 book organizations. Published annually in April by R.R. Bowker Co.

international mailings, collecting payment A notice within any international promotion specifying the type or types of currency in which payment must be made. For most U.S. international promotions, publishers usually indicate payment must be in U.S. dollars or a draft on a U.S. bank. Many also indicate they will accept UNESCO coupons, or payment on any of the well-known bank credit cards: American Express, MasterCard, Visa. See also *UNESCO coupons.*

international medical lists A major source of international medical lists is IBIS Information Services. Lists include medical faculty staff by category, medical libraries worldwide, staff by category, medical libraries worldwide, European hospitals by size and country, and senior physicians in the U.K. by medical specialty. The address of IBIS Information Services is 152 Madison Avenue, Suite 803, New York, NY 10016-5424. Phone: 212-779-1344.

International Organization for Standardization (ISO) An international body charged with developing and promulgating standards. ANSI (American National Standards Institute) is affiliated with ISO and sends its standards to ISO for international adoption.

international paper sizes Sizes founded on the metric system. The basic paper sheet size (AO) is one square meter in area. Hence the weight of one sheet of paper equates to gram per square meter—the measurement used to differentiate between

grades of paper, e.g. $70g/m^2$ and $80g/m^2$.
A sizes untrimmed (in millimeters)
AO = 841 × 1189 (33⅛″ × 46¾″)
A1 = 594 × 841 (23⅜″ × 33⅛″)
A2 = 420 × 594 (16½″ × 23⅜″)
A3 = 297 × 420 (11¾″× 16½″)
A4 = 210 × 297 (8¼″ × 11¾″)
A5 = 148 × 210 (5⅞″ × 8¼″)
A6 = 105 × 148 (4⅛″ × 5⅞″)
A7 = 74 × 105
RA sizes for printing and cutting to A sizes
RAO = 860 × 1220
RA1 = 610 × 860
RA2 = 430 × 610
RA3 = 305 × 430
RA4 = 215 × 305
SRA for bleed printing where extra is required to produce A
sizes
SRAO = 900 × 1280
SRA1 = 640 × 900
SRA2 = 450 × 640
SRA3 = 320 × 450
SRA4 = 225 × 320
See also *paper sizes.*

International Periodicals Directory   See *Ulrich's International Periodicals Directory.*

international pricing   Some U.S. publishers mark up prices for books sold directly in international markets. The higher prices are required to cover additional costs of doing business in international markets.

international promotion, foreign language use   See *translations in international promotion.*

International Publishers Association (IPA)   The international body that represents national publishing associations such as the AAP before UNESCO, WIPO, and other quasi-governmental organizations involved in copyright and other publishing-related matters. Secretary general of IPA is J.A. Koutchounow. Address: Avenue de Miremont 3, 1206 Geneva, Switzerland. Phone: 463018.

International Publishers Bulletin/IPA Bulletin   A quarterly publication of the International Publishers Association, edited by J. Alexis Koutchounow, secretary general of IPA. See also *International Publishers Association (IPA)*.

International Publishing Newsletter   A monthly newsletter of international publishing with emphasis on book fairs, trade events, promotional opportunities, trade regulations, and copyright matters. Address: K.S. Giniger Co., Suite 1301, 1133 Broadway, New York, NY 10010. Subscription address: International Publishing Newsletter, 80 South Early Street, Alexandria, VA 22304. Phone: 703-823-6966.

International Standard Book Number (ISBN)   An international system of book numbering, providing a unique 10-digit identifier for each book published. All U.S. and English-speaking countries carry as the first digit in any ISBN a "0" or a "1." This first digit shows that the book was published in an English-speaking country. The second three-digit group usually identifies the publisher (the identification for The Oryx Press, for example, is 897). The third group identifies the book. The last digit is the "check digit." It discloses any error in the preceding group. The final digit ranges from 0 to 10, with X being used in place of 10. The U.S. ISBN agency is administered by the R.R. Bowker Company. See also *International Standard Serial Number (ISSN)*.

International Standard Serial Number (ISSN)   A unique number assigned to a serial publication. The number remains unchanged as long as the title of the serial remains unchanged. The ISSN is the internationally accepted code used for identification of all serial publications. For ISSN information, write to: National Serials Data Program (NSDP), Library of Congress, Washington, DC 20540.

International Standard Serial Number (ISSN), origin of   A Standard Serial Numbering plan was prepared by the American National Standards Institute Committee Z39 in the late 1960s and presented at the 1970 Oslo meeting of the International Organization for Standardization. Following the meeting, a block of ISSN numbers were assigned to the United States, using the R.R. Bowker Company Serials Bibliography file as the starting point. Subsequently, the Bowker Serials Bibliography in 1971 and 1972 included a combined alphabetical index with ISSNs for every entry. Volumes I and II were published in 1972 as *Ulrich's International Periodicals Directory, 14th Ed.*

international student edition   A reduced-price, exportable edition of a textbook designed for sale in third world countries and/or certain restricted markets.

International Surface Air Lift   See *ISAL.*

International System of Units (SI)   The system of weights and measures, commonly known as the metric system, that is accepted by most countries in the world. When promoting scientific and technical books outside the U.S., it is important to call attention to those that contain metric or SI units or equivalents. Derived from Systém International d'Unités.

International Tradeshow Directory   Detailed information on approximately 4,500 national and international trade fairs and exhibitions in 95 countries. Third English Edition covers years 1987-1989 and includes exhibitor registration deadline. Published by M+A, Frankfurt, West Germany. Distributed in North America by Gale Research Company.

interspersed advertising (periodical)   The practice of interspersing advertising within the editorial content of a periodical. Typically done with magazines, but not journals. See also *stacked advertising (periodical).*

in the mail cost   Total cost to produce and mail a promotion piece.

introductory-level text   A college textbook at the freshman or sophomore levels. Also called *low-level text.* See also *graduate-level text; intermediate-level text.*

introductory price   A special price at which a book is offered, either prior to publication, or for a period that may include time before and after publication. The advantage of an introductory price over a prepublication price is that the expiration date may be extended if promotion and sales results warrant, while a prepublication price usually terminates on publication date. See also *prepublication price.*

inventory reduction sale   See *sale, inventory reduction.*

inventory reduction sale cutoff date   See *sale response time.*

inventory turnover, bookstore   See *turnover (bookstore)*.

inverted pyramid style (publicity)   The preferred writing style for most news releases. This calls for the basic story in the first paragraph or two, with details in the paragraphs following. Thus, if the release is cut, the important information will still be included. See also *publicity/press release*.

invoice stuffer   See *statement stuffer*.

invoice symbols   The following symbols are sometimes used on publisher invoices, although the recent trend has been to spell out the complete message:

BO	Back order
CWO	Cash with order
NEP	New edition pending
NOP	Not our publication
NYP	Not yet published
OP	Out of print
OS	Out of stock
OSC	Out of stock, canceled
OSI	Out of stock indefinitely
TOS	Temporarily out of stock
XR	No returns permitted

involvement device   A specific type of direct-mail enclosure designed to get the reader involved in the offer or the message once the envelope is opened. Tokens, stamps, and sweepstakes are such vehicles. See also *stamps (in book promotion)*.

Inward-WATS   See *AT&T 800 Service*.

IPA   See *International Publishers Association (IPA)*.

ISAL   International Surface Air Lift. A service of the United States Postal Service available for books, periodicals, and advertising matter that provides faster delivery than surface delivery to 125 countries at slightly lower cost. Mail must be eligible for third-class rates, bundled in sets for each country of destination, and delivered to any of 10 U.S. "gateway" cities. Most U.S. journal publishers with European distribution transport their periodicals to Europe via ISAL, or other air freight carriers with competitive rates. See also *ISAL consolidator*.

ISAL consolidator   A company that will take a publisher's (or other client's) mail, bag, label, or document, and deposit the mail at various U.S. airports, or else fly the mail to certain points throughout the world and have the post offices of the different countries deliver it.

ISBN   See *International Standard Book Number*.

island display unit   A display unit that can be seen from all four sides.

island exhibit (exhibits and conventions)   A display area with aisles on all four sides. See also *island display unit*.

island position (advertising)   A fractional-page advertisement entirely surrounded by editorial matter.

ISO   See *International Organization for Standardization*.

ISSN   See *International Standard Serial Number; International Standard Serial Number, origin of*.

IST   Division of Information Science and Technology, National Science Foundation.

ital   Instructions to set copy in italics. An underline is used in typed copy to indicate copy to be set in italics. See also *italic/italics*.

italic/italics   Type based on script and slanting to the right. It derives its name from the fact that it originated in Italy. It is more difficult to read than roman type and should be used sparingly in text matter. Studies have shown that readers prefer roman to italic. See also *oblique (typography); roman, roman type*.

J

jacket Paper cover around a bound book originally used to protect a book prior to sale. The jacket now serves primarily as an advertisement, giving information about the book and its author. Most trade publishers include the list price on the front jacket flap. Text, professional, and reference books are often published without jackets.

jacket band A paper strip around a book jacket bearing an advertising message. See also *wrap-around*.

jacket copy Generally refers to the copy appearing on the jacket flaps. However, jacket copy also includes the back panel, where publishers sometimes carry over information about book and author, or else list books of related interest. See also *flap copy/jacket flap copy/jacket copy; jacket; trade book jacket functions*.

jacket copy, scientific, technical, and scholarly For such books, the front jacket flap generally tells what the book is about, what need it fills, its audience, and the credentials of the authors. The back flap provides detailed biographical notes of the author or editor, credentials, and other written works in the same or a related field.

jacket copy approval, clearance For scientific, technical, professional, or scholarly works, it is good practice to have author or editor review and approve jacket copy before it is released to the printer. Such clearance can prevent misstatements and costly errors and ensures that the jacket statement properly represents the book. See also *flap copy/jacket flap copy/jacket copy; jacket; jacket copy*.

jacket flap copy See *flap copy*.

jacket purposes, trade book   See *trade book jacket functions.*

jargon (copywriting)   The use of uncommon words or specialized terms in place of words from the general vocabulary. Book marketing and bookselling personnel tend to slip into jargon with associates, but should avoid it in communication with outsiders or in copy reaching outsiders. A frequent failing of promotional copy is that it includes "insider" words that are not readily understood by the general public.

job (advertising)   A single complete project within a promotion effort. It may refer to an advertisement, a mailing, or a particular piece of literature, etc. All costs related to the particular job bear the job number for final accounting and budgeting purposes. See also *job number (advertising).*

job, closed   See *closed job (advertising).*

job, open   See *open job (advertising).*

jobber   The term used intermittently with "vendor" or "wholesaler" by librarians for their supplier of books. There is a tendency among veteran librarians to refer to all wholesale booksellers as "jobber," although the term is technically incorrect for those who supply books to the retail book trade. It is, however, appropriate for the specialist library supplier. See also *jobber, library; medical book distributor; wholesaler (book)/jobber* .

jobber/dealer, approval plan   See *approval plan jobber/dealer.*

jobber, academic library   A supplier of books to libraries whose operation is geared to the special needs of academic libraries.

jobber, contract   A wholesale bookseller who specializes in school, institutional, and governmental book requirements under terms of a specific contract and usually for a specified period of time, usually a year, called the contract year.

jobber, library   A specialist library supplier who acts as buying agent or order consolidator, serving as an intermediary between the publisher and the publisher's library customers. Jobbers offer the library a convenient way to buy the books of dozens or hundreds of publishers and to receive a consolidated invoice for all of their purchases. U.K.: library supplier. See also *library wholesaler.*

jobber, school   A supplier of books to the school market at all levels including building, district, county, and state.

job function (direct mail)   A descriptive line added to a business address to direct a mailing piece to an individual in a business with that specific responsibility. Used most often in publishing mail promotions when either the name of the recipient is unknown or the job responsibility may fit more than one job title. For example: Printing Buyer. See *title slug (direct mail)*.

job number (advertising)   A number assigned to a particular advertisement, effort, single activity, or project to facilitate tracking of costs involved. Also sometimes used for tracking results. The job is usually considered officially started or "opened" with assignment of the job number. See also *job (advertising)*.

job printer   A commercial printer who performs a wide range of miscellaneous or small printing jobs such as business forms, letterheads and stationery, advertising circulars, etc. See also *lettershop, basic services; quick printing*.

job requirements, sales rep   See *sales call (retail accounts); sales conference; sales rep/sales representative; sales territory (sales rep)*.

job shop   See *job printer*.

job title (advertising)   The title given an opened job on a particular advertising or promotion activity identified by an assigned job number. See also *closed job (advertising); job (advertising); job number (advertising); open job (advertising)*.

job title (direct mail)   A descriptive line added to a business address to direct a mailing piece to an individual with that specific job title, such as president, or personnel director. See *job function (direct mail); title slug (direct mail)*.

jog (printing)   To push or shake printed sheets so as to align them in a compact pile.

joint imprint   The imprint of two publishers on the title page of an edition of a book being marketed and distributed by each in a different country. See also *co-publishing (book)*.

joint mailing   Two separate but complete direct-mail packages of different advertisers mailed in a common mailing envelope, thus sharing cost of postage and list rental. See also *cooperative mailing/co-op mailing; shared mailing.*

joint publication   Publication of a book in two editions by two different publishers, e.g., between a trade publisher and a university press, where one might do a paper edition and the other a cloth edition. See also *co-edition; co-publishing (book).*

journal   1. Usually a periodical that publishes original research papers and other research material that has not previously appeared, generally written by the person who conducted the research and reviewed by peers. By contrast, magazines do not carry original research papers. 2. A periodical for practitioners in a specific field or profession, with editorial coverage designed to provide coverage of the field. See also *hybrid journal; scholarly journal; primary scientific journal.*

journal, archival   See *archival journal.*

journal, core   See *core journal.*

journal, hybrid   See *hybrid journal.*

journal, primary scientific   See *primary scientific journal.*

journal, refereed   See *refereed journal.*

journal, scholarly   See *scholarly journal.*

journal, scientific   See *scientific journal.*

journal, typewritten   A journal the editorial content of which is produced from camera-ready manuscripts submitted by the authors, usually on typewriters or letter-quality printers connected to word processors.

journal advertising income   Moneys derived from space advertising sales in a journal. For most scientific and technical journals, advertising revenue is minimal. In the medical area, however, advertising revenue may account for about a quarter of the total revenue.

journal advertising positioning   See *stacked advertising (periodical).*

journal break-even   The number of years required before subscription income matches publishing cost. Most publishers seek to achieve break-even in three to five years.

journal catalog   A publisher's catalog devoted exclusively to journals, and used as a promotion vehicle, primarily to libraries and periodical subscription agents. Publishers with few journals rarely issue a catalog. Instead, they favor individual informational sheets or folders for each journal.

journal expires   See *expires.*

journal gracing policy   1. A policy set by a journal publisher on how long a subscriber will continue to receive the journal beyond expiration. 2. The up-front credit policy period on new subscriptions.

journal market segments   See *periodical market segments.*

journal ordering patterns   See *periodical ordering patterns, library.*

journal overrun   An overprinting of a single journal issue for a specific reason. Some publishers who devote an entire journal issue to a conference proceeding overrun the issue, add an ISBN number, and sell the "journal overrun" as a book. Others overrun an issue to use the extras as samples or handouts.

journal page charges   A charge levied by some scientific and scholarly journals against authors whose articles they publish to help reduce cost of publication. Such charges are sometimes a survival factor, tend to increase income, and often help keep subscription costs down. On the other hand, they are resented by authors and may discourage contributions from leading researchers.

journal pagination sequence   In journal publishing, pages are frequently numbered consecutively for all issues within a volume. Accordingly, the pagination of each issue after the first will begin where the previous issue left off. See also *magazine pagination sequence.*

journal payment method   Journal subscriptions, as a rule, are paid in advance. However, a few publishers will offer a "bill-me" option with a three-month credit grace period. For the vast majority, promotions usually state "Prepayment is required on all orders" or "Service will begin when payment is received" or some similar statement. See also *journal gracing period.*

journal payment rate/pay rate See *payment rate/pay-up rate (subscription product).*

journal prepayment requirement See *prepayment required (journals).*

journal price sensitivity Institutions and businesses subscribe to a journal as a rule because the journal is important to their reference collection or serves ongoing research needs. Consequently, pricing is not a critical factor in subscription consideration if the journal is considered important. Subscriptions are dropped when a price is deemed to be beyond the publication's value or contribution to the program. Price sensitivity increases when there are many individual subscribers.

journal promotion mailing lists Rental lists, to be successful for journal promotions, must be to individuals whose professional or personal interests closely match the aims and scope of the journal being promoted. Most professional associations and societies rent their mailing lists, and are often ideally suited for journals promotions. Individual subscriber lists to similar journals are also ideal and may be secured on an exchange basis. For association/society names, addresses, and phone numbers, refer to the Gale associations encyclopedia. See *Encyclopedia of Associations.*

journal promotion timing Since most journal subscriptions start in January and run the calendar year, the vast majority of library subscribers plan their upcoming year budgetary requirements by early fall. Consequently, journal promotions timed prior to this period have the best chance of getting into the upcoming year's budget.

journal promotion yield Journal mail promotions, as a rule, are not expected to produce a subscription yield that exceeds promotion cost. Rather, success is measured by lifetime value of subscriptions received. Rate of renewal, when known, is often a key factor. See also *subscription promotion yield rule.*

journal publishers, encyclopedia of See *Ulrich's International Periodicals Directory.*

journal publishing house   1. A publishing operation in which most of the publishing activity is devoted to journals. Books may also be published, but the book publishing is considered a secondary activity. 2. Some houses prefer to be known as book publishing establishments but derive their major income from journals. 3. Any publishing operation that also includes one or more journals. Worldwide, most journal publishers of record issue less than two journals.

journal rate of renewal, annual   See *renewal rate (subscription product)*.

journal reprints   See *offprint*.

journals, bonus distribution   See *bonus distribution (periodicals)*.

journals, consolidated billing   As a service, subscription agents combine all of the different journal subscriptions for a library into a single consolidated invoice. A number of publishers also offer libraries consolidated billing on their journals.

journals, foreign subscriptions   Most foreign journal subscriptions sold in the U.S. are placed through subscription agents to minimize currency exchange problems.

journals air service charge   See *air service charge (journals)*.

journals consortia   Centralized organizations that handle all details of production and distribution for a group of journals. Editorial control, as a rule, remains with the individual periodicals when the periodicals are owned by outside organizations. Among the more successful are the Transaction Periodicals Consortium, The Johns Hopkins University Press Journals Section, and the Heldref Foundation. (Heldref is an acronym for Helen Dwight Reid Educational Foundation.)

journals copy approach   Journals sell largely on their perceived need and their role as a forum for research results within their specialized field. Journals copy should therefore stress how content provides latest research results, satisfies information needs, and keeps readers informed on current developments within the journal's scope.

journals markets (1) Subscribers (individual and institutional); (2) subscription agents (domestic and foreign); (3) bookstores; (4) newsstands; (5) periodical distributors.

journal subscriber patterns/makeup The ratio of individual subscribers to institutional subscribers. Journals produced by commercial publishers are subscribed to mainly by institutions. What few individual subscriptions exist are often tied to research grant moneys. Journals published by societies generally have a large number of individual subscribers in addition to library subscribers. Societies often have a built-in subscriber base in their membership. At the American Chemical Society, for example, the split between individual and institutional subscriptions is about 50-50.

journal subscription agent See *European subscription agent; subscription agency, full service; subscription agent/agency.*

journal subscription cycle As a rule, journal subscriptions are sold on a calendar-year basis, starting in January and expiring in December. See also *magazine subscription cycle.*

journal subscription decision-makers See *academic library subscription decisions.*

journal subscription list A mailing list of individuals who regularly receive a scholarly, scientific, or professional periodical.

journal subscription payment requirement. See *subscription payment requirement, periodical.*

journal subscription price, foreign See *foreign subscriber price (journal).*

journal subscription price, institutional See *institutional subscription price (journal).*

journal subscription price, member See *member subscription price (journal).*

journal subscription price, personal See *personal subscription price (journal).*

journal subscription pricing, two-tiered See *differential pricing (journals).*

journal subscription renewal rate The percentage of subscribers who renew their subscriptions each year. The rate varies widely from one journal to another. In the scientific, technical, and medical fields, however, renewal rates tend to be very high—upwards of 80% for many. By contrast, in a field such as nursing, the renewal rates tend to be much lower because of the high work turnover rate in this profession. Within any particular journal subscription base, library and other institutional renewal rates tend to be much higher and more stable than those for individual subscribers.

journal subscription turnoffs (1) Redundancy of material; (2) publication off schedule; (3) unreasonable pricing.

journal supplier See *subscription agent/agency.*

journals U.S. currency requirement Most journals originating in the U.S. require advance payment in U.S. currency or a draft on a U.S. bank. Many will also accept UNESCO coupons in payment. See also *UNESCO coupons.*

journal volume frequency The issues of a scientific or scholarly journal issued during a normal subscription cycle (one year) may be part of a single volume, or a number of different volumes. See also *magazine volume frequency.*

jump page/pages A page inside a newspaper or periodical on which lengthy articles started on the first page are continued to completion.

junior college library market Approximately 1,125 libraries. See also *college and university library market.*

junior college textbook decision-making months See *college textbook decision-making months.*

junior high school library collection development These libraries buy both fiction and nonfiction from children's book lists, and an equal amount of adult books, reference materials, software, audio tapes, etc.

junior high school library market (public) Approximately 12,500 libraries.

junior spread (advertising) An advertisement in a periodical that occupies only a portion of two facing pages.

justification   Type composition set so both left-hand and right-hand margins align vertically. See also *flush (in type composition); flush left; flush right.*

juvenile   The former classification for children's books. The term "juveniles" for children's books is still used, but infrequently. See *children's books.*

K

kerning (typography)　In typesetting, the adjustment of space between two letters so they are closer together than normal, often to the point where part of one letter overlaps with the adjacent character. See also *typography*.

key　An identifying device or code in an advertisement or promotion to indicate the source of responses. See also *keyed advertisement*.

keyboard, qwerty　See *qwerty keyboard*.

keyboarding　1. The process of striking keys to create or enter information. 2. A present-day substitute for typewriting and typesetting, although keyboarding does not necessarily produce printed output immediately. 3. Producing type, proofs, tape, or film by manual operation of a machine with a keyboard. U.K.: keying.

key code　See also *code (direct mail)*; *keyed advertisement*.

key contact list　A list of key outside contacts, especially reviewers, with whom direct communication can sometimes produce better results than other more general forms of communication. Most book marketers and book publicists maintain their personal lists, though sometimes these are restricted to use within a single department.

keyed advertisement　A space or direct mail advertisement that is marked with a code, letter, or number to facilitate tracking of responses. A different key is normally used for each mailing list or for each periodical in which an ad is placed. In direct mail, the best location for a key is on the back of a business reply card or in the upper left-hand corner on a business reply envelope. Keyed space advertisements are almost always coupon ads and the key is placed in a corner of the coupon.

keying (v.) 1. Coding a promotion with numbers or letters as a response identification device. 2. Sometimes an equivalent term for keyboarding, especially in the U.K.

key library new-book information sources See *library new-book information sources.*

keyline Outlines on mechanical art showing the proper positions for stripping in copy or illustrations. See also *colors in mechanical preparation.*

key market See *target market.*

kick-off date The official starting date of a promotional campaign or sales drive.

kill (manuscript acquisitions) To reject a proposal or manuscript, or to cancel a contract.

kill (typography) 1. To delete one or more words from typeset copy. 2. Instructions to printer to destroy unwanted type composition.

The Kirkus Reviews A bimonthly professional book reviewing service that provides critical prepublication reviews of fiction, nonfiction, children's books, and young adult books. Reviews over 4,000 books a year. Subscribers are libraries and booksellers. Address: 200 Park Avenue South, New York, NY 10003. Phone: 212-777-4554.

kit/education kit Nonprint items purchased for use in elementary and secondary school libraries. A kit is classified as something that serves as an educational tool, and may include filmstrips, cassette tapes, transparencies, and reel-to-reel tapes.

kraft board A strong quality of board made from kraft wood pulp, a pulp made largely from spruce or pine by the sulphate process.

kraft paper A strong, unbleached brown paper, familiar to most users as brown wrapping paper and used as outer wrapper by many periodicals.

K-8 market 1. The elementary school market. 2. Books or materials intended for grades from kindergarten through 8th grade.

K-12 market See *elhi/el-hi market.*

L

label (n.)   A paper form bearing a name and address which when affixed to a mailing piece serves as the mailing address.

label, permission   See *permission label (bookselling)*.

label, pressure-sensitive   See *pressure-sensitive label*.

label format, standard   See *cheshire label format (mailing list)*.

label key   A code added to mailing list labels to identify list source. So as to permit tracking response, promotions must be designed in such a way that label is returned with the order.

label paper, gum-perforated   Labels on perforated sheets with gum backing that will adhere when moistened.

label paper, heat transfer/heat activated   Label paper that becomes adhesive when heating is applied.

label paper, plain   Usually 16- to 20-pound white offset stock.

label paper, pressure-sensitive   Label paper that adheres when pressed on to an envelope or mailing piece.

labels, mailing, for publicity   See *Bacon's Computerized Media Bank (publicity)*.

label types   Most labels on which mailing lists are supplied are provided ready for affixing by a Cheshire machine. They may be supplied 1-up (one name on top of another); 3-up (3 across and 11 down); 4-up (4 across and 11 down); and 5-up (5 across and 11 down). When no preference is specified, most list suppliers will provide a rental list on 4-across labels.

laid paper   When held up to light, laid paper reveals fine parallel lines (wire marks) and cross lines (chain-marks).

language for foreign promotions   See *translations in international promotion.*

language rights   The granting of a license to another publisher to translate and publish a book in another language. The licensee usually has world rights on the edition in the specific language of the translation (Spanish is an exception: The Spanish American rights and rights for Spain may be sold separately).

large print books   Books set in larger-than-normal type size, usually 16 or 18 points, contrasted with the 9-, 10-, or 11-point typesize normally used. Primary markets: The visually impaired and elderly readers. LP books meeting certain standards and criteria may carry the Seal of Approval from the National Association for the Visually Handicapped. See also *point (typography).*

large type books   See *large print books; Large Type Books in Print.*

Large Type Books in Print   An index of over 5,000 titles available from large-type publishers and associations. Available from R.R. Bowker Company.

laser-printed letter   Letters produced by a computerized imaging method on a laser printer at extremely high speed.

laser printing   A printing technology that offers great flexibility and high speed to provide an attractive alternative to impact printing. In laser printing, a computer-controlled laser is used to scan an imaging surface. The imaging surface picks up an electrostatic toner which is transferred and fused on to the paper. Most laser printers can print characters in any two dimensional orientation and can be programmed to print with a number of fonts and sizes.

LaserSearch   An advanced book-information system for retail booksellers using a CD-ROM disc containing 350,000 book titles. The system will search by title, author name, or other variants, including subject category. Any title thus found can be ordered electronically from Ingram. Contact: Ingram Book Co., 347 Reedwood Drive, Nashville, TN 37217. Phone: 800-251-5900.

launch meeting   A session prior to publication of a book during which editorial, marketing, and publicity personnel review a book's plans and discuss marketing plans and procedures.

law library mailings   See *direct-mail to law libraries, key ingredients.*

lawyers, copy approach to   Emphasis should be on information from competent authority and how the book will speed their work.

layout   A type specification diagram showing arrangements of elements of printed matter—page, piece—for a printer to follow. A preliminary quick pencil sketch is called a *rough* layout. A more precise drawing, closely approximating a final advertisement, for example, is called a *comprehensive.*

LC   Library of Congress. See also *Library of Congress Proof Slips.*

lc   Lowercase; small letters.

LCCN   See *Library of Congress catalog card number.*

lead book   A title in a publisher's seasonal trade list expected to lead the list in sales volume and to generate a substantial advance sale.

leaders (typography)   Dots (...) or short strokes (--) used in copy to direct the reader from one part of the copy to another. Usually specified in linear measurement, such as 2, 4, or 6 units per em. Common in tables of contents. Also called *dot leader.*

leaders in the field   See *influentials; opinion leaders (publicity).*

lead generator/lead producer   A promotional effort designed to produce an inquiry for subsequent follow-up.

leading (typography)   The additional white space inserted between lines of type to permit easier reading or achieve a more open aesthetic effect. Originally was used to specify the piece of metal that was inserted between lines of type in metal type composition. In modern systems, this space is achieved with machine spacing. Type specified as 10/12 (referred to as "ten on twelve") is 10-point type on a 12-point body, which includes 2 points of leading. See also *body (typography).*

lead label card (card deck)   A lead-off or top card in a card deck mailing bearing one to six pressure-sensitive preaddressed labels. These labels may be removed and applied to individual cards within the deck for easy response.

lead producer   See *lead generator/lead producer.*

lead time   The time needed from implementation of a promotion job to deadline.

leaflet   U.K. and European term for flier, a small inexpensively produced advertising piece; it is usually on a single sheet of paper. See also *flier/flyer.*

learned journal   See *scholarly journal.*

learned society publishing mandate   In their publishing programs, learned societies support the profession or field of knowledge they represent largely by disseminating the fruits of scientific, technical, or scholarly research or by producing reference works that support further research.

leased bookstores   Bookstores, mainly in colleges and other institutions, leased to outside operators. A 1986 estimate of the National Association of College Stores indicated that approximately 15% of the 2,700 college bookstores were leased to outside operators. The two largest are Follett Retail Group (Chicago) and Barnes & Noble (New York City).

lease operators   See *leased bookstores.*

lease plan (library)   See *book lease plan.*

leftovers (direct-mail)   The materials remaining after a mailing house has completed a mailing. Mailing instructions should also include instructions for this material—either returned to mailer, destroyed, or stored for future use. If stored for future use, inquire about storage charges. Also called *overages.* In the U.K., such leftovers are incorporated into mailings on related subject titles on a "use until exhausted" basis.

legs   A term used to describe a trade book so popular, it "walks" right out of the bookstore.

letter, comp and colleague   See *comp and colleague letter.*

letter, fill-in See *fill-in letter.*

letter, personal See *personalized letter; personal letter.*

letter, underlining in In promotional letters using typewriter typefaces or simulated typewriter typefaces, stress is given to words, phrases, or lines by underlining. When more than one color of ink is used, often the underlining is in the second color of ink. Underlining plays the same role as italics in regular type composition, but is more prominent in letters. Heavily used in newsletters.

letter enclosure readership study In direct-mail letter promotions, the enclosure is usually the third item referred to by the recipient after the outer envelope and letter. The enclosure is quickly scanned, and, if considered worthy of further attention, such attention begins with the cover. About 50% of readers open and look at the inside; the other 50% first go to the back cover. (Source: Clark-O'Neill, *Indicia*, January 1987.)

letter eye flow, personalized The common pattern of eye flow by the recipient of a personalized letter is as follows: From (1) name and address; to (2) salutation; to (3) end of letter to the signature; to (4) postscript, if included. Between (2) and (3) the eyes tend to skip the page to scan highlighted words inside the letter (Source: Clark-O'Neill, *Indicia*, January 1987). See also *envelope eye flow.*

letter fold A sheet of paper folded two or more times in the same direction.

letter format A sales message, usually printed or written on the mailer's letterhead and enclosed in an envelope for mailing. In some promotional letters, a headline will be substituted for the letterhead.

letterhead, standard-size The standard size in the U.S. for most letterheads and business forms is 8½″ × 11″. U.K. size: 8¼″ × 11¾″ (A4).

letterhead test (direct mail) Test mailing to an audience in which different letterheads are sent to differing segments of the same audience.

letter insert   Advertising matter added to outgoing mail. Usually referred to as bill stuffer or statement enclosure. Sometimes letter inserts may accompany outgoing correspondence.

letterpress printing   A printing process in which ink is transferred from raised surfaces such as metal type directly onto the paper. While no longer widely used, it originally offered a number of advantages over offset, among them higher quality printing, and the opportunity to correct the printing plate easily with hot-metal type and to leave type standing for later reuse. Further, letterpress can accommodate numbering, scoring, and other attachments. See also *offset printing (offset lithography)*.

letter quality   A computer printout that produces text similar in appearance to that produced by a high quality typewriter.

letter salutation   The greeting in a letter. In promotion letters, the salutation is often omitted and, instead, a headline is used as an opener.

lettershop/mailshop   A service company that will prepare promotional mail in accordance with postal regulations (labeling, metering, sorting, bagging, etc.), deliver it to the post office on specified dates, and provide the mailer with proof of delivery to the post office. Lettershops, also called mailing houses, provide numerous other services which may include creating and printing promotional mail and mailing list maintenance. U.K.: mailing house.

lettershop, basic services   Addressing; inserting; sealing; bagging; mailing; list acquisition and/or maintenance; art and design services; printing; imprinting; duplicating; composition; folding and binding; computerized letter preparation; literature storage; ZIP sorting. See also *job printer*.

lettershop, recognized   Many publishers who rent mailing lists ask that they be shipped to their mailing house or lettershop, where a planned mailing will be processed and placed in the mail. List owners, as a rule, require that such list rentals will be made only to recognized lettershops identified as such through association affiliation or directory listing.

letterspacing (typography)   The addition of space between letters in typesetting, thereby altering the line proportions. See also *kerning (typography)*.

Levin's Law (for direct-mail book promotion)   Any direct-mail promotion consistently forces the total sales curve to rise dramatically from its prepromotion level. Other promotion devices such as advertising and reviews do not have this effect. (Howard M. Levin in *The Evaluation of Book Promotion Devices*, Printers Devil Press, 1976.)

liability insurance   See *certificate of liability insurance.*

librarian, authorized (telemarketing)   A librarian with the authority to place an order for a book or periodical in response to a telemarketing inquiry or solicitation.

librarian, collection development   See *collection development librarian.*

librarian, special   See *special librarian.*

librarian, subject   See *subject librarian (college).*

librarian media preferences, school   See *school library selection media.*

libraries, federal   Libraries funded by and supporting various branches of the United States Government. Their fiscal year starts October 1. See also *Directory of Federal Libraries; government, federal, and armed forces library market.*

libraries, major categories of   (1) Public; (2) school; (3) academic and research; (4) special; (5) government.

library, academic   See *academic library; college library collection.*

library, book publishing   See *Crouse Library.*

library, elementary   See *school library, elementary.*

library, high school/secondary school   See *high school library collection development.*

library, junior high   See *junior high school library collection development.*

library, public   See *public library.*

library, special   See *special library.*

library, stock   See *photo agency.*

library approval plan   See *approval plan; approval plan profile.*

library approval plan jobbers   See Appendixes 8 and 9.

library approval plan profile   See *approval plan profile.*

Library Associations Marketing Directory   See *Marketing to Libraries.*

library awareness plan   See *forms only library awareness plan.*

library binding   A book bound according to standards established by the American Library Association and the Library Binding Institute. Library or class A bound books are covered in buckram cloth, with round corners, strong endpapers, muslin-reinforced end signatures, and sewing with four-cord thread and canton flannel backlining.

Library Binding Institute   Organization of firms and certified library binders doing library binding in accordance with LBI Standard for Library Binding, including rebinding of worn volumes, prebinding of new volumes, and hardcover binding of periodicals. Address: 1421 Wayzata Boulevard, Wayzata, MN 55391.

library book selection specialist   See *bibliographer.*

library direct mail, approach to schools   See *school library direct mail approach.*

library direct ordering advantages   See *direct ordering, library.*

library discount   A discount given to libraries off the list price of a book by most publishers and library jobbers. Discounts tend to be higher for trade books and lower or nonexistant for more specialized works. Jobber discounts may be tied to volume of purchases or size of order, while in many instances, a publisher will have a flat library discount, such as 5% or 10%. Some publishers and jobbers also extend a courtesy discount to librarians for personal purchases when submitted on library stationery.

library jobber   See *jobber, library.*

library jobber with approval plan   See *approval plan; approval plan jobber/dealer.*

Library Journal   A leading twice-a-month periodical for librarians that carries approximately 4,500 adult book reviews a year with emphasis on value of books for a library collection. Published by R.R. Bowker Company, 245 W. 17th Street, New York, NY 10010.

library lease plans   See *book lease plan.*

library lists, college   See *departmental library representatives; college library lists, CMG Information Services; college library subject area generalists; college library subject area specialists; library lists, Market Data Retrieval.*

library lists, Market Data Retrieval   Market Data Retrieval offers lists of a wide range of public, school, and college libraries. Also offers lists of librarians by title, such as director, reference librarian, or young adult librarian. Other lists by librarian name. Numerous other library selection options. See also *Market Data Retrieval.*

library list sources, major   Major sources for library lists are R.R. Bowker Co., 245 W. 17th Street, New York, NY 10010; IBIS Information Services Inc., 215 Park Avenue South, New York, NY 10003; Market Data Retrieval, Inc., 16 Progress Drive, Shelton, CT 06484. Other library list sources are found in Category 91 of *SRDS Direct Mail List Rates and Data.*

library mailings   Mailings to libraries. Response from such mailings is difficult to trace, even when a reply card or envelope is enclosed, since most libraries order through jobbers or use purchase orders that show up as white mail, untraceable to any source. Nevertheless, studies show that librarians do respond to direct mail, their orders contributing to echo effect. See also *direct mail to libraries, rule for.*

library markets, size of   See *college and university library market; elementary school library market (public); junior college library market; high school library market (private and Catholic)* or *(public); public library market, U.S.; special library market, including business and technical libraries.*

library new-book information sources   Publisher direct mail and catalogs, book reviews, publisher space advertising, word of mouth, *Weekly Record* (from R.R. Bowker), *Alert* services (from Catalog Distribution Service of the Library of Congress) based on C.I.P. (Cataloging in Publication) data, approval plan books, and/or form slips.

Library of Congress catalog card number (LCCN)   A number assigned by the Library of Congress to each catalog record. The number can be applicable to a single book or to a multivolume work if cataloged as a set.

Library of Congress CIP Program   The Cataloging-in-Publication Program of the Library of Congress facilitates the inclusion of LC cataloging data on the copyright page of new books. To participate, publishers submit a completed CIP data sheet and front matter and representative pages from the book in either galley or page proof. Within 10 days, LC will assign CIP data, including the LC catalog card number. Details from CIP Division, Library of Congress, Washington, DC 20540. In the U.K., the CIP program is operated by the British Library.

Library of Congress Proof Slips   Descriptive book cataloging copy sold by the Library of Congress to public and academic libraries for their use in cataloging and book selection. The CIP Program enters information into the proof slip system in advance of publication.

library periodical ordering patterns   See *periodical ordering patterns, library.*

library prices for journals   See *differential pricing (journals).*

library publications   Periodicals keyed to librarians or various segments of the library market. They include: *American Libraries; Library Journal; Booklist; Choice; Special Libraries; School Library Journal; RQ; Wilson Library Bulletin.* While not a library publication, *Publishers Weekly* has approximately the same number of library subscribers as it does bookseller and publisher subscribers.

library rate (postage)   A preferential rate for the mailing of books and other educational materials by libraries and kindred nonprofit institutions. In 1976, the law was amended to permit publishers and book distributors to use the preferential rate for shipments to libraries. See also *book rate (postage)*.

library rep   1. A member of a publisher's library field sales staff. 2. A publisher sales representative who calls only on libraries. See also *college rep; sales rep/sales representative; trade rep*.

library review media   See *review media, library oriented*.

library review media, primary, for academic books   *Choice; Library Journal*.

library review media, primary, for children's and young adult books   *Booklist/Reference Books Bulletin; The Horn Book; School Library Journal*.

library review media, public library   Public libraries prefer *Library Journal, The Kirkus Reviews*, and *Publishers Weekly*.

library routing card/slip   An enclosure with mailings to academics or individuals who can influence library purchases. Such enclosures may be for a specific title, or may be an open recommendation accompanying a multiple-book offering. It is hoped that the individual will add his or her name and department or title to the preprinted recommendation and then route it to the librarian, who will order the book or books named.

library sale   See *sale, inventory reduction*.

library slush fund   A fund of surplus or unbudgeted capital held by a library that may be used for attractive acquisitions. The acquisitions may not be considered essential. The fund may also be used for miscellaneous unreportable expenditures.

library subscription agency   Another name for periodical subscription agent.

library supplier   U.K. favored usage for library jobber.

library technical services   Those functions involved with acquisition of materials and preparation of them for access and shelving by library clientele. Includes acquisitions (purchasing), continuations and serials, and cataloging and binding departments. May include collection development (book selection), although in smaller libraries this is more often part of library public services.

library vendor See *approval plan jobber/dealer; jobber, library; library wholesaler.*

library wholesaler The library wholesaler is similar in operation to the trade book wholesaler, with fast shipment, reports on titles short from initial shipment, and good discounts, plus benefit of consolidated billing. Various library wholesalers also offer other services. The oldest and largest of the library wholesalers is Baker & Taylor, founded in 1828 and exclusively in wholesale bookselling since 1912. Many librarians use the term "jobber" rather than "wholesaler" when referring to book suppliers. See also *jobber, library.*

library wholesaler preview program A program of certain publishers under which wholesalers receive on an automatic basis as published one copy of each title, based on a specific ordering or subject profile at special terms that are higher than their normal discounts. Purpose of such programs are to aid with early ordering either for stock or for ongoing library approval programs.

licensed book publishing Creation of books based on copyrighted characters or products (such as toys or media characters) through a licensing agreement granted by the owner of the copyrighted source. It is said to have started with the licensing of a greeting card character (Strawberry Shortcake) by Random House from American Greetings in 1978. Booksellers like licensed books because of their instant recognition value, such as Disney characters, popular toys, or TV show heroes. The grantor of the license is the *licensor;* the recipient is the *licensee.* Such arrangements are done usually through licensing companies.

life cycle The active selling period of a published work. Trade books, as a rule, have a relatively short life. Scientific and scholarly books have a much longer life. Scholarly works by university presses are often available over many years. The life cycle of many professional and scholarly books can be extended by their inclusion in ongoing direct-mail campaigns within their market. See also *sales life (of a book).*

life of a campaign (promotion) The time during which response may be expected from an advertisement or mail promotion. See also *campaign length (direct mail); half-life formula.*

lifetime value of periodical subscription The amount of income that can be expected over the life of a typical subscription. For many periodicals, lifetime value is calculated on five years. It is arrived at by multiplying the annual subscription rate by the renewal rate. A $50 journal with a 75% subscription renewal rate would have a (five-year) lifetime value of about $150.

lifetime value of subscriber product An estimate of total income anticipated from a customer or subscriber over the customer's or subscriber's active buying or subscription life.

lift letter An enclosure added to a mail offer inviting recipients to read only if they have decided *not* to respond. Copy is usually in the form of a postscript, is signed by someone (often of higher authority) other than the signer of the letter enclosure, and offers a short, added, strong selling point.

lightface type Type in which the thickness of the strokes comprising each character is thinner than in the regular or normal type of the same face. See also *typeface.*

lighting (exhibits) See *exhibit lighting.*

limited edition 1. A predetermined number of copies printed at one time, after which no more will be printed. 2. Generally refers to a small or limited number of copies in a single printing, each signed and numbered and carrying a high retail price.

limp binding A book covered with a flexible material. In lieu of a stiff board, there may be a thin card or paper, or none at all.

limp cover See *limp binding.*

line art See *line copy.*

line copy 1. Any copy or artwork suitable for reproduction without using a halftone screen. 2. Any art consisting of solid blacks and whites, with no shading or contrast. See also *line drawing.*

line drawing A drawing done in lines only with no shading. See also *line copy.*

line length See *column width rule (typography).*

line length rule   One formula is typeface point size × 2 as maximum picas line width. Thus a line in 12-point type should have a maximum line length of 24 picas for greatest readability.

line negative   A photographic negative of a line drawing, made without the use of a halftone screen.

Linkline 0345   A U.K. service of British Telecom similar in some respects to the American AT&T 800 Service, except that with the 0345 number, a customer or prospect can call the advertiser from anywhere in the U.K. and pay only the cost of a local call. Advertisers then pay the difference between the local phone call rate and what they would pay if it had been an 0800 toll-free call. See also *Linkline 0800*.

Linkline 0800   A U.K. service of British Telecom that parallels the AT&T 800 Service in the U.S. See also *Linkline 0345*.

list (n.)   1. All of the books a publisher has for sale, both current and forthcoming. 2. A specific segment of a publisher's list such as a spring list. 3. List price. 4. A mailing list. See also *backlist; frontlist; list price/retail price; mailing list; midlist title*.

list, academic   See *compiled list (academic)*.

list, compiled   See *compiled list*.

list, mailing   See *mailing list*.

list, marginal   See *marginal list (direct mail)*.

list advertisement/list ad   Ad in which a number of different titles are listed with or without brief descriptions.

list affinity (direct mail)   The connection between the interests or needs of the names on a particular mailing list and the book or periodical being offered to that list. Affinity is the key to success in all mail promotion—the greater the affinity, the greater the chances for success.

list arrangement   See *mailing list arrangement/sequence*.

list broker   An individual or organization engaged primarily in arranging mailing list rentals between list owners and business mailers. The broker may assist and guide in locating and obtaining rental lists for mailers, but payment comes in the way of commission from the list owner, usually 20%. Some broker functions: List research and recommendations, clear approval for rentals and ensure timely delivery, supply information on lists that have worked for others in related areas.

list-building premium   See *premium, list-building*.

list cards/data cards   See *mailing list cards/list data cards*.

list catalogs   See *SRDS Direct Mail List Rates and Data*.

list cleaning   See *mailing list cleaning*.

list compiler   See *mailing list compiler*.

list computerization   See *list conversion/computerization*.

list conversion/computerization   Preparation of a mailing list in computerized format and entry into a computer which makes it possible to handle electronically various aspects of the list in many different ways.

list count (direct mail)   1. The number of names on a mailing list, as indicated on the list owner's or compiler's catalog or on a list data card. 2. The actual number of rental names delivered, as indicated with delivery of the rented list. There is sometimes wide variation between announced list count and actual names delivered. Delivery counts should be checked.

list data cards   See *mailing list cards/list data cards*.

list deliverability   See *mailing list deliverability*.

list duplication   See *duplicate (mailing list); duplication rate (mailing list)*.

list duplication rule, telemarketing   See *telemarketing list duplication rule*.

list exchange (direct mail)   The exchange of mailing lists by two list owners with no payment involved, or the exchange of a mailing list for some other consideration such as advertising space. See also *mailing list exchanges, bookbuyer; mailing list exchanges, subscriber*.

list formats   See *mailing list formats*.

list guarantee See *deliverability guarantee.*

list house A supplier of mailing lists; typically a compiler.

list maintenance See *mailing list maintenance.*

list manager An individual who handles all details of mailing list rentals for the list owner. List managers may be employed by the list owners, or operate independently for a share of rental income.

list minimum (direct mail) See *mailing list minimum order requirement.*

list owner The final authority on list rental or exchange for a particular list that may have been acquired in the course of business, by compilation or outright purchase. List renters usually deal with the list owner's designated list manager or through a list broker.

list pretest A test of a mailing list before its actual use in a mailing. One way to test a list to ascertain its currentness, appropriateness, and acceptability is by a telephone test of a small segment.

list price/retail price 1. Suggested retail or published price of a book. 2. The price appearing in the publisher's catalog. 3. The price against which discounts are given to booksellers and jobbers. 4. The book's price as it appears on the jacket. See also *introductory price; net price; net pricing; prepublication price.*

list profile (direct mail) A description of a mailing list, including details of the special common characteristics of those comprising it. The list profile usually will tell you if the list is appropriate for the market you are seeking to reach.

list rental See *mailing list rental.*

list rental checking Persons renting mailing lists should have lists delivered to their place of business, not their lettershop, so the lists can be checked for accuracy, format, and actual list count. See also *mail monitoring.*

list rental letter of agreement A letter required by a mailing list owner from someone wishing to rent the list. The renter states in the letter that the list as provided on a rental basis will be used for a single one-time mailing. The renter agrees to other specifications that the owner requires. Some list owners include a sample letter of agreement in their list catalogs. The mailing list owner requires that the letter be copied and returned on the list renter's letterhead.

list rental reciprocity requirement (direct mail) A requirement of a few list owners that rental of their lists is conditional on the list owner being able to rent lists owned by the individual requesting the rental. (American Chemical Society lists carry this requirement.)

list responsiveness (direct mail) Response from a particular mailing list may vary from one mailing to another, based on timing, nature of offer, and many other factors. New or newer books, for example, will have a better response rate than older books because they have greater sales potential. See also *response rate (direct mail)*.

lists, association and society See *association list (direct mail)*.

lists, bookbuyer See *bookbuyer lists*.

lists, bookseller See *bookseller mailing lists, major sources*.

lists, college faculty See *college faculty lists*.

lists, rules-of-thumb for See *mailing lists, rules-of-thumb for*.

list salting See *salting*.

list segmentation A means of targeting a mailing to a selected segment of a larger mailing list, from which one or more common characteristics can be isolated, such as buyers of books in a certain subject area or above a certain price, buyers from a given geographic region or from a certain year, and the like.

list selection A selected part of a mailing list that may be rented separately from the entire list. See also *list segmentation*.

list sequence The sequence or order in which names appear on a mailing list.

list sources, school library The three major sources are R.R. Bowker Company, Market Data Retrieval, and QED (Quality Education Data). Bowker is at 245 W. 17th Street, New York, NY

10010; Market Data Retrieval is at 16 Progress Drive, Shelton, CT 06484; QED is at Suite 340, 1580 Logan Street, Denver, CO 80203.

list sources, school market   Major sources are Market Data Retrieval, 16 Progress Drive, Shelton, CT 06484; and Quality Educational Data (QED), Suite 340, 1580 Logan Street, Denver, CO 80203.

list suppression, database   When selecting mailing lists from a database from which names have been selected for previous mailings of the same offer, renters may request that the database owner suppress the names that have been used before to avoid costly duplication.

list targeting   See *target marketing.*

list test for telemarketing   See *telemarketing list sampling rule.*

list testing   A sample mailing to a portion of a mailing list to determine its responsiveness. Many list owners set minimums on orders for test mailings, which may be in names, such as a 3,000 or 5,000 minimum, or in dollar amount, such as $100 or $150. Minimums vary with each list. Also used to test a list sample prior to full telemarketing effort. See also *list test size rules; mailing list test; rollout/roll out/rollout mailing.*

list testing, alphabetical   It is unwise to test a list by letters of the alphabet. Random letter selection is not representative of any list and will give an unbalanced result.

list test size rules   The larger the test group, the more accurate are the results. For example, a test of 10,000 names of a 50,000-name mailing list will give more accurate results than a 3,000-name test of the same list. As few as 2,000 names will usually be satisfactory for a test, although many owners of large lists have minimum rental requirements of 3,000-5,000 names, sometimes 10,000 when some ordered on magnetic tape. Some marketing "pros" say the test segment should be sufficiently large to produce a minimum of 25 to 50 responses. See also *list testing; rollout/roll out/rollout mailing.*

list turnaround   The time it takes a mailing list house to fill and ship a rental order after it is received. In planning mailings to rented lists, it is good practice to ask the turnaround time on orders so as to ensure that lists will be on hand for the planned mailing date.

list universe (direct mail)   1. All the names available for a particular mail promotion. 2. All the names in a publisher's customer/bookbuyer file. 3. All the names available for promotion to a particular market.

list use frequency, law for   Mail to the same list as often as it continues to be profitable.

literary agent   An individual or organization who acts on behalf of an author on publishing and rights matters for a commission or percentage of the proceeds from the author's work.

Literary Market Place (LMP)   A comprehensive and useful directory of companies and individuals in U.S. and Canadian publishing and related industries and support activities. However, does not list publishers who produce less than three books a year. Published annually by R.R. Bowker Co., 245 W. 17th Street, New York, NY 10010. Phone: 212-645-9700. See also *International Literary Market Place (ILMP)*.

literature table (exhibits and conventions)   At some meetings, a table or group of tables placed in the registration area or near the entrance to the exhibits where various types of literature are placed to be taken by those interested. Such tables may have a charge of so-much-per-piece, or may be available free to exhibitors. The literature table can be useful for a nonexhibitor to use for promotional items.

litho   Abbreviation for lithography. See *offset printing (offset lithography)*.

lithography   See *offset printing (offset lithography)*.

live area (advertising)   The area advertising will occupy. For a *Time* magazine size publication, for example, the usual live area measures 7″ wide by 10″ high. By contrast, the "page size" or "trim size" of *Time* is 8½″ × 11″. See also *image area (printing)*.

live matter   1. Type composition. 2. The printed message of a promotion piece.

LMP   See *Literary Market Place*.

local agent   See *European agent.*

local conversion rate   When books published in the U.S. are sold directly through booksellers in foreign countries, the booksellers convert to local currency based on their country's bookseller conversion rate for U.S. and U.K. published books.

local pricing   Billing an export book in the currency of the country to which the book is sent.

logotype   Identifying device or trademark. Abbreviation: logo. See also *colophon; signature (in advertisement).*

long discount   See *trade discount (bookseller).*

loose deck (direct mail)   A card deck format containing a loose pack of postcards, each bearing a separate message, and each returnable, usually postpaid, to the advertiser. See also *bound deck (direct mail); card deck.*

loose-leaf binding   A binder, usually with rings, posts, or screws that holds perforated sheets, signatures, or printed sections in place between covers. See also *loose-leaf edition; loose-leaf publishing.*

loose-leaf edition   A version of a book bound in a loose-leaf binder. Individual leafs can be added, removed, or rearranged.

loose-leaf publication   A publication bound in a loose-leaf binder. See also *loose-leaf publishing.*

loose-leaf publishing   This format is ideally suited for publications containing information that requires regular updating to retain its value. Loose-leaf publications are often sold on a subscription basis. Purchasers are initially sent a binder and a set of loose-leaf pages containing the current contents. Updates, with information that supplements or supersedes the original content, is sent periodically thereafter. Especially well-suited for certain business, legal, and professional reference publications. See also *cumulative supplement approach (loose-leaf publishing); loose-leaf publishing, origin of; pocket part (loose-leaf publishing); replacement pages (loose-leaf publishing); upkeep service (loose-leaf publishing).*

loose-leaf publishing, origin of   Started in 1919 by Richard Prentice Ettinger and Charles W. Gerstenberg, when a book they collaborated on and jointly published contained an obsolete chapter because of a change in the law. They removed the binding and inserted the book in loose-leaf binders after replacing the obsolete chapter. Their newly established publishing operation was named Prentice-Hall, the combined maiden names of their mothers.

loose-leaf reference   One or more volumes on a specific topic published in a loose-leaf binder, updated by supplements and revisions, either on a regular basis or as required.

low bulk (paper)   See *bulking paper.*

lower case (typography)   Uncapitalized letters of the alphabet. Type set in lower case is easier to recognize and can be read 13.4% faster than type set in upper case or all in caps. See also *caps (typography); upper case, all caps (typography).*

low-level text   See *introductory-level text.*

LP books   See *large print books.*

LTV   Lifetime Value. Often used in periodical subscription promotion efforts and market forecasts to estimate how many dollars will be earned during the active life of a subscription. This can be determined by projecting the subscription rate times the renewal rate. See *lifetime value of a periodical subscription; lifetime value of a subscription product.*

Lufthansa   The West German airline that provides package flights for the Frankfurt Book Fair. The airline controls a block of hotel rooms in Frankfurt and, in conjunction with air passage, may be helpful in arranging hotel accommodations for the Frankfurt Fair.

M

machine acceptable (direct mail)   Designing mailing enclosures that can be inserted by machine. When a piece is not machine acceptable, it must be hand inserted at considerably higher cost.

machine coated   Coating applied while the paper is still on the paper machine. Also called *MC paper*.

machine readable   1. Any data recorded in a form that can be sensed or read by a computer or other machine. 2. Information stored in digital form that can be processed by a computer. 3. Information in a form that can be translated by machine into bit patterns for computer storage and applied to such input media as magnetic tape, paper tape, and punched cards. See also *magnetic tape*.

machine readable codes (MRCs)   Printing codes on book covers that can be read by machine. Such codes may identify ISBN, ISSN, or price. Two systems in use are the EAN bar code and the OCR-A code.

magazine   A paper covered periodical containing a collection of articles, stories, pictures, or other features, and, usually advertising. They differ from scientific or scholarly journals in that they almost never carry results of original research as do journals. Some business and professional magazines use "journal" in their titles, but are classified as magazines. Advertisers and publishers usually refer to such publications as a "book." See also *book (as magazine); journal.*

magazine, functional   A magazine that tells readers how to improve their performance in their places of work.

magazine, horizontal   See *horizontal publication.*

magazine, industry   See *industry magazine; vertical publication.*

magazine, product news   See *product news magazine.*

magazine, single-advertiser   See *single-advertiser magazine.*

magazine billing practices   Magazine order forms invite customers to submit payment with their order or to request billing. If the latter option is chosen, the subscription is entered and copies of the magazine are shipped prior to billing. However, if payment is not received within a reasonable time, the subscription is discontinued.

Magazine Industry Market Place (MIMP)   An annual publication offering information on more than 2,800 consumer, trade, professional, literary, and scholarly periodicals and their publishers, plus support professionals in the field. Published by R.R. Bowker Co., 205 E. 42nd Street, New York, NY 10017.

magazine insert   An insert enclosed with a periodical. Typically, most are in card form, either blown in during the binding process or bound in. Catalogs and other advertising matter may also be used as inserts. Book publisher advertising matter is systematically enclosed with periodical mailings in the U.K. and Europe, and 1986 changes in U.S. postal regulations now permit such advertising enclosures in U.S. periodicals.

magazine pagination sequence.   In a magazine, the page numbers start from one with each issue. See also *journal pagination sequence.*

magazine subscription agency   See *subscription agency, full service.*

magazine subscription cycle   Most magazine subscriptions can start any month of the year and expire one year later. See also *journal subscription cycle.*

magazine subscription payment requirement   See *subscription payment requirement, periodical.*

magazine volume frequency   One volume of a magazine includes all published issues within a one-year period. See also *journal volume frequency.*

magnetic tape   A common data storage medium that consists of a plastic tape with a magnetizable surface coating capable of storing magnetic patterns on which data may be stored via electrical impulses.

magnetic tape/mag tape (direct mail)   A primary means of recording, storing, and retrieving data for computerized mailing list operations.

mail, minimum size (USPS standards)   Under U.S. Postal Service regulations in effect since July 15, 1979, all mail must be not less than 3.5″ high and not less than 5″ long to be mailable. It must also be at least seven-thousandths (.007) of an inch thick. Applicable only to first-class pieces of 1 ounce or less, and single-piece, third-class mail weighing 1 ounce or less.

mailer   1. A mailing piece; 2. One who does volume mailings. 3. A lettershop or mailing house.   See also *self-mailer*.

mail forwarding (USPS regulations)

- First-class mail gets free forwarding for 12 months. If not forwardable, it will be returned to sender free with new address or reason for nondelivery.
- First-class mail marked "Address Correction Requested" will not be forwarded; it will be returned with new address free for 18 months.
- First-class mail marked "Forwarding and Address Correction Requested" will be forwarded for 12 months with address corrections returned to the mailer at a cost of 30¢ per piece.
- Second-class mail gets free forwarding (in U.S.) for up to 60 days.
- Third-class mail over 1 ounce and endorsed "Address Correction Requested" on undeliverable mail will bring mailer new address for 30¢ for 18 months.
  If under one ounce, the address-correction charge is 22¢ per piece. Third-class mail without the endorsement will be destroyed at the delivery office.

mailing (n.)   1. A number of pieces of identical or virtually identical pieces of mail, addressed to individuals, companies, or institutions and dispatched through the postal system at the same time with a predetermined objective. U.K.: mail shot. 2. Any mail effort meeting USPS requirements for second- or third-class mail. See also *Bulk Business Mail; direct mail advertising; direct marketing.*

mailing, announcement   See *announcement mailing.*

mailing, direct response   See *direct response mailing.*

mailing, dry-test   See *dry-test mailing.*

mailing, follow-up   See *follow-up mailing.*

mailing card   A self-mailer printed on card stock with a minimum thickness of seven thousandths of an inch to conform with U.S. Postal Service regulations.

mailing date   Date a mailing is delivered to the post office. Also called *drop date.* See also *half-life formula; response time (direct mail).*

mailing date, assigned   See *assigned mailing date.*

mailing frequency   1. The number of times a year that a particular mailing is made. 2. The number of times a year a particular audience is mailed to.

mailing frequency to same list   See *list-use frequency, law for.*

mailing house/mailshop   See *lettershop/mailshop.*

mailing life cycle   See *campaign length (direct mail).*

mailing list   A collection of names derived from a common source. Some mailers refer to each list used in a mailing as a "market."

mailing list, academic   See *academic mailing lists, U.S.*

mailing list, academic (compiled)   See *compiled list (academic).*

mailing list, association and society   See *association list (direct mail).*

mailing list, bookbuyer   See *bookbuyer lists; CMG Data Base.*

mailing list, compiled   See *compiled list.*

mailing list, database   See *database mailing list.*

mailing list, directory compiled   See *directory list.*

mailing list, external   See *external mailing list*.

mailing list, horizontal   See *horizontal mailing list*.

mailing list, marginal   See *marginal list (direct mail)*.

mailing list, response   See *response list*.

mailing list, telemarketing   See *telemarketing mailing list*.

mailing list, vertical   See *vertical mailing list*.

mailing list affinity   See *list affinity (direct mail)*.

mailing list arrangement/sequence   The order in which names are kept on a mailing list. It may be ZIP code sequence, alphabetically by state, alphabetically by individual name, alphabetically by company, etc. Most rental lists are supplied in ZIP code sequence.

mailing list broker   See *list broker*.

mailing list cards/list data cards   Cards provided by list owners, managers, or brokers that provide a detailed description of that list and other rental information such as price, format, minimum quantity, test arrangement, etc. They are usually provided free.

mailing list cleaning   The practice of keeping a mailing list up to date by eliminating nondeliverables, correcting address changes and misspellings, and keeping the list accurate. See also *directory list recompilation*.

mailing list compiler   A person who develops or compiles lists of names and addresses from available sources such as directories, newspapers, trade show registrants, or other sources. Names on completed lists have one or more common characteristics.

mailing list count   See *list count (direct mail)*.

mailing list deliverability   The percentage of a particular mailing list that gets delivered in a third-class bulk mailing. The older the list (or the longer the period since it was last updated), the lower is the deliverability. Lists, as a rule of thumb, lose deliverability at the rate of about 20% a year from the date of compilation. See also *deterioration index*.

mailing list deterioration   The tendency of mailing lists to go out of date or cease to be deliverable with the passage of time. See also *deterioration index*.

mailing list duplicate copies   A duplicate copy of a rental mailing list. Many list owners will supply a second (usually computer-generated) copy of a rental list when requested on the list rental order. The most frequently cited charge is 50% of the list rental charge.

mailing list exchanges, bookbuyers   The practice of some publishing marketers to exchange names of bookbuyers on their house list for a like number of bookbuyer names from a competitor. Usually, no payment is involved unless the exchange is arranged by a list broker, in which case they split the broker's commission (usually 25%). See also *list exchange (direct mail); mailing list exchanges, subscriber*.

mailing list exchanges, subscriber   The practice of periodical publishers exchanging subscriber names for those of a competitor on a barter basis with no payment involved to either. See also *list exchange (direct mail); mailing list exchanges, bookbuyers*.

mailing list formats   The various ways in which mailing lists may be reproduced or supplied to list renters. When not otherwise specified, most rental lists will be supplied in 4-across east-west cheshire label format. Other formats include the use of pressure-sensitive labels, magnetic tape, printed sheets or 3″ × 5″ cards, or floppy disks. See also *cheshire label format (mailing list); label types*.

mailing list maintenance   An ongoing program for making changes in existing names and addresses on a list as they occur, converting information from typed or written sources into additions to the mailing list, correcting ZIP codes, deleting names that have ceased to be useful, etc. See also *merge-purge (mailing list)*.

mailing list manager   See *list manager*.

mailing list minimum order requirement   A requirement by a mailing list owner that payment be made for a minimum quantity or amount for a list rental. On large lists the minimum quantity may be 3,000 to 5,000 names, or, for a magnetic tape rental, 10,000 names or more. On a very small list, the minimum charge may apply to the entire list.

mailing list order dates   Different list suppliers require varying amounts of time for list rental fulfillment. All list rental orders should be sent sufficiently early so that all will be on hand well in advance of the mailing house's assembly date. See also *direct mail promotion assembly date.*

mailing list protection   See *decoy.*

mailing list rental   A list released by an owner or owner's agent for a fee with permission for the renter to use it one time only for a mailing on or about a mailing date either assigned by the list owner or mutually agreed upon. See also *assigned mailing date; list broker; list manager; one-time use; sample mailing piece requirement.*

mailing lists, college   See *college faculty lists; graduate-level faculty lists.*

mailing lists, daily and weekly newspaper   See *Bacon's Computerized Media Bank (publicity).*

mailing lists, journal promotion   See *journal promotion mailing lists.*

mailing lists, magazine   See *Bacon's Computerized Media Bank (publicity).*

mailing lists, news services and syndicates   See *Bacon's Computerized Media Bank (publicity).*

mailing lists, publicity media   See *Bacon's Computerized Media Bank (publicity).*

mailing lists, radio and television station   See *Bacon's Computerized Media Bank (publicity).*

mailing lists, rules-of-thumb for   See *competitor mailing list, rules-of-thumb for; customer mailing list, rule-of-thumb for; multiple book buyer lists, rules-of-thumb for;*

mailing lists, scholarly, association and society   The prime list-broker source of such lists is Thor Information Services Inc., P.O. Box 158, Great Neck, NY 11022. Phone: 516-829-5151.

mailing lists, U.K. and European academic   See *IBIS Information Services* and various entries under *lists*.

mailing list science   An understanding of the general body of knowledge covering practices and procedures involving mailing lists—acquisition, testing, use, maintenance and evaluation. For broad coverage of this area, see *Encyclopedia of Mailing List Terminology and Techniques* by Nat Bodian, published by Bret Scot Press, 50 Cross Street, Winchester, MA 01890. Phone: 617-719-7865.

mailing list segmentation   See *list segmentation*.

mailing list sequence   See *mailing list arrangement/sequence*.

mailing list source code   See *source code, mailing list*.

mailing list sources, school library   See *list sources, school library*.

mailing list split test.   See *split test (direct mail)*.

mailing list test   A test mailing in which different lists are used and the responses from each compared. This is in contrast with list testing, which involves testing a small sample of a single list. See also *list testing; test campaign (direct mail)*.

mailing list testing, alphabetical   See *list testing, alphabetical*.

mailing list test sample   A number of names taken from a larger list and used in a test mailing to gain an indication of the list's responsiveness. See also *direct mail testing; list testing; list test size rules; market testing; pyramiding*.

mailing list universe   See *list universe (direct mail)*.

mailing list usage agreement   The terms under which a mailing list owner permits use of the list in a rental. Virtually all such agreements stipulate that list rentals are for one-time use only and by the renter or renter's recognized lettershop.

mailing list variables   Identifiable and measurable characteristics of a list that can be applied in selecting names or tracked in a mailing's results.

mailing objective   The intended purpose of a mail promotion. The objective of most mailings is to generate orders or inquiries. They may also serve to inform, to help build store traffic or convention display traffic, or to generate leads for the field sales staff. A mail promotion also serves as a preliminary to "soften the market" for a telemarketing campaign.

mailing package   See *direct-mail package; mailing package eye flow studies.*

mailing package enclosure eye flow   The common pattern of eye flow by the reader of an enclosure in a mailing package is from (1) illustrations, the eyes jumping from one to another, to (2) large and midsize headlines, to (3) inside spread, with eye path starting at upper left and moving to upper right (Source: Clark O'Neill, *Indicia,* January 1987).

mailing package enclosure instructions   Instructions to a mailing house or lettershop with a scheduled mailing indicating not only package components, but also—if portions are being supplied from outside sources—quantity, name of supplier or printer, telephone number, contact name and telephone number, and date of delivery.

mailing package eye flow studies   See *envelope eye flow; letter enclosure readership study; letter eye flow, personalized; mailing package enclosure eye flow; response device effectiveness.*

mailing receipt, USPS   See *proof of mailing.*

mailing title   The title assigned to a mailing so that it can be identified both internally and on list and mailing house orders. Every mailing should have a title that will be universally applicable to all communications relative to it.

mail-inquirer list   See *inquiry list.*

mail monitoring   1. Procedures available to list owners to ensure compliance with terms of their list rental agreement. For example: Is the mailing piece essentially the same as the sample submitted with the list rental order? Was the mailing made on or about the authorized mailing date? Was the list used by the original renter? 2. A check by a volume mailer to establish mail delivery time, condition of mailing package contents, and other factors.

mail monitor service   A professional outside service used by mailers to verify mailing content, original mailing date, and delivery time. Also used by list owners and compilers as a control against unauthorized usage of their mailing lists.

mail offer   See *offer (direct mail)*.

mail order (direct mail)   1. A mailing designed strictly to sell by mail a product (or service) on a profitable basis. Cost-per-order is evaluated in terms of cost-per-thousand to mail, and number of orders received per thousand pieces mailed. 2. A book order received by mail, phone, or other medium and shipped to the customer through the mail or another carrier such as UPS.

mail-order advertising   A method of sales promotion in which the entire sales transaction is done through the mail.

mail-order book   Books designed to be sold primarily through large mail-order campaigns.

mail-order bookseller   A bookseller whose primary selling activity is through the mails. Because most use catalogs, they are also referred to as catalog houses. See also *catalog house*.

mail-order buyer (MOB)   An individual known to have made a mail-order purchase, and, therefore, more likely to respond to a mail offer. See also *bookbuyer lists*.

mail-order catalog house   See *mail-order house*.

mail-order catalogs, publisher   Publisher catalogs listing forthcoming titles and bestselling backlist titles in specific subject areas and designed to elicit mail orders from those to whom mailed.

mail-order drop   A direct-mail effort designed to generate mail orders.

mail-order FTC (Federal Trade Commission) delivery rule   See *30 Day Delayed Delivery Rule (mail order)*.

mail-order house   One whose business is devoted to the sale of products by mail. Many mail-order houses include professional and reference books in their catalog offerings.

mail-order publication   A book, series, or set that is designed and produced primarily for sale by mail.

mail-order publisher A publisher who produces books specifically designed for sale by mail. Examples: Reader's Digest Books; Time-Life Books; Dover Publications.

Mail Preference Service (MPS) A centralized delisting program operated by the Direct Marketing Association for individuals who do not want to receive unsolicited mail. The information is circulated to 1,200 DMA members.

mail-responsive list A list of people who have previously responded to a mailing offer. See also *mail-order buyer (MOB)*.

mail-responsive month, best For consumer mailings, most book promotions do best in January and next best in September.

mailshop See *lettershop/mailshop*.

mail shot (U.K.) A single mailing. See also *mailing*.

mail size surcharge, USPS Mailing piece,s over 6⅛″ high, over 11½″ long, or over ¼″ thick are subject to a special surcharge. This rule applicable only to first-class pieces of 1 ounce or less, or single piece, third-class mail under 1 ounce.

mail universe/mailable universe All of the *available* lists considered to be appropriate for an anticipated mail promotion. See also *market*.

main selection (book club) The primary or first-choice offering of a book club during one of its cyclical offering periods to book club members. See also *alternate selection (book club)*.

major trade book markets New York, Los Angeles, Chicago, San Francisco, Boston, Houston, Detroit, Philadelphia, Dallas, Minneapolis, Denver, District of Columbia, Seattle, Atlanta, and Miami.

makeready (printing) 1. Setting up a press prior to printing a job. 2. Adjusting printing plates to ensure a uniform printing impression. See also *press proofs*.

making the numbers Meeting a projected target over a publishing season or year, either in terms of number of titles published, in terms of unit sales, or in terms of dollar volume.

making the rounds   Sales calls by a publisher representative on his or her established bookseller accounts.

making the sales   Meeting a projected sales goal for a given period, usually the publishing season or year.

managed book   A book in which the publisher selects the topic and manages all aspects of its creation. Usually, the scope of the work is outlined, and then staff or outside professional writers develop the text around the outline. The book may have a designated author or editor, or be authorless, depending on subject or discipline.

management mailings, rule for   See *direct mail to top management, rule for*.

manager, list   See *list manager*.

manila envelope   A light brown envelope made of manila paper, a strong, durable paper useful for mailing large items.

A Manual of Style   See *The Chicago Manual of Style, 13th Ed.*

manufacturing costs   The costs of paper, printing, binding, and delivery to publisher's warehouse. See also *unit cost*.

MARC   Machine Readable Cataloging, a Library of Congress program providing machine-readable cataloging in the LC form.

marginal book   1. A book that is not directly compatible with a publisher's list, or outside the subject area normally covered by the publisher. Marginal books that are outside the normal range of a publisher's promotional effort require excessive time and expenditure, and extraordinary promotional efforts. They often are unprofitable. 2. A book with minimum sales expectations.

marginal book, strategies for   A marginal book that is not selling can be disposed of in a number of ways short of remaindering. One is to repackage it. Another is to sell it to another publisher with a compatible list. A third is to offer it to a specialized book club that has an audience for it. Still another is a white sale (pre-remaindering).

marginal list (direct mail)   1. A mailing list not to a primary market or audience. 2. A list that in a prior test or mailing did not prove to be cost effective.

market   1. The logical audience for a published work. 2. Those who are likely to benefit from a published work and either are likely to purchase it, or influence its purchase by others.

market (direct mail)   1. When multiple lists are available for a mail promotion, each list is sometimes considered a market. 2. Some mailers consider all of the lists available for a planned mailing as *the* market.

market, author   Authors represent a potential market for other books of a publisher in the same area. Publishers cognizant of this frequently offer authors liberal discounts not only on the author's own book, but also on other books on the same list.

market, primary   1. The main market or audience for a book. 2. The audience for which a book or journal will have greatest appeal, or for which it is deemed to have greatest appeal. Sometimes, after promotion, a market considered to be the primary market does not do as well as other markets considered to be of lesser importance. 3. The audience in mind when writing or publishing the book or journal. See also *target audience*.

marketability   The perceived saleability of a book.

market clustering   Publishing in closely related areas or disciplines. This enables a number of different titles to share promotional costs, making for greater marketing strength and editorial visibility.

Market Data Retrieval   See *library lists, Market Data Retrieval.*

marketing (publishing)   All activities related to directing the sale and movement of books and publications from publisher to user, either directly (as in mail order) or through agents such as booksellers, jobbers, professors, cooperative sale accounts, etc.

marketing plan   1. A written plan for the promotional launch of a new publishing project. It usually outlines a budget, time frame, and measurable objectives, and lists all media and the basis on which they will be used. 2. A written plan by marketing management for moving published products to their likely or logical markets. Plan may be an overall one for the line for a season or fiscal year, or for a group of related books, or on a book-by-book basis. 3. A written plan of all activities involved in achieving a particular marketing objective.

marketing plan (journal)   A written plan for the launch of a new journal, usually covering a prolonged period of three or five years. It shows budgeted expenditures for each of the years in the plan and includes such items as universe, price, promotional vehicles and their cost, payment rate (percentage of subscribers who actually pay), renewal rate after each subscription year, and, often, lifetime value of each subscription.

marketing plan (newsletter)   See *marketing plan (journal)*.

marketing plan, annual   A written game plan for the coming calendar or fiscal year, often serving as the basis on which promotional funds are allocated. It should be elastic and capable of modification as circumstances warrant.

marketing plan, annual, key elements   (1) Position in the marketplace; (2) marketing goals and objectives in order of priority; (3) courses of action to be taken vis-a-vis product mix, pricing, promotion, and distribution; (4) implementation timetable; (5) responsibility assignment; (6) plans for subsequent evaluation.

marketing plan, strategic   A formal long-range plan that includes long-term objectives and strategies and provides a blueprint for specific directions, taking into account competitive threats and opportunities, organizational strengths and weaknesses, and how environmental conditions are likely to provide positive or negative reinforcement. Acquisitions and divestments are sometimes factored into such plans.

marketing plan activities   Depending on the publishing project for which the plan is developed, it may, depending on budget, include such activities as (1) publicity; (2) advertising; (3) direct-mail promotion; (4) exhibit and convention display; (5) point-of-sale materials for retail places of sale; (6) field sales efforts; (7) export sales efforts.

marketing questionnaire   See *author questionnaire/marketing questionnaire*.

marketing research   1. Investigation of a segment of a particular market geared to a particular objective. Research may test either a product or a market. Most marketing research is done by mail. 2. "Asking the right questions to the right group."—Carol

Stuckhardt, at a seminar of the Professional Publishers Marketing Group in New York, May 14, 1986.

marketing research, qualitative See *qualitative marketing research.*

marketing research proposal A set of guidelines for how a marketing research investigation will be conducted. It usually incorporates information on background, purpose, methods to be used, budget, and time frame for completion.

Marketing to Libraries A directory of useful marketing information about North American libraries based on a study of more than 90 library associations conducted by Sandy Whiteley, editor, and the staff of the (ALA) *Reference Books Bulletin*. Provides details on all library groups, with information on rental of their member lists, advertising in their publications, and exhibiting at their conferences. Published 1987, available for $24.95 from ALA Publishing Services, 50 E. Huron Street, Chicago, IL 06611.

market niche Sales potential within a given market for a product or group of products.

market penetration (of a book or journal) The number of books or subscriptions sold in a particular market when compared with the perceived size of the total market. See *market share.*

marketplace/market place The existing customer universe. Sometimes also used to signify the business world in general.

market position The status of a publisher in a particular market relative to that of other publishers selling to the same market.

markets, major trade book See *major trade book markets.*

markets, traditional See *traditional markets (book).*

market segmentation Subdivision of a market by geographic, demographic, psychographic, usage, or other characteristics. See also *list segmentation.*

market share 1. A portion of a definable and often measurable market. 2. The relationship of the sales volume for a product or group of products within a given market to the total volume for that market, either actual or potential. See also *market penetration (of a book or journal).*

market test Test of a product among different groups or in different markets to determine which offers the best sales potential. See also *product test*.

market testing Tests of small segments of new, different, or untried markets in fields related to a book to ascertain whether the tested market has potential for the book(s) in the mailing offer. See also *direct mail testing; list testing*.

markup The difference between the established net price and the retail or selling price. Booksellers who buy books through net pricing usually mark up a book to reflect what they would have paid net had they purchased the book at a desirable discount off list price. See also *net pricing markup formulas (bookselling)*.

mass market house See *mass market publishing*.

mass market paperback See *rack-size paperback; trade paperback*.

mass marketplace (book) 1. The market for paperback books. 2. Generally that aspect of publishing in which publications are sold through drugstores, supermarkets, airports, bus depots, and railroad stations, as contrasted with bookstores. 3. That part of the book market handled by IDs or independent distributors.

mass market publishing Companies engaged in the publication of mass market paperbacks, both original works and reprints of hardcover works. (There are less than 25.) The license to reprint an original hardcover work is purchased from the hardcover publisher and covers a period of five to ten years. See also *mass market paperback*.

master data card See *mailing list cards/list data cards*.

match An addition to an already printed letter—either date, salutation, address, or other text—aimed at giving the printed letter a personalized look. See also *match letter*.

matchcode A coded distillation of the elements of a name and address, which enables a computer to match identical addresses on different lists and cast out duplicates in a merge-purge operation. See also *merge-purge (mailing list)*.

match letter See *fill-in letter*.

match rate analysis A technique for testing the perceived quality of a mailing list. It is based on the concept that a high rate of duplication between lists is an indication for a high degree of affinity.

matte finish Papers with little or no gloss that are suitable for all types of lithographic reproduction.

mature market/mature product Market in which sales are fairly stable and in which there is little opportunity for major future growth.

mature product See *mature market/mature product.*

maximum address size, cheshire label See *cheshire label maximum address size.*

McNaughton Plan A rental plan through which public libraries rent high-demand books fully cataloged and processed for immediate circulation. Offered by Brodart Company, 500 Arch Street, Williamsport, PA 17705.

McPublishing A descriptive term for desktop publishing coined by Peter Hodges, publishing consultant, in conjunction with November 18, 1987 seminar of Professional Publishers Marketing Group, held at McGraw-Hill Building, New York. See also *desktop publishing; desktop publishing, professional.*

MDMO Medical Direct Mail Organization, Ltd. The leading mailing and list source in the United Kingdom for medical and healthcare lists. Address: South Down House, Station Road, Petersfield, Hampshire GU32 3ET, England.

MDMS A system developed by Pergamon in England that can create promotion pieces and catalogs from information stored in a single database.

mechanical/mechanical paste-up Camera-ready copy for any printed piece that shows the precise placement of each element and that is comprised of actual or simulated type and artwork. See also *board artist/mechanical artist; camera-ready copy.*

mechanical, colors used on See *colors in mechanical preparation.*

mechanical binding   Pages held together by a mechanical device. They require the punching of holes in the paper so that metal or plastic wire, strips or rings may be threaded through them. Several common types are spiral wire binding, plastic comb binding, and loose-leaf binding. Mechanical binding permits a bound work to open flat. See also *comb binding; loose-leaf binding; spiral-bound edition.*

mechanical requirements   The specifications to which print advertising material must conform in order to meet a periodical's layout and makeup requirements.

media (for book promotion)   The various advertising channels for reaching potential markets: periodicals, newspapers, direct mail, telephone, radio, TV, etc.

Media Guide   An annual publication of Steven K. Herlitz, Inc., providing detailed information on more than 300 publications in the medical and allied health fields that accept advertising. Address: Steven K. Herlitz, 404 Park Avenue South, New York, NY 10016.

media kit   A portfolio of information sent to potential advertisers, containing advertising rate card, sample issues, and demographic information. See also *advertising rate card.*

media plan   1. A plan listing advertising vehicles to use for the launch of a single book or journal or group of books. 2. The space advertising plan for a specific book that will enable advertising to reach its primary markets. 3. A plan of mailing lists to use for a direct-mail campaign.

media relations (publisher publicity)   See *publicity department media relations.*

media rep   A sales representative of an advertising medium. Sometimes called space rep or space salesman (salesperson).

Medical and Health Care Books and Serials in Print   A two-volume annual listing approximately 65,000 books by subject, author, and title under more than 5,000 Library of Congress subject categories. Includes over 11,000 periodicals and journals by subject and title. From R.R. Bowker, 245 W. 17th Street, New York, NY 10010.

medical and nursing school faculty lists See *college faculty lists.*

medical book 1. A book designed for someone in medical practice or research. 2. A book applicable to the care of people who are sick, and of interest to physicians and other medical practitioners, including nursing and the allied health care professions, students, and others concerned with health care.

medical bookbuyer lists Individuals who have bought medical books by mail. A major U.S. source of medical bookbuyer lists is CMG Information Services. See also *CMG Information Services, Inc.*

medical book distributor The medical book distributor operates differently from the trade book wholesaler or library jobber. Medical book distributors aim to serve as a single source for all medical book needs within their market. They maintain a balanced stock of books for immediate shipment; supply books to booksellers as well as to libraries; act as a direct seller to medical practitioners and supply the textbook needs of medical schools, nursing schools, and hospitals. They may also serve as a subscription agency for journals in the health sciences. They establish exclusive distribution arrangements with major medical publishers, negotiating favorable discounts in exchange for specific inventory maintenance arrangements.

medical book exhibits, cooperative Exhibits or book and journal displays at meetings of medical and health care professionals where the output of many different publishers is displayed by a single exhibitor. Participants pay so much per book. Inquiry leads are forwarded to respective publishers. The leading sponsor of cooperative book exhibits at medical meetings is Conference Book Service, 80 South Early Street, Alexandria, VA 22314. Phones: 703-823-6966; 800-366-4776.

medical book market The medical market is divided into about 20 or more specialties. Within each specialty, there are four publishing levels: (1) reference texts; (2) clinical books; (3) student textbooks; (4) books for the nursing and paramedical professions.

medical book salespeople, commission See *commission salespeople, medical.*

medical card decks See *Publishers Row card deck program.*

227

medical clinical book See *clinical book.*

medical jobber See *medical book distributor.*

medical libraries, international Over 9,500 medical libraries worldwide, outside the U.S., are available by category: university; research; corporate; government; subject; and country. From: IBIS Information Services, 152 Madison Avenue, Suite 803, New York, NY 10016-5424.

Medical Library Association (MLA) A 5,000-member national association of librarians and others engaged in professional library or bibliographical work in medical and allied scientific libraries. Founded in 1898, with annual meeting and convention held in May or June. A prime exhibit opportunity for publishers seeking exposure to the medical library market. Address: 919 N. Michigan Avenue, Ste. 3208, Chicago, IL 60611.

medical library market Approximately 2,100 libraries located in medical schools, schools of nursing, veterinary schools, Veterans administration hospitals, other hospitals, pharmaceutical companies, university libraries, and public libraries.

medical mailing lists, U.K. See separate entries under *international medical lists; MDMO; medical libraries, international.*

medical mailing lists, U.S. The medical and health care industry is one of the most highly segmented of all industry or professional groups. Lists are available for virtually any segment or level of the profession or industry. For doctor lists, the American Medical Association has the AMA Masterfile, available through a number of authorized agents. Various publishers of medical periodicals also make their lists available with a variety of list-selection options. CMG Information Services has the names of over 100,000 buyers of medical books by subject. See also *AMA Masterfile; CMG Information Services, Inc.*

medical media, guide to See *Media Guide.*

medical publisher Publisher involved in publication of books, periodicals, and/or educational or informational materials for the medical community and its suppliers. See also *medical book; medical book distributor; medical book market.*

medical reference texts High-level works in narrow areas of medicine, usually produced for a limited international market and sold at high prices.

meeting and conference exhibits See *convention exhibits.*

megabook A book by a celebrity or big name author expected to have wide sales appeal; such books often sell a million or more copies, and authors may receive advances of as much as a million or more dollars. The large advance payment is based on the publisher's expectation the book will become a lead title on a seasonal list.

member-get-member (book club) A promotion to existing members offering a gift or premium for enrolling a new member. This technique is used by some book clubs which ask a member to sign up a new member, for which both member and new member receive a premium. The offer travels with a regular member mailing and is therefore an economical form of book club new member solicitation.

member price (book club) The price paid for a book by a member of a book club. Typically, book club prices are about 20% less than publisher list prices, although in some instances the discount may be much larger.

membership discount 1. A discount afforded by some publishers to members affiliated with an association or society. There may be special requirements. For example, one society group gives its members four discount coupons with membership renewal; these are honored by numerous publishers, provided prepayment in precise net amount is furnished with order and coupon. 2. A discount offered to members of an association or society by the publishing arm of that association or society.

member subscription price (journal) 1. The subscription price charged by an association or society for a subscription to one of its publications by a member. 2. A special subscription price afforded to members of a compatible association or society by a journal publisher.

menu-driven computer program A computer program that progresses or proceeds on the basis of choices presented on the monitor. The choices are made by a yes/no alphanumeric entry or by a selection of options.

merge-purge (mailing list)   To combine two or more mailing lists into a single list with duplicate names eliminated. Mailers using rented lists from various sources can eliminate duplications between lists by having them merge-purged by a computer service bureau. As a rule, the list must be of sufficient quantity to merit being placed on a magnetic tape essential for a merge-purge. The resulting list from a merge-purge is usually furnished in one continuous ZIP code sequence. As a rule, a list must be 10,000 or more names to go on a tape, so a merge-purge requires a combination of lists, all of which consist of over 10,000 names. See also ZIP string.

merge-purge package (mailing list)   A package that not only merges two or more mailing lists into a single list with duplications omitted, but also identifies names of individuals appearing on more than one list. Duplicate names are called multihit names, or multibuyers, if the lists are names of mail order buyers. See also multibuyer (mailing lists).

metered mail, first-class vs. third-class   See metered mail effectiveness.

metered mail, postal requirements   See metering.

metered mail effectiveness   For most mailings to rented lists, metered third-class mail is more effective than mail with printed indicia and, as a rule, will produce about the same response as metered first-class postage. Metered first-class mail, however, will have a higher rate of deliverability. See also metering; postage meter usage.

metering   Applying postage to mail by means of a postage meter. See also postage meter usage.

metric system   See International System of Units (SI).

Mezhdunzrodnya Kniga (also known as V/O Mezhdunarodnaya Kniga)   1. The USSR governmental association for international book and journal trade. 2. The USSR agency that sells and distributes to foreign markets all books and journals produced in the USSR. 3. The USSR agency that acts as importer for all foreign journals brought into the USSR. Address: 39 Dimitrova Ul., 113095, Moscow, USSR.

microcomputer A small computer, usually a portable or desktop unit with a keyboard and a display device.

microfiche A plastic sheet of photographic film, usually 4″ × 6″ in size, on which as many as 200 or more pages or frames can be stored, greatly reduced in size. They can be seen enlarged on a projection machine or reader. See also *microform.*

microfiche price lists A publisher's price list supplied to booksellers on microfiche. John Wiley & Sons Ltd. initiated this practice in the U.K. and supplies free fiche readers to booksellers.

microfilm A microform on which images are stored on a film roll, greatly reduced in size. See also *microform.*

microform 1. A general term embracing microfilm, microfiche, and micro-opaque processes. 2. Graphic materials photographically reduced to extremely small size. A number of scientific and scholarly journals are offered in this format and as a substitute for back issues in hard copy format.

micropublishing The publishing of information in microform.

midlist title 1. A trade title of a general nature, or one viewed by its publisher as having limited sales potential. 2. Neither frontlist nor backlist.

mini catalog A miniature catalog of 8 to 16 pages and measuring approximately 3¾ ″ × 5¾ ″. Used by some publishers as envelope stuffers or as inserts with card deck mailings. Available from Web Specialties, Inc., Milwaukee, WI.

minimum order (bookseller) A special minimum size order set by a publisher to achieve a certain benefit such as a special discount, free freight, etc. See also *special deal.*

minimum order (mailing list) See *mailing list minimum order requirement.*

minimum purchase requirement (bulk sale of books) In order to qualify for a particular discount, publishers may require that a minimum number of assorted books or copies of a single title be ordered at the same time.

mining the backlist A growing practice by publishers of searching out once-popular titles in the backlist and reissuing them in more attractive formats, more often than not in low price paperback. See also *repackaged edition*.

mini sales conference A meeting held by a trade sales manager and the sales reps after a seasonal sales conference. The purpose of the meeting is to determine account reaction to a new title list and to make adjustments as appropriate. See also *sales conference*.

mint (antiquarian bookselling) A copy of a book that looks brand new. See also *antiquarian bookselling terms*.

missionary book The first book on a particular subject.

MK Abbreviation or shortened name for Mezhdunzrodnya Kniga, the USSR governmental association responsible for the export and import of books and journals. See full entry under *Mezhdunzrodnya Kniga*.

MLA (abbreviations) Maine Library Association; Manitoba Library Association; Maryland Library Association; Medical Library Association; Michigan Library Association; Minnesota Library Association; Mississippi Library Association; Missouri Library Association; Modern Language Association; Montana Library Association; Music Library Association. See also *Medical Library Association*; *MLA Directory of Periodicals*.

MLA Directory of Periodicals: A Guide to Journals in Languages and Literatures A directory of over 3,000 journals and series indexed in *Modern Language Association International Biography*. Covers journals concerned with language, literature, folklore, and linguistics. Provides detailed information, including whether book reviews are included. Published in even-numbered years by Modern Language Association of America, 10 Astor Place, New York, NY 10003.

MMD Manager of Merchandise Distribution, also called merchant. The title of a particular type of bookbuyer in the B. Dalton book chain. See also *buyer/distributor system (bookstore chain)*.

MOB A mail-order buyer.

mobility of college faculty   The annual rate at which college faculty members change their mailing addresses. The U.S. percentage was calculated at 21% in a 1979 study by CMG. The U.K. estimate is 20%.

mobility of professionals   The annual rate at which professionals change their mailing address, estimated to be approximately 20%-30%.

model a title   The practice by book chain buyers and large bookstores of selecting a book either because of its substantial advance or because of its prior sales record and entering it into a computerized reordering system. The reordering system ensures that a certain stock level will be maintained at all times. When the stock falls below this level, a reorder is automatically generated.

modeled book   A book entered in a bookstore's inventory system at a specific level. Automatic reorders are called for when the level is reached. The reorders ensure continuing sales. See also *model a title.*

Modern Language Association   See *MLA Directory of Periodicals: A Guide to Journals in Languages and Literatures.*

mom and pop store   A small, family-operated retail establishment. See also *bookstore; independent/independent bookstore/independent bookseller.*

monetary value   Total expenditure by a customer or subscriber over a specified period or for the active life account or subscription.

monitoring service   See *mail monitor service.*

monograph   1. A short treatment of a single subject, theoretical or applied, written by a specialist for fellow specialists. 2. Any single or multiauthored manuscript or collection of manuscripts published as a single unit.

monograph, research   See *research monograph.*

monograph, social science   See *social science research monograph.*

montage   A grouping of photographs or parts of photographs, joined one to the other, usually without separation lines and presented so as to form a single impression.

"more" line (news releases) On any news release more than a page in length, the word "—more—" must be inserted at the bottom of all but the last page. If the "more" line is omitted and the succeeding pages become separated, it will not be possible for the recipient to know if the complete release is at hand. See also *end marks (news/press releases)*; *news release*.

mortise (printing) A hole or open space cut out of a printing plate so that type matter or an illustration plate can be inserted. Virtually obsolete as most printing is now done by offset.

motor freight convention shipments See *common carrier convention shipments*.

MRCs See *machine readable codes*.

multibuyer (mailing list) A name found on two or more mail-order buyer lists. Multibuyer lists are considered to have greater potential than buyer lists. See also *merge-purge package (mailing list)*; *multiple book buyer lists, rule-of-thumb for*.

multihit names (mailing list) Names appearing on several different mailing lists during a merge-purge program. See also *merge-purge package (mailing list)*; *multibuyer (mailing list)*.

multilingual dictionary A dictionary, often on a special subject, that provides for words in one language equivalents in two or more languages. Definitions may or may not be included. See also *multilingual edition*.

multilingual edition A book in which some or all of the text is in three or more languages. See also *multilingual dictionary*.

multipart volume A single work published in parts, the various parts of which comprise a volume. This is sometimes done with a reference work considered too large to be inserted in a single binding (or too high-priced to be offered as a single book).

multiple book buyer lists, rule-of-thumb for A mailing list of multiple book buyers will usually produce a higher response than one of the same size containing names of buyers of only one book.

multiple buyer One who has placed an order two or more times. See also *multiple book buyers lists, rule of thumb for*.

multiple-product direct-mail promotions   A direct-mail promotion in which a number of different products are offered, such as in a card deck, catalog, or cooperative mailing. See also *card deck; cooperative card deck/co-op deck/co-op pack; cooperative mailing/co-op mailing; solo mailing.*

multivolume work   A single work published in more than one volume. Such publication may be offered simultaneously, or a volume at a time over a protracted period. See also *multipart volume.*

multivolume work, sales erosion rule   When books are published in multivolume sets with separate volumes at spaced intervals, sales will generally decline from one volume to the next. The greater the time gap between published volumes, the greater is the sales decline.

Murphy's Law   "If anything can go wrong, it will."

museum publishing   A publishing program conducted by a museum, usually associated with education or art. Major museum publishers are the Metropolitan Museum of Art and the Museum of Modern Art (MOMA).

M weight (of paper)   The weight of 1,000 sheets of any given size of paper.

N

NACS See *National Association of College Stores.*

name-get-a-name See *referral names.*

NAPRA New Age Publishers and Retailers Alliance. A group formed in 1987 to aid marketing efforts and publisher/retailer relations for new age books. See also *new age books.*

National Association of College Stores (NACS) A trade association of retail stores that sell books and supplies to students and faculties of educational institutions. Members also include publishers and suppliers to the college store market. NACS sponsors an annual Trade Fair, always in April, that is the college store industry's only trade show. Publishes *The College Store Journal,* a bimonthly, and *NACS Weekly Bulletin.* Founded in 1923 under the name College Bookstore Association. Address: 528 East Loraine Street, Oberlin, OH 44074. Phone: 216-775-7777.

National Association of College Stores Trade Fair See *Campus Market Expo (CAMEX).*

national book wholesalers, main Back-to-Basics Books, Hendersonville, NC; The Baker & Taylor Co., Bridgewater, NJ, and other locations nationwide; Blackwell North America, Beaverton, OR, and Blackwood, NJ; Bookpeople, Berkeley, CA; Bookslinger, St. Paul, MN; Brodart Inc., Williamsport, PA; China Books and Periodicals, San Francisco, CA; Golden-Lee Book Distributors, Brooklyn, NY; Ingram Book Co., Nashville, TN; International Scholarly Book Services, Inc., Beaverton, OR; J.A. Majors Co., Irving, TX; Matthews Book Co., Maryland Heights, MO; Midwest Library Service, Bridgeton, MO; Norman Book Distributing Co.,

Lansing, MI; Nutri-Books Corp, Denver, CO; Small Press Distribution, Berkeley, CA; Suits News Co., Lansing, MI.

National Business Telephone Directory A national directory by Gale Research of over 350,000 businesses, professional associations, trade associations, services, and publishers in a single alphabetical sequence.

National Directory of Newsletters and Reporting Services See *Newsletters Directory*.

National Information Standards Organization (NISO) A standards developing organization that develops and reviews standards relating to the communication needs of libraries, information services, the publishing industry, and the book trade. Originally created as Committee Z39 of the American National Standards Institute (ANSI), it was responsible for the development of the International Standard Book Number (ISBN) and the International Standard Serial Number (ISSN). Address: National Bureau of Standards, Administration 101, Library E-106, Gaithersburg, MD 20899. Phone: 302-921-3241. See also *American National Standards Institute (ANSI)*.

National Periodicals Center See *National Periodicals System*.

National Periodicals System A concept calling for a program or center, funded by the Federal Government that would maintain a comprehensive collection of periodical titles and provide on-demand document delivery service by loan, photocopy, or microform to participating libraries.

National Trade & Professional Associations of the United States An annual paperback directory covering 6,000 organizations with details of each organization. Extremely useful and an alternative to *Encyclopedia of Associations*, though less detailed—but at about one fourth the cost. Published by Columbia Books Inc., Washington, DC 20005.

NATURE A weekly publication in England of news of the world scientific community and scientific book reviews. Considered by many scientists the world's foremost scientific journal. Published by Macmillan Journals Ltd., 4 Little Essex Street, London WC2R 3LF, England. Phone: (01) 836-6633. Published weekly on Thursday. Copy for advertising in the international edition due 14 days preceding publication date. U.S. subscribers receive the U.S. demographic edition, with advertising appearing only in that edition. U.S. office: 65 Bleecker Street, New York, NY 10012. Phone: 212-477-9600. See also *scientific book review media, major*.

NBA See *Net Book Agreement*.

NCR No Canadian Rights. On selling U.S. publishers rights to their books, many U.K. publishers retain Canada as part of their market and include an "NCR clause" in their contracts, meaning no Canadian rights.

need (copywriting) Building into advertising copy the promise that the offering will fill an essential requirement that the reader has, or may have in the future. A handbook on a particular aspect of engineering may offer to meet a future need and this may provide sufficient buying motivation. See also *want*.

"need to know" (book pricing and promotion) A book containing information or material that is central to the prospect's needs— information they must have. A publication that offers "need to know" information can be priced higher without encountering price sensitivity and get exceptional results from promotion. See also *"nice to know" (book pricing and promotion)*.

negative A reverse photographic image in which black becomes white and white becomes black.

negative check-off option An option given to customers or periodical subscribers by list renters to check off on their order or subscription renewal form if they object to having their names rented out.

negative option The successful mail-order technique used by most book clubs whereby a book is shipped and billed to a member automatically unless the member writes in advance and asks that it not be sent. The practice is also called inertia selling in Great Britain. See also *automatic shipment; positive option*.

negative-option publishing Sometimes used as another name for book clubs. See also *no-commitment book club*.

NE/NEP Publisher's abbreviation for new edition pending.

nesting An enclosure placed within another (nested) before being inserted into a mailing envelope.

net Price to be paid. No further discount. See also *net price*.

net book (U.K.) A book that must not be sold to the public in the U.K. at less than list price.

net book agreement (NBA) An agreement by U.K. publishers under which books are published at net prices—net prices being the prices at which such books must be sold to the public. Net books may not be offered for sale at less than net published prices unless and until the book has been held in stock by the bookseller for more than a year and has been offered back to the publisher at cost price or at the proposed reduced price. A net book may, however, be sold to certain libraries, book agents, and quantity buyers authorized by the Publishers Association.

net names (mailing lists) Names remaining after a merge-purge of two or more lists to eliminate duplications. See also *merge-purge*.

net 90 days (college stores) Extended terms granted by some publishers on customer request for college store adoption orders. Sometimes done during summer and winter season to encourage stores to send orders in advance of normal selling periods.

net 90 days (export sales) Extended dating given by some publishers to retail export accounts for shipments to foreign locations, or to export accounts in foreign countries.

net 90 days (school market) Extended terms granted by some publishers to encourage early orders for the fall and spring semesters. See also *extended credit*.

net 90 days (wholesale booksellers) Extended dating occasionally given by publishers on special stock orders placed by wholesalers. A few publishers allow extended dating on one order per year.

net orders per hour (telemarketing) The actual number of orders per hour based on paid sales from a telemarketing sales effort. See also *gross orders per hour (telemarketing)*.

net price The bookseller's cost for a book, usually the list or suggested resale price less discount. Shipping or transportation charges, when levied, are usually added onto the net price. See also *list price/retail price*; *net*; *net pricing*.

net price (U.K.)   The price for a book fixed by a publisher, below which the net book shall not be sold to the public. Also called net published price. See also *net book (U.K.)*.

net pricing   Publishers' billing for a book at an established net price, with no suggested retail price. Booksellers then set retail selling prices on an individual basis. See also *list price*.

net pricing markup formulas (bookselling)   One popular formula for markup on books sold by publishers with net pricing is 1.4 times the net price, rounded off. Most booksellers who buy books through net pricing view the net price as what they would have paid net with a desirable discount and mark up accordingly.

net profit   The "paper" profit a publisher makes when the sale of a book is made, regardless of whether payment is ultimately collected.

net response   The true response from a mailing, i.e., orders received and paid for.

net sales   The balance after deducting all credits and allowance for returned books from gross sales. See also *gross margin on sales*.

net 30 days   Standard terms of payment for most publisher accounts. See also *cash with order (CWO)*.

new age books   A generic term for contemporary books on topics such as holistic healing techniques, natural foods and alternative diets, spiritual and metaphysical subjects (especially those derived from Eastern philosophies and religions, crystals, channeling, reincarnation, and so on). See also *NAPRA*.

New Age Publishers and Retailers Alliance   See *NAPRA*.

new book information sources for academics   See *book information sources for academics*.

new books received listing   The practice of many scientific, scholarly, and trade periodicals to list all new books received for review, irrespective of whether they are subsequently reviewed or not. In some media, the listing is sufficiently informative to induce ordering.

new edition   An edition containing substantial changes from the previous edition, and printed from new, revised plates.

new edition frequency   There is no rule for how soon a new edition should be introduced. In mature subject areas, or fields not experiencing rapid development or change, one consideration is a minimum of 25% to 30% new material. Another may be when the earlier edition has achieved at least two-thirds of its lifetime sales projection. Still, a third may be when an early period of high-volume sales is followed by a relatively long period of flat sales.

newsletter   A concise periodical, often composed on a typewriter and mailed in a #10 envelope to simulate a letter. Provides late-breaking information in a particular area of interest. Most newsletters are sold by subscription, and generally do not contain advertising.

newsletter publishing   See *Publishing Newsletters, Revised Edition.*

newsletters, publishing industry   See *publishing newsletters.*

Newsletters Directory   A descriptive guide to more than 8,000 subscription, membership, and free newsletters, bulletins, digests, updates, and similar serial publications issued in the United States and available in print or online. (Former title: *National Directory of Newsletters and Reporting Services*). A typical entry provides up to 22 points of information, including scope, audience, and circulation. Many entries also indicate whether book reviews are included. Published by Gale Research Company, Book Tower, Detroit, MI 48226. See also *Oxbridge Directory of Newsletters.*

newsletter seminars   One-day seminars, held in various cities during the course of the year, geared to starting and improving performance of newsletters. Contact: Newsletter Clearinghouse, 44 W. Market Street, P.O. Box 311, Rhinebeck, NY 11572.

newsletter success criteria   (1) A broad market with a great deal of time lag between writing and publishing; (2) a narrow market with poor or insufficient coverage by other periodicals; (3) a particular market in which there is a lack of professional information in other published sources; (4) an evolving market in which information becomes obsolete at a very rapid rate; (5) a highly specialized market in which there is strong interest in information among those active in it.

Newsletter Yearbook/Directory   See *Hudson's Newsletter Directory*.

newspaper insert, freestanding   Advertising inserts in newspapers are called freestanding inserts. They are preprinted and added to the paper when the sections are assembled.

newsprint   An inexpensive grade of paper made mainly from groundwood pulp. Its primary use is for newspaper printing. See also *paper sizes*.

news release   A written communication, usually consisting of one to three pages and distributed for the purpose of obtaining news space in a publication. In publishing, it is used often to elicit a request for a review copy of a book. A general news release, in theory, is sent with the intent it will be viewed as "news" by the recipient. A news release designed to elicit a review copy request is usually written to generate enough interest in a published work to ensure that the publication receiving the release will request the book for review purposes. A news release may also be sent along with a review copy of a book as an aid in the review process. If not already included, the release should add at the bottom such basic bibliographic information as title, author, ISBN, publication date, and price.

news release (sent with review book)   News releases often accompany books sent for review, the idea being that such releases offer a summary of the book for those media that either do not have reviewers or do not wish to spend the time reviewing the book. Reviewers for such media frequently write the review based on information provided in the news release accompanying the review book. Book publicists, aware of this practice, often include good quotable phrases in their releases and later pick them up when a review appears, using the exact wording of the news release.

news release, inverted pyramid style   See *inverted pyramid style (publicity)*.

news release, release date   See *release date (news releases)*.

news release assembly   The pages of a news release, if more than one, should be numbered. The pages should be in order and stapled (one staple, upper left-hand corner). A line illustration may be stapled to a release, but never to a glossy print.

news release guidelines   (1) Insert heading "NEWS RELEASE"; (2) include not only name and address of issuer, but also name and telephone of contact individual, should additional information be desired or a clarification wanted; (3) show release date, usually near top, flush left. Unless there is a reason for release to be held up to a certain date, use "For immediate release"; (4) a headline of one or two lines length that gives main thrust of release is helpful to the recipient; (5) release should be typed double-spaced on one side of an 8½″ × 11″ sheet; (6) releases are best kept to one page. However, if longer, use word "more" centered at bottom of page; (7) if longer than two pages—for example, three pages long—put at the top of the second page "#2 of 3 pages," and at the top of the third page "#3 of 3 pages"; (8) at end of release seeking news space, signify by either "###" or the journalist symbol "-30-". Another ending is "-0-"; (9) at the end of a release written to elicit requests for a review copy of a book, insert a coupon request form that can be completed and returned. See also *end marks (news/press releases)*; *"more" line (news releases)*; *news release assembly*.

New Technical Books   A monthly publication of the New York Public Library that is considered the standard review medium on new technical books by many librarians. Arranged by subject and based on recent additions to the NYPL's Science and Technology Division collection. Used as a book selection aid by many librarians. Published continuously since 1915. See also *ASLIB* for U.K. equivalent publication.

New York Review of Books   A major review medium for popular and semipopular books with appeal to well educated and scholarly readers. An important medium for university press and scholarly publishers. Published biweekly (monthly in certain months) by NYREV Inc., 250 West 57th Street, New York, NY 10107. Phone 212-757-8070.

New York Times Book Review (NYTBR)   The single most important trade book advertising medium in the United States, and one of the most prestigious and influential review mediums. Most trade advertising campaigns start with this publication, which, in addition to the *Times* readership, is subscribed to by most leading libraries and by over 35,000 people who subscribe to this section only. Further, it is available for sale nationwide at hundreds of bookstores. Address: 201 E. 50th Street, New York, NY 10022-7703.

nice spread　See *book distribution jargon (bookstores).*

"nice to know" (book pricing and promotion)　A book containing information that may be useful but is not essential and, therefore, may be price sensitive. Such a book may require a harder sell to convince prospects to buy. See also *"need to know" (book pricing and promotion).*

niche marketing/publishing　Concentration on a specific pocket of a larger market. Invariably, this type of specialization reduces ratio of promotion cost to sales, especially with an ongoing program and increasing market share. Such concentration also helps attract new authors who favor being published by the same houses as their peers.

nine-digit ZIP code　See *ZIP+4.*

NIPP　A physician newly in patient practice. They are excellent prospects for a variety of medical and other reference-type products. Lists of such physicians are available from Clark-O'Neill/Fisher-Stevens, Fairview, NJ 07022-1570. Phone: 201-945-3400.

NISO　See *National Information Standards Organization.*

nixie　A piece of mail returned by the post office because it is undeliverable. See also *mail forwarding (USPS regulations).*

NMA　National Micrographic Association.

no Canadian rights　See *NCR.*

no-commitment book club　A book club that requires no commitment of a minimum purchase of books as a condition of membership. See also *negative-option publishing.*

nonexclusive book club rights　Rights to a book club that permit the publisher to offer the book to other book clubs at the same time. See also *book club rights; book club rights, first use; exclusive book club rights.*

nonimpact printing　Any method of printing done without the impact of an image-bearing surface upon the surface being printed. See also *ink-jet printing.*

nonrepro pencil   A light turquoise-blue pencil that will not reproduce when copy is photographed. Used for paste-up guidelines and markings.

nonreturnable discount   A preferential discount offered to booksellers who agree to purchase books from a publisher on a nonreturnable basis.

nontraditional market (books)   1. A market other than a bookstore, library, school, or normal retail channel. 2. Any market not normally known to sell or buy books. 3. A term used to identify books sold by publisher special sales departments. 4. Any untapped market that represents a potential source of new sales to a publishing establishment.

NOP   Publisher's abbreviation for "not our publication."

no-return policy   See *return policy.*

notch binding   A signature of folded and gathered sheets with spine notched and glue affixed in the notches. Almost as strong as a smyth sewn binding and stronger than perfect binding.

notification slip   A new book announcement sent to a library by an approval plan vendor for a title in conformity with the library's approval plan profile. The book is for acquisition consideration. See *approval plan; forms only library awareness plan.*

Nth name selection   A method of selecting a portion of a mailing list (every other name or every fifth name, etc.). The method provides a means of sampling the larger list. Sometimes it is used when, for budgetary reasons, only a small portion of a larger list is affordable.

nursing school faculty lists   See *college faculty lists.*

NYP   Abbreviation for "not yet published."

NYTBR   See *New York Times Book Review.*

O

oblique (typography)   Roman characters that are electronically slanted to the right.

oblong   1. The longer of two dimensions. 2. Designation for a book wider than it is high. 3. In binding, a booklet or catalog bound on the shorter dimension.

OCR   See *optical character recognition*.

OCR-A code   A magnetic character typeface that both a machine and a human being can read. Used by some publishers on book covers.

off color   Ink or paper that does not match the sample it is supposed to duplicate.

offer (direct mail)   The terms under which a particular product or service is promoted.

offer, prepublication   See *prepublication offer*.

offer, subscription   See *subscription offer (book)*.

offer test (direct mail)   A test mailing in which different types of offers are used to different segments of the same audience. Such tests may include prepub price vs. list price or book with premium vs. book at discount, etc.

official closing time (convention exhibits)   The hour at which exhibits officially close. No dismantling of displays, packing of equipment, literature, etc. is generally permitted until the official closing time.

offprint   Copies of a journal article made available in quantity, apart from the original journal issue. Offprints are made from sheets run simultaneously with and in addition to journal printing. They may start with the last page of the previous article, and may also contain the first page of the article following. Many journal publishers view offprints as an added revenue source. A few claim as much as 5% to 10% of income derived from this source.

offset lithography   See *offset printing (offset lithography)*.

offset paper/stock   A book stock characterized by strength, cleanliness, and pick-resistance, that is also relatively impervious to water (sized). It is manufactured for use on an offset press. See also *paper sizes; sizing (of paper)*.

offset printing (offset lithography)   A printing process utilizing a rotary press in which a plate wrapped around a cylinder (plate cylinder) transfers an inked image onto a sheet or rubber blanket wrapped around an abutting cylinder (blanket cylinder), from which it is then transferred (offset) to the surface of the paper being printed. The offset platemaking process is faster than letterpress and considerably less expensive. The offset process permits quality printing on a variety of materials and can accommodate virtually any layout. See also *letterpress printing*.

off-the-book page publicity   Publicity about a book treated as news or editorial matter in sections of a newspaper or magazine other than the book page or book review section. Such publicity may be released to a syndicate or wire service. The publicity may consist of a feature article about the author or of an article based on guidelines set forth in the book. Publicity sometimes appears in special heading sections or departments of newspapers or magazines. Columnists and editorial writers are good prospects for publicity about books dealing with topics they are inclined to write about.

on approval   Books sent to a library, usually by a wholesaler, for purchase subject to approval after inspection. On-approval books do not obligate the library to buy and are not subject to billing. See *approval plan*.

on consignment   Books supplied with the understanding that they will be paid for when sold. Supplier retains title until sold and can recall books not paid for at any time. U.K.: sale or return.

on-demand edition   A book reproduced on demand by xerographic process from a microfilm of the book.

on-demand publishing   Supply of books, either singly or in small quantities, in response to individual orders by means of photographic reproduction from a microfiche or typescript.

one-color printing   A reference to printing in one color ink on white paper.

one-free-for-10   A publisher offer to give a bookseller one free copy for every ten ordered. An incentive used frequently at the American Booksellers Convention to get a bookseller to place a stock order for a particular trade title at the convention. Rarely, if ever, done for nontrade titles. See also *one-free-with offers*; *special deal*.

one-free-with offers   A publisher special offer to a bookseller as an ordering incentive. A frequent incentive at publisher exhibits at the American Booksellers Association Convention. Most typical of such offers is one-free-with-10, although 12 or some other quantity is sometimes used. These types of offers are called "Special Deals," although such deals are not limited to one-free-with offers only. See also *special deal*.

100% co-op ad   An ad in which the publisher agrees to pick up all the costs of placement. Most co-op ad agreements do not call for 100% payment, and agreements are often verbal ones with the sales rep. See also *co-op ad*.

one-shot book   A randomly published title that is not tied to a publishing program. A single book by a publisher who may or may not publish other books on a regularly scheduled basis.

one-time buyer (mail order)   A buyer who has not made a second or repeat purchase.

one-time rate   Basic advertising rate in a publication. Rate applied to advertising in a publication when the number of insertions is insufficient to earn a contract or frequency discount or rate. See also *advertising contract*; *card rate*; *contract rate*; *contract year (advertising)*; *earned rate*; *frequency discount*; *short rate*.

one-time use   An understanding that a rented mailing list will not be used more than once without the consent of the list owner.

One Touch   An electronic book ordering service of the Ingram Book Company.

one-year contract (mailing list)   1. An arrangement for a list rental with unlimited use of the list for one year. Occasionally done for compiled lists. 2. An agreement by a list renter to use a minimum number of names from a mailing list database within a one-year period in exchange for a preferential rental rate.

online/on-line   A term applied to a system or to facilities that provide an interactive data processing service at a location physically separated from the computer that performs the processing.

online access   Information retrieval from a database through a computer terminal.

online catalog   Catalog from which information is electronically retrievable.

only to order   See *OTO*.

on-request publishing   See *on-demand publishing*.

onsert   A freestanding or loose advertising insert or enclosure sent along with a periodical to its subscribers. The term is used to distinguish them from bound-in supplements. See also *bind-in card; blow-in card; insert*.

OP   Abbreviation for "out of print." See also *out of print*.

opacity   The amount of show-through on the opposite side of a printed sheet or the adjoining sheet. A high-opacity paper has less show-through. See also *show-through (paper)*.

open check/open draft   A vehicle used by many booksellers when special ordering a book from a publisher under the ABA STOP plan. The bookseller issues an "open check" with no amount listed. The publisher's order department fills in the amount to reflect correct discount and postage charges based on the list price existing at the time the order is filled. Most open checks have a printed limitation on them, such as "Void over $50." See also *Single Title Order Plan (STOP)*.

open draping (exhibits and conventions)   Draping over risers and tables that hangs loose like a woman's skirt. When risers are draped, it is best to request "open draping" which permits access to the area underneath risers for storage. See also *closed draping; risers (exhibits and conventions)*.

open-end (catalog) envelope An over-sized envelope on which the opening is on the short end.

open-ended series See *series, open-ended*.

open-face window envelope See *window envelope, open-face*.

open job (advertising) Job on which activities are still pending, or for which all charges have not been fully accounted for. In some promotional activities, such as in advertising departments, jobs opened and open jobs are measurement criteria for the facility's activity.

open-side (booklet) envelope An over-sized envelope on which the opening is on the long side.

open-to-buy system (bookstore chain) A buying system used by some chains in which purchases are based on a fixed allocation of dollars deemed essential for inventory control. The inventory is kept at the level required to meet sales projections for a given year. See also *buyer/distributor system (bookstore chain); category buying system (bookstore chain)*.

open-window envelope A window envelope in which the opening is not covered. This type of envelope is not permitted in certain international mailings, Canada included. Window envelopes in these countries must have a glassine covering.

opinion leaders (publicity) An important publicity channel for scientific, technical, professional and scholarly books is the small group of opinion leaders in the book's field. Many publishers send complimentary copies of books to them with the knowledge that they can spread the word on such specialized books to a book's prime audience in ways that other types of promotion cannot match.

optical character reader See *optical character recognition*.

optical character recognition 1. Copy prepared using OCR-readable typefaces can be "read" by electronic scanning machines (optical readers). This information can then be used to produce photocomposition. 2. Optical character readers are used by the U.S. Postal Service to read ZIP numbers for mail sorting.

3. Some scholarly journals ask authors to prepare submissions in an optical character recognition (OCR) typeface, which can be machine read by scanning. See also *camera-ready copy.*

optical illusions in color   (1) If two complementary colors are placed side by side, both seem to be brighter; (2) a color appears to be lighter if it is seen against a darker color; (3) a light surface on a dark background appears to be larger than a dark surface of the identical size on a light background. This applies to type in color on color backgrounds. Type in a light color on a dark background will appear larger than type in a dark color on a light background.

optical reader   See *optical character recognition.*

optical scanning   Direct input of data into a computer by use of a character reader rather than by keyboarding.

option   A license to buy or sell a specific property such as a manuscript or the rights to a book, usually in a legally binding written agreement, in reciprocation for some consideration and within a specific period of time.

order/open check   See *open check/open draft.*

order blank   See *order form/order blank.*

order form/order blank   A vehicle accompanying a promotional effort that the recipient or reader may complete and return as a means of ordering. Such forms may be part of a larger printed piece, in which case they should always be enclosed in a broken-line or dash-line border to denote action by the reader. They may also be an independent unit such as a business reply mail card or a business reply envelope. If in a catalog or periodical, a bind-in card or order form may be detached along a perforation line. Most card decks or card packs consist entirely of order forms, since each of the enclosures may be returned separately.

order form, duplicate in direct mail   With catalog mailings or multiple-title book offers, a duplicate order form, included with the mailing, will often increase response.

order form format, recommended   An order form that looks too valuable to throw away will receive a better response than a routinely conceived one.

order form options (direct mail)   (1) Reply card postpaid; (2) reply card postage required; (3) reply envelope, postpaid; (4) reply envelope, postage required; (5) telephone number, caller paid; (6) toll-free 800 number; (7) reserve charge telephone call; (8) clip-out order coupon; (9) perforated order form or coupon; (10) credit card payment; (11) promotional order stamp affixed to card, form, or letter; (12) self-stick customer return address label; (13) fully prepared and completed order for customer to sign and return. See also *stamp promotions.*

order form signature   See *signature line.*

ordering, library   See *acquisitions librarian; approval plan jobber/dealer; jobber, library; library wholesaler; wholesaler (book)/jobber.*

order stamp   A stamp bearing the appearance of a postage stamp and used as an ordering vehicle or involvement gimmick with a promotion package. Both book publishers and periodical mass mailers such as Publishers Clearinghouse have used this device effectively for generating orders. When used in book publishing promotion, it may or may not have a cover illustration and is likely to carry title, author, price, and page count. The leading book publisher-user of stamps is W.B. Saunders Company. See also *stamp formats (for book and journal promotions); stamps (in book promotion).*

orphan (typography)   A widow carried over to the top of the next column or page. This is considered poor typographic design and should be avoided.

orphans (on publisher's list)   Isolated titles not in keeping with the publisher's regular publishing program and therefore requiring special effort or attention because they cannot be marketed in clusters with related titles.

OS   Abbreviation for "out of stock." See also *out of stock.*

otabind   A style of paperback binding in which cold glue is applied to the backbone and a paper cover is affixed only along the hinge. This permits the backbone of the book to be free of the cover as with a hardcover book, but also permits the pages to lie flat. See also *perfect binding.*

OTO   U.K. term meaning "only to order." The equivalent of the U.S. term "special order." An OTO book is one which is not normally stocked but only to order when a customer request is received. See also *special order (n.).*

outbound telemarketing   See *telemarketing, outbound.*

outlet manager   The coordinator for all sales and promotion activities related to a specific book sales outlet. He or she may be trade sales manager, library sales manager, special sales manager, or college marketing manager.

outline letters/open-faced letters (typography)   Types that comprise only the outline of the letter, in contrast to solid types that print in full face. Outline typefaces are generally used sparingly and only to create special effects. See also *typeface; typography.*

out of print (OP)   A book no longer printed or stocked by the publisher, and publisher has no intention of reprinting. When a book is declared out of print, stock still remaining in the publisher's warehouse may either be destroyed or sold off at a greatly reduced price, usually to wholesalers or booksellers. Books thus sold are called *remainders.* See also *remaindering.*

out-of-print book searching   Booksellers seeking out-of-print books regularly list what they seek in the *AB Bookman's Weekly.* This publication is read by some 8,000 specialist and antiquarian dealers who respond to these ads by sending "quote cards" to the advertisers which indicate the condition and price of items being sought. Booksellers may then buy and mark up according to their own profit needs. See also *AB Bookman's Weekly.*

out-of-print dealer   A bookseller who buys and sells out-of-print or hard-to-find copies of books. Such dealers do business by mail, selling to collectors, libraries, and reading-copy customers. See also *antiquarian book dealer; rare book dealer; used book dealer.*

out of stock (OS)   A book temporarily out of stock, with a new shipment or printing awaited by publisher.

overlay (artwork)   A protective covering for artwork or photographs. Also a transparent covering consisting of low opacity paper or clear plastic. Sometimes used to show corrections or instructions for the platemaker.

overlay (mailing list)   Use of two mailing lists, whereby information appearing with names and addresses on one list is transferred to the same names and addresses on the other list through a computer match. Most frequent use: Adding phone numbers.

overmatter   See *overset*.

overprint   Printing over an already printed area.

override   A bonus or commission, usually a percentage of revenue, profits, or sales, paid to executives or sales management. Sometimes based on attaining specific sales goals.

overrun (journal)   See *journal overrun*.

overrun or underrun (printing)   As a rule, most print jobs are either more or less than the quantity ordered. Under printing trade practices, this is permissible and the customer is billed for the exact quantity shipped. On small quantities (up to 10,000) an allowance of up to 10% is considered acceptable. Over 10,000 the tolerance percentage should be agreed upon in advance. Underruns are usually caused by spoilage in printing and binding.

overs   1. Surplus materials at a lettershop after a mailing has been completed. 2. A preplanned overprinting of a planned promotion to allow additional copies for in-house distribution, sales force handouts, convention give-aways, or other uses, including literature requests. See also *leftovers (direct mail)*; *overrun or underrun (printing)*.

oversell   Advertising copy that promises more than a book can deliver. Such practices can lead to unusually high book returns.

overset   Type composition in excess of the space permitted in a particular job.

oversize mail surcharge   See *mail size surcharge, USPS*.

overstock   In terms of books, surplus inventory in excess of what is likely to be sold. The overstock is considered uneconomical. On the basis of previous sales history, there is no profit in warehousing the books or in trying to sell them. See also *remaindering.*

over the transom   A book proposal or manuscript received unexpectedly or without prior solicitation or invitation.

overworked list (mailing lists)   A mailing list that has diminished effectiveness because it has been used too frequently. Owners are able to prevent this from occurring by assigning mailing dates spaced well apart from one another. See *assigned mailing date.*

Oxbridge Directory of Newsletters   A directory of over 14,000 U.S. and Canadian newsletters. Includes complete details on each including name, address, phone number, date of origin, contents and material used, and frequency. Classified by subject. Published biennially in odd years by Oxbridge Communications Inc., 150 Fifth Avenue, New York, NY 10011. Phone: 212-741-0231. See also *Newsletters Directory.*

P

P.A.   See Publishers' Association.

package, direct-mail   See *direct-mail package*.

packaged book   A book produced for a publisher entirely or in part by an agency that specializes in writing, editing, designing, and producing books for hire. According to the terms of its agreement with an originating publisher, the packaging agent's assignment may range from writing and copyediting a manuscript to designing and even printing and binding a finished book. See also *packager*.

package enclosure campaign   See *package insert campaign*.

package insert   A card, folder, or booklet included in a package or outgoing book shipment. Also called a *bounceback*. See also *bounceback (direct mail); freestanding insert*.

package insert campaign   A catalog or enclosure sent with outgoing book shipments. By limiting the campaign to a specific number of inserts with the same key or identifying number, it is possible to track and record the response to the specific campaign and to evaluate results based on the cost of the campaign.

package insert program   1. The systematic practice of conducting individual package insert campaigns. 2. The practice of including advertising inserts with outgoing shipments on an unstructured basis. See also *package insert campaign*.

packager   An independent individual or organization that produces books off the premises for distribution by a book publisher. The "package" may be a finished manuscript, camera-ready copy, or a complete book. Also called book producer. See also *American Book Producers Association (ABPA); packaging (in publishing).*

package stuffer   See *package insert.*

package test (direct mail)   A test of two or more direct-mail packages, one being the currently used standard mailing package or "control" and the other(s) containing variations. Following such tests, the subsequent expanded mailings to the same lists tend to utilize the more successful package based on test results. See also *control (testing); direct-mail package.*

packaging (in publishing)   Any deviation from standard methods of presentation, pricing, and/or distribution of a publication as a means of increasing its sales potential.

packaging, journal format   The packaging of a book, deemed of limited commercial potential, as a journal publication. The three possible formats: (1) as a special issue or a special volume of the journal; (2) as installments in the journal; (3) as a supplement to the journal.

packaging requirement (printing)   Instructions to a printer indicating how printed matter is to be packaged—cartons, skids, etc. Labeling for such packages should also be furnished.

packing crate (exhibits and conventions)   The permanent case in which a convention display unit is packed and shipped.

packing list/pick list   A list to be inserted with a book shipment to be used by the customer to check off books received against those that were ordered. See also *picking list/pick list.*

packing slip (printer's)   A document enclosed with a printing shipment that indicates (1) the contents of each carton; (2) the number of pieces in each carton; (3) the number of cartons in the shipment; (4) whether it is a complete or partial shipment; (5) if a partial shipment, what is still to come; (6) whom to contact if there are any questions about the shipment.

padded van (conventions)   One of two ways to ship convention books and display materials. Whereas the alternate means, motor freight, does not guarantee delivery on any particular date, shipment by padded van does guarantee delivery on a specified date. See also *common carrier convention shipments.*

page charges, journal   See *journal page charges.*

page proofs   A complete set of composed pages ready for final checking before publication is printed.

pagination sequence, journals   See *journal pagination sequence.*

pagination sequence, magazines. See *magazine pagination sequence.*

paid actives, periodical   See *periodical mailing list, paid actives.*

paid-space advertising   See *space advertising.*

pamphlet   1. An unbound single sheet folded into smaller panels. 2. Anything in a paper cover less than 49 pages long. 3. Anything without hard covers and relatively inexpensive or free. See also *booklet.*

P&R title   P&R refers to professional and reference. A P&R title would be either a professional or reference book, usually published under a single divisional responsibility, often called the P&R division.

Pantone® Matching System   See *PMS colors.*

paper (book format)   A term commonly used in publisher catalogs and advertising to indicate that a book is bound in a paper cover and also to differentiate it from a hardcover edition of the same book if one is available. See *paperback/paperbound; paperback edition/paper edition; cloth (book format).*

paper, bible   See *bible paper.*

paper, board   See *board (paper).*

paper, bond   See *bond paper*

paper, book   See *book paper.*

paper, coated   See *coated stock (paper).*

paper, cover   See *cover paper.*

paper, high-bulk   See *bulking paper.*

paper, index   See *index paper.*

paper, kraft   See *kraft paper.*

paper, offset   See *offset paper/stock.*

paper, pressure-sensitive   See *pressure-sensitive paper.*

paper, short-grained   See *short-grained paper.*

paper, text   See *text paper.*

paperback/paperbound   A book bound with a paper cover. Usually priced less expensively than the same title in hardcover when available both ways. See also *hardcover.*

paperback, rack-size   See *rack-size paperback.*

paperback, trade   See *trade paperback.*

paperback edition/paper edition   The issuance of a hardcover book in paper covers. There are three types: mass market, which are rack size, trade editions, which are usually the same size as the hardcover edition, and textbook, which is similar to a hardcover book except for the cover and which may or may not have a hardcover counterpart.

Paperbound Books in Print   Lists paperbound books in all fields by author, title, and subject. Also lists over 5,000 publishers of paperbound books. Published semiannually, spring and fall. Sold by copy or by year. From: R.R. Bowker Co., 245 W. 17th Street, New York, NY 10010.

paper characteristics   (1) *Weight* (calculated by the ream); (2) *Opacity* (show-through; greater capacity, less show-through; (3) *Brightness* (brighter sheets have more contrast); (4) *Grain* (the direction in which the paper fibers lie); (5) *Bulk* (thickness of paper, i.e., pages per inch); (6) *Surface* (the finish of the paper, rough or smooth).

paper edition   See *paperback edition/paper edition.*

paper finish   See *finish (paper).*

paper grain   See *grain paper.*

paper sizes   The various types of papers are manufactured in different basis sizes (the standard size in which it is normally and most conveniently produced). Following are the sheet basis sizes for the most frequently used printing papers, given in both inches and millimeters:

Bond	17″ × 22″	432 × 559 mm
Book or Text	25″ × 38″	635 × 965 mm
	17½″ × 22½″	445 × 572 mm
Cover	20″ × 26″	508 × 660 mm
Printing Bristol	22½″ × 28½″	572 × 724 mm
	22½″ × 35″	572 × 889 mm
Index Bristol	25½″ × 30½″	648 × 775 mm
Newsprint (tag)	24″ × 36″	610 × 914 mm
Postcard stock	28½″ × 45″	724 × 1142 mm

See also *international paper sizes*.

paper smoothness   See *finish (paper)*.

paragraph (typography)   A copy block, often defined by an indent at the beginning of the first line. Where paragraphs have no first-line indent, they are separated by extra line spacing. Short paragraphs offer these three benefits over longer ones: (1) attract greater attention; (2) have greater legibility; (3) are more readily understood.

parallel fold   See *accordion fold*.

parallel importation   A doctrine that gives access in copyright in the same market to legitimately produced editions of the same book from different sources. (Definition from: *The Bookseller*, May 1, 1987).

Pareto's Law   A general law stating that 80% of the total results in a given situation are produced by 20% of the participants. For example: 80% of sales come from 20% of the titles, or 80% of the orders are brought in by 20% of the sales reps. Also referred to as the "*80-20 principle*."

pass (bookselling)   A decision by a bookstore or chain buyer not to order a particular title during a sales rep presentation. "The buyer told me he had decided to pass on that title."

pass (printing)   One run of paper through a printing press.

pass-along effect   The tendency of professionals receiving mail or periodicals at their place of employment to share materials received with associates.

pass-along instructions See *routing instructions.*

pass-along notice An enclosure with a mailing or a block of copy on a promotion asking the recipient to pass material along to a friend or associate.

pass-along reader Reader of a publication who has not purchased or ordered the publication from the publisher.

pass-along readership The readership of a periodical, advertisement, or direct-mail promotion piece beyond that of the original recipient. Many book mail promotions encourage such circulation by including a message suggesting the recipient pass it along to a friend or colleague. Card deck mailings to business or professional addresses have a high pass-along value.

paste-up See *mechanical/mechanical paste-up.*

paste-up artist See *board artist/mechanical artist.*

payment method, journals See *journal payment method.*

payment method, magazines See *magazine billing practices.*

payment rate/pay-up rate (subscription product) The percentage of those respondents to a subscription product promotion who, after sampling or subscribing, actually remit payment. Also known as percentage of paid or net paid.

payment terms, special sale See *special sales terms of payment*

payment test (in mailing) A mailing in which different recipients of the same mailing will be offered different payment options. The results are tallied and compared for responsiveness for each type of payment offer. Typical tests: Cash-with-order vs. 15-day free examination; offer with and without credit card payment option, etc.

pay rate (subscription product) See *payment rate/pay-up rate (subscription product).*

payup Rate of payment.

PBB Professional Business Book.

P.E./PE See *printer's error.*

peel-off label   A self-adhesive label that can be peeled off a wax-finish backing and reapplied elsewhere, usually on an order form, envelope, or response device. See also *pressure-sensitive label*.

peer-reviewed journal   See *refereed journal*.

peer-reviewed research   A process used in scholarly publishing whereby a research article to be published (book or journal) is reviewed by two or more peers as to accuracy, clarity, and correct scientific procedure.

peers   Those of equal position or engaged in like activities at a similar level. One of equal standing with another. In scientific and scholarly publishing, research monographs are written by authors for their peers.

percentage of return   See *response rate (direct mail)*.

perfect binding   A binding method in which the folds of the signatures are trimmed and the spine edges of all sheets are glued together by means of an adhesive. Almost always used for papercover books. Also called *adhesive binding*. See also *otabind*.

perfect press/perfecting press   A printing press that prints both sides of the paper in a single pass through the press.

perforation   The process of punching small holes or slits in paper stock to facilitate tearing along a desired line. Usually used for order coupons in mailing piece. Removable reply cards utilize a 10- or 12-tooth perforation, or an 8-tooth large gap perforation.

perforation lines   Dashed nonrepro blue pencil lines on mechanical artwork to indicate where perforations are to be made.

per inquiry   Some advertising sources will accept payment based on the number of responses drawn by an advertisement. This is known as "per inquiry" payment. See also *PI campaign; PI deal*.

periodical   1. A publication appearing, usually, at stated intervals. Each issue is complete in itself and indicates a relation with prior and subsequent issues. 2. A term used by librarians when referring to both magazines and journals. See also *serial*.

periodical, specialized   See *specialized periodical*.

periodical circulation regulations/intelligence   Postal regulations require periodical publishers who use second-class mailing permits to post their circulation figures in an issue appearing closest to October. Otherwise unpublished circulation figures can be located through postal records or by checking the issue in which this figure is posed.

periodical mailing list, free controlled subscriber   A list of subscribers who receive a controlled circulation periodical free of charge because of special qualifications such as job title, occupation, or industry affiliation. Not as good as a list of "paid actives" since they might not be subscribers if payment were required. See also *periodical mailing list, paid actives*.

periodical mailing list, paid actives   A list of current subscribers who have paid for their subscriptions. This is the most reliable type of periodical subscriber list since it is kept up to date by the subscriber. See also *periodical mailing list, free controlled subscriber*.

periodical mailing list, subscriber   A list of subscribers to a periodical. For journals and publications requiring prepayment, this is as good a list as "paid actives." However, if subscriptions are on a "bill me" basis, such lists may also include names of people who subscribed and never paid. See also *periodical mailing list, paid actives*.

periodical market segments   There are three distinct market segments in periodicals promotion. For the most effective promotion, each requires its own distinctive approach. The segments are: (1) current subscribers; (2) cold prospects, individuals with whom there has been no prior contact who may or may not be subscribers to other periodicals; (3) expires (former subscribers who have not renewed).

periodical ordering patterns, library   (1) Ordering is either direct or through a subscription agency at specific times of the year; (2) expensive periodicals are ordered only as a result of staff or administrative discussion and then sometimes only as replacements for periodicals for which little demand has been shown; (3) ordering decisions are influenced by patron request or demand and by whether the contents of the periodical are accessible through various abstracting and indexing sources.

periodical pagination sequence   See *journal pagination sequence; magazine pagination sequence.*

periodicals, bonus distribution   See *bonus distribution (periodicals).*

periodicals consortium   See *journals consortia.*

periodicals directories   See entries under *Serials Directory; Standard Periodical Directory; Ulrich's International Periodicals Directory.*

periodical subscription   See *subscription (periodical).*

periodical subscription agency   See *subscription agent/agency.*

periodical subscription lifetime value   See *lifetime value of periodical subscription.*

periodical subscription payment requirement   See *subscription payment requirement, periodical.*

period of eligibility for return   The period during which publishers will accept returns from a bookseller account. Typically not before three months or after one year from date of invoice, although some returns policies extend only to six months, others are good for as much as 18 months.

peripheral universe   Secondary market.

permission   The granting of permission or authorization by a copyright owner to use copyrighted material in printed form. Such permissions may or may not involve a fee.

permission (bookselling)   An authorization, used by most publishers, to a bookseller for the return of certain books. The permission may be in the form of a letter or a permission label.

permission, photo   See *photograph release.*

permission label (bookselling)   A requirement of most book publishers who permit book returns. The label must accompany the returns and indicate that publisher permission for the return has been granted.

personal bookstore   See *independent/independent bookstore/independent bookseller.*

personalized letter   A letter used in mailing in which the name of the recipient has been included in both the salutation and the body of the letter. Recommended for small markets where maximum penetration is needed, and for special offers, or for a timely news announcement. See also *computer letter*; *personal letter*.

personalized letter eye flow study   See *letter eye flow, personalized*.

personal letter   A letter addressed directly to a specific person. It bears the recipient's name and address and the salutation on the letter is to that person. See also *personalized letter*.

personal subscription price (journal)   The price charged by a journal publisher for a subscription placed by an individual for his or her personal use. For many journals targeted to the institutional market, discounts of as much as 50% are given for personal subscriptions that accompany an institutional subscription. For society or association journals, discounts to individual subscriptions can be much larger. See also *institutional subscription price (journal)*.

photo agency   A commercial organization that supplies photographs for commercial purposes on a fee basis. Also called photo service or stock library. Photographs supplied are called stock photographs. One of the largest is the Bettmann Archive in New York City, which houses the entire collection of United Press International. Address: 136 E. 57th Street, New York, NY 10022. Other photo agencies are listed in *Literary Market Place (LMP)*.

photocomposer   A photomechanical machine used to set type, in position, on photo sensitive paper plates.

photocomposition   The process of producing type photographically onto film or film paper.

photocopy   1. A photographic copy of an existing photograph. Such a print may be enlarged, reduced, or screened. 2. A xerographic copy.

photograph release   A form signed by an individual appearing in a photograph to be used for advertising or promotion. With the individual's release, the photograph can be used without liability.

photography book 1. A book the content of which consists primarily of photos. 2. A book with primary appeal to photographers, camera buffs, or those who view photography as an art form.

photo offset lithography See *offset printing (offset lithography)*.

photostat/stat A fast method of making photocopies of black-and-white original copy. Photostats may be direct positive (DP) or negative-to-positive (negative made first). A photostat may be made larger, smaller, or the same size. A requested change in size is usually expressed as percent of original copy (e.g., photostat to 85% size). If used for reproduction, a glossy stat is to be specified. See also *PMT; Velox*.

pica (typography) A standard unit for measuring width and depth of lines of type, equivalent to approximately ⅙″ or 12 points. In printed promotion, many other elements may be measured in picas, such as width of margins or space between columns of type. Picas are not quite 6 to the inch, 30 picas measuring 4.98″.

P.I. campaign A per inquiry campaign, i.e., the promotion, whether print or broadcast, is paid for on the basis of inquires or orders received. Usually there is prior agreement on the amount of payment per inquiry. See also *per inquiry; P.I. deal*.

picking list/pick list A list prepared for the warehouse to use in picking books off the shelf in fulfillment of a book order. See also *packing list*.

PICS See *Publishers Information Cards Service (PICS)*.

P.I. deal Payment for advertising based on the number of orders or inquiries received. Payment is a fixed amount per inquiry or per order. See also *per inquiry*.

piggyback label See *peel-off label*.

pilot book club A book club with the minimum number of members necessary to reveal predictable behavior characteristics in such areas as sales, returns, payments, resignations, etc.

pilot study A study undertaken on a small scale to establish whether a larger study is needed.

P.I. program for medical publishers   See *Publishers' Row card deck program.*

pirated edition   An edition of a book reprinted and distributed without permission or of payment to the copyright owner.

pitch letter   A letter component of a press kit sent to the producer of a radio or TV show aimed at obtaining an author booking. Its purpose is to tell the producer why the author or the book's subject is either newsworthy or appropriate for the producer's program. The letter should be followed by a phone call to the producer to try to schedule the interview.

place stamp here   Instruction on the mailing face of reply card or envelope when mailer does not wish to pay return postage. Occasionally the instruction will specify a specific amount of postage, which may be the postcard rate or the prevailing first-class letter rate. Mailers of catalogs, expensive brochures, or free examination materials sometimes require payment of return postage as an indication of the respondent's sincerity in making the request or placing the order. It is considered a form of response qualification. See also *qualify a lead.*

plans, special, for booksellers   See *backlist stock plan; bookseller agency plan.*

plant costs (for book)   All production costs incurred by the publisher before a book goes to press. Includes cost of composition, plates, proofs, jacket art, etc.

plastic comb binding   See *comb binding.*

plate   1. The printing surface used in any contact printing process. Also called printing plate. 2. A printed illustration. Often implies a high-quality illustration printed separately from a book and inserted into the printed pages. See also *size indications in printed matter.*

plate size   See *size indications in printed matter.*

plug   1. A favorable mention of a book in a print medium or broadcast. 2. Any endorsement or favorable commentary about a book, whether or not solicited by the publisher, that can be used in publicity or advertising.

PMS colors   A system of over 500 ink colors that can be matched from 10 basic inks. Each of the colors is numbered, and most printing orders specify ink colors by PMS number. PMS is an abbreviation for Pantone Matching System.

PMT   Photomechanical transfer, made with process camera. A diffusion transfer process that allows original line art to be reduced or enlarged. See also *Velox*.

PN   Abbreviation for *Publishing News*, a U.K. book trade weekly.

P.O. advertising   See *P.I. deal*.

pocket part (loose-leaf publishing)   Pocket parts are issued by loose-leaf publishers as small supplements to the main body of a work that had been published earlier. They are designed to slip into a pocket in the back of the binder. See also *loose-leaf publishing*.

point (typography)   A unit of measurement used for size of type faces, rules, borders, and other elements used in typography. It is in universal use in English-speaking countries. A point measures .013837 of an inch or approximately $\frac{1}{72}$ of an inch. Seventy-two points are equal to 0.996 inches.

point-of-sale   A retail place of sale, such as a bookstore.

point-of-sale advertising   Advertising in the place where a book is offered for sale.

point-of-sale display/point-of-purchase display   Any advertising materials displayed where customers can make a purchase. Includes counter cards, posters, banners, headers, etc. See also *easel*.

point-of-sale kit   A kit of advertising materials provided to a bookseller to enhance promotion in-store of a single book, project, or publishing event. See also *window display kit*.

polybag   A mailing envelope made of polyethylene film.

polywrap (plastic wrap)   A wrapping used in place of envelopes because of its light weight and great strength. 1. A wrap favored for foreign mailings because it is lighter in weight than paper and reduces postage costs. 2. A wrap almost universally used for card deck mailings. Most employ clear wrap, although some are printed in one to four colors.

poor (antiquarian bookselling)   A book in obviously poor condition, adequate only for reading content. See also *antiquarian bookselling terms*.

popular reference   See *reference, popular*.

pop-up   A die-cut folder or other form of direct-mail advertising, the opening of which causes a figure or illustrative element to "pop up." Also referred to as "dimensional printing."

pop-up book   A book in which folded down figures pop up when the facing pages are spread apart. A popular type of book for very young children.

portable display (exhibits and conventions)   A light weight, compact exhibit that can be hand-carried to a show by a sales rep or other individual and set up on the spot, usually on a rented table.

POS   See *point-of-sale*.

position   Placement of an advertisement on a page and location of the page in the publication. See also *preferred position*.

position charge   An added charge over standard space rates; charged by some publications for guaranteed placement of advertising in specific locations within the publication. Inside or back covers are usually offered at a percentage rate over black-and-white page rates inside the publication, or at a stated higher price. See also *run-of-paper position*.

position guarantee   A guarantee that an advertisement will appear in a specific position within a publication, or that a card in a card deck will be placed in a specific location. See also *position charge*.

positioning   See *price positioning*.

positioning (book)   1. The status a book enjoys in a specialized field relative to its competition, or share of the available market. 2. Strategic placement of a book in ways that will aid its success in terms of competition, price, or its ability to meet the needs of its market. 3. The categorization of new titles on a trade publisher's upcoming list relative to marketing opportunities and market needs, taking into consideration pricing, design, printed and point-of-sale promotion, and advertising and publicity.

positioning of advertising   See *advertising positioning.*

position request   A request by an advertiser for a particular location for a placed advertisement if that position is available. By prefacing such a request with the words "Would appreciate...", the advertiser does not commit himself or herself to pay a special position charge. See also *preferred position.*

positive option   A book club arrangement whereby books are shipped only in response to orders from members that are generated through regular promotional announcements. This is in contrast to negative option clubs wherein books are shipped automatically unless the member orders that they not be sent. See also *automatic shipment; negative option.*

postage instructions (direct mail)   Instructions on an order to a lettershop or mailing house advising the type of postage to be used for a mailing. Any deviation from these instructions becomes the responsibility of the mailing service.

postage-metered courtesy reply envelope   If a postage-metered courtesy reply envelope is used as a mailing enclosure and has the *printed* words "No postage stamp necessary—postage has been prepaid by" and payee's name and address in the center of the envelope, the month, day, and year may be omitted from the meter impression and the envelope may be mailed at any future date from any part of the United States. See also *postage meter usage.*

postage meter usage   Meter stamps may be used on all classes of mail, but requirements vary. *First-class:* Must be mailed the same date as metered and must show month, day, and year. May be deposited in collection boxes. *Other classes:* Omit month, day, and year. This enables sender to run envelopes or mail through machine at any time prior to mailing. Bulk rate third-class must show words "Bulk Rate."

postage-paid business reply mail   A card or envelope enclosure sent with a mailing, both as a reminder that an order is expected and also as a vehicle for mailing back the order or response. The mailer pays the return postage. A postage-paid reply card or envelope will usually produce a better response than one requiring payment of return postage on mailings to individuals. See also *business reply mail*.

postage test Test mailings in which different segments use different rates of postage, such as first-class vs. third-class, or metered postal indicia vs. printed indicia, or stamp vs. metered indicia.

postal code An international term for a combination of numbers only or numbers and letters used to aid processing and delivery of mail. See also *postcode (U.K.); ZIP code*.

postal indicia/indicia Imprinted designation used on mail to denote payment of postage. Postal regulations require that the printed postal indicia always be on the side along the fold of a self-mailer.

postcard A single-sheet self-mailer meeting USPS requirements both as to dimensions and thickness (.007″ minimum). See also *paper sizes*.

postcard mailing 1. A mailing of postcards. 2. Another term used to describe a card deck. See *card deck*.

postcard packs See *card deck; card pack*.

postcode (U.K.) Term of reference for the United Kingdom postal code—the counterpart of the U.S. ZIP code. See also *postal code*.

poster A sheet, usually of cardboard or heavy paper, with an announcement on one side affixed to a panel or window at point of sale, on a bulletin board, or at a book display. When attached to an easel, it stands on a counter or table. See also *poster cardboard sizes*.

poster cardboard sizes Standard sizes of poster cardboard are 28″ × 44″, 22″ × 28″, 14″ × 22″, 11″ × 14″, and 11″ × 28″.

poster reproduction When a single poster is needed, usually it is best to have it photocomposed and mounted or hand painted. For larger quantities, duplicates of photocomposed matter are useful on quantities up to five or ten. Beyond that, silk screening may be most economical. For larger runs or large quantities, offset printing is most economical.

postscript, sales letter   The "P.S." is the most highly read part of a sales letter. Its primary objective should be to urge the reader to take a desired action.

PPB   The three primary manufacturing costs of a book: paper, printing, and binding.

ppi   pages-per-inch. The number of sheets in a stack of paper one-inch high. See also *bulking paper.*

PPMG   See *Professional Publishers' Marketing Group (PPMG).*

PR Aids   A computerized system of publicity activities developed by PR Aids, Inc., for distributing news releases and announcements, as well as review copies, to critics and editors in all media. Address: 330 West 34th Street, New York, NY 10001. Phone: 212-947-7733.

prebinds/prebinding   A special reinforced binding done to standards of the Library Binding Institute and desired by librarians, particularly for children's books to ensure longer wear and more circulations. Process includes oversewing, rounding and backing of the spine, and cloth hinges.

precanceled-stamp mailing   Mailing in which postage is paid by stamps that are canceled before they are sold by the USPS. Use of precanceled stamps precludes having them canceled after mailing. For some promotions, precanceled stamps have been found more effective than a metered or printed postal indicia.

precanceled stamps, use of   Precanceled stamps are used mainly for payment of postage on bulk mailings. However, they may be used on single-piece or limited size mailings as long as proper amount of postage is paid. To use precanceled stamps, you must have an approved USPS permit Form 3620. See also *precanceled stamps, USPS usage rules.*

precanceled stamps, USPS usage rules   (1) Permit (Form 3620) required; (2) must be delivered to post office where permit is on file; (3) precanceled stamps may be used along with regular stamps on the same mailpiece for full payment of postage; (4) no Form 3620 is necessary if not used for a bulk mailing. See also *precanceled stamps, use of.*

preemptive bid   An aggressive bid by a reprint house to buy the rights of a trade book. So called when the bid is so high that no other offers are considered by the publisher, and the rights are immediately awarded to the preemptive bidder. This usually occurs after a reprinter has got an "early" or "first look" at the manuscript. See also *floor (reprint auction rights)*.

preferred position   A desired position for an advertisement in a magazine or journal for which an advertiser must pay a premium over the basic rate. For magazine covers a premium over the earned rate is almost always charged. See also *earned rate; run-of-paper position*.

prelims   The front matter of a book, usually folioed by lowercase roman numeral page numbers.

premium, list-building   A free offer in an advertisement or mailing designed to elicit names and addresses in the subject area related to the offer for mailing list building purposes.

premium book   1. A book used as a prize, bonus, or award given as an inducement for some action such as recommending a new customer or entering a periodical subscription. 2. A book used to induce larger purchases of products or services, or for good will or other public relations purposes.

premium bulk sales   See *special sales, premium*.

premium customer   One acquired as a result of a premium offer.

premium offer (book club)   See *book club premium offer*.

premium sales   A term used by some publishers to describe special sales activity. See *special sales*.

premium test (direct mail)   1. A test mailing in which different segments of the same audience are offered different premiums. A comparison is then made of the response from each type of premium. 2. Testing a mailing with and without a premium to determine if response rate will increase sales measurably more than the extra costs of the premium.

prepack   A counter display holding 10 to 20 copies of a book, and designed to be placed on a bookstore counter for impulse selling. See also *impulse purchase*.

prepack system (paperback)   A method of paperback distribution used by independent distributors (IDs). Under the system, the ID sends each book outlet a monthly selection of new titles appropriate for the rack space and book categories carried by that outlet. See also *routemen (paperback)*.

prepayment discount   A discount offered by some publishers for payment with order. Such discounts are usually about 5%, and some "bury" the discount by offering free shipment with prepayment.

prepayment required (journals)   A basic precept of all journal publishing programs. Payment must be received before a subscription will be entered.

preprint   Copies of a book or section of a book or periodical produced prior to publication for some special purpose. Preprints are sometimes used to generate early reviews or to stimulate bookseller interest at bookseller conventions.

prepub   Prior to publication.

prepublication discount   A discount off the list price offered for book orders placed with a publisher prior to publication.

prepublication offer   An offer of a discount off the announced list price of a book on orders received prior to the stated publication date. See also *prepublication price*.

prepublication orders/prepub orders   Orders received prior to the official publication date of a book, usually as a result of early promotion or sales solicitation. When used in reference to orders from booksellers, they are referred to as *advance orders*, or, simply "the advance."

prepublication price   A price offered by a publisher for orders placed prior to the publication date of a book. The price is usually less than the established list price. Where a high advance order volume is desired, the prepublication price may offer a considerable saving. See also *introductory price*; *prepublication discount*; *prepublication offer*.

prepublication review   A review published in advance of the book's official publication date.

preremainder sale   A sale by a publisher of surplus inventory directly to retailers at remainder prices on a nonreturnable basis.

presenting a book   1. A sales presentation of a book by a sales rep to a bookseller or to the buyer for a chain. See also *subscribing a book*. 2. Any sales conference presentation devoted to a single title prior to publication.

presort mail   See *first-class voluntary presort*.

press, good (book reviews)   See *good press/excellent press (book reviews)*.

press clipping service/bureau   An organization that employs readers trained to spot newspaper or periodical mentions of their clients. When such mentions are located, they are clipped, identified as to source, and mailed to clients on a regularly scheduled basis. The three largest are Burrelle's Press Clipping Service, 75 E. Northfield Avenue, Livingston, NJ 07039; Luce Press Clippings, Inc., 420 Lexington Avenue, New York, NY 10017 (other offices throughout the U.S.); and Bacon's Clipping Service, 14 E. Jackson Boulevard, Chicago, IL 60604. See also *press cutting agency*.

press conference   A meeting called to inform members of the press about a special or extremely newsworthy project or happening. Those present are permitted to ask questions in the development of news coverage of the subject. When held to promote a newsworthy book, press kits are often distributed. See *press kit*.

press cutting agency   U.K. usage for press clipping service. See also *press clipping service/bureau*.

press kit   An information package for publicity campaigns, usually a folder with flaps or pockets. Press kits for book promotions usually contain a news release, a glossy photo of author, information from the book, an author biography, quotes or reviews about the book, and articles about the author. See also *pitch letter*.

press proofs   A printed sheet drawn from the press before the start of the pressrun. If not requested as part of the printer's price quotation for the job, publishers will be charged for printed sheets, unless they can examine them at the press on the printer's premises at the time of makeready.

press release   See *news release; publicity/press release.*

pressrun   The quantity of books to be produced in a single printing.

pressure-sensitive label   An adhesive-backed label that will adhere to a mailing piece when applied with pressure. When computer prepared, such labels are 4 across and 12 deep per section. See also *peel-off label.*

pressure-sensitive paper   Paper stock with an adhesive coating that is protected by a backing sheet until used. When the backing is removed, the paper will stick without moistening with just the application of pressure.

previous year's net billing   The net amount billed during a one-year period by a publisher to a bookseller, after allowing for returns and credits. Often the basis for co-op advertising allowances. For example, a number of publishers provide cooperative advertising money equal to 5% of the previous year's net billing to the bookseller.

price, in advertising   The use of a price in advertising is a critical factor in buying decisions. A study by Cahners Publishing Company in 1986 indicated that 16% more people remembered ads bearing price than those that did not. See also *in press.*

price, introductory   See *introductory price.*

price, prepublication   See *prepublication price.*

price add-on (bookseller)   Some booksellers charge their retail customers a fixed percentage above the announced list price on books that are sold to them without any discount from the publisher.

price change timing   Trade publishers with active backlist sales should provide their bookstore customers with sufficient notice of impending backlist price increases to stock up at the current prices or to change the prices listed on their current inventory. Such notice can be provided via a price change listing in the classified section of *PW.*

price increases, end of edition   An occasional practice in some publishing establishments of increasing prices on an established work with a relatively stable sales pattern when it appears likely that inventories will not last until the appearance of the next edition and no further reprints are planned, or when no new edition is planned and it is felt the remaining inventory will sell out at any price.

price increases for inflation   The practice in some publishing establishments to increase prices selectively on a given date each year to reflect inflation and/or higher reprint costs. As a rule, highly competitive textbooks and other price-sensitive works are passed over or increased in price less frequently.

price positioning   1. Pricing a book with a view toward similar or competitive works. 2. Pricing a book at a level where it is less likely to meet sales resistance. 3. Pricing a book to ensure earliest possible commercial success or acceptance.

price protection   A publisher's guarantee to an account that a book's price will be guaranteed for a specified period of time. This is particularly applicable to mail-order catalog houses that offer books for sale and request such protection for the life of their catalog.

price resistance   1. The price level for a book at which it meets customer resistance or is perceived not to be of good value. 2. The level at which books will not be stocked or purchased. A number of libraries and booksellers on standing order ask publishers not to ship books over a certain price. 3. In college texts, the price a professor considers excessive for a text to be considered for his or her course needs. See also *price resistance point*.

price resistance point   The list price level for a particular book at which it meets customer resistance. A college text, for example, viewed as a good buy up to $39.95, might not be viewed as favorably at a price over $40, although the difference is small. See also *price resistance*; "*need to know*" (*book pricing and promotion*; "*nice to know*" (*book pricing and promotion*).

price sensitivity (books)   See "*need to know*" (*book pricing and promotion*) "*nice to know*" (*book pricing and promotion*).

price sensitivity (journals)   See *journal price sensitivity*.

price sensitivity, book   A book is said to be subject to price sensitivity when at a certain price or price range a perceived market or component of the book's market becomes reluctant to buy. The textbook market is considered the most price sensitive.

pricing, based in inventory availability   In the remainder end of the book trade, retail pricing often is based on available inventory, higher when available quantities are small, lower when quantities are ample. See also *remainder pricing*.

pricing, charging what the market will bear   The practice of setting a book or journal price as high as it is felt the market will accept without encountering serious sales resistance, or in the case of a journal, subscription cancellations. See also *differential pricing (journals)*.

pricing, encyclopedia   See *encyclopedia pricing*.

pricing, international   See *international pricing*.

pricing, remainder   See *remainder pricing*.

pricing differential in journal subscriptions   See *differential pricing (journals)*.

pricing factors for professional and reference books   See *yardsticks for pricing and promotion*.

pricing on industrial training sales   See *special sales, industrial training*.

pricing on initial STOP order   Approximately 700 publishers participate in the ABA Single Title Order Plan (STOP). These publishers generally will permit booksellers to calculate discounts using the prices shown in the current issues of either *Books in Print* or *Publishers Trade List Annual*. Because some publisher prices change after publication of these two works, they accept the *BIP* or *PTLA*-listed price only for the *first* STOP order of a given title. See other entries under *STOP*.

pricing on premium sales   See *special sales, premium*.

pricing studies, book   Studies conducted either to indicate which specific book prices are more likely to inspire book purchases or to ascertain established pricing patterns of a majority of publishers within a specific area of publishing. A published study made in 1984 of 35 U.S. chemistry book publishers indicated that most chemistry books under $40 had a price ending in ".95" while in the $40-$60 range, prices that did not end in even dollar amounts ended with a ".50". (From: *The Bookseller*, Jan. 12, 1985; study by Nat Bodian).

pricing what the traffic will bear   Pricing a work higher than similar works or works produced at similar cost to provide a higher-than-usual profit for the publisher. Sometimes done because the work is deemed to be essential and unlikely to meet price resistance, or to counterbalance other works that have been underpriced for competitive reasons. See also *price increases, end of edition*.

primary journal   See *core journal; primary scientific journal*.

primary letters   Letters of the alphabet having no ascenders or descenders. See also *ascender (typography); descender (typography)*.

primary market   The most likely buyers of a book or periodical.

primary prospect   The most appropriate prospect for a mail or telephone offer. For example, chemists would be prospects for a book on organic chemistry, but *organic chemists* would be primary prospects.

primary scientific journal   A journal that provides a forum for ongoing researchers in a particular scientific field and is recognized as the primary medium for publication of peer-reviewed research papers. It usually has an editorial board of acknowledged leaders in the field. Also referred to as a *core journal*.

print advertising   See *space advertising*.

print-and-tumble   See *work-and-tumble*.

print-and-turn   See *work-and-turn*.

printed matter, size indications in   See *size indications in printed matter*.

printer's error (PE)   An error in printing composition attributable to the compositor or printer. Such errors are not chargeable to the customer. Also called *compositor's error*.

printing, crash   See *crash printing.*

printing (book pressruns)   The output of a single pressrun of any edition of a book is called a printing. Printings after the first that are made from the same type, print negatives, or plates, are often enumerated on the copyright page, sometimes indicating the date of each printing. For book collectors, the first printing of the first edition of a book usually has a special value.

printing broker   A seller of printing who subcontracts the work to a printer having the right equipment for the job and who can meet the timely delivery requirements of the customer.

printing completion date (direct mail)   The date by which all the printed components of a mailing must be completed and in the hands of the mailing house. Ideally, this date should precede by several days the assembly date. See also *direct-mail promotion assembly date.*

printing process   See *letterpress printing; offset printing (offset lithography); one-color printing; web-fed offset press; web-fed rotary letterpress.*

printing quotation   A price supplied in writing by a printer for a particular job describing all of the services involved in the fulfillment of that job. When signed by the recipient, it becomes a binding contract, subject to all of the printing trade customs usually printed on the reverse side. See also *printing trade customs.*

printing trade customs   The commonly accepted rules of the printing industry. They are usually in fine print on the back side of a printing quotation. Quotations from printers are good for 30 days.

print product   A product printed with ink on paper.

print quantities (promotion)   In determining the print quantity for a job, persons ordering promotion materials should allow for a legal underrun from their printer as well as for spoilage during addressing and inserting. See *overrun* or *underrun (printing); spoilage.*

print run   The number of copies of a publication produced at one printing.

proceedings, published   See *conference proceedings.*

process color See *color printing.*

process printing Printing from two or more halftone plates to produce intermediate colors and shades. See also *four-color process printing (4/C).*

product advertisement Advertisement designed to sell the products listed. See also *institutional advertisement.*

production (book) In the U.S., all necessary steps to produce a book up to, but not including, the actual manufacture, i.e., printing, binding, and jacketing of a book. In the U.K., all of those steps necessary to produce a complete book, including manufacturing.

product line A group of related products, or a group of products within a publishing establishment that have been grouped for reasons of affinity, convenience, or more efficient control. Examples: A product line of all professional books, all encyclopedias, all books on computer science and engineering, etc.

product manager An individual within a publishing establishment who is responsible for coordinating, scheduling, and managing all aspects of marketing and promotion for a specific product, product group, or product line. In some publishing establishments, product managers have complete editorial and design control as well.

product mix 1. The types of books available for a promotion or offering. 2. The mix of products and product lines that make up a publisher's list. 3. The mix of publications offered in a mailing or catalog.

product news magazine A magazine, usually controlled circulation and in tabloid format, providing literature or information on equipment or services for a business or professional audience. Most enable the reader to obtain desired literature by circling a number on a reader service card. See also *reader service card.*

product-oriented tabloid See *product news magazine.*

product test Test of different products or variations of the same product to a given market, audience, or group of markets. See also *market test.*

professional and reference book publishing   1. Publication of books for professional audiences and the reference collections of libraries. Such books often have limited appeal and short pressruns and, therefore, are usually sold at short discount. P&R books are not normally stocked in bookstores, and publishers rely on direct marketing to reach their primary audiences. Some stores will special order such books when requested to do so. 2. In a few publishing houses, the term "professional and reference" is reserved for loose-leaf services, encyclopedic references, and highly specialized reference works. See also *textbook publishing; trade publishing*.

professional association book publishing   (1) Publishing proposals usually originate with the membership; (2) the membership provides a ready source of buyers; (3) the publishing program is viewed as a member service; (4) the organization relies heavily on its own publications and membership lists for space ads and mailings. See also *commercial publisher; university press*.

professional association co-publishing   An association may strike an agreement with a commercial publisher whereby the latter handles some or all marketing aspects of the association's publishing program. Sometimes the association or society will retain sales rights for its membership only, while the commercial publisher will hold all other rights. Other times, the commercial publisher will hold all sales rights, but with special prices to association or society members. Still another way is for the association to hold domestic rights, but give foreign rights to a commercial house.

professional book club   A book club offering books related to a single profession or scientific discipline, in which all offerings appeal to the members' work-related interests. See also *book club; special interest book club*.

professional books   1. Books directed at professional people and specifically related to their work (AAP definition). 2. Books that satisfy the continuing educational needs of practicing professionals after they have finished using textbooks (Adapted from article by Harry R. Most in *Publishers Weekly*, March 21, 1977). 3. A work by a practicing or teaching professional or scholar and intended for the author's peers in the same activity.

professional books, sales patterns See *sales patterns for technical, professional and reference books (rule-of-thumb)*.

professional business book (PBB) A book of interest to professionals working in a business area. Sales of such titles take off much more quickly than scientific or technical books, are likely to be candidates for large-chain purchases and book club adoptions, can be produced more readily than a scientific work, and are not heavily affected by competitive titles in the same subject area. They require a trade-type jacket, may need solo mail promotion, and usually will not do well in either the college or international markets.

professional desktop publishing See *desktop publishing, professional*.

professional discount Typically a discount afforded by some publishers to school and college faculty or staff who order books on institutional stationery.

Professional Publishers' Marketing Group (PPMG) An organization of marketing executives concerned with improving the marketing of professional books and journals. Organized January 16, 1981, in New York City, PPMG's originator was Peter Hodges, formerly of John Wiley & Sons, Inc., and now an independent publishing-marketing consultant. The organization conducts day-long marketing seminars in New York City, usually in May and November.

professional, technical, and reference books See *P&R title*.

professional trade book A book aimed at professionals, but with sufficiently high sales potential to be offered at trade discount. A professional trade book will have a more attractive jacket than its short-discount counterpart in order to have more shelf-display appeal.

profile, approval plan See *approval plan profile*.

pro forma invoice An invoice that must be paid before the publisher will dispatch the book or books that have been ordered. Pro forma invoices are used to preclude collection problems when the buyer does not have an established account with the publisher, for journal subscriptions, and on international orders.

program (computer)   A collection of instructions designed to make a computer perform a specific task.

progressives/progressive proofs   Individual impressions taken from color printing plates showing the reproduction of each color alone. Impressions are combined and rotated with succeeding colors. The final combination of all of the colors then shows the final color reproduction.

progs   See *progressives/progressive proofs.*

project   In publishing promotion, a specific activity involving a book, event, or well-defined activity with a specific time frame. Also used to define a specific segment of a program.

projected conversion rate   An estimate of the annual percentage of responders or inquirers over a period of years who will enter subscriptions for a particular subscription product. Projections are often made on a year-by-year basis for five years in journals and newsletter sales forecasts.

projected renewal term rate (subscription products)   An estimate of the rate at which new subscribers will convert to a first-year renewal on their subscriptions. In subsequent years (from the third year on) of a subscription, these subscribers are considered official renewals and are part of the renewal rate of the publication.

promotion   (1) All activities involved in communicating the desirable qualities of a published project or about-to-be published product to its markets and/or to the public at large; (2) any effort intended to produce sales advertising, publicity, displays, etc.; (3) all aspects of a single marketing or promotional effort or event. Individuals responsible for management of book promotion were at one time referred to as *promotion managers,* but are now known as *marketing managers.*

promotion, cluster   See *cluster promotion.*

promotion, three-step   See *three-step promotion.*

promotion, two-step   See *two-step promotion.*

promotional book   Usually out-of-print former trade titles, often heavily illustrated, on any of a wide range of popular subjects. They are inexpensively reprinted to sell at low prices to bargain-minded individuals, especially as holiday gift items. Most are produced by remainder dealers in-house or are obtained from outside packagers. See also *bargain books; remainder.*

promotional video   The use of a publisher's promotional videotape in a bookstore or at a trade show display to call attention to a specific book. For certain types of trade books, such videotapes are very effective.

promotion budget   An allocation devoted to promotion of new and backlist books. Often a percentage of previous year's sales and tied to sales forecast for budgeted year including an adjustment for inflation. See also *contractual promotion commitment.*

promotion plan   See *marketing plan.*

proof of ad (bookseller co-op advertising)   To receive reimbursement for an authorized cooperative advertisement from a publisher, booksellers must submit proof of ad and original invoice by the advertising medium, usually within 90 days of insertion date.

proof of mailing   When a lettershop or mailing house deposits a mailing at a postal facility, it is issued a Form 3602 or a Form 3602PC. This serves as proof of mailing and provides weight per piece mailed, total number of pieces, rate charged, and name of permit holder.

proofreader's marks   A group of standardized indications used to correct a printer's proof when comparing it with the original manuscript.

proofreading   The act of reading copy or a printer's proof against the original manuscript for the purpose of detecting and correcting errors.

proofs   Sample impressions of type composition supplied by a printer or compositor for checking and correction. After proofreading, one set, marked "master set," is returned, signed, and appropriately noted with "O.K." or "approved with corrections," etc.

proprietary publishing/private labeling   The practice of a publisher giving exclusive distribution rights on a book to a store or group of stores, or a single distribution source for a specified period of time. Example: When *USA Today* published *BusCa-*

pade in late 1987, it gave the 950-store Waldenbook chain exclusive retail rights to the title until the summer of 1988.

prospect list See *inquiry list*.

prospectus A detailed, formal presentation describing a forthcoming major publication. Usually prepared for serial works, encyclopedias, and major works that require detailed information for a purchasing decision. An elaborate, illustrated prospectus is appropriate, even necessary, to convey the merits of a high-ticket publication. See also *brochure*.

protected A book trade term meaning a book that may be returned to the publisher for credit if unsold. The term "fully protected," when applied to a publisher's list, means all unsold books are returnable. U.K.: sell safe. See also *return privilege*.

protected mailing date A mailing date is said to be protected when a list owner guarantees that a list will not be rented to any other user for an agreed upon period prior to and following the mailing of a particular list renter. See also *assigned mailing date*.

protection (book price) See *price protection*.

PSP The professional and scholarly publishing division of the Association of American Publishers. This division incorporates publishers of books, journals, loose-leaf, and other media in technology, science, medicine, business, humanities, law, and the social and behavioral sciences. See also *PSP book*; *PSP publisher*.

PSP book 1. A professional or scholarly book, so named because of the renaming in November 1979 of the AAP division for publishers of such publications as the Professional and Scholarly Publishing Division. Previously, when the AAP division was known as the Scientific, Technical, and Medical Division, or STM Division, such books were known as STM books. 2. A book bought by a person who is seeking professional information, or how to succeed in his or her profession. See also *professional books*.

PSP publisher A publisher of professional and scholarly books, though not necessarily a member of the PSP division of the Association of American Publishers.

psychographics   Study of differences in personality and life-style (psychographic characteristics) within a demographic group. Provides insights into individual psychological characteristics and their possible influence on buying patterns and preferences. See also *demographics/demographic characteristics.*

PTLA   See *Publishers Trade List Annual.*

PTLA **price**   The price shown for a published work in *Publishers Trade List Annual (PTLA).* Under the ABA's single title order plan, many of the participating publishers will honor bookseller orders at the price listed in the current edition of either *Publishers Trade List Annual* or *Books in Print.*

PTR title   Refers to professional, technical, and reference books. See also *P&R title.*

pub date   See *publication date/pub date.*

publication advertising   See *space advertising.*

publication date/pub date   The publisher's official or record date a book becomes available for sale. A publisher often ships a book to the trade in advance of this date with instructions not to release until publication date. 1. The publication date, when applied to trade titles, is mainly for the benefit of the major media reviewers (particularly the *New York Times Book Review*) to give them sufficient lead time to review a book on publication date. 2. The publication date, when applied to scientific, technical, and reference books, and textbooks, often refers simply to the year of publication, giving librarians and scholars an indication of the newness of the material. Some publishers protect PSP and textbooks published in the last quarter of a calendar year by assigning a copyright date for the upcoming year. See also *availability date; bound book date.*

publication dates, backlist   Promotional material for backlist titles should always include publication dates so customers, especially librarians, can distinguish between forthcoming and previously published titles.

Publication Reference File   A biweekly microfiche publication of the U.S. Government Printing Office listing the more than 14,000 titles it has for sale.

publication-set advertisement   An advertisement for which the type has been set for the advertiser by the publication that will run the ad. Many publications do not charge for normal publication-set advertisements when provided with copy, layout, and clear instructions for composition. Most require that copy be in 20 to 30 days prior to official closing date for advertising.

publication slip   See *review slip*.

publication year (mail-order catalog)   Some mail-order catalog houses issue annual catalogs. They refer to the active life of the catalog as the publication year, and often ask participating publishers to provide price protection during that period for each book listed in the catalog. See also *price protection; year of publication (directories and annuals)*.

publicist, book   An individual, usually in the publicity or promotion department of a publishing establishment, whose primary responsibility is to generate media attention for the books published by and the authors connected with his or her house. Specific duties include establishing and maintaining contact with reviewers, sending out review copies and press releases, organizing publication parties, scheduling book-and-author luncheon talks, and arranging author interviews in newspapers or guest spots on a local radio or TV program.

publicity (book)   1. The news aspect of book promotion. 2. Any activity designed to bring a book's message to potential buyers that is not directly paid for. 3. Actions on behalf of a book that will generate interest in it by consumers, booksellers, reviewers, or others. 4. Any activity that gets the author's name before the public and reinforces his or her reputation and credentials. 5. Sometimes refers to book reviews, a primary channel of book publicity.

publicity (general)   Generally used to describe all media attention generated in support of a product, service, or effort that is not directly purchased. However, most book marketers agree that the best publicity for a book is "word of mouth." The term "publicity" also includes mentions of a book or author exposure on radio and TV. See also *publicity (book)*.

publicity/press release   A statement issued to the press for publicity purposes. While the intent of the publicity release sender is to obtain publicity, for the release to be considered or effective, it must be viewed by the recipient not as "publicity," but as "news." Consequently, publicity releases look better and appear to be more acceptable if headed "News Release." In publishing, a "release" is frequently an enclosure with a review copy of a book providing detailed information on the accompanying work. For many types of books, the review is often a pickup from the accompanying release. This is particularly true of trade or general publications that have a single individual responsible for preparation of all book reviews. It would not apply to professional, scientific, or scholarly periodicals that publish reviews by individuals who are experts in the field covered. See also *news release*.

publicity, word of mouth   The most frequent and strongest reason why individuals read trade books. Any and all other forms of publicity contribute to this strongest and most effective aspect of book publicity.

publicity department media relations   Dealings between publisher publicity staff and the media. Such relationships must always be on a highly ethical basis, consistent, and oriented toward the editorial interests and needs of the media.

publicity information sheet   A sheet used by the publicity department in a publishing establishment to obtain background information from an author such as business or professional affiliation, educational background, honors and awards received, and other published works. See Appendix 4.

publicity mailing lists   See *Bacon's Computerized Media Band (publicity)*.

publicity off the book page   See *off-the-book-page publicity*.

publicity tour   See *author tour*.

public library   A noncommercial library for the use of the general public. The programs and purposes of public libraries vary with their communities, but generally seek (1) to support the development of individuals and groups of all ages through educational materials; (2) to satisfy the information needs of patrons and community; (3) to provide a center for cultural life within a community; (4) to encourage the positive use of leisure time by providing material for pleasure reading and relaxation. Public libraries buy books throughout the year within budget limitations, although their fiscal year usually runs from July to June.

public library book budgets in the U.S. (1) More than $100,000: 342 libraries; (2) $50,000-$100,000: 942 libraries; (3) $25,000-$50,000: 1,483 libraries; (4) $10,000-$25,000: 2,655 libraries; (5) $5,000 to $10,000: 3,833 libraries; (6) $1,000-$5,000: 6,986 libraries.

public library market, U.S. Approximately 8,800 main libraries and 6,350 branches.

public library primary review media See *library review media, public library.*

public record A means of establishing the existance of a published work. New books are entered on the public record by sending finished copies to the R.R. Bowker Weekly Record Department, 245 W. 17th Street, New York, NY 10011, and to the H.W. Wilson Co., *Cumulative Book Index,* 950 University Avenue, Bronx, NY 10452. Books then are listed in *The Weekly Record* (Bowker), *The American Book Publishing Record* (Bowker), and in *Cumulative Book Index* (Wilson). U.K.: *Whitaker's Forms* achieve this; also *Blackwell's Bookline* and *Perline,* and *Teleordering.*

PubLinx An online service for publishers of the Faxon Company of Westwood, Massachusetts, one of the world's largest subscription agents. It offers publishers, at minimal cost, the capability of receiving and responding online to claims, cancellation requests, customer address change notifications, and back issue orders.

published price Price set by the publisher at the time of publication. See also *list price/retail price.*

publisher, A&I See *A&I Publisher.*

publisher, CD-ROM See *CD-ROM; CD-ROM publishing.*

publisher, children's books See *children's book publisher; children's books.*

publisher, college textbook See *college textbook publisher.*

publisher, ELT See *ELT publisher.*

publisher, ESL See *ELS publisher.*

publisher, frontlist See *frontlist publisher.*

publisher, healthcare See *medical publisher.*

publisher, loose-leaf See *loose-leaf publishing.*

publisher, mail-order See *mail-order publisher.*

publisher, medical See *medical publisher.*

publisher, PSP See *PSP publisher.*

publisher, regional. See *regional publisher.*

publisher, sci-tech. See *sci-tech publisher; STM publisher.*

publisher, serial See *serial publisher.*

publisher, short-discount See *short-discount publisher.*

publisher, society See *professional association book publishing; society publisher.*

publisher, STM See *STM publisher/company.*

publisher, textbook See *textbook publisher.*

publisher, university press See *university press.*

publisher cooperative advertising policies See *retail cooperative advertising policy.*

publisher distribution arrangements, foreign See *distributing booksellers, international; European agent; U.K. and European distribution sources.*

publisher 800 telephone ordering See *800 telephone numbers, book publisher.*

publishers, major types (1) commerical publisher; (2) university press; (3) association and society.

The Publishers' Association (P.A.) An organization founded in 1986, and open to any United Kingdom publisher whose business is the publication of books. Its membership produces over

90% of all books published in the U.K. Address: 19 Bedford Square, London WC1B 3HJ, England.

Publishers Book Exhibit   A cooperative book exhibit service dealing primarily in library meetings. Covers approximately 50 conferences and association meetings a year. Displays books, periodicals, audio cassettes, and video tapes. Address: 86 Millwood Road, Millwood, NY 10546. Phone: 914-762-2422.

The Publisher's Direct Mail Handbook   A comprehensive volume by Nat Bodian on all aspects of direct-mail promotion, including guidelines, techniques, and case histories based on the experience of leading mail marketers in book and journal publishing. The first comprehensive work devoted exclusively to publisher mail marketing techniques and research. Published in 1987 by ISI Press, 3501 Market Street, Philadelphia, PA 19104. Phone: 800-523-1850.

Publishers, Distributors and Wholesalers (PAD) Online Database
An online database identifying over 44,000 U.S. publishers, 1,500 distributors, 1,500 wholesalers, 1,800 book trade associations, and 3,500 software publishers. From: R.R. Bowker, 245 West 17th Street, New York, NY 10011.

publisher's imprint (in advertising)   The publisher identification in a book advertisement is a key selling feature. Many librarians and booksellers will buy a book sight unseen if the advertising for it indicates it is from a publishing establishment with a good reputation and a strong established list in a particular field. In advertising in specialized journals, the publisher's imprint at the top of the advertisement often is the strongest headline possible, and many houses regularly head their new title offerings "New from _____ " and draw highest readership scores for ads.

Publishers Information Cards Service (PICS)   Small cards designed to present the information that librarians in the U.K. require. Produced by IBIS Information Services, London, which will produce and supply to subscribing publishers, or mail directly to U.K. libraries. See also *IBIS Information Services*.

Publishers in the UK & Their Addresses   A directory of more than 2,000 publishers and their addresses, with publisher prefixes in ISBN sequence. Printed single column on double-column pages and issued annually in April by J. Whitaker & Sons Ltd., 12 Dyott Street, London WC1A 1DF, England.

publishers' invoice symbols See *invoice symbols.*

Publishers' Library Marketing Group (PLMG) An organization of employees of publishing companies engaged in the promotion of trade books and paperbacks of interest to schools and libraries. Founded in 1965. Monthly meetings in New York City. Write c/o Donne Forrest, E.P. Dutton Co., Two Park Avenue, New York, NY 10016.

Publisher's Multinational Direct A monthly methods-oriented newsletter for publishers using direct marketing to reach international markets. Published by Direct International Inc., 150 E. 74th Street, New York, NY 10021.

Publishers Publicity Association (PPA) An association of publicity directors of publishing houses and their staff members, as well as media representatives. The 250-member organization holds monthly luncheon meetings in New York City. Write c/o Jill Danzig, Peter Bedrick Books, 125 E. 23th Street, New York, NY 10010.

publisher's representative A salesperson who calls on the publisher's customers and prospective customers is referred to as a *sales rep.* See also *pub rep; sales rep/sales representative.*

publisher's row An area at a trade show or convention limited to publishers' exhibits. See also *exhibit floor plan.*

Publishers' Row card deck program A program of card deck mailings to individuals in various medical specialties. Participating publishers of medical products participate by paying a percentage commission on each title sold. In 1987, the program's fourth year, over 25 publishers had participated. For information, write: Publishers' Row, Suite 441, 59 Temple Place, Boston, MA 02111. Phone: 800-222-3790.

Publishers' Trade List Annual (PTLA) A hardbound collection of the catalogs and booklists of more than 1,500 publishers in the United States. Published annually in six volumes by R.R. Bowker. This is Bowker's oldest publication, issued since 1878.

Publishers Weekly: The Journal of the Book Industry The weekly periodical of the U.S. book industry, its circulation of approximately 36,000 is spread among individuals in the publishing industry, booksellers, and librarians. It is the primary advertising announcement vehicle to the retail book trade. Because it carries about 5,000 reviews a year on new and forthcoming books, it has a substantial library circulation. The 1986 Bowker catalog showed 5,907 bookseller subscribers in the U.S., and over 10,000 library subscribers, including over 6,100 U.S. public libraries. Published by Bowker Magazine Group at 249 West 17th Street, New York, NY 10011. Phone: 212-645-9700.

publishing, learned society   See *learned society publishing mandate.*

publishing, licensed book   See *licensed book publishing.*

publishing, professional desktop   See *desktop publishing, professional.*

publishing, religious book   See *religious book.*

publishing, travel book   See *travel book publishing.*

publishing, university press   See *university press publishing mandate.*

Publishing Marketplace   A special section of *Publishers Weekly* designed to make advertising affordable for small publishers. Consists of ⅑ page ads printed on bright yellow background for high visibility and priced at $395 per $2\frac{1}{8}'' \times 3\frac{1}{16}''$ unit, composition included, payable in advance to *Publishers Weekly Marketplace.*

Publishing News (PN)   A British biweekly publication for the book industry published on alternate Fridays by Gradegate Ltd., 43 Museum Street, London WC1A 1LY, England.

publishing newsletters   See *AAP Newsletter; Book Marketing Update; Booknotes; BP Report; COSMEP Newsletter; International Publishing Newsletter; Publisher's Multinational Direct; Publishing News (PN); Publishing Northwest; Resources for Book Publishers; Society for Scholarly Publishing Letter.*

Publishing Newsletters, Revised Edition   A comprehensive reference and sourcebook on newsletter publishing by Howard Penn Hudson of Newsletter Clearinghouse and published in 1988 by Charles Scribner's Sons, New York.

Publishing Northwest   A bimonthly newsletter promoting books published by presses in the Northwest. Address: Te-Cum-Tom Enterprises, 5770 Franson Court, North Bend, OR 97459.

publishing on demand   See *on-demand publishing.*

publishing war stories   Informal case histories generally pointing out some lesson learned or making a significant point about a sales or promotion effort.

PUBNET   An electronic book ordering system for college bookstores, jointly sponsored by the Association of American Publishers and the National Association of College Stores, and developed by the General Electric Company.

pub rep   The advertising sales representative for a magazine. Also called *media rep or space salesman.*

pubset ad   See *publication-set advertisement.*

pubset type (publication-set type)   Type matter set by a periodical or newspaper from copy supplied by the advertiser, for an advertisement to be published at a future date. Most newspapers and larger periodicals will charge only for the space purchased, the composition being supplied free when requested by the advertiser. Most smaller circulation and scholarly periodicals charge for composition at their cost, or at a nominal fee.

pull   The rate of response on a mail promotion effort. U.K.: also refers to a letterpress proof. See also *response rate (direct mail).*

purge   Eliminating duplicate or undesirable items from a file, e.g., unwanted names from a mailing list. See also *merge-purge (mailing list).*

PW   See *Publishers Weekly: The Journal of the Book Industry*

pyramiding   Testing a mailing list by mailing to increasingly larger quantities of the same list, based on success of the smaller samples. See also *list testing; rollout/roll out/rollout mailing.*

Q

quad left   Flush left.

quad right   Flush right.

qualified bidder   Bidder deemed qualified to enter a bid for a book supply contract. A book supplier who has held a contract and performed poorly may be disqualified as a bidder when the contract is up for renewal.

qualified inquirer/prospect   Person who, by the nature of his or her job function, profession, or place of employment is viewed as a likely buyer of an offering.

qualified lead/inquiry/response   Any respondent to a promotional effort whose interest in making a purchase is likely to be high on account of measures (qualifiers) taken by the sponsoring publisher to discourage casual responses. A mail marketer may qualify an inquiry by requiring payment of postage; a textbook publisher may require full course information before sending an examination book; a catalog house may ask a nominal charge for a catalog; or an inquirer may be telephoned to establish serious interest.

qualified person (telemarketing)   The essential practice in all telemarketing campaigns of establishing that the person taking the call is qualified, by title or job function, to respond to the offer.

qualified readership   A preferred term for recipients of controlled circulation business and professional publications. See also *controlled circulation; unqualified reader.*

qualify a lead   To establish a prospective buyer's interest before sending a catalog, brochure, or sample copy. One way is to have inquirer pay own postage on inquiry, or by asking a token payment for a catalog or sample.   See also *place stamp here.*

qualitative marketing research   An in-depth analysis of responses from a research study without use of statistical measurements. The most effective form of qualitative market research is the focus group interview. See also *focus group.*

quality of response (direct mail)   An important factor in the measurement of any direct-mail effort is not only the response rate (number of responses), but also the quality of response— how many paid up, how many returned the ordered book or product, how many of those receiving books on approval failed either to pay up or return the book. A small response from a high-quality (well targeted) list is often better than a larger response from a poor-quality list. See also *back end results.*

quality paperback   See *trade paperback.*

quantity, estimated mailing   See *estimated mailing quantity.*

quantity, print   See *print quantities (promotion).*

quantity, total mailing   See *total mailing quantity (direct mail).*

quantity discount   A discount offered by a publisher (or wholesaler) to booksellers who purchase a required number of books, either assorted titles or multiple copies of a single title. Such discounts may also be offered to other types of buyers for multiple book purchases on the same purchase order.

quarterly   1. A journal or other publication having four issues per year. 2. The frequency designation in catalog copy for journals having four issues a year.

questionnaire (author)   See *author questionnaire/marketing questionnaire.*

questionnaire (special sales)   See *special sales questionnaire.*

quick copy   See *quick printing.*

quick copy shop   A printing trade term for a neighborhood retail printing establishment that does quick printing. See also *quick printing*.

quick printing   Printing done by small establishments that are able to produce simple printing jobs in one color on standard size sheets of paper either while you wait or within a few hours. A valuable aid for publishing promotion when a few hundred fliers are needed instantly for an upcoming convention or when convention price lists run out midway through an exhibit. Such shops can print a quick letter promotion. Also called *instant printing* or *quick copy*.

Quill & Quire   The monthly news magazine of the Canadian book trade. Address: Suite 213, 56 The Esplanade, Toronto, Ontario M5S 1A6, Canada. Phone: 416-364-3333.

quotation/quote (printing)   An estimate from a printer for a pending job. A quotation is usually good for 30 days. See also *alterations; press proofs*.

quote (book publicity)   A passage or phrase, usually between quotation marks, that says something positive about a book. See also *review excerpt/book review excerpt; review quote*.

quote cards (bookselling)   Cards used by specialist and antiquarian booksellers to respond to advertisements placed by other book dealers in *AB Bookman's Weekly* for "wanted" lists of out-of-print books. Booksellers receiving such cards have a period, usually 30 days, to respond with an order. See also *AB Bookman's Weekly; out-of-print book searching*.

quotes (advertising)   Favorable comments, endorsements, or recommendations in book advertising or on a book jacket, designed to encourage interest in a book. Quotes are often obtained in advance of publication from manuscript or galleys so as to be received early enough to include on the book's jacket. See also *review excerpt/book review excerpt; review quote; testimonials (promotion)*.

quotes, cover   See *cover quotes*.

quote source   The originator or source of material used between quotation marks either on a book jacket or in advertising or promotion about a book. Quotes lacking a source are uneffective and should not be used.

qwerty keyboard   A term applied to a keyboard using the same letter arrangement as that of a standard typewriter. The qwerty arrangement originated with the introduction of the first Remington typewriter on September 12, 1873.

R

rack jobber Independent distributors who fill the mass market paperback racks in retail outlets of non-book-oriented businesses, such as drug stores. Title choice and display position are determined by the ID rather than the retail outlet. See also *independent distributor (ID)*; *rack-size paperback*.

rack-size paperback Paper covered books mass-produced to a standard size (approximately $4\frac{1}{16}''$ wide by $6\frac{7}{8}''$ high) for sale from racks in news stands, drug stores, supermarkets, and other nonbook outlets, as well as in traditional bookstores. See *mass market paperback*.

ragged right/rag right Copy with unjustified right-hand margin.

rag rt An instruction in art and type composition to indicate that composition is to be set flush left and ragged or unjustified on the right.

rail/side rail (conventions and exhibits) A low, usually metal rail, or divider used to separate exhibits. It is often useful, when in an end-of-aisle booth, to take down the rail so that access to the exhibit may be gained from the side as well as the front.

random selection See *Nth name selection*.

rare book dealer A buyer and seller of expensive, hard-to-find copies of out-of-print books, who serves mostly collectors, often by mail, working out of a shop, office, or home. See also *antiquarian book dealer*; *out-of-print dealer*; *used book dealer*.

rate See *contract rate*; *short rate (direct mail)*.

rate card See *advertising rate card*.

300

rate of return (direct mail)   Usually expressed as a percentage that compares the number of responses generated by a mailing with the number of pieces mailed or delivered. See *response rate (direct mail)*.

rate of returns (bookstore)   Generally refers to ratio of books returned by a bookseller as a percentage of total books ordered. A bookseller returning 30 books out of every 100 ordered would have a 30% rate of returns.

rate of sale (bookstore)   The sales movement of a title regularly stocked in a bookstore—sometimes monitored on a weekly basis, sometimes less frequently. See also *stock on hand (bookstore)*.

RBB   See *Reference Books Bulletin*.

reader   1. Book publishers refer to those who buy and read books as "readers," and they track the habits of readers through survey research. In the world of trade books, for instance, there are more readers among women than men. Books on some topics may not sell because there are few readers among those interested in the subject. 2. An individual employed to read and evaluate manuscripts for their publishing potential. 3. A device capable of transcribing data from an input medium. 4. A device that enlarges a microform image so that it can be read by the naked eye. See also *optical character recognition; optical scanning*.

reader-printer   A dual purpose device that enlarges microimages for viewing and that can produce a paper copy of the enlargement.

reader service card   A business reply card that is bound into a periodical to facilitate reader inquiries about products and services advertised or mentioned in the publication. The ads of participating advertisers are numbered so prospects can circle the corresponding number on the reader service card and mail it in. Inquiries are then forwarded from the publication to the advertiser for follow-up. In some cases, reader service cards can be used for ordering advertised books. Also called *bingo card*.

reader-service-card book ad   A book advertising technique pioneered by Nat Bodian at American Elsevier in the 1960s and refined at Wiley in the 1970s and 1980s for the direct sale of professional and reference books. It is based on multi-book advertising in a business periodical carrying a reader service card. Each book in the advertisement bears an order number that is matched by a like number on the reader service card. The reader of the publication circles the reader service card matching number to order the book.

readership   The number of people who read a publication as contrasted with the number of subscribers. See also *circulation; pass-along readership; readership study.*

readership study   A study conducted on behalf of a publication in an effort to acquaint current and prospective advertisers with the readers of the publication.

ream   A unit of 500 sheets of paper in a given size.

rebate   See *advertising rebate.*

recency (of names)   A mail-order term meaning the amount of time elapsed since the customer's last purchase, or the most recent activity recorded. See also *frequency; hotline list (direct mail).*

reciprocity requirement (mailing lists)   See *list rental reciprocity requirement (direct mail).*

recommended supplementary reading   Books recommended but not assigned as required texts by a professor for a course to be read on a voluntary basis. In the social sciences, such lists can be extensive. See also *required text.*

recommended text   See *recommended supplementary reading.*

recto   The right-hand page of a printed publication, usually odd-numbered. See also *verso.*

reduction   Photographically decreasing an image to a desired size. An 8″ × 10″ photo or block of copy reduced to 4″ × 5″ would be "scaled 50%." See also *scale.*

referee   An expert on a subject to whom an editor sends a manuscript of a journal article or book for evaluation. Also known as a *reviewer.*

refereed journal   Journal in which all of the articles appearing have been reviewed by competent peers of the authors who attest to their originality, quality, completeness, and clarity. Referees also establish whether the articles fall within the scope of the journal. Also known as *peer-reviewed journal*.

reference, direct   A one-stop source that provides the user with the information being sought, such as a dictionary or encyclopedia.

reference, indirect   Source that tells the user where to find desired information, such as an index or bibliography.

reference, popular   A general reference work intended for large audiences, such as an income tax guide or world almanac, in contrast to one intended mainly for use by librarians and other professionals.

reference book/reference   A work containing a body of information that is organized to provide convenient access to specific items or aspects of that information, rather than to be read from cover to cover. Most are purchased by libraries and educational institutions. See also *reference, direct; reference, indirect.*

reference books, sales patterns   See *sales patterns for technical, professional, and reference books (rule-of-thumb).*

Reference Books Bulletin (RBB)   A major source of in-depth reference books reviews, *RBB* appears as a bound insert in the center of the American Library Association semimonthly (monthly in July and August) evaluation publication, *Booklist.* It has its own review board, operating independently of *Booklist* and reviews products *not* recommended for purchase as well as recommended ones. See also *Booklist/Reference Books Bulletin.*

reference discount   A discount classification applied to reference books. Reference discounts are generally less than trade discounts. In many types of contract bidding, the book supplier must bid by discount for each class of books, with one of the discount classes being reference books. See also *contract bid; discount categories/classes (contract bidding); textbook discount; trade discount (periodical).*

Reference Quarterly   See RQ.

referral names   The practice of some periodicals asking subscribers to submit names of friends, or of business or professional associates who might be interested in subscribing to the publication. Such names are then either sent a sample or otherwise solicited in subscription efforts. In book club promotion, the term for referral names is member-get-a-member. Also known as name-get-a-name. See also *member-get-member (book club).*

regional book   A book designed to appeal to readers within a specific area of the country. Usually offered at a trade discount, such books are sold through book outlets and by direct mail to individuals within that region. They include such types of books as Who's Who directories and yellow pages; tourist, activity and consumer guides; historical works; nature field guides; cook books; and coffee table books.

regional publisher   A small press that publishes regional books. In most instances, topics published cover a small geographic region. Says Michael Coffee, editor of *Small Press,* "There are lots of books known only within a 300-mile radius, but they are selling hundreds of thousands of copies a year."

Regional, State, and Local Organizations directory   See *Encyclopedia of Associations: Regional, State, and Local Organizations.*

register (printing)   The fitting of two or more printing images on the same sheet of paper in exact alignment. When improperly aligned, the images are said to be "out of register."

release   1. In book promotion, generally refers to news release or press release. 2. Term for any newsworthy announcement issued by a publicist. 3. A form signed by individuals whose quotations are used in advertising and by models whose photographs are used in advertising. The signed form releases the advertiser from any liability in using the quotation or photo. See also *news release; publicity/press release.*

release date (news releases)   An instruction at the top of the first page of a news release specifying exactly when the release may be used. Most releases carry the heading "For Immediate Release." Others may bear a specific date, indicating that the release may not be used before that date. Some releases show a date and add "or thereafter," indicating the release will still be pertinent after the indicated release date.

relief printing   See *letterpress printing.*

religious book   "...books published by religious book specialists, reviewed and advertised largely in religious book outlets to people interested in religion." —Chandler Grannis in *What Happens in Book Publishing, 2nd Ed.* (Bowker, 1967). Categories include: (1) Bibles and devotional manuals; (2) inspirational books for laypeople; (3) materials for professional clergy and theologians; (4) textbooks for religious education programs. (Source: John Dessauer in *Book Publishing: What It Is, What It Does, 2nd Ed.* (Bowker, 1981). See also *religious bookstore.*

religious book club   Book clubs catering to various religious interests, mainly in three categories: Protestant, Catholic, and Jewish. Offerings may be religious and inspirational, but often include selected popular fiction and nonfiction. Religious clubs are included in the Book Clubs section of *Literary Market Place.* See also *book club.*

religious bookstore   Bookstore with inventory of mostly religious books. There are over 2,000 bookstores in the United States that classify themselves as religious bookstores. See also *religious book.*

remailing   A repeat mailing of a direct-mail package to a previously used list, often after enough time has elapsed to indicate good results. Such remailings often pull as well as the first mailing.

remainder   A book considered by the publisher to be surplus inventory unlikely to ever be sold and therefore disposed of at a fraction of its production cost to a remainder dealer. According to *Publishers Weekly* (April 17, 1987) "about 50% of all books published eventually go on the remainder block." See also *remainder dealers, major; remaindering.*

remainder dealer, specialist   Remainder dealer who specializes only in specific types or categories such as religious or children's books.

remainder dealers, major   The major remainder dealers for trade books are Book World Promotions (Newark, NJ, and New York, NY); Booksmith Promotional Co. (New York, NY) Bookthrift (New York, NY); Marboro Books Corp. (New York, NY, and Moonachie, NJ); Outlet Book Company (New York, NY); Pop-M

Company (Ivyland, PA), and Publishers Marketing Enterprises, Inc. (New York, NY); Publishers Overstock Co. (New York, NY); Horizon Book Co. (New York, NY).

remainder dealer supply sources   (1) Publishers' surplus stock; (2) reprints; (3) books packaged by remainder houses; (4) books bought from outside packagers.

remainder house   A specialist dealer who buys publishers' overstocks and sells to bookstores (and sometimes also to individuals by mail).

remaindering   The practice of selling, at greatly reduced prices, all or part of a publisher's overstock of slow-moving books, or of those being dropped from the publisher's list. Any book thus sold is called a *remainder*. See also *remaindering, partial*.

remaindering, partial   The partial sell-off of a publisher's stock at very low (remainder) prices to dispose of surplus inventory. The publisher will continue to sell the remaining inventory at usual prices. See also *remaindering*.

remainder pricing   Pricing decisions often depend on available quantities. J.P. Leventhal of Outlook Book Company, New York, said in *Publishers Weekly*   (April 6, 1984), "A $19.95 book can be sold for $7.95 or $1.98....We might sell a theatre book for $6.95, but if we have only 1,500 copies and know there is a passionate audience out there, we can price it up to $10."

renewal billing cycle (periodical)   The various times when a periodical publisher mails renewal notices to subscribers. For scholarly journals, most publishers send three notices. For scientific and scholarly periodicals, the cycle should start sufficiently early so that it terminates simultaneously with the mailing of the last issue of the paid subscription. Also called *renewal program* or *renewal series*.

renewal campaign, business directory   The mailing of renewal notices to previous buyers of a directory or other business reference issued annually, or in periodically updated editions. Business directory renewal campaigns typically start three months before publication and end about two months after the new edition is published.

renewal notice/invoice A notice issued by a periodical publisher to a subscriber. If the subscription is through a subscription agent, the notice may go to the agent only. However, if no renewal is subsequently received, a notice may also be sent directly to the customer, or the customer may be contacted by phone.

renewal program (journals) An organized effort to retain current subscribers to a periodical. It is an integral part of the marketing plan for any journals publisher. See *renewal billing cycle (periodical)*.

renewal rate (subscription product) The rate of renewal for a subscription product—usually a periodical or newsletter—after the second subscription year. See also *conversion rate; retention rate (periodical)*.

renewals, first (periodical) See *first renewal (periodical)*.

rental list label format See *cheshire label format (mailing list)*.

rental plan See *book lease plan*. See also *approval plan; blanket order; McNaughton Plan*.

reorder (bookseller) Any stock order placed after the initial order for a book. Many trade booksellers place initial orders with the publisher and rely on wholesalers for reorders or special orders. This is particularly true of larger stores that can earn maximum publisher discount with their initial order.

rep A publisher's sales representative. U.K.: agent. See *sales rep/sales representative*.

rep, commission See *commission rep*.

rep, house See *house rep*.

repackaged edition The reintroduction and republication of a book in a format other than that of any previously published edition of the work. The book being repackaged may or may not currently be in print. Repackaged editions include paperback versions of cloth books, revised and updated editions of older works, and large print editions. See also *large print books*.

repackaging (book)   Reissuing a book in a different format to make it more appealing to others outside its primary market, or more affordable to those within its primary market. See also *repackaged edition*.

replacement pages (loose-leaf publishing)   Pages sent by a loose-leaf publisher to update and replace parts of a work sent at an earlier date. see also *loose-leaf publishing*.

reply card   A self-addressed card included as part of a mailing to facilitate response from the addressee. See also *business reply mail; return envelope*.

reply card bearing address   Reply cards bearing recipient's name and address have been found to be more effective than those that require the respondent to add such information.

reply card bearing stub   Reply cards with tear-off stubs are generally more effective than ordinary reply cards because they give the respondent a receipt.

reply card effectiveness   See *response device effectiveness*.

reply card placement (direct mail)   The reply card in a mailing should be inserted in such a way that it is seen first when the main components of the mailing are removed from the envelope. If it is not, it could be left in the envelope and could diminish the mailing's effectiveness.

reply envelope   See *envelope, reply*.

Reply-O-Letter   A patented mailing format with a die-cut opening on the face of the letter and a pocket on the reverse side. An addressed reply card or envelope inserted into the pocket shows through the die-cut opening, providing an address for both the letter and the window mailing envelope.

repping group   An independent sales group that sells books to the retail and wholesale trade for publishers who do not have their own sales force. A repping group, also often called a *commission group*, typically has exclusive rights to sell a publisher's list within a given geographical territory. U.K.: agent.

reprint (book)   A return to press of an existing work, often with corrections of minor typographical errors.

reprint (journal)   Pages of a published journal article reimposed in such a way that only the text of the article is reprinted. See also *offprint.*

reprint book   A book consisting of a collection of journal articles in which the original articles were used as camera-ready copy.

reprint edition   Any reprinting of a book subsequent to the first printing. Such editions may be without change or with minor typographical corrections. Reprint editions also include new editions of a work that has been sold by its original publisher to a reprint publisher or reprinter. Such books may no longer be profitable for the originating publisher, but may be kept in print profitably by the reprint house because of its specialization in this type of publishing or because of economies of scale.

reprint publisher   A publisher that specializes in reprinting, usually in small editions, older titles of value that have gone out of print. See also *on-demand publishing.*

reprint rights   1. The sale of rights to a work to a reprint house for a reprint edition. 2. The sale by a publisher of the right to publish and distribute a title either in the original language or in translation by a publisher in another country within that publisher's sales territory.

repro/repro proof   See *reproduction proof.*

reproduction proof   Clean and sharp typeset copy suitable for photographic reproduction and platemaking.

republisher   Generally refers to a paperback publisher. See also *reprint publisher.*

required text   The official text for an academic course of study. See also *recommended supplementary reading.*

resale and/or exemption certificate   A form supplied by publishers to retail and cooperative accounts that buy books for resale and, therefore, are exempt from payment of sales tax. They must supply either a copy of their Exemption Certificate, or a Sales Tax Permit License number, certifying their eligibility for such exemption.

Research Centers Directory   A directory of over 6,000 university-related and other nonprofit research organizations. Arrangement is by subject and then alphabetically by unit name. Includes alphabetical, institutional, and subject indexes. Published summer of odd numbered years by Gale Research Company, Book Tower, Detroit, MI 48226.

research journal, primary   A journal that publishes reports of new and original research. It is the initial published source for a specific identifiable advancement in knowledge.

research monograph   A book dealing with one subject or research area, designed to inform and summarize that area for other scientists.

Resources for Book Publishers   A newsy and well-written bi-weekly newsletter concerned with book publishing, particularly in small publishing firms. Features include book reviews, announcements of meetings, resources available, and marketing tips. From: The Huenefield Company, P.O. Box U, Bedford, MA 01730. Phone: 617-861-9650.

respondent   Individual who has responded to a mail survey.

responder   An individual who has responded to a direct-mail offer.

response (direct mail)   1. The number of individuals receiving a mailing who have completed and returned a reply card, order form, or envelope. 2. Replies received from a mail promotion. See also *response rate (direct mail)*.

response, inquiry-qualifying   See *direct-mail response, inquiry qualifying*.

response card   See *response device/vehicle*.

response deck   See *card deck; card pack*.

Response Deck List & Media Planner   A source of card deck information. The spiral-bound directory lists full details on over 600 regularly published decks, including cost-per-thousand circulation. From: Thinkbank Publishers, PO Box 1166, Arlington, TX 76004. Phone: 817-640-5495.

response device/vehicle   Any medium supplied to a direct-mail recipient to facilitate a response to an offer. Such devices include business reply cards and envelopes, order forms or coupons, and even toll-free telephone numbers or the stamps supplied by some medical publishers.

response device effectiveness   The loose response device has been found to be up to three times more effective than one that must be cut or torn from another enclosure. Source: Clark-O'Neill, *Indicia*, January 1987.

response dropoff, credit card   See *credit card response dropoff*.

response envelope   See *envelope, reply*.

response forecasting   Estimating response from a mailing or mail order ad based on early rate of orders received after mailing or ad publication date. See also *half-life formula*.

response handling (direct mail)   All mail promotions seek some kind of response. If the anticipated response includes orders, inquiries, and possibly telephone calls, full arrangements should be made for dealing with all possible types of responses in advance of the mailing. If all mail is opened in a central place, such as a mail room, instructions should be given as to who gets the orders and who gets the literature requests. Telephone operators should be informed as to whom phone inquiries should be directed.

response instructions, stamp promotion   See *stamp promotion response instructions*.

response list   A mailing list consisting of people who have responded to some kind of offering, usually by mail. See also *compiled list; database mailing list*.

response month, best   See *mail-responsive month, best*.

response percentage   See *response rate (direct mail)*.

response quality (direct mail)   See *quality of response (direct mail)*.

response rate (direct mail)   The number of responses from a mailing or percentage of return. A mailing producing two replies per one hundred pieces mailed would have a response rate of 2%. Sometimes expressed as percentage of return, although this term, popular up until the 1950s, is now rarely used. See also *list responsiveness (direct mail).*

response speed of advertising   See *advertising format response speed.*

response stamps   See *stamps (in book promotion); stamp promotion response instructions.*

response time (direct mail)   As a rule, a bulk third-class promotional mailing will have a meaningful response about 10 days after the mailing date and draw about half of the total campaign response within about two weeks after that.

response time for sale offerings   See *sale response time.*

response vehicle test (direct mail)   A test mailing in which different segments of the same mailing have different types of response vehicles. The response from each type is then measured and compared with the others. Such tests may include business reply card vs. business reply envelope, or *both* reply card and envelope vs. no reply enclosure at all, or postpaid reply card vs. reply card on which postage must be added. See also *response device.*

responsive list, proven   See *proven mail responsive.*

retail cooperative advertising policy   A detailed policy of most trade publishing establishments that spells out in detail the terms and conditions under which the publisher will participate in cooperative advertising with bookseller accounts. In most instances, the policy calls for an allowance that is a percentage of either (a) a full calendar year's billing history or, (b) for those with less than a year's billing history, a percentage of net billings to the date of the co-op request. See also *co-op ad.*

retail outlets (bookstore)   See *bookstore; bookstore chain; college store; independent bookstore; leased bookstores.*

retention rate (periodical)   The annual percentage of all current subscribers to a periodical who renew their subscriptions. See also *conversion rate; renewal rate (subscription product).*

retitled edition   A reissuing of a previously published book under a changed title.

return, on mail promotion   See *response rate (direct mail)*.

return card   See *reply card*.

return eligibility period (bookstore)   See *period of eligibility for return*.

return envelope   A self-addressed envelope used as a mail enclosure to facilitate a reply, order, or payment from the addressee.

return period (bookstore)   See *period of eligibility for return*.

return policy   Established terms of a publisher regarding the return of unsold books. Most publishers accept returns without penalty. A few offer an option of normal discount with return privilege or a higher discount to those willing to forego the returns option. There are also publishers who do not accept returns or assess a penalty for return of books by booksellers.

return postage (U.K. Post Office policy)   The British Post Office will return all mail with sender's address on envelope free of charge when undeliverable.

return postage guaranteed   A line added to pieces in a third-class bulk mailing that instructs the Postal Service to return any undeliverable mailing piece. The straight third-class postage rate is charged for the return. See also *address correction requested*.

return postcards   Another name for cards in a card deck.

return privilege   Granting a bookseller the right to return unsold books for credit, sometimes within a specified period of time. Those who do not allow booksellers to return unsold books are said to sell nonprotected books. See also *protected*.

returns   1. Books returned by a bookseller for credit. 2. Books sent to a potential buyer for examination and returned. 3. Response from a mailing, also called *response rate*.

reverse   See *negative*.

reverse echo effect   The impact on a book's total sales that occurs when direct-mail promotion is suspended. Reverse echo studies have shown that a cessation of direct-mail promotion results in diminished sales from all other sales outlets. For more, see *The*

Publisher's Direct Mail Handbook, Chapter 2, ISI Press, Philadelphia, 1987.

reverse out   A technique used to create a reverse effect by printing all areas except the type characters, leaving the type characters in the original color of the paper or other background material.

reverse plate   A printing plate photomechanically reversed from type so that black design on white paper becomes white design against black background. See also *reverse type.*

reverse type   White printing on a black background. Research has shown that reverse printing is read 10.5% slower than black-on-white printing.

review (manuscript)   A critical evaluation of a work under consideration for publication, often with suggestions or recommendations for improvement.

review chasing   A follow-up inquiry to a review medium after a book has been sent for review to inquire as to whether the review has appeared or will appear at some future time.

review copy   1. A book sent to a publication to obtain publicity or a review for a book. 2. A book sent to individuals who have the authority to purchase books in quantity or to influence their purchase by others. 3. A book sent to influential individuals within the field of the book in recognition of their role as opinion leaders in the field. See also *advance copies; advance galleys; desk copy; examination copy/exam copy.*

review copy (special sales)   In the special sales category of book marketing, a sample copy of a book sent to an account or prospective account for evaluation as to its appropriateness for the account's audience. In some instances, no order will be placed without evaluation of the actual book, which is retained and used in the preparation of promotional copy.

review excerpt/book review excerpt   An extract of one or more passages or a continuous portion from a book review.

review file   A central location where all reviews of a particular book may be readily accessed in a publisher's promotion department. A useful resource in preparation of promotion copy, since book reviews are generally regarded as more credible than the publisher's copy. Useful in book club or subsidiary rights sales, in making offers to potential buyers seeking a book as a premium, and in identifying review sources for related titles. Also useful in promotion of new editions.

review label   See *review slip*.

review lag   The elapsed time between the publication date of a book and the date a review of it is published. In some newspapers and magazines, a zero lag is achieved by sending advance galley proofs or else sending out review copies in advance of the official publication date.

review list   All the publications that are likely to review or otherwise publicize a book. Usually compiled by the publicist or publisher's publicity department. For specialized and scholarly books, it will usually closely follow and expand on suggestions made by the author and by the in-house sponsoring editor.

review media, library-oriented   *Booklist/Reference Books Bulletin*; *Choice*; *The Kirkus Reviews*; *Library Journal*; *Publishers Weekly*; *School Library Journal*. Also, for many special libraries, *New Technical Books*. See separate entries for each publication.

review media, library-oriented (U.K.)   *The Bookseller*; *Library Association Journal*; *The Book Exchange*; *Reference Librarian*.

review media file   A file of review media pertinent to a press's publishing program. Contains name and address for each review medium to which appropriate books are regularly sent, as well as names of freelance writers and reviewers who regularly contribute to appropriate media. The mailing address is often different from that of the medium's main business address. The individual file for each medium may also include special information relative to review policies, such as whether reviews will be done only from page proofs, or whether more than one review copy is required. All such files should show most recent update, since some publications change reviewers regularly.

review medium   One known to carry book reviews. Review copies should be addressed to a specific individual whenever possible. Books should not be sent for review to publications that do not carry book reviews. To ascertain whether a publication carries book reviews or not, check these publications: *Ulrich's Interna-*

tional Periodicals Directory; Bacon's Publicity Checker; and *The Standard Periodical Directory.*

review note   See *review slip.*

review quote   A quotation from a book review and usually used either between quotation marks or in a different type face than accompanying text. Such quotes, to be effective, must be attributed to their source. See also *review excerpt/book review excerpt; testimonial.*

reviews, book   A review, notice, or record of a published work in a publication, usually with an evaluation. A critical aspect of all book marketing strategy. For virtually every type of book published, the review is considered the primary publicity form. In some areas, it is also the primary advertising form. In the academic and scholarly world, many book purchases are made only after reviews have been read. Library acquisitions also rely heavily on reviews. Reviews represent the best and least expensive form of book marketing since the basic cost to the publisher is only that of the unit manufacturing cost of the review copies plus shipping. Unfortunately, many scholarly journal reviews appear a year or more after a book's publication and have less impact on sales than those appearing within the first year. See also *abstracting and indexing services; publicity (book).*

reviews, scholarly book   See *Choice.*

review slip   An enclosure in a book sent by a publisher for review. Usually includes such information as title, author, pub date, and price; also a request that the publication send copy(ies) of published review. U.K.: review note.

revised edition   The reissuing of a book with sufficient changes or new material to enable it to be offered and treated as a new work by the publisher. Opinion varies on the amount of change or new material necessary to warrant a revised edition. Most publishers consider 25% to 30% a minimum amount. However, for textbooks, a revision will often be done with a lesser amount to kill off competition from used copies of the current edition.

risers (exhibits and conventions)   Elevated platforms that stand on exhibit tables. Used for display at exhibits and conventions. Risers are usually draped with a colored material. Draping stapled at top and bottom is called *closed draping.* When stapled only at top and hanging free, it is called *open draping*. See also *open draping (exhibits and conventions)*.

Robinson-Patman Act   A law passed in 1936 calling for a seller to treat all competitive customers of a product on proportionally equal terms with regard to discounts and cooperative advertising allowances, and other terms, for the purpose of prohibiting discrimination or favoritism "in restraint of trade."

ROI   Return on Investment. The amount of money returned per unit invested.

rollout/roll out/ rollout mailing   Mailing to the remaining part or portions of a mailing list after a successful test of a portion of it. See also *follow-up mailing; list testing; list test size rules; pyramiding*.

rollout drop-off   The difference in response rate between a test mailing to a list and the response rate for a subsequent mailing to the remainder of the list. The rate of response usually will be lower for the rollout than for the test.

rollout rule-of-thumb (direct mail)   Test 5% of a very large list (100,000 or more), then 20%, then the balance of the list.

rollout universe   All of the names remaining on one or more mailing lists after a test mailing.

roman/roman type   1. Normal upright type as opposed to slanting or italic type. 2. An all-inclusive term for the various families of serif typefaces.

ROP/r.o.p. space   See *run-of-paper position*.

ROS   Return on sales, or profit as a percentage of sales.

rotating circulation   1. The practice of some high-circulation publications mailing their publication to rotating segments of their total circulation, so that different names are used in each segmental mailing to prevent the same names from receiving promotional mailings too frequently. 2. A practice used by some paid circulation publications to add additional nonpaid circulation to their subscription list in certain desired areas or groupings (i.e., top management) and still qualify as a paid circulation publication by the rules of the audit bureaus (ABC and BPA).

rough layout See also *layout.*

routemen (paperback) Sales representatives employed by independent distributors. They call on paperback book outlet accounts, deliver books and stock racks, and write reorders. See also *prepack system (paperback).*

routing card See *library routing card/slip.*

routing instructions An instruction added to the face of an envelope, mailing piece, or catalog that asks the primary recipient to forward the mailing to others for whom the offer may also have interest. Pass-along instructions may be general, such as "Please pass along to a friend or colleague," or to specific job functions, or they may be general and request the pass-along with blank lines to be filled in by the recipient.

royalty A percentage of the earnings on a book that a publisher pays to the author of the book. The royalty is based either on the list price or net price for each copy of the book sold. The percentages vary from one type of book to another. For high-potential books or established authors, the royalty may be individually negotiated irrespective of the publisher's stated royalty policy.

r.p.m. (U.K.) Resale Price Maintenance. See also *net book agreement.*

RQ (Reference Quarterly) A quarterly publication of the Reference and Adult Service Division of the American Library Association. Used by librarians as a selection aid for reference books. Carries about 35-40 book reviews annually. Published by American Library Association, 50 E. Huron Street, Chicago, IL 60611.

r.r.p. (U.K.) Recommended retail price.

RSC ad See *reader service card book ad.*

rule Black line used to create borders or boxes. Rules come in a range of thicknesses measured in points.

rule of nine Publisher's discount policy that assumes that an order for more than nine copies of a title suited for use as a textbook is considered an adoption and invoiced at textbook discount.

rule-of-thumb for clear copy See *copy, effective (direct mail)*.

run in Setting type without paragraph breaks, or adding copy without starting a new paragraph or new line.

run (mailing list) A single, continuous pass of a mailing list through a computer. When only a small segment of a large list is rented, the list owner may assess a run charge.

run (printing) See *pressrun*.

run-around A change in the size of a column of type, usually to accommodate an illustration. It may be shortened from the left or right as required. The type is said to run around the illustration. Sometimes called *set-around*.

running charge (mailing lists) The price a list owner charges a renter for names run or passed but not used for a specific rental. Such charge may be based on number of names run or passed, or it may be a fixed charge.

running head The line that appears across the top of the printed page in a book or catalog. In a catalog, it usually denotes the subject matter of the entries on the page.

run-of-book See *run-of-paper position*.

run-of-paper position Placement of an advertisement in a publication anywhere in the edition, at the publisher's discretion. *Run-of-book* has the same meaning, but usually applies to magazine advertising only. See also *position charge*.

run-of-publication See *run-of-paper position*.

S

saddle binding   See *saddle stitching*.

saddle stitching   Binding method for a booklet by which wire staples are driven through the back fold of the booklet. (This enables booklet to lie flat when open.) This method is not adequate for thick publications. See also *side wiring/side stitching*.

safe book   A book the publisher is reasonably sure will earn a profit if published.

sale   1. A transaction in which merchandise has been delivered and paid for. 2. An offering, at a reduced price, usually for a specified time period. See also *sale, inventory reduction*.

sale, coupon   A device used by some publishers to reduce surplus inventory, particularly on a high-priced work. A coupon is printed and distributed that states its face value will be applied to any purchase of the stated work prior to the expiration of the date shown. Such sale coupons, often identified as "Valuable Coupon," are either mailed or distributed at meetings and conventions.

sale, extended offer   A sale offer in which the original sale expiration date has been extended. One technique used is to overprint on the cover copy or front panel of a sale catalog or promotion piece announcing that the sale has been extended.

sale, half-price   A surplus inventory sale in which all offerings are 50% off list price. Also referred to as a *white sale*.

sale, inventory-reduction Usually a mail-order sale offering selected titles from the active list at special prices or discounts to encourage sales of titles considered to be surplus inventory or thought to be over-priced for certain markets. Such sales invariably cover a specific time span and have a cut-off date after which they return to regular prices. See also *sale, coupon; sale, half-price; sale, premium offering; sale, single flat price; sale, variable discount; sale, varied net price.*

sale, premium offering To encourage larger orders, publishers may permit customers to select a free book from a premium list, or to receive a specified title without charge if they order more than a certain number of other books being offered, or if their total order exceeds a set dollar amount.

sale, seasonal Sale tied to a particular season, such as spring or fall.

sale, single flat price A surplus inventory sale in which all books are offered at a single flat price. One publisher celebrating his 95th anniversary had a number of high-price works all on sale at $95.00.

sale, variable discount A surplus inventory sale in which discounts may vary from book to book within the sale offering.

sale, varied net price A surplus inventory sale in which each title shows two prices—the established list price and the sale price. Discount is not mentioned.

sale books See *bargain books.*

sale catalog Catalog in which currently available books are offered at reduced prices or at discounts off the established list price. Many publishers have periodic sale catalog offerings to reduce surplus inventory.

sale catalog advertisement An advertisement in a periodical offering a publisher's sale catalog on return of the coupon included in the advertisement.

sale cutoff date See *sale response time.*

sale discount A discount offering on books by a publisher during an inventory reduction sale. Usually applied to older, slow-moving books considered to be in surplus inventory. Discounts may vary according to the publisher's anxiety to dispose of stock and the age of the work.

sale insert   A sale offering inserted in another publication. In countries where customer and bookbuyer lists are not readily available, some book publishers produce sale fliers or offerings that are inserted into association, society, and commercial publications in the same or a related subject area.

sale or return (SOR)   A publisher term in the U.K. meaning books are fully returnable. "Our books are fully SOR."

sale response time   Publisher sales, to be effective, should provide adequate response time. A cutoff date of at least three months from mail date is advised. Some publishers allow up to six months. A short response time tends to diminish response. Many publishers will honor sale orders up to 30 days after cutoff date.

sales call (retail accounts)   A call on a retail bookseller account by a sales rep. Usually made at least once a selling season to present the books of the publisher or publishers he or she represents. Salaried reps may also check inventory on backlist steady sellers, and write up or recommend stock replacements. Some reps follow up in between calls by phone. Sales calls are scheduled in advance and routes are planned to keep travel time at a minimum and to make the largest number of calls each day. See also *seasonal calls (bookstore); tri-season schedule.*

sales conference   A meeting, usually held semiannually, during which field sales reps are brought together and presented with details and promotion plans for the major books of the forthcoming season and to provide a forum for idea and information exchange with in-house publishing personnel. See also *mini sales conference.*

sales conference, mini   See *mini sales conference.*

sales forecast   Estimated sales volume for a publisher's list for a given future period. Most marketing and promotion budgets are tied to such forecasts. See also *sales projection (book).*

sales handle   See *handle/sales handle.*

sales history (book)   A record of how a book has sold year by year, and usually broken down by outlet to indicate where sales were made. A useful tool in estimating or forecasting sales of new editions, or of comparable titles.

sales letter connectors   See *connectors (in direct-mail copy)*.

sales letter headline   See *headline/head (in sales letter)*.

sales letter postscript   See *postscript, sales letter*.

sales letter salutation   See *salutation, sales letter*.

sales letter underlining   See *underlining in sales letters*.

sales life (of a book)   The period of time during which a book sells actively or according to minimum requirements. George Pratt of Little Brown & Co. defines it as having four stages: (1) launch stage; (2) growth stage; (3) maintenance stage; (4) death stage. Also, the selling period of a book before a new edition is launched. See also *shelf life (bookstore)*.

sales manual, college   See *college sales manual*.

sales package   See *direct mail package*.

sales patterns for scholarly books (rule-of-thumb)   For scholarly books, the pattern, according to one leading university press, in recent years was 70%-80% in the first year. A possible reason: The primary market for scholarly books is the library market, and as a rule such acquisitions are made either through approval plans or other means shortly after the books are published, or after the early appearance of reviews.

sales patterns for technical, professional, and reference books (rule-of-thumb)   Based on estimated five-year life, most do 40%-50% of the five-year total in the first year, about 20%-25% the second year, about 10%-15% the third year, about 5%-10% the fourth year, 0%-5% the fifth year.

sales patterns in rapidly changing fields   Books in rapidly changing areas of science and technology enjoy the bulk of their sales activity during the first year after publication and little thereafter.

sales patterns of serials   See *serials, sales patterns*.

sales presentation (by sales rep)   A presentation of new and forthcoming titles to the buyer for a bookseller. See also *sales conference*.

sales projection (book)   Estimated sale of a book over a given period, or book's estimated active sales life, usually three or five years for most professional and scholarly books.

sales promotion   Any effort to encourage the purchase of a product or service.

sales rep/sales representative   A sales person representing a publisher or group of publishers within a specific geographic area or sales territory. If employed by the publisher, he or she is called a house rep. If self-employed and representing a number of publishers, he or she is called a commission rep or a commission sales rep. A sales rep selling books for adoption in academic institutions is called a *college traveler*. See also *book traveler; college rep; college sales representative; commission rep; house rep; library rep; trade rep; traveler*.

sales rep, commission   See *commission rep*.

sales rep, library   See *library rep*.

sales representative   See *commission rep; sales rep/sales representative*.

sales territory (cooperative publishing)   The countries or regions to which the originating publisher of a work grants exclusive sales rights in a cooperative agreement with another publisher. U.S. publishers, for example, sometimes get North American sales rights in a cooperative arrangement with U.K. publishers.

sales territory (sales rep)   The geographic region a sales rep is assigned to cover, or is responsible for. The rep is expected to allocate time in order to cover his or her sales territory, usually making at least one call during each of the two major selling seasons—spring and fall. For large or important accounts, the rep may follow up with monthly visits or be in contact with the account by telephone. The necessary paperwork is often done at home or in a hotel room at night and/or on weekends. See also *sales call (retail accounts)*.

salting   Decoy or dummy names inserted in a mailing list to test for delivery of mailings, or unauthorized use of list. Also called *seeding.*

salutation, sales letter   "Dear Reader" is the best salutation to use in sales letters that cannot be personalized by name or when recipients may hold different job junctions or be high-level business professionals.

sample   A representative portion of a total group involved in a survey.

sample letter of agreement (mailing list)   See *list rental letter of agreement.*

sample mailing piece requirement   A sample of the copy for a proposed mailing, supplied to the mailing list owner with a list rental order. Many list owners will not release their lists without a sample of the intended mailing.

sample package (lettershop)   A sample, supplied to a lettershop or mailing house prior to a mailing, to indicate the desired assembly sequence of the materials to be included in the mailing. See also *folding dummy.*

sampling (journals)   The practice of journals publishers of providing a free sample issue to a prospective subscriber.

sampling in special sales   See *special sales inquiry handling.*

SAN   See *Standard Address Number.*

sans serif   A typeface without cross-strokes (called *serifs)* projecting from the extremities of the letters. Sans serif is considered to be more legible for headlines, less legible for textmatter. See also *serif.*

saturation campaign   Campaign in which a number of different media are used simultaneously. When space advertising is used in conjunction with direct mail, space ads should precede mail by about a month so as to reinforce the mailing effort.

SBN   See International Standard Book Number.

sc Proofreader's mark for small caps (small capital letters). These are capital letters approximately the height of lowercase (small letters). See also *small caps (typography); x-height (typography)*.

scale Term used in preparation of printing or advertising to denote size of reduction or enlargement. When expressed as a percentage, "scale 50%" would be used for a reduction to 50% of size before reduction. See also *reduction*.

scanning See *optical scanning*.

SCF (Sectional Center Facility) A centralized mail-processing hub in the U.S. Postal Service. The first three digits of the Zip code identify the sectional center area; the last two identify the associate offices and also stations and branches of the sectional center. There are 313 SCFs in the Postal Service.

scholarly book characteristics (1) They are specialized and for a well-defined market; (2) They have few sales outside their primary market; (3) They are not in competition with one another; (4) They, as a rule, have a very long life; (5) They have a large imprint loyalty. Customers of a scholarly publisher will favor books from that press; (6) Price is often not a factor in their sale; (7) They generate little subsidiary rights income; (8) They tend not to be highly profitable; (9) They are usually published by university presses.

scholarly book reviews See *Choice*.

scholarly journal 1. A scholarly or learned journal is a periodical primarily devoted to the publication of original research and/or scholarship. 2. Journal in which the material is a continuous presentation of research materials from one issue to another, no issue being a single entity but rather components of a volume. Typically, all of the issues within a single year constitute a single volume. 3. Journal published by a learned society or university press.

scholarly publisher Publisher primarily concerned with publishing works of intellectual and academic interest.

scholarly publishers, types (1) Commercial publishers; (2) university presses; (3) learned societies.

Scholar's Bookshelf   This mail-order operation based in Princeton, New Jersey, provides professional and scholarly publishers with a source for selling surplus inventory. Founded and operated by Abbot M. Friedland, former marketing director of Princeton University Press. Interest areas: humanities, the fine arts, science and technology. Contact: Scholar's Bookshelf, 51 Everett Drive, Princeton Junction, NJ 08550. Phone: 609-799-7233.

school books   See *elhi text.*

school bookstore   A store, usually affiliated with an elementary or secondary school, that purchases books for resale to students.

school jobber   See *jobber, school.*

school library, copy approach   In describing materials to be used by students in school libraries, it is important to identify the reading or grade level of the books being offered. Relationships to course materials or curriculum programs should be specified. Full bibliographic details and author information should be included, particularly in copy describing professional books for school librarians.

school library, elementary   See *elementary school library buying pattern.*

school library, high school   See *high school library collection development.*

school library, junior high school   See *junior high school library collection development.*

school library direct-mail approach   (1) Indicate importance of content on outer envelope; (2) offer books that meet a curriculum need; (3) show net price—what it will cost the library; (4) keep order form simple.

School Library Journal   A monthly publication catering to the interests of school librarians and public librarians concerned with new books for children and young adults. Carries about 2,500 book reviews a year, of which about 10%-15% are young adult books. Reaches over 28,000 elementary, junior high, and high school libraries, as well as 4,600 public libraries. From: Bowker Magazine Group, 249 W. 17th Street, New York, NY 10011.

school library mailing list categories   Public high school; public junior high school; public elementary school; private high school; private elementary school; Catholic high school; Catholic elementary school. See also *list sources, school library.*

school library mailing lists   See list *sources, school library.*

school library selection media   Primary book selection media used by school libraries. A 1977 American Library Association study indicated 98% of librarians questioned used *School Library Journal*, and 70%-81% said they used *Booklist*.

SCIENCE   A weekly publication of the American Association for the Advancement of Science (AAAS) and the leading overall periodical for advertising and reviews of high-level scientific publications. From: AAAS, 1515 Massachusetts Avenue NW, Washington DC 20005. See also *scientific book review media, major.*

scientific and technical book copy approach   Stress should be given to changing developments in the field and the currency of the work. Content is extremely important; many such works will sell on the strength of the contents listing. The authority of the author is also important.

scientific and technical publisher   Publisher primarily engaged in the publication of specialized works for scientific and technical audiences, and for educational programs and library reference collections in areas such as engineering diciplines—civil, chemical, mechanical, electrical and electronic, industrial, aeronautical, and the various branches of science—physics, chemistry, biology, mathematics, and computers. The current AAP designation for a scientific and technical publisher is "PSP publisher," for one engaged in professional and scholarly publishing. See also *PSP; PSP book; PSP publisher.*

scientific book review media, major   The two major review media worldwide for high-level scientific books are *SCIENCE* and *NATURE*. See separate entries for each.

scientific journal   Journal designed primarily for the transfer of scientific information.

scientific journal, international   Journal serving a worldwide constituency in a scientific or other special field.

scientists, advertising appeals to See *scientific and technical book copy approach.*

sci-tech General reference to scientific and technical books. See *scientific and technical publisher; PSP book; STM book.*

sci-tech publisher See *scientific and technical publisher.*

score To emboss or impress a rule on a thick sheet of paper, or several thicknesses, so that it will fold evenly without cracking or distorting the paper.

score (when printing on card stock) On heavier stocks, the paper must be scored or dented to ensure a clean fold. See also *folding (paper); grain (paper).*

screen Usually a brief form for *halftone screen.* In advertising, a screen refers to the process by which a continuous tone photograph is converted or broken into dots. Line screen number signifies number of dots per square inch. Most frequently used screens are 120-line and 133-line screens, for magazines and direct mail. Screens in newspaper advertising are coarser— 65-line or 85-line. The coarsest screen available is 50-line. See also *benday (or Ben Day); halftone screen.*

screen print See *Velox.*

screen size The number of lines per linear inch in a screen. The finer the screen, the greater the number of lines. The number of dots per inch on a 133-line screen will be more than twice that with a 65-line screen and provides more minute details. Screen size is closely tied to the type of paper used and the quality demanded from the illustrations. See also *benday (or Ben Day); halftone screen; screen.*

screen tint A mechanical tone created by a uniform pattern of tiny dots over its entire area and rated by its approximate dot-size value, such as 20%, 30%, 50%, etc. The eye sees the tone when in black ink as gray, or if in another color as a tint of that color. See also *benday (or Ben Day).*

seasonal calls (bookstore) The traditional visits to bookstores by publisher reps to introduce the books of the forthcoming season—either spring or fall. See also *sales call (retail accounts); tri-season schedule.*

seasonal catalog   A catalog used as a vehicle for announcing all new titles for a forthcoming publishing season. Some large houses will issue a special seasonal catalog for trade titles only; others a general seasonal catalog for distribution to both bookstores and libraries. Titles may be by subject or month of publication. In seasonal catalogs for trade bookstores, titles may be by perceived order of importance. Academic librarians favor seasonal catalogs as a checking and ordering vehicle. Library jobbers with approval plans carefully examine listed forthcoming titles against library profile requirements. See also *announcement catalog; catalog.*

seasonal catalog, trade   The seasonal catalog for a trade publisher is a selling tool for the trade rep as well as for the publicity and subsidiary rights departments. The library sales department may also distribute the catalog either direct to libraries or as a handout at library meetings. Booksellers use the trade catalog as a buying resource of the publisher's books for the coming season.

seasonal dating   In trade publishing the strongest retail sales of the year occur between Thanksgiving and Christmas. Some publishers encourage the placing of Christmas season stock orders well before the season by offering seasonal dating, i.e., dating the invoice December 1, so that payment will not be due until after the Christmas selling season. See also *December dating; extended credit.*

seasonality   The tendency for particular types of promotions to perform better in certain seasons of the year than in others. Seasonality is a factor in all promotions to individuals, bookstores, schools, and libraries. Full discussion of seasonality factors in book promotion may be found in *The Publishers Direct Mail Handbook*, ISI Press, 1987. See also *timing (book promotion).*

seasonality of college promotions   See *college textbook decision-making months.*

seasonal list   All of the books issued during a particular publishing season. Publishers traditionally have two seasonal lists, a spring list and a fall list. Scholarly presses with limited output deal with yearly lists and may issue a catalog in the fall bearing a cover date of the following year.

seasonal sales conference   A meeting used by publishers to present books of the forthcoming season to the field sales reps. Usually, sponsoring editors introduce their books and provide the reps with sales handles they can use in selling the books to bookstore buyers.

secondary audience (advertising promotion)   See *pass-along effect.*

secondary audience (book)   1. A market for a publication other than its primary market, and so regarded because it is either smaller, more costly to reach, or in some way likely to be less responsive than the primary market. 2. Readers or researchers who are likely to purchase a publication even though it lies outside their area of primary interest or research.

secondary school library   See *high school library collection development.*

second-class mail   Includes newspapers and other periodical publications issued at least four times per year. In order to mail publications at the second-class rates, a publisher must first obtain a permit.

second-class mail, forwarding of   See *mail forwarding (USPS regulations).*

second cover   The front inside cover of a periodical, catalog, or booklet. When this position is specified for an advertisement, it is usually charged at a premium over the page rate. See also *third cover; fourth cover.*

second serial rights   The selling of an excerpt from a book to another print medium after publication. See also *first serial rights.*

seed, telephone list   See *telephone seed/telephone-list seed (telemarketing).*

seeding   See *salting.*

seeds   Names included in a mailing list to enable the list owner to check on list usage. The names may be fictitious or, with permission, of real individuals. Also known as *decoys.* U.K.: *sleepers.*

segmentation   See *list segmentation.*

selective order plan (bookseller)   A book ordering plan offered by some publishers whereby a bookseller places an initial stock order and thereafter receives periodic announcements from which subsequent optional purchases may be made. See also *bookseller agency plan.*

selectivity   Selection options of certain mailing lists that enable the list user to focus on a desired segment of a market.

self-cover   A printed piece with a cover of the same paper as the inside text pages.

self-mailer   Any direct-mail piece that can be mailed without an envelope or separate wrapping. In the U.S., it must meet a minimum thickness requirement of .007″. Self-mailers are banned in the U.K.   See *trap envelope.*

self-mailer, dead back   One in which one of the outer sides is blank.

sell copy/selling copy   Advertising copy devoted to encouraging sales of a product or service. It usually emphasizes benefits rather than features. See also *benefit (in book advertising); feature (n.) (book advertising); "nice-to-know" (book pricing and promotion).*

selling title   A title given a book with sales appeal the primary consideration. Many business books build into the title a benefit that, for other types of books, would serve as a headline.

sell safe   Term used in the U.K. for the sale of books to a bookshop with the understanding that any unsold copies may be returned to the publisher. See also description of "fully protected" under entry for *protected.*

sell-through (books)   The sale to the ultimate consumer, usually through a bookstore.

sell-through (paperback)   The number of mass market paperbacks placed through IDs, or independent distributors, that are eventually sold. A figure used by some industry experts is 35% to 40%.

seminars, book marketing   See *Professional Publishers' Marketing Group (PPMG).*

seminars, newsletter   See *newsletter seminars.*

serial   A publication issued under the same title in successive parts, bearing numerical or chronological designations, and intended to be continued indefinitely. Normally, only the dates or volume numbers change from one issue to the next. Falling within the classification of serials are journals, periodicals, newspapers, annuals, proceedings, transactions, and numbered monographic serials. See also *series (book).*

serial publisher   1. Another name for publishers of periodicals and journals. 2. A generic term used by periodical subscription agents for publishers with whom they do business.

serial rights   The legal permission granted by a book publisher to another print publication to publish an excerpt or portion of a book before or after the book is published. See also *first serial rights; second serial rights.*

serials, sales patterns   Serials thrive in new fields or in established areas experiencing rapid change as a result of new research. Sales of serials tend to grow in such areas and then to stagnate or diminish as the field matures or stablizes.

Serials Directory   A comprehensive directory listing over 114,000 serials published worldwide, including LC, Dewey Decimal, National Library of Medicine, and Universal Decimal classification numbers and coden designations. Thirty-eight separate items of data are given on each title. Issued annually with three updates. Also available on CD-ROM. From: Ebsco Publishing, Box 1943, Birmingham, AL 35201. Phone: 1-800-826-3024.

Serials Industry Systems Advisory Committee (SISAC)   A group formed to develop voluntary standardized formats for electronically transmitting serial information and to present formats to be adopted as American National Standards.

series (book)   A collection of books or monographs within a defined discipline or subdiscipline. In some scientific and technical publishing areas, and particularly where the series is by the same author or editor, books in a series may be published in uniform sizes, have similar bindings, and have similar jacket designs. These serve as an aid to series recognition, especially in libraries, the main buyers of series. See also *serial.*

series (typography)   All the sizes available in a particular typeface. Typically range from 5 points up to 80 points. See also *family (typography)*.

series, open-ended   An ongoing series of books in which each new volume adds new information to the series as a whole. Volumes may be published irregularly or annually.

series book, advantages   Libraries tend to subscribe to series that fit their collections. This means automatic sales of each new volume. A lesser-known author of a series volume benefits from the attention drawn to the series by better known authors. A series may continue for many years and serve as a magnet for new authors writing in the same field.

series book, disadvantages   Some marketers feel a book blended into a series may not achieve the true sales potential it would if promoted as an individual title. Well-known authors may share this attitude since the partnership with the series may be viewed as a submerging of their own individuality.

series subscription (books)   A subscription to a series of books to be published over a period of time. The subscription signifies a commitment to the entire series and usually calls for a preferential price or discount over single-volume prices. See also *subscription discount (book)*; *subscription price (book)*.

serif   A bracketed cross stroke or projection at the extremities of type of letter forms. There are many varieties: square serif, old style serif, modern serif, etc. Serif typefaces are said to be more legible than sans serif faces for textmatter. See also *sans serif*; *typeface*.

serif, square   See *square serif*.

service ad   An advertisement in a media directory such as *Standard Rate & Data*, usually in the same section and/or adjacent to the advertiser's directory listing. The advertisement provides additional information in support of the listed entry. For those interested, such advertisements provide much useful information.

service charge   1. A charge to libraries imposed by some jobbers for books on which they have received little or no publisher discount. 2. A charge imposed by some jobbers for special services requested in fulfillment of an order. 3. A charge by a subscription agent on library orders for fulfilling periodical subscriptions. It is usually calculated as a percentage of the total annual cost of subscriptions.

service kit, convention exhibit   See convention exhibit service kit.

set (books)   A group of related books or any combination of books grouped and sold as such by the publisher. Books may be available separately or in some instances sold only as a single unit comprising a set. This includes works such as multivolume encyclopedias or lengthy reference works. When books are sold individually as well as in sets, the set price is usually less than the total of the individually priced books. See also *set discount*.

set-around   See *run-around*.

set discount   A discount on a grouping of books when purchased collectively as a set. Typically set discounts vary from 5% to 20%.

set line-for-line (typography)   Instruction to set copy exactly as submitted, so that each typeset line has exactly the words that appear in a line of manuscript.

set price   See *set discount*.

set solid (typography)   To set type without any leading, or spacing, between lines. See also *leading (typography)*.

set to fit (typography)   An instruction to a compositor to set a block of copy in a typesize that will fit a designated area. A useful instruction, especially for those unfamiliar with type sizing or copyfitting.

set-up (exhibits and conventions)   Assembly of all exhibit components exactly as they will or should appear in a show.

set-width (typography)   The width of an individual type character, including an amount of space on either side to prevent the characters from touching. In phototypesetting, this space can be adjusted electronically to produce condensed or expanded type.

sexism (in copywriting)   The use of terms designating only one gender, usually the masculine, to refer to people in general in copy. Sexist language should be avoided in all promotion copy.

This should be done by using words having no sexual connotation such as humankind for mankind, salesperson for salesman, supervisor for foreman, personnel for manpower, etc. A useful guide for preventing sexist usage is *The Nonsexist Word Finder*, by Rosalie Maggio, published by The Oryx Press, 2214 North Central at Encanto, Phoenix, AZ 85004.

shared mailing   Literature of two or more advertisers mailed in the same envelope. This term is the United Kingdom preference for the term cooperative mailing favored in the United States. See also *cooperative mailing/co-op mailing; joint mailing*.

sheet-fed press   A printing press in which the stock to be printed is fed in sheets, rather than being fed in a continuous roll. See also *web press*.

sheetwise imposition   Printing one side of the sheet from one plate or set of plates, and then the other side from another plate or set of plates. See also *work-and-tumble; work-and-turn*.

shelf life (bookstore)   The length of time a book will remain on a bookstore shelf before it is displaced by another title. Also the length of time a mass market paperback will remain on a paperback display rack before it is displaced. See also *sales life (of a book)*.

shilling mark   See *slash (typography)*.

shipping crate (exhibits and conventions)   A shipping case for exhibit components.

shipping options, special sale   See *special sale shipping options*.

ships (sales rep terminology)   Books due to be shipped. Sales reps may report that they tried to present their "May-June ships" during a January sales call, but were told it was too early, and to present them at a later date.

S-hook (exhibits and conventions)   Hardware shaped in the form of an "S" and used to hang objects from the top back rail or side rails of an exhibit booth. Usually the sponsor of an exhibit or convention will supply a card that is suspended from the top back rail by two or more "S" hooks. The card identifies a convention exhibitor. A booth number sometimes is suspended.

short course   A brief course, conducted for practicing professionals, on a narrow topic within a specific scientific or professional area to enable attendees to keep up to date on latest techniques and research. Given at meetings and conventions, in hotel rooms, at sponsor headquarters, or, sometimes, in an industrial location for employees of a particular company. A professional reference book is often included as part of the course materials package.

short discount   1. A discount that is lower than the discount of 40% or more typically given bookstores for trade books. 2. A discount scaled down from that given normal trade books and usually applied to textbooks, professional and reference books, and books sold primarily to users. See also *trade discount (bookseller)*. 3. Typically, books with discounts ranging from 5% to 35%.

short discount book   Typically, a nontrade book.

short discount publisher   A publisher of nontrade books.

short-grained paper   Paper in which the grain runs parallel to the shortest sheet dimension.

short rate   An advertising rate billed to an advertiser that is higher than a rate previously billed because the advertiser has not purchased the amount of space or met the minimum insertion requirement on which the lower rate was based. See also *contract rate; contract year; frequency discount; one-time rate.*

short-run publishing   The practice of publishing a book economically in a reasonably short time for a small market. Sometimes done from typewritten sheets supplied by the author. See also *camera-ready copy.*

shorts   See *short shipment.*

short shipment   A shipment of a book order in which one or more titles are unavailable and, therefore, back ordered. Books omitted from initial shipment are referred to as *shorts.*

short title   An abbreviated or shortened title of a book used to identify it in a computer printout, on a price list or order form, or in a bibliography.

short-title catalog   A shortened version of a publisher's full catalog, usually giving bare bibliographic details, such as author, title, publication date, ISBN, pages, and such other information that may aid ordering.

shot down   A proposal that has been disapproved.

show   Another term for an exhibit at a meeting or convention.

show decorator (exhibits and conventions)   The contractor at an exhibit or convention designed by the show sponsor to provide on a rental basis for the duration of the show all booth furnishings desired—tables, risers, chairs, waste baskets, smoking stands, carpeting. Such items are usually ordered in advance of the show and are in place before the show's opening. Exhibitors should ensure that all furnishings billed are actually provided.

show discount   See *convention discount.*

show kit   See *exhibitor's kit.*

show-through (paper)   The degree to which printing on one side of a sheet can be seen from the other side. See also *opacity.*

shrinkage (bookstores)   Inventory missing from a bookstore's stock that has not been recorded as sales. Shoplifting is the main source. Others include poor checking of incoming stock and nonrecorded removal of damaged stock.

shrink-wrap insert   An advertising insert placed inside the shrink-wrapping on top of a book.

shrink-wrapping   A process where plastic packaging is applied by machine to a book to form a tightly sealed plastic skin that is airtight, waterproof, and offers protection.

SI   See *International System of Units (SI).*

SIC   See *Standard Industrial Classification.*

sidebar   A related piece of information placed alongside the major textual information, usually in a box, in a shaded area, or visually set off in some way.

sidelines   Nonbook items sold in a bookstore.

side wiring/side stitching　A publication that is bound by placing staples through the signatures, near the spine. Although very strong, this method does not allow pages to lie flat. See also *saddle stitching*.

signature (in advertisement)　Name and address at the end of an advertisement, usually accompanied by the publisher's colophon or device. The signature is sometimes called a *logotype* or *logo*.

signature (in bound publication)　A printed sheet folded to page size for binding by itself or with other such folded sheets to form a book, periodical, catalog, etc. Most signatures are in multiples of 8, i.e., 8, 16, 32, 64, and 128. The norm for most book signatures is 32 pages. Three factors in signature size are sheet size, press size, and trim size. A four-page signature is not usual, but can be done on a small press when required as an insert.

signature line　A line on an order form calling for the respondent's signature. This is an important factor in free examination offers to consumer mailings, since it provides proof of the order should it later be denied.

signature-with-order　See *signature line*.

silk screen process　A form of stencil printing. The master may be hand cut out of a film, or made photographically. This master or stencil is then adhered to a fine mesh silk, fiber, or metal screen and a backing material peeled off the stencil. The screen, with master attached, is then laid on top of the surface to be printed, and ink is forced through the stencil to form the printed impression. Often used for making signs and posters.

silver print　See *blue (blueprint or blueline)*.

simultaneous publication　Publication of both cloth and paper editions of a book at the same time.

single-advertiser magazine　A controlled circulation publication with editorial content aimed at a specific market and containing a single advertising insert bought and paid for by a single sponsor. Typically, circulation of a single-advertiser magazine is 20,000 to 40,000, although some go higher.

Single Title Order Plan (STOP) An arrangement administered by the American Booksellers Association whereby booksellers can special order books not normally carried in stock from the approximately 700 participating publishers in the STOP plan. By following the instructions listed for each publisher, the bookseller sends in a check with a STOP order, which the publisher accepts as payment in full and ships the book promptly at a discount equal to or close to normal trade discount. Some publishers recommend that booksellers send in an open check rather than one with the amount filled in so that price increases or changes in postage charges can be accommodated. See also *open check/open draft*; *STOP form.*

sinkage The amount of space left blank at the top of a page before the first line of type, properly measured from the top of the normal text page.

SISAC See *Serials Industry Systems Advisory Committee*; *SISAC code.*

SISAC Code A code developed by the Serials Industry Systems Advisory Committee to provide a standard means of uniquely identifying serial issues and articles. The code contains all of the information normally used to identify serial publications, presented in a strictly defined standard code suitable for transcription into a machine readable form. It permits publishers, libraries, and vendors to communicate about serial publications.

SI units (copywriting) See *International System of Units (SI).*

size indications in printed matter Sizes are stated as width by depth (8½″ wide × 11″ deep). *Trim size* indicates the actual extremities of a printed piece. *Bleed size* is ⅛″ on each side of a printed sheet that is to bleed. Thus an 8½″ × 11″ sheet that is to bleed four sizes should be 8¾″ × 11¼″. *Plate* size is overall size of printing plate, including bleed (where applicable).

sizing (of paper) Treatment of the surface of paper to make it less porous and to prevent penetration of water. Offset papers require sizing.

SKU Originally Stock Keeping Unit. Now used to mean "store control unit." See also *SKU system.*

SKU system   A stock control system widely used in the retail book trade, especially by the larger chains, such as Walden and Dalton. SKU, an internal version of the ISBN numbering system, is derived from Stores Keeping Unit.

SLA   See *Special Libraries Association.*

SLA conference   The annual meeting of the Special Libraries Association, held in June in various cities. A major exhibit opportunity for publishers with publications, products, and services of interest to special librarians. All major library jobbers also participate. 1989, New York City; 1990, Cleveland. See also *Special Libraries Association.*

slanted shelving   Bookshelves for exhibits and bookstores that are designed to facilitate face-out display of books and other publications. See also *easel.*

slash (typography)   The term used for a diagonal mark or slant line as in and/or. Also called *solidus, shilling mark, virgule.*

sleeper   A book that had poor initial sales, but later became a substantial seller. May also refer to a book that sells much better than projected.

slipcased edition   An edition of a work furnished in a protective open-ended boxlike container. See also *boxed edition/boxed set.*

slippage (of titles)   Delay of books in production beyond originally scheduled publication dates.

slug   A line of composition or spacing material cast by a Linotype or similar machine. Also a temporary line inserted as an identifying reminder of a line or of lines to be supplied later. See also *title slug (direct mail).*

small buy (bookstore)   A minimal order for a trade title the bookseller feels has limited sales appeal.

small caps (typography)   Small capital letters, shaped like capital letters but only the height of a lower-case (small) x. Indicated in copy by two lines drawn underneath. See also *c & sc (typography); caps (typography); sc; upper case, all caps (typography); x-height (typography).*

small press A small, independent publisher with limited finances and resources. Michael Coffey, editor-in-chief of *Small Press* magazine, offers this definition: A press "with revenues of less than $5 million, fewer than 24 titles a year, fewer than 12 employees."

Small Press A bimonthly magazine devoted to the small, independent publisher. Covers all aspects of publishing, including production, pricing, marketing, promotion, distribution and fulfilment, and new technologies. Carries approximately 100 small press book reviews per issue. From: Meckler Publishing Corp., 11 Ferry Lane West, Westport, CT 06880. Phone: 203-226-6967

SMP required See *sample mailing piece requirement.*

smyth sewing/Smyth sewing Fastening side-by-side signatures so that each is linked with thread to adjacent signatures, as well as saddle sewn through its centerfold. Stitching is on the back of the fold. Smyth sewn books open flat.

social science research monograph A work presenting the results of original research on a topic and thereby making a substantive contribution to social science knowledge.

society book publishing program See *professional association book publishing.*

Society for Scholarly Publishing (SSP) A national association of individuals involved in scholarly publishing, including scholars, editors, publishers, librarians, printers, booksellers, and others. Publication: *SSP Letter*, published six times a year. Annual meeting late May. Address: 2000 Florida Avenue, NW, Washington DC 20009. Phone: 202-328-3555.

Society for Scholarly Publishing Letter See *Society for Scholarly Publishing.*

society list (direct mail) See *association list (direct mail).*

society publisher A publishing arm of a learned or professional society. Society publishing programs originate with the membership, and the publisher is answerable to the organization's membership. See also *professional association book publishing.*

softbound See *paperback/paperbound; softcover.*

soft copy   Information displayed on a video terminal, from digital storage, or in microform; also unedited manuscript copy. See also *hard copy*.

softcover   A nonrigid paper book cover. Also called *paperbound* or *paperback*.

software   1. Computer programs. 2. The application programs and system programs of a computer system required to perform any operation. 3. A program or group of programs needed to perform or accomplish a particular function on a computer.

solidus   Slant line. Also called *slash, shilling mark, virgule*.

solo direct-mail effort   See *solo mailing*.

solo mailing   A mailing in which only one book is offered. U.K.: solus mailing. See also *multiple-product direct-mail promotions*.

solus mailing   See *solo mailing*.

SOR   See *sale or return (SOR)*.

source   See *credit line; quote source*.

source code, mailing list   An identifier on a mailing label or an order form that enables a mailer to identify responses from a particular list or promotion.

source database   A full text database containing the complete body of a source of information and that can be searched electronically via a computer.

source key   See *key*.

space (magazine publishing)   1. A general reference to advertising in periodicals. The word *space* is often synonymous with *advertising*. See also *time*. 2. That portion of a periodical that is available for advertising.

space advertising   Advertising inserted in a print medium and paid for according to its size, or the amount of space it occupies. Sometimes referred to as *paid space advertising*, or *print advertising*. Book marketers often have separate budgets for space advertising and for direct-mail advertising. See also *editorial matter; space contract*.

space advertising response speed   See *advertising format response speed.*

space contract   An agreement between an advertiser and the publisher of an advertising medium that specifies the terms according to which advertisements will be placed during the term of the contract, usually in compliance with the current rate card. Such contracts may guarantee special positions, space discounts, and so on.

space discount   A discount given by a publication based on a commitment by an advertiser to purchase a certain amount of advertising space over a given amount of time, usually a year. See also *contract year (advertising); frequency discount.*

spaced mailing   A practice in direct-mail promotion of mailing different lists at different times, particularly where there is a possibility of a high rate of name duplication between the lists.

space rep   Sales representative of a print advertising medium. See also *media rep.*

space salesman/space salesperson   See *media rep; pub rep.*

special charges, special sale   See *special sales shipping charges.*

special deal   A special offer by a publisher to a bookseller as a buying incentive, for example, a special discount for an order beyond a minimum size. Dozens of publishers offer special deals to booksellers at the annual convention of the American Booksellers Association. Special deals may include high discount, free shipping, extended billing, or extra free books. Most special deals are listed in the ABA convention issues of *American Bookseller* and *Publishers Weekly.*

special edition   An edition of a book published for a special purpose, or in a special format. A special edition may be done for premium or book club purposes, for participants in a conference or seminar, or for government use. It may also be packaged as a special volume or issue of a journal, as installments in a journal, or as a supplement to a journal. Some publishers also issue special editions in less expensive paper and binding to be sold at reduced prices to third world countries.

special fourth-class mail   See *book rate; library rate (postage).*

special interest book A book on a particular subject or one aimed at a specific audience. See also *general interest book*.

special interest book club A consumer book club catering to a specific audience with a special interest such as astronomy, electronics, gardening, or military history. See also *book club; professional book club*.

special interest magazine Generally a publication catering to a special interest that may be related to a hobby, pastime, profession, or business.

special issue An issue of a periodical that is devoted to or features a single topic, such as spring announcement issue, instruments issue, or convention issue. See also *convention issue*.

special issues directory See *Guide to Special Issues and Indexes of Periodicals*.

specialist bookshop U.K. term for a specialty bookstore. Specialist bookshops tend to be more common in the U.K. than in the U.S. See also *specialty bookstore/specialty bookselling/specialty bookseller*.

specialized catalog A catalog designed for a specific outlet. A trade catalog, for example, is issued spring and fall expressly for bookstores and trade wholesalers and may be restricted to titles offering full trade discounts only. Other catalogs may be produced for libraries, for special sale accounts, for educators, etc., or on specific subjects or subject groupings.

specialized periodical A periodical that caters to the interests of a specific field or to individuals interested in a particular topic or area of activity.

special librarian One of a group of information managers and librarians who work in special libraries and information centers. They are skilled in searching for and locating specialized information for the clientele served. The managers and librarians not only hold advanced degrees in library and information science, but also have special training and skills in the fields they serve. Most hold membership in the Special Libraries Association and are affiliated with one of the 29 SLA divisions related to their specialty and also with one of the 53 SLA regional chapters that meet on a regular basis.

Special Libraries   A quarterly publication of the Special Libraries Association containing news and information of interest to special librarians. See *Special Libraries Association.*

Special Libraries Association (SLA)   An international organization of professional librarians and information specialists who serve business, industry, institutions, government and research organizations, and departments of public and university libraries. Approximately 12,000 individual members participate in some 29 specialized divisions and various state and regional chapters, many of which publish bulletins and newsetters. Membership list available for rental. Founded in 1909. SLA, 1700 18th Street, NW, Washington, DC 20009. Phone: 202-234-4700.

special library   1. A library or information center the primary purpose of which is to provide information to support the goals and activities of its parent organization or sponsor. The latter may be an individual, corporation, association, government agency, or other group. 2. A specialized departmental collection within a library responsible for the organization and dissemination of information on a specific subject, primarily offering service to a specialized clientele through the use of varied media and methods. See also *special librarian.*

special library market, including business and technical libraries Approximately 11,000 libraries in the U.S.

special markets   A term used by some publishers to describe special sales activity or sales to markets not considered traditional outlets for books. See *special sales.*

special offer   1. An advertised offering providing a special benefit, such as a reduced price, discount, premium, free copy, or trial subscription to those using the special offer response vehicle— coupon or order form, during a specified period or during a telephone solicitation. 2. An offer made by a rep on a sales call. 3. An offer made at an exhibit or convention as a sales inducement. See also *coupon program.*

special order (n.)   A book order placed by a bookseller with a publisher to fill a specific customer request. UK: OTO (only to order).

special sales   The generic term for all publisher sales made to or through nontraditional outlets; i. e., any outlet other than a bookstore or library. Special sales is the most rapid growth area in publishing and the one offering the most potential for the future. Special sales may be known by many other names, depending on the publisher, but the publishing industry recognizes "special sales" as the basic identifier. The primary special sales outlets are mail-order catalog houses and professional associations and societies that offer books to their members through their publications. Industrial firms that use books as premiums are another nontraditional outlet, and a few publishers also include book clubs in this category.

special sales, industrial training   Usually bulk sales of publications to be used in conjunction with on-site training programs for business or industry. Discount is usually based on quantity.

special sales, premium   A sale usually to a company or institution for the one-time purchase of a bulk quantity of a specific book for a specific purpose. Price often is a critical factor and a quotation based on a unit price rather than a discount is usually the best approach.

special sales accounts, copy approach   Typically, most prospects who may be sought after as special sales accounts, such as professional associations and societies, mail-order catalog houses or business firms unfamiliar with bookselling practices, require special promotional approaches. These six benefits have been found helpful in special sales promotional approaches: (1) full selection option from publisher's active list; (2) opportunity for product or service diversification; (3) opportunity to broaden customer base; (4) for member organizations, opportunity to improve member services; (5) increase income/earnings with little or no effort or investment; (6) complement or enhance their current offerings.

special sales account turnoffs   Experienced special sales marketers have found the following six pointers to be strong deterrents to either maintaining existing special sales accounts or establishing new ones: (1) avoid subscription offers; (2) avoid prepublication offers; (3) avoid books with a content difficult to comprehend; (4) avoid books with little or no discount; (5) avoid sale requirements that require tieing up cash for inventory; (6) avoid sale requirements that require a long-term commitment.

special sales discount   Some special sales accounts, especially mail-order booksellers, favor a high discount to other types of arrangements. Many will opt for the higher discount with no return privilege to a lesser discount with a returns option. A two-tier discount schedule covering both options is recommended for one type of account. Association and society special sale accounts often give a discount to members and expect to receive fairly substantial discounts from publisher.

special sales inquiry handling   When handling inquiries from special sales outlets that could lead to bulk sales of a book or books, it is often best to send sample copies of the books in question, since buying decisions for such large orders cannot be based on promotional literature alone.

special sales outlets, primary   (1) Mail-order catalog houses; (2) trade associations (or their publications); (3) professional societies; (4) business publications and journals; (5) industry (for industrial training, premiums, etc.).

special sales questionnaire   An author questionnaire issued by some publishers' special sales departments to elicit information that may lead to bulk sales arrangements of the author's book. See Appendix 13.

special sales review copy See *review copy (special sales)*.

special sales shipping charges   A charge added on to the net price for shipping a book to a special sales account, or for dropping to the account's customer. Most publishers ship at the book rate (Special Fourth Class Rate), or when requested to do so, by UPS. See also *special sales shipping options; special sales terms of payment.*

special sales shipping options   (1) Bulk shipment directly to account; (2) drop shipment to the account's customer. See also *special sales shipping charges; special sales terms of payment.*

special sales terms of payment   For most publishers, special sales book shipments are due and payable 30 days from date of invoice. See also *special sales shipping charges; special sales shipping options.*

special to (publicity)   A heading used on a news release written in a nonexclusive but special way for the publication to which it is being sent. Releases to other publications can be sent simultaneously, if written somewhat differently. See also *exclusive to (publicity)*.

specialty bookstore/specialty bookselling/specialty bookseller   A bookstore or shop specializing in a particular subject or related group of subjects, such as travel, food, or cooking. Such stores, because of their special nature, are less sensitive to competition from chains or discount operations, and less subject to seasonal fluctuations in sales than a general bookstore. See also *specialist bookshop*.

specialty retail store/specialty retailer   A retail outlet for books that is not a bookstore. These may include computer stores, craft shops, health food stores, sporting goods stores, or any store catering to a special interest group.

specialty wholesaler   A wholesaler of specialty items who also supplies his or her accounts with books in the same specialty area. For example, a pet food distributor who also carries books about pets.

specs   Type specifications.

spine out   Book displayed on a counter or shelf with only the spine showing. At some cooperative book exhibits, there are different exhibit rates for "spine out" or "face out" display of a book. See also *face out*.

spin-off (book)   A volume with the content consisting of selected material taken from a larger work. Various encyclopedia publishers publish spin-off segments of the larger work as smaller independent books.

spin-off (journal)   Occasionally a segment or department of a journal, representing an emerging branch within the larger field, is spun off into a separate publication. *School Library Journal* is a spin-off of a former department of *Library Journal*. *AB Bookman's Weekly* is a spin-off of a former department of *Publishers Weekly*.

spiral-bound edition   An edition in which all pages, including paper covers, have been hole-punched and bound with a spiral binding that permits pages to lay flat. See also comb binding.

split galleys   Galley proofs half the usual length. Occasionally done for ease of use by reviewers.

split run   In space advertising, split runs permit different advertisements or different versions of the same advertisement to appear in alternate copies of the same issue simultaneously.

split-run edition   A pressrun for which a publisher has designated a number of books to be bound in hardcover and the remainder to be bound in paperback. See also pressrun.

split-run test   An option offered by some magazines permitting two different advertisements, copy approaches, or coupon offers to run in alternate copies of the same issue for testing purposes. Split-run can also be used in direct mail with alternate mailing list names, or to reach two distinct groups, both included in the same circulation of a particular promotion.

split test (direct mail)   A test mailing of two or more portions of the same mailing list. See also list testing.

spoilage   The percentage of any printing job spoiled by the printer in the various processes related to printing, folding, and binding. It is wise to order in excess of actual needs to allow for such spoilage.

sponsored book   A book issued by an established publishing house in behalf of a company or organization with a special interest in having it published. Sometimes a payment is made to insure the publisher against loss from a small sale through normal channels, or the sponsor may agree to buy a sufficient number of copies at an agreed-upon price to ensure profitable publication. Usually such books require no royalty.

sponsored edition   An edition of a book in which all or part of the costs of producing the particular edition have been subsidized by a company, organization, or individual other than the publisher.

spot light (exhibits and conventions)   A lamp focusing extra illumination in a controlled area of an exhibit booth—usually within the booth or a portion of it. A well-lighted booth is an important prerequisite of a convention book display. Conversely, a well-planned booth lacking sufficient illumination can lose or discourage traffic.

spotty coverage (bookstore) See book *distribution jargon (bookstores)*.

spread (advertising) Short for two-page spread, meaning an advertisement on two facing pages. See also *center spread (advertising)*.

spread (bookstore) Distribution of a book among various bookstore accounts visited by a sales rep.

spread, half-page (advertising) See *half-page spread (advertising)*.

spread, junior (advertising) See *junior spread (advertising)*.

spread, three-page (advertising) See *three-page spread (advertising)*.

spread is good (trade book) Sales rep language for a book that has had wide acceptance among bookstore accounts.

spring list (publishers) 1. Usually books published during the first half of the calendar year. 2. Those books published after the publication date of the spring catalog. 3. Those books published in the six-month period since the issuance of the preceding fall catalog.

spring season (trade bookselling) Usually mid-January to mid-June.

square serif A typeface with serifs usually as heavy as or heavier than the body of the type. Such faces are used mainly for headlines and display purposes. Such faces include Barnum, Beton, Cairo, Clarendon (and Craw-Clarendon), Karnak, Memphis, and Stymie.

SRDS Standard Rate and Data Service. SRDS produces the most widely used directories covering advertising rates and data for space advertising, mailing lists, and broadcast media. Advertising and marketing people frequently refer to these directories simply as SRDS. Address: 3002 Glenview Road, Wilmette, IL, 60091. See also *SRDS Business Publication Rates and Data; SRDS Direct Mail List Rates and Data*.

SRDS Business Publication Rates and Data A monthly catalog listing more than 4,200 U.S. business publications in 175 market classifications. Includes advertising rates, contract and copy regulations, mechanical requirements, issuance and closing dates, and circulation statements, as well as a direct response advertising media section, listing cooperative card deck availabilities. From: Standard Rate and Data Service, Inc., 3002 Glenview Road, Wilmette, IL 60091.

SRDS Consumer Magazine and Agri-Media Rates and Data A monthly publication that gives all the rates and advertising specifications for consumer magazines and for farm publishers and broadcasters. From: Standard Rate and Data Service, Inc., 3002 Glenview Road, Wilmette, IL 60091.

SRDS Direct Mail List Rates and Data A directory sold on a yearly subscription basis containing over 55,000 business and consumer mailing list selections in 227 market categories. Each rental list included has 11 points of information from list source to test arrangement. A subscription includes six bimonthly issues and 24 update bulletins with late additions and changes. From: Standard Rate and Data Service, Inc. 3002 Glenview Road, Wilmette, IL 60091.

SRDS Newspaper Rates and Data A monthly publication that gives all the rates and advertising specifications for newspapers. Published by Standard Rate and Data Service, Inc., 3002 Glenview Road, Wilmette, IL 60091.

SSP See *Society for Scholarly Publishing.*

stable of journals 1. A term occasionally used to refer to a wide-ranging journals publishing program. 2. All of the journals of one publisher.

stacked advertising (periodical) The practice of bunching up or "stacking" all advertising by a periodical publisher—either in front of a periodical or in back, or in both locations, but nowhere else. Both *New England Journal of Medicine* and *Annals of Internal Medicine* stack advertising both in front and back. See also *interspersed advertising (periodical).*

staggered mailing See *spaced mailing.*

stamp, live An actual postage stamp affixed to a mailing piece as contrasted with a metered or printed postal indicia.

stamp formats (for book and journal promotions) (1) Folded sheet of stamps enclosed with an outgoing book shipment to a mail-order customer; (2) bound into catalog; (3) enclosed in standard letter package; (4) tipped onto cover letter; (5) separate "yes" or "no" stamps for affixing to order card. See *stamp promotions; stamps (in book promotion).*

stamp promotion, printing source Specialty Printers of America, 201 East 42nd Street, New York, NY 10017 Phone: 212-697-0820.

stamp promotion response instructions Directions on how stamps are to be used in order placement. Typically, with a stamp sheet covering many books, the instruction will be "To order these titles, paste stamps on order card or your letterhead and return to (publisher name and address)."

stamp promotions Publisher promotions in which postage-stamp-like printed sheets are used as order vehicles. Printed stamp sheets may contain anywhere from 1 to 120 stamps. Stamps may accompany direct-mail efforts or be used as book or envelope enclosures. See also *stamps (in book promotion); stamp formats (for book and journal promotions); stamp promotion, printing source.*

stamps (in book promotion) A number of publishers use stamps to promote book sales. Each stamp usually illustrates a book jacket or cover and sometimes an order number. The stamp is perforated and gummed and is removed and applied the same as any postage stamp. The recipient of a stamp promotion need only moisten the back of the stamp and affix it to an order vehicle or on a letterhead to place an order for the book illustrated or described on the stamp. Most publishers issue sheets of stamps. The leading producer of stamps for publisher book promotion is Specialty Printers of America, 201 East 42nd Street, New York, NY 10017.

stamps, precanceled See *precanceled stamp mailing; precanceled stamps, use of.*

stand-alone store/bookstore A separate entity separated from a larger group or chain. For example, the software departments of the B. Dalton book chain in late 1987 were spun off and became independent selling units, or "stand-alones," under a separate corporation.

standard (print publication)   A volume of accepted products or practices for an industry, trade, product, or profession. Generally published by or on behalf of an association, society, or regulatory voluntary agency in the field covered. Two major publishers of standards are the IEEE (electrical engineering) and the ASME (mechanical engineering).

Standard Address Number (SAN)   A unique seven-digit numeric identifier preceded by the letters SAN and used by book buying and selling organizations to permit easier and more accurate communications. Initiated in the U.S. in 1980 and administered by the R.R. Bowker Company, the SAN is a standard of the American National Standards Institute (ANSI).

Standard Industrial Classification (SIC)   A government-assigned code number by function and product for every U.S. business. Many mailing list compilers rent lists by SIC classification.

standard No. 10 package   See *direct-mail package.*

Standard Periodical Directory   A biennial publication listing 65,000 U.S. and Canadian periodicals arranged by subject. Published by Oxbridge Communications Inc., New York, NY 10011.

Standard Rate & Data Service, Inc.   A publisher of advertising media reference directories located at 3002 Glenview Road, Wilmette, IL 60091. See entries under *SRDS.*

standing order   A single written order authorizing automatic shipment of each edition of a work that appears periodically or annually. Such an order can also be placed for each new volume of an ongoing series. The book is shipped upon publication; the order remains in effect until a request to discontinue it is submitted. Such orders may or may not offer a preferential discount. There is no penalty for discontinuance. Also called *continuation order.* See also *approval plan.*

standing order customer   U.K. term for bookseller agency account.

standing order discount   A discount given by a publisher to a library, company, or facility that places a standing order for automatic shipment of new books in a particular area or for a particular work published serially. Some publishers of reference annuals give a 5% discount for standing orders.

standing order plan (bookstore)   See *bookseller agency plan.*

stat (n.)   Abbreviation for photostat. See also *photostat/stat.*

stat (v.)   An instruction to make a photostatic enlargement or reduction. Example: Stat to 85% of copy size.

statement stuffer   A term generally applied to advertising enclosed with an invoice or statement. Also called bill or envelope stuffer. See also *bag stuffer; envelope stuffer; flier/flyer; insert.*

stet   Proofreading term for "let it stand as it is."

sticker (v.)   1. The practice of inserting a label in a book to identify its distribution source. Used by publishers who market import books that are received bearing only the name of the originating publisher. The sticker not only identifies the domestic publisher or distributor but also the domestic ISBN number. 2. Adding a sticker to a book's cover or jacket to accommodate price changes.

STM   International Group of Scientific, Technical, and Medical Publishers. Based in Amsterdam, the group was established in 1969 in Frankfurt and now has nearly 150 member companies. Paul Nijhoff Asser is executive secretary. Address: International Group of Scientific, Technical and Medical Publishers, Keizersgracht 462, 1016GE, Amsterdam, Holland.

STM book   A scientific, technical, or medical book. Also a book issued by a member of the International Group of Scientific, Technical, and Medical Publishers.

STM bookseller   Bookseller carrying substantial inventory of scientific, technical, and/or medical books.

STM booksellers, largest U.K.   The two largest and leading booksellers in England are Foyles in London and Blackwells in Oxford. Blackwells does the larger business, but most of it is in mail order and goes overseas. Foyles, with nearly twice the floor selling area, does most of its selling on the premises. See separate entries for each. Three other substantial STM booksellers are Dillons, Modern Book Company, and H.K. Lewis. All are located in London.

STM library market, U.K. Approximately 40% academic, 40% special libraries in industry and government, 10% public libraries, and 10% other.

STM market The market for scientific, technical, and medical books.

STM publisher/company Publisher engaged in the publication of scientific, technical, and/or medical books. Within the U.S., the term PSP publisher is more common. See also *PSP publisher*.

stock Generally refers to the material that will be printed, such as paper, plastic, foil, cloth, etc.

stock list A selected list of titles used by a publisher's trade sales reps for inventory checking and writing of orders during sales calls. Typically, a stock list will carry author's name, title, price, and blank spaces for quantity-to-order and inventory-on-hand.

stock on hand (bookstore) The number of copies of a specific book available for sale in a particular bookstore. Also called inventory on hand. See also *rate of sale (bookstore)*.

stock photograph See *photo agency*.

stock plan, backlist See *backlist stock plan*.

stock turn See *turnover (bookstore)*.

stop A term used by sales reps to refer to a single bookstore sales call. See also *making the rounds; Single Title Order Plan (STOP); STOP form; subscribing a book*.

STOP See *Single Title Order Plan (STOP); STOP form*.

STOP form A special order form made available by the American Booksellers Association to facilitate delivery of bookseller special orders at the lowest cost to both bookseller and publisher and to speed the book to the customer before the need for it has passed. A single form can be used for single or multiple copies of any given title and, so long as cash accompanies the order, it will be filled. Publishers discount book orders according to publisher STOP discounts listed in the "Single Title Order Plan" guide issued by the ABA. Approximately 700 publishers participate in the plan. See also *Single Title Order Plan (STOP)*.

STOP order   An order placed by a bookseller on a STOP order form in accordance with the Single Title Order Plan policies of the American Booksellers Association. See also *drop shipment, STOP order; Single Title Order Plan (STOP); STOP form.*

STOP order drop shipments   See *drop shipment, STOP order.*

STOP order pricing   See *pricing on initial STOP order.*

store control unit   See *SKU system.*

strike-on composition/direct-impression composition   Copy prepared for platemaking and printing using a typewriter or other keyboard device that makes a physical impression on the paper. See also *cold-type composition/cold composition.*

strip-in   See *stripping (printing).*

stripping (mass-market paperbacks)   Ripping off the cover of an unsold paperback and returning it to the publisher for credit.

stripping (printing)   The assembling, usually in negative form, of the elements that are to appear on the printing plate.

stub on reply card   See *reply card bearing stub.*

stuffer   See *flier/flyer; statement stuffer.*

sub. (abbreviation)   1. Subject (as in subject catalog). 2. Subscriber (periodicals and subscription services). 3. Substance (basis weight in paper).

subhead   A secondary headline between the main headline and the main body of the advertisement. It may also be a single-line insert every two or three paragraphs in text matter, usually in a different typeface from the text.

subject catalog   A catalog that contains information about a publisher's list in a specific subject or grouping of related subjects. Such catalogs enable scholars, instructors, professionals, and special collection librarians to locate titles that are related to their special interests or needs. Librarians prefer subject catalogs where possible.

Subject Guide to Books in Print   A three-volume annual supplement to *Books In Print*, published by R.R. Bowker, 245 W. 17th Street, New York, NY, 10011. All of the entries in *Books in Print* are listed under their subject headings.

Subject Guide to Forthcoming Books   See *Forthcoming Books*.

subject librarian (college)   A librarian in a college or university library responsible for collection development on a particular subject. Subject librarians often make the buying decision for ordering new research monographs and journals.

sub rights   See *subsidiary rights/sub rights*.

subscriber mailing list exchanges   See *mailing list exchanges, subscriber*.

subscriber mailing lists   See *periodical mailing list, free controlled subscriber; periodical mailing list, paid actives; periodical mailing list, subscriber*.

subscribing a book   A U.K. term for the practice of sales reps calling on bookshops and soliciting orders for new trade books. See also *making the rounds*.

subscription (book)   An order for a defined series of books published at variable intervals. The subscription implies intent to purchase the entire series or set in exchange for a price consideration that may be either a subscription price or a subscription discount off the price of individual volumes. See also *standing order; subscription discount (book); subscription discount (periodical); subscription price (book)*.

subscription (periodical)   An agreement between a publisher and an individual or organization to deliver a fixed number of issues of a periodical in exchange for payment or other consideration. Most subscriptions are either for a subscription year or a calendar year. A subscription year is one year from date of first issue sent. A calendar year is all issues produced between January and December of a specific year. For irregular serials published on a subscription year that is different from a calendar year, all new subscriptions begin with the current or next subscription year, say, July through June. See also *journal subscription cycle; magazine subscription cycle*.

subscription, bulk   See *bulk subscription (periodical or newsletter).*

subscription, direct (periodicals)   A subscription from a library placed directly with the publisher.

subscription agency, full service   A periodical subscription agency that functions as an extension of the library's periodicals acquisitions department, handling periodicals, annuals, serials, newspapers, newsletters, continuations, and more. Where customer service requirements are extensive and complex, customers are charged a service fee.

subscription agent/agency   The principal medium through which libraries place periodical subscriptions. Agents receive orders for periodicals from libraries and group them by publisher before forwarding them. Most publishers allow a small discount for this service. The library benefits by having a single source for all its periodicals, monthly billing, and reliable claims service. In Europe, libraries are more likely to place periodical subscriptions through their bookseller, who, in effect, serves as the periodical subscription agent.

subscription agent, European   See *European subscription agent.*

subscription agent, health sciences   A subscription agent specializing in health science journals. The J.A. Majors Company is recognized as the largest subscription agent in this field.

subscription agent fees   Payment to a subscription agent for orders rendered to publishers. Two methods of reimbursement by publishers: (1) a discount off subscription price; (2) a flat payment per subscription. The discount is the most common method used, though some publishers neither grant discounts to agents nor pay any fees.

subscription agents, largest   EBSCO Subscription Services; F.W. Faxon Co; Moore-Cottrell Subscription Agencies, Inc.; Swets North America, Inc.; McGregor Magazine Agency; Turner Subscription Agency, Inc.

subscription decision-makers, academic   See *academic library subscription decisions.*

subscription discount (book)   A discount given by a book publisher to customers who subscribe to a group of books published
in series over a period of time, such as an encyclopedia. When
the price of individual volumes is not set or is subject to change
from one volume to another, the publisher, in lieu of a subscription price per volume, may offer a subscription discount which
will be applicable to all volumes, irrespective of price.

subscription discount (periodical)   A discount given by the publisher of a periodical to a subscription agent. Traditionally, the
discount reflects the saving by the publisher of billing and
processing individual subscription orders, since most subscription agents group their subscriptions to each publisher, rather
than sending them one at a time.

subscription offer (book)   An offer to supply more than one book,
either by group as in a set of encyclopedias or in serial format
for an indefinite period, as with an updating service offer or
continuing series, sometimes at a price advantage over the
single-copy price, or with a premium for signing up.

subscription payment requirement, periodical   Magazine publishers typically will enter a subscription order and bill for subsequent payment. Journal publishers, with few exceptions, will ask
for prepayment before starting a subscription.

subscription price (book)   A stated price per book for a series of
books published at variable intervals. Price is usually less than
the price of books purchased as individual units, and will hold
for the duration of the subscription. See also *subscription discount (book)*.

subscription product/subscription-based product   1. A product
sold on a subscription basis. Customers subscribe either for a
fixed time period, such as a year, or until they serve notice that
they wish to discontinue their subscription. 2. A subscription for
a closed-end series with the subscriber agreeing to enter an
order for the entire series or set in exchange for a guarantee that
billing will be at the subscription price, or discount. 3. A loose-
leaf publication with an updating service. 4. Any periodical for
which a renewal must be made after a prescribed subscription
period.

subscription product lifetime value   See *lifetime value of subscriber product*.

subscription product pay rate   See *payment rate/pay-up rate (subscription product)*.

subscription product renewal rate   See *renewal rate (subscription product)*.

subscription promotion yield rule   A periodical with a 75% renewal rate will yield revenue equal to three times the initial year's subscription rate over a five-year period.

subscription rates (journals)   Rates charged by journals for subscriptions. Many journals have rates for individuals that are different from the rates for libraries and institutions. Orders placed through subscription agents are always charged at the institutional rate.

subscription reference books   Reference books designed for sale one book at a time.

subscription year   The annual publication cycle on which a subscription fee is based. See also *journal subscription cycle; magazine subscription cycle*.

subsidiary company   See *foreign subsidiary*.

subsidiary rights/sub rights   All those rights of a literary property beyond original publication rights. These may include: first serial; second and subsequent serial; digest; book condensation; dramatic/performing; broadcast/television; anthology and quotation; mechanical reproduction; merchandising; foreign/translation.

subsidy publisher   See *vanity publisher*.

substance/substance weight (paper)   See *basis weight (paper)*.

subtitle   An additional or secondary title of a book, often used to explain the book's content or intent. When omitted from advertising copy, it can often destroy the value of the ad. Increasingly, the subtitle is separated from the book's title by a colon.

Successful Direct Marketing Methods, 3rd Ed.   A useful reference on direct marketing by Bob Stone. Published by Crain Books, Chicago, 1984.

sunned (antiquarian bookselling)   A book faded or discolored as a result of exposure to sunlight. See also *antiquarian bookselling terms*.

superior characters/superior letters/superior figures/superscript (typography)   Small type characters, usually numerals or asterisks, printed above x-height that are used to cite reference notes, or superscript characters used in chemical or mathematical formulas. See also *inferior characters (typography)*; *x-height (typography)*.

supplementary reading list (academic)   A list of titles prepared by an academic instructor that are supportive of the adoptive text but are not required reading.

supplements (book)   Published products related to a previously published work. Supplements, when free, are sent automatically. If sold, they may be ordered at the time of original purchase, or in response to a notification from the publisher.

suppress   To hold back or eliminate a segment of a mailing list run. See also *merge-purge (mailing list)*; *list suppression, database*.

suppression of database names   See *list suppression, data base*.

surprint   To print type over a halftone, block of color, or other type.

swapping, mailing list   See *list exchange (direct mail)*.

sweepstakes   An advertising or promotion effort in which prizes are awarded by chance, such as a lottery, to those who respond to the promotion. Book sweepstakes offerings should not be undertaken without competent legal advice. There are federal and often state laws that must be complied with in such offerings.

swipe file   A file maintained by many creative people, copywriters in particular, of advertising ideas from other sources, often competitors. Swipe files represent the best efforts of others and are useful idea stimulators for writing ad copy or creating a mailing piece. In publishing, samples of competitive mailings can keep you abreast of what the competition is doing as well as provide a source of ideas on new advertising innovations that you can adapt to your own efforts.

symposia   Books that offer a collection of papers on one subject, usually given at a meeting after which they are published in one volume known as a "symposium." See also *conference proceedings*.

synoptic format   A synopsis of a larger work; a brief summary of the most important features of the full text.

synoptic journal   A publishing format used in some scientific or scholarly journals in which only summaries of the authors' full papers are presented. Full copies of any paper are supplied on demand from a data bank.

synoptic microform journal   A journal that prints only synopses or summaries of scientific papers. It simultaneously publishes the full papers in a microfiche edition of the journal.

T

tables, exhibit See *exhibit tables.*

tabloid A newspaper or business publication about half the size of a standard newspaper and sometimes printed on newsprint. Magazines in tabloid format with reader service cards (product news magazines) are said to produce faster responses than magazines in conventional format. See also *product news magazine.*

tabloid, product oriented See *product news magazine.*

tabloid size Typically from 11″ to 11¾″ wide and 15″ to 17″ long.

tactical test (direct mail) See *test, tactical (direct mail).*

tagline A line added to a mailing piece to help direct it to a specific job title or function (marketing director, publicist, vice-president, etc.).

tape/mag tape See *magnetic tape.*

tape conversion The conversion of copy printed on paper to magnetic tape.

target audience 1. The desired or intended audience for a planned promotional effort. 2. The primary audience or market for a publication. 3. Experts in a given field or on a given topic for whom a particular book will serve as a reference tool or information source.

targeted copy Advertising copy tailored to the specific or specialized interests of the group or audience that the advertising will reach.

target market   The most likely buyers of a promotional offering. In publishing, the most likely buyers of a publication.

target marketing   1. Concentrating a marketing effort on specific segments within the perceived total market. 2. The practice of directing mailings to the primary audience for the product offered.

Target Marketing   A monthly trade periodical for the direct marketing industry. Formerly called *ZIP: Target Marketing*. Published by North American Publishing Co., 401 North Broad Street, Philadelphia, PA 19108.

tear sheet   A page torn from a specific issue of a publication containing an advertisement and sent to an advertiser or advertising agency as proof of insertion.

teaser   An advertisement or promotion designed to generate curiosity for a subsequent advertisement or promotion.

teaser copy   Copy on the mailing face of an envelope or self-mailer that attempts to capture the attention of the recipient and to entice him or her into reading the inside matter.

technical book definition   See *technical book publishing; technical book types.*

technical book publishing   Curtis Benjamin, in *What Happens in Book Publishing* (Bowker, 1967) describes technical book publishing as covering five distinctive fields: (1) mechanical arts; (2) mathematics and natural science; (3) engineering and all other applied sciences, including agriculture, forestry, military science, medicine, hygiene and public health, psychology, psychiatry, nursing, pharmacy, dentistry; (4) the social sciences—anthropology, economics, sociology, and government; and (5) industrial and business administration, which are based on both natural and social science. See also *technical book types.*

technical books, sales patterns   See *sales patterns for technical, professional, and reference books.*

technical bookstore   A bookstore carrying a large inventory of books on technical subjects, but with an inventory that may not be restricted to such books. See also *technical book publishing.*

technical book types Curtis Benjamin, in *What Happens in Book Publishing* (Bowker, 1967) describes five major kinds of books in almost every technical field: (1) practical how-to-do-it manuals; (2) technical tests; (3) purely theoretical treatises; (4) monographs; (5) handbooks. See also *technical book publishing.*

technical, business, and special library market See *special library market, including business and technical libraries.*

technical services, library See *library technical services.*

technical text A book on a technical subject, often used as a classroom textbook, and combining theory and application, at a particular level of the subject.

telegram format See *gram format (printed promotion).*

telemarketing/telephone marketing Use of the telephone in conjunction with the generation of sales.

telemarketing, inbound Receiving calls generated by the customer or prospect. The 800 toll-free number is designed to encourage this type of activity. See also *800 number (telephone).*

telemarketing, medical specialty Telephone marketing to physicians by medical specialty. One source of AMA physician phone numbers by medical specialty is Clark-O'Neill/Fisher-Stevens, One Broad Avenue, Fairview, NJ 07022. Phone: 201-945-3400.

telemarketing, outbound Telephone calls to customers or prospects for sales purposes.

telemarketing, subscription product renewals The practice of following up mailed renewal invoices for a subscription product with a telephone inquiry to the subscriber. Seasoned practitioners say the best timing is the period between the mailing of the second and third renewal invoices.

telemarketing list duplication rule List rentals for telemarketing purposes sometimes have the same name appearing more than once on a page. When several pages have been checked, if the rate of duplication is two or more names per page, the entire list should be checked for duplications before the list is used.

telemarketing list sampling rule A sample of 100 calls usually will give a response equal to that of a 1,000-name direct-mail test of the same list.

telemarketing mailing list A mailing list that includes telephone numbers and is suitable for telephone selling.

telemarketing pitch, sample size rule A telemarketing sales pitch that works well after 50 calls will work well for 500.

telemarketing rule, book See *50-50-50 rule (in book telemarketing)*.

telemarketing service bureau A service bureau that handles either inbound or outbound calls, or sometimes both, on a prearranged fee basis. Inbound service usually involves use of 800 toll-free numbers used in conjunction with the publisher's advertising and promotion. Calls are received by the service and transmitted to the publisher. Outbound telemarketing may involve preparation of sales scripts and sales campaigns on specific publishing projects, using the publisher's customer list or other appropriate lists.

telemarketing test A test usually conducted through an independent telemarketing service. Payment may be at a fixed rate per hour for an agreed upon number of hours. Test may be of an offer, a mailing list, a price, or a script. Some telemarketers will test 50 to 100 names on a list just to establish the correct contact for subsequent calls.

Teleordering A system under which bookseller (in U.K.) calls a publisher on a modem to place an order by computer. Invoices and orders are filled through the publisher's computer system with no human input. The computerized service is interfaced to the *British Books in Print* database and is also operational in a number of European countries, including Finland, Sweden, France, Holland, Denmark, and Italy. As of spring 1987, 310 U.K. booksellers representing 980 SANS (standard account numbers) and over 40 publishers representing 631 SANS were using the system.

telephone list In publishing promotion, usually either a list of customers acquired through a telemarketing effort or a mailing list with telephone numbers appended.

telephone list enhancement   Adding telephone numbers to a mailing list.

telephone list test See *list pretest.*

telephone marketing See *telemarketing/telephone marketing.*

telephone seed/telephone-list seed (telemarketing)   A fictitious name included in a telephone marketing rental list by the owner to detect improper use of the list. The seed is an individual who has agreed in advance to accept calls to that fictitious name and to record the name of the caller.

telepublishing Electronic means of disseminating information, in contrast with print on paper. See also *folio publishing.*

10 EOM cash discount   A cash discount for payment within 10 days of the end of the month in which billed. The larger national wholesalers have been giving booksellers this type of discount.

ten percent formula   A formula used by some trade publishers to establish a budget for advertising, publicity, and promotion of a particular new trade title during a forthcoming season. The formula: Book's net price times 10% times either the anticipated advance orders or the first printing.

terminal   A device by which information can be sent to or received from a computer. Operation is governed by a typewriter-like keyboard.

terms (booksellers)   Discount schedule and credit period offered to booksellers by a publisher. Terms may vary according to type of account and nature of order.

term test (journals)   Test of a journal subscription offer for two different time periods, usually for one year against a longer term such as two years. Some journal publishers have tested a one-year offer against a same-price offer good for two years; others have tested a one-year full price offer against a slightly discounted two-year subscription.

test, approach (direct mail) See *approach test (direct mail).*

test, color See *color test (direct mail).*

test, copy   See *copy test (direct mail)*.

test, envelope   See *envelope test*.

test, format   See *format test (direct mail)*.

test, letterhead   See *letterhead test (direct mail)*.

test, mailing list   See *mailing list test*.

test, market   See *market test*.

test, offer   See *offer test (direct mail)*.

test, package   See *direct-mail package test*.

test, payment   See *payment test (in mailing)*.

test, postage   See *postage test*.

test, premium   See *premium test (direct mail)*.

test, product   See *product test*.

test, response vehicle   See *response vehicle test (direct mail)*.

test, tactical (direct mail)   Tactical tests in direct mail are designed to evaluate variables other than the physical format of the direct-mail package. They include tests of lists or segments of lists, or of such factors as timing. See also *approach test; (direct mail)*.

test, term (journals)   See *term test (journals)*.

test, telemarketing list   See *telemarketing list sampling rule; term test (journals)*.

test campaign (direct mail)   Test mailings to a number of different mailing lists to establish which are the best, most responsive, or most appropriate for subsequent mailings. See also *mailing list test*.

testimonial   A quotation, usually positive, used in conjunction with advertising or promotion of a book. In trade publishing, quotes are often obtained in advance of publication by sending galley proofs. The testimonials are then used on the book's printed jacket. See also *review quote*.

testimonials (promotion) Favorable quotes included in space ads or promotion literature from user's comment about the product (book or periodical).

test list A mailing list under consideration or used for a test to establish its suitability or sales potential.

test list (direct mail) See *list testing; mailing list test sample.*

test mailing, dry See *dry-test mailing.*

test market One of a number of groups, audiences, or lists used in a test.

test minimums See *list test size rules.*

text 1. A textbook. 2. The body matter in an advertisement or promotion piece or any printed medium as differentiated from headlines and other display matter. See also *body copy/body matter.*

text, advanced-level See *graduate-level text.*

text, intermediate-level See *intermediate-level text.*

text, introductory-level See *introductory-level text.*

text, junior level See *intermediate-level text.*

textbook Also referred to as a text. A book used for a course of study.

textbook, college See *college text, textbook.*

textbook adoption See *adoption.*

textbook adoption reasons See *college textbook adoption considerations.*

textbook awareness sources See *college textbook awareness sources.*

textbook buybacks The practice of college bookstores buying back used textbooks from students after they are no longer needed for classroom use.

textbook buying season See *book rush.*

textbook decision month   The month in which an individual instructor or faculty committee selects a textbook for a course of study during an upcoming semester. See also *college textbook decision-making months.*

textbook discount   The publisher discount given for textbooks adopted for classroom use and ordered in quantity, traditionally 20%.

textbook edition   See *text edition.*

textbook publisher   Publisher concerned primarily or solely with publication of books for educational purposes.

textbook publishing   Publication of books for classroom needs. Less risky than trade publishing, since textbooks can sell for more than one year, often have established sales patterns, and can be reissued periodically in new editions. See also *professional and reference book publishing; trade publishing.*

textbooks, elhi   Textbooks produced for students in elementary and high schools.

text edition   Some books may be issued in more than one edition, a text edition being one designed to be used in a course of study and usually offered at short discount. The same book may also be issued in a trade edition that is offered at trade discount for resale through bookstores.

text paper   An uncoated book paper characterized by a relatively rough surface, opacity, and strength. Used for books, promotion pieces, and envelopes. The term "text" is derived from the fact that the paper was used mainly for the printing of books. Standard size: 25″ × 38″.

text reference   A book that can be used as a text by students in the classroom and as a reference by practitioners. See also *graduate-level text.*

text type (promotion)   Type composition forming the body matter of any printed promotion. Any such composition set wider than 60 characters or narrower than 20 characters may be difficult to read.

text type area   The rectangular area on a page on which all type composition appears, excluding running head and folio.

t.f. ad   See *till forbid (advertisement)*.

T4S   Abbreviation for trim paper four sides.

thematic catalog   A catalog dealing with books on a single theme, or in one subject area.

theological bookshop   Term used in U.K. for religious bookstore.

theoretical text   See *theoretical treatise*.

theoretical treatise   A book written at the frontiers of knowledge within a field, usually reporting on research by leading authorities. Such books are sold to libraries, to professionals in the field, and, in some cases, to graduate students as supplemental reading material.

third-class bulk rate   Special postage rate for mailings of 200 or more identical pieces and/or weighing 50 pounds or more, and meeting other special postal requirements.

third-class mail   The class of mail used for advertising and printed promotions as well as parcels or catalogs that weigh less than 16 ounces. It is also referred to by the USPS as Bulk Business Mail. Third-class mail receives deferred handling; this means it is processed and delivered after all other classes of mail have moved through the USPS system.

third-class mail, forwarding of   See *mail forwarding (USPS regulations)*.

third-class mail delivery standards   See *USPS delivery standards for third-class mail*.

third cover   The inside back cover of a periodical, catalog, or booklet. This is the recognized and preferred form, although some individuals prefer to use "Cover 3." The numerical designation is shown as "3rd cover" in all SRDS directory entries. See also *second cover; fourth cover*.

-30-   A typical ending for a news story, news release, or publicity release. Placed at center of page under last line of release. Favored most by writers with journalistic backgrounds. Most other release writers end their releases with "###".

30 Day Delayed Delivery Rule (mail order)   A ruling of the Federal Trade Commission, passed on February 2, 1976, relative to fulfillment of orders for books or merchandise to be shipped. Essentially, the rule states that unless shipment can be made within 30 days of receipt of the order, all advertising for the offer must clearly state the anticipated time of shipment. The 30 days begin when full or partial payment is received, or when, on a charge sale, the seller charges the customer's account. When shipment cannot be made within the period, the seller is obliged to inform the buyer by first-class mail before the expiration of the original 30-day period and to give the buyer the option of accepting the delay or of cancelling the order for a full refund. (Many direct marketers add the line "Please allow 4-6 weeks for delivery" to their promotions.)

Thor Information Services, Inc.   A leading broker for academic mailing lists, operated by list professionals formerly associated with *The Educational Directory.*

three-for-one formula   A system used by some book publishers to remove surplus inventory of slower moving backlist professional and scholarly books. Under the formula, inventory retained is three times the number of copies sold in a preceding 12-month period. Any surplus over that amount is disposed of.

three-page spread (advertising)   Three consecutive pages devoted to a single advertisement, or to a specific publishing project or offering within a catalog.

three-step promotion   A promotion scheme with as many as three distinct contacts with a potential customer. The first step may be a mailing designed to generate an inquiry for literature or a prospectus. Those responding would be sent full details of the product or service being offered. Those who don't respond to the second mailing within a certain time would be called by telemarketers. Such campaigns can be costly on a per-order basis and are profitable only for high-ticket items or for subscription products or serial publications. See also *two-step promotion.*

three-up   See *two-up/three-up/four-up (printing).*

till forbid (advertisement)   An advertisement placed with the instruction that it be run in every issue until the advertiser orders it to stop, or until forbidden to run. Such ads are called *t.f. ads.*

till forbid (subscriptions)   An instruction that a continuation order or subscription order be continued indefinitely until forbidden to continue. Then called a *t.f. order.*

till-forbid offer (book club)   See *automatic shipment.*

time (broadcasting)   A general reference to broadcast advertising, whether radio or television. The word "time" being synonymous with the purchase advertising time. See also *space (magazine publishing).*

Times Book Review   See *New York Times Book Review (NYTBR).*

Times Educational Supplement   A weekly book supplement published in the United Kingdom covering books primarily of interest to teachers in secondary schools. Sold on newsstands and in college and university bookstores. Published on Friday; carries advertising.

Times Higher Education Supplement   A weekly book supplement published in the United Kingdom for people in or interested in higher education. Sold on newsstands and in college and university bookstores. Published on Friday; carries advertising. Address: Priory House, St. John's Lane, London EC1M 4BX, England.

Times Literary Supplement   The most influential book review source published in the United Kingdom. *TLS* carries reviews on current fiction and nonfiction with especially good coverage of literary topics. Many university press and scholarly books are reviewed and advertised in *TLS*, which has a good readership in North America. Published on Friday; carries advertising.

timing (book promotion)   1. Any temporal or seasonal factor in a promotional effort that will bear on the outcome of a campaign. Such factors might include textbook decision months, the impact of holidays on mail delivery and the responsiveness of recipients, and the relative strength of certain months or seasons for mailings as reflected in earlier efforts. 2. A promotion so timed that if a test is successful, follow-up mailings to larger segments of the same audience can be made in prime seasons. Full discussion of timing factors in book promotion may be found in *Publishers Direct Mail Handbook,* ISI Press, 1987. See also *seasonality.*

timing (journal promotion)   See *journal promotion timing.*

timing (textbook promotion)   See *college textbook decision-making months; textbook decision month.*

tint   A pattern of dots that reproduces as a tone.

tint block   A block of solid color on a printed piece on which type or an illustration may be printed.

tip-in   A page pasted or glued into a bound publication.

tissue overlay   A transparent or translucent sheet placed over artwork for various purposes such as (1) a protective covering; (2) to bear copy to be surprinted; (3) to indicate a color separation.

title, selling   See *selling title.*

title, working   See *working title.*

title addressing   Addressing a mail promotion to a job title or job function rather than to a specific person by name. See also *job function (direct mail).*

title announcement form   See *forms only library awareness plan; notification slip.*

title of mailing (direct mail)   See *mailing title.*

title slug (direct mail)   A generic job title added to organization names and addresses on mailing labels, and used to direct a mailing to persons with a specific job title or function. See also *job function (direct mail).*

TLS   See *Times Literary Supplement.*

TMM   Textbook Marketing Manager.

toll-free WATS line   See *800 number (telephone).*

topping privileges   During auctions for reprint rights, the first bidder who establishes the floor or minimum bid has the right to top the final bidder when the auction has been completed. The topping bid is usually required to be 10% over the final bidder's offer in order to be accepted. See also *floor (reprint rights auction).*

total circulation   see *circulation, total.*

total mailing quantity (direct mail)   The total estimated number of names on the mailing list or lists to be used. The actual number of names may be significantly different, since list counts are constantly changing as a result of new additions and cleaning out of old undeliverable names.

total net paid   Total number of buyers of a single issue of a periodical whether by subscription or by single-copy sales.

tote bags   See *carry-away bags (exhibits and conventions).*

touch-up paints (exhibits and conventions)   Some exhibit and display units include kits of appropriate-color paints so that scratches or dents incurred during shipping can be touched up prior to the opening of the show.

tracking of results (direct mail)   Data collected on the results of a mail campaign. Tracking can indicate which lists produced a certain response and the quality of one list when compared with another. It can reveal the variations in pay-up rates from on-approval shipments sent to various lists. Tracking also reflects the responsiveness of various title slugs. All of this and much more can be obtained from tracking after a mail campaign, provided the mailing is designed so as to make this information easily accessible after all of the responses have been received and/or acted upon.

track record   A record of prior performance, usually measured in sales.

track record, author's   See author's track record.

trade (n.)   Often used as synonym for retail book trade. Sometimes also used in catalog listings after price to indicate a trade discount.

trade advertising   Any advertising done to support the sale of trade books to or through bookstores.

trade advertising media, primary   *American Bookseller; New York Times Book Review; Publishers Weekly.*

trade book/trade title   1. Generally any popular fiction or nonfiction book carried in the average bookstore or well-stocked public library. 2. Any book sold at a trade discount. See also *trade discount (bookseller)*; *professional trade book*.

trade book, children's   See *children's trade book*.

trade book jacket functions   The trade book jacket serves four purposes: (1) to attract the potential reader's eye; (2) to present pertinent information; (3) to express the tone and mood of the book; (4) to lead the reader into the text. Source: David Bullen, designer, in *Small Press*, May-June 1984 issue.

Trade Book Marketing   A guide to marketing of trade books with contributions by various industry professionals. Edited by Robert Carter and published in 1983 by R.R. Bowker.

trade book markets, major   See *major trade book markets*.

trade book wholesaler   A wholesaler of books who deals mainly in current general books of the type found in most bookstores or on the current fiction and nonfiction shelves of large public libraries. The largest is the Ingram Book Company, based in Nashville, Tennessee.

trade discount (bookseller)   Terms of sale to booksellers on current popular fiction and nonfiction—usually at least 40%. Also called *long discount*. See also *trade edition*.

trade discount (periodical)   A discount for periodical subscription agents or booksellers placing journal or periodical subscriptions. The discount the publisher will permit when remitting subscription payments. For scientific and scholarly journals, only a small discount is usually given. For broad-based and popular periodicals, the discount is much larger.

trade edition   A book intended for sale primarily through general bookstores and for the general circulation collections of public libraries. See also *trade discount (bookseller)*.

trade paperback   A book bound in a soft cover and sold through bookstores at trade discount that is produced in a format other than that of a rack-size mass market paperback. Most trade paperbacks are reprinted from the same plates that were used to print earlier hardcover versions of the same books. However, an increasing number of trade paperback originals, particularly in fiction, are being published today. Publishers reissue their own books in trade paperback editions or sell rights to these books to trade paperback publishers when the original cloth verison has achieved its projected level of sales. Trade paperback editions are also published when it is felt that a lower-priced edition may encourage classroom use. Occasionally out-of-print works are reissued in a trade paperback format, perhaps with the addition of a new introduction or preface. See also *rack-size paperback.*

trade publication   A periodical devoted to the interests of a particular business, industry, or vocation. Sometimes also referred to as *trade journal, business paper,* or *business publication. See also business paper/publication; journal.*

trade publishing   Publication of hardcover general interest books, both fiction and nonfiction, designed for consumer audiences and sold through normal book channels. See also *professional and reference book publishing; textbook publishing.*

trade rep   A publisher's sales representative who calls on the retail book trade. See also *library rep; sales rep/sales representative.*

trade show   A grouping of exhibits related to a specific trade or industry. Suppliers rent space to display goods or demonstrate services. Useful for display of books and periodicals that are of interest to the sponsoring organization. See also *book exhibit; exhibits, convention.*

Trade Shows and Professional Exhibits Directory   A reference listing over 3,500 events worldwide with essential information for exhibitors, including U.S. contact for foreign shows. Entries grouped by subject in a single hardbound volume. From: Gale Research Co., Book Tower, Detroit, MI 48226. Phones: 313-961-2242; 800-521-0707. See also *AAP Exhibits Directory.*

trade terms   See *terms (booksellers).*

trade wholesaler   See *trade book wholesaler.*

traditional market (books)   Those markets to which books are normally sold, such as bookstores, schools, and libraries. See also *nontraditional market (books).*

translation rights A form of subsidiary rights by which an originating publisher of a work grants permission to another publisher to issue the work in a language other than that of the original edition. The publisher purchasing the rights oversees and produces the translated edition and handles its own marketing and distribution. Where there are buyers for both editions in the same region, they may be sold alongside one another. See also *foreign publication rights; reprint rights.*

translations in international promotion Occasionally, promotional mail to foreign countries is translated into the local language. Caution is advised, however, since the recipient may erroneously conclude that the publication being offered is in his or her native language as well.

trap envelope U.K. term for a self-mailer, or a mailing piece capable of entrapping other mail. Trap envelopes are banned by the British Post Office. See also *entrapment.*

travel book publishing Generally, books that serve as guides for those who travel, both domestically and abroad. Some 28 million Americans travel abroad each year. While many books have their biggest season around Christmas, travel books do well all year, with peaks around Christmas, then March/April, and then again June/July.

traveler A term formerly used to identify publisher sales representatives who traveled from city to city and called on bookstores. The word "traveler" is still used to identify publisher college sales representatives who are commonly called *college travelers.* See also *Association of Book Travelers; Book Traveller; college traveler; commission rep; sales rep/sales representative; trade rep.*

travels well (book) See *book that travels well, easily.*

trial offer See *free examination offer.*

trim To reduce overlong copy. Also, abbreviation for "trimmed size" of a printed piece.

trim size The final size of any printed piece after trimming, i.e., cutting away excess paper so that it conforms to job size specifications in printed matter. See also *size indications in printed matter; text type area; type area; undertrim.*

tri-season schedule   The practice of a few publishers issuing new books and making sales calls on a schedule of three separate seasons, rather than the traditional spring and fall schedule.

TSM   Former name of the Technical, Scientific, and Medical Division of the Association of American Publishers. Division was renamed Professional and Scholarly Publishing Division in November 1979. See also *PSP; STM.*

TSM book   Formerly used to describe a technical, scientific, or medical book when there existed within the American Booksellers Association the TSM division for such books. When the divisional name was changed to the PSP division for professional and scholarly publishing, the term TSM book gave way to PSP book. See *PSP book.*

turn   Bookseller term for inventory turnover. See *turnover (bookstore).*

turnaround time (journals)   The elapsed time from when an article is written and when it is published.

turnaround time (mailing list)   See *list turnaround.*

turnover (bookstore)   The number of times a year stock turns over in a bookstore, i.e., the ratio of retail dollar value of inventory to yearly retail sales. A store with $75,000 retail inventory that does an annual retail volume of $300,000 is said to be getting four turns a year. This is the number of turns considered essential for successful bookstore operation, although few independent bookstores achieve it.

turnover (U.K.)   Annual net sales.

twig books   Advanced treatises and monographs with limited markets, deriving from increasingly specialized subbranches, or "twigs," of broader disciplines. See also *twigging.*

twigging   The proliferation of publications in progressively narrow, specialized areas of a scientific or scholarly discipline. A term coined by Curtis Benjamin.

two-color printing   The use of two different ink colors on a single printed job. See also *process printing.*

two-step inquiry   See *two-step promotion.*

two-step promotion   A promotion requiring two separate efforts to complete a sale. This is usually done for high-price or multivolume reference works. The initial step is an advertisement or mailing designed to generate an inquiry. The second step is a follow-up mailing, usually a detailed brochure or prospectus with sufficient detailed information to help complete the sale. See also *three-step promotion*.

2/10 net 30   See *cash discount (booksellers)*.

two-up/three-up/four-up (printing)   When more than one copy of an item is printed at the same time on the same sheet with a single pass through the printing press. Two-up means two at one time; three-up means three at one time, etc. After printing, the individual components are cut apart. See also *work-and-tumble*; *work-and-turn*.

two-year college library market   See *junior college library market*.

type, compact   See *kerning (typography)*.

type, inline   See *inline letters/open-faced letters (typography)*.

type, narrow measure   Type composition set to a narrow width. Studies have shown that body type set to a width of less than 20 characters is difficult to comprehend for most readers. See also *type, wide measure*.

type, outline   See *outline letters/open-faced letters (typography)*.

type, wide measure   Type composition set to a wide width. Ideal line width is considered 40 to 60 type characters. See also *type, narrow measure*.

type area   That area within the trim size of any printed piece on which type and illustrative material will appear. See also *text type area*; *trim size*.

type emphasis   When a word, title, or phrase is to be emphasized typographically. The three primary methods are: (1) italic; (2) boldface; (3) underscore.

typeface   1. A style or design of type, sometimes named after its designer. 2. The printed character left on the paper by the printing surface of the type or printing plate. See *sans serif*; *serif*; *typography*.

typefaces, readability of   Generally, readability is higher with roman (serif) typefaces than with same-size sans serif typefaces.

type high (relief printing)   The height of a unit of metal type from the bed of a letterpress printing press (.918″). With most composition now done by electronic or photographic means, the term is rarely used.

type page   Area of the page that type will normally occupy, margins not included.

type readability, rule-of-thumb for   The more quickly type is meant to be read, the narrower the column should be. Newspapers, for example, designed for fast reading, have narrow columns. Magazines have somewhat wider columns. Books have widest columns.

typescript   See *copy.*

typesetter   See *compositer.*

type shop   A business establishment that sells type composition.

type sizes, commonly used (in points)   6, 7, 8, 9, 10, 11, 12, 14, 18, 20, 24, 36, 42, 48, 72.

typewriter composition   Composition prepared for reproduction with a typewriter or similar strike-on device. See also *camera-ready copy; strike-on composition/direct impression composition.*

typewritten book   Generally refers to a book in which the composition has been prepared by a typewriter, often by the author.

typo   A typographical error made by the typesetter.

typographer   One who sets type. See also *compositor.*

typography   The selection and arrangement of type for use in printed matter. Also, the business of typesetting.

Tyvek® envelope   A strong, lightweight envelope produced by the DuPont Company and favored by international mailers because of the savings in postage cost due to its light weight.

U

U.K. and European distribution sources (1) Library suppliers/ jobbers; (2) retail and academic booksellers. It is important to note that all three sources are frequently one and the same, since retail booksellers are also library suppliers and academic booksellers. See also *European agent*.

U.K. and Europe distributing booksellers See *distributing booksellers, international*.

U.K. book distribution channels Retail outlets accounted for 85% of U.K. book distribution in 1985. Another 11% were distributed through book clubs, and the remaining 4% through other direct channels. Source: *International Publishers Bulletin*.

U.K. Booksellers Association See *The Booksellers Association of Great Britain and Ireland*.

U.K. book trade weekly See *The Bookseller*.

U.K. business reply mail system See *Freepost; Freepost address*.

U.K. CIP Program See joint entry under *Library of Congress CIP Program*.

U.K. direct purchasing organizations See *DPO (British)*.

U.K. equivalent of AT&T 800 telephone service See *Linkline 0800*.

U.K. equivalent of *SRDS* See *BRAD (British Rate and Data)*.

U.K. foremost book review medium See *Times Literary Supplement*.

U.K. foremost scientific journal See *NATURE*.

U.K. Freepost See *Freepost*.

U.K. high school mailing lists See *high school lists, U.K.*

U.K. largest bookshop See *Foyle's*.

U.K. library market for STM books See *STM library market, U.K.*

U.K. mailing entrapment rule In the U.K., the Post Office will not permit the use of self-mailers. Promotional mail as well as catalogs and periodicals must be encased in an envelope. The reason, according to the Post Office, is that mail traveling in an envelope cannot "entrap" other mail traveling in the same container.

U.K. mailing lists See *IBIS Information Services; MDMO*.

U.K. net book agreement See *net book agreement (NBA)*.

U.K. net price See *net price (U.K.)*.

U.K. postcode See *postcode (U.K.)*.

U.K. publication rights See *foreign publication rights*.

U.K. Publishers Association See *Publishers' Association (P.A.)*.

U.K. Times Supplements See *Times Educational Supplement; Times Higher Education Supplement; Times Literary Supplement*.

Ulrich's International Periodicals Directory An essential reference tool for anyone involved in book marketing or publicity. Carries a subject-arranged list of approximately 70,000 periodicals published worldwide, with such information as frequency, subscription price, publisher name and address, whether periodical carries advertising and book reviews, online availability, format, and services that abstract or index the periodical. Published annually in September by R.R. Bowker Co., 245 W. 17th Street, New York, NY 10011. See also *International Standard Serial Number (ISSN), origin of*.

unabridged The most complete version of a published work, especially a dictionary that may be published in different-size versions.

undeliverable mail See *mail forwarding (USPS regulations); nixie*.

underbid (n.)   Government agencies and other bulk buyers of books will sometimes invite bids from wholesalers as well as from the books' publishers. When a publisher does not wish to underbid wholesalers also bidding on the same order, the publisher will throw in a purposely low-discount bid that will not be competitive.

undergraduate text   A text appropriate for students enrolled in a course of study at a college or junior college.

underlined copy   1. Copy in body text that has an underline for emphasis or to highlight an important point. Used mainly in sales letters and in newsletters. Eye camera tests have shown that underlined copy in body text will be noted before regular text. 2. In copy markup, an underline is used to indicate "set in italic."

underlining in sales letters   Underlines (underscores) are used in a sales letter to call attention to important words, phrases, or sentences, or as a substitute for what might be set in italic or boldface, or to synthesize the letter's message for those who scan rather than read. See also *letter eye flow, personalized.*

underrun (printing)   See *overrun or underrun (printing).*

underscoring (typography)   1. A major means of typographic emphasis. 2. An underline in typed or keyboarded matter to indicate copy is to be set in italics. See also *underlining in sales letters.*

undertrim   To trim a finished printed piece to a size smaller than the trim size specified. See *trim size.*

undupe/unduping   See *merge-purge (mailing list).*

unduplicated audience   1. Audience not reached by any other mailing list or advertising medium in a promotion campaign or effort. 2. Resulting names after a mailing list merge-purge program.

UNESCO coupons   Coupons issued by UNESCO having a value expressed in various U.S. dollar denominations from $1 to $1,000. These are purchased and used to order U.S. publications by customers in countries with a shortage of foreign currency. Most publishers agree to accept these coupons as payment and subsequently redeem them with the coupon office of the United Nations Educational, Scientific, and Cultural Organization or UNESCO-appointed agents. UNESCO charges the publisher a handling fee for this which ranges from 3% to 5%, depending on the amount of each transaction.

unique selling proposition (USP)   1. A unique feature or benefit. 2. In promotion copy, the uniqueness of the offering in contrast with all other similar products currently available.

unique ZIP code   A five-digit ZIP code assigned to a single large office building, company, or organization with a high volume of incoming mail to speed up delivery.

unit cost   Cost per copy to produce a book. Obtained by dividing manufacturing costs by number of units produced.

United Parcel Service   See *UPS*.

units   A term used by some publishing professionals as a reference to single copies of books. Example: "We sold 1,250 units of [title]."

universal negative letterspacing (typography)   Removing space from all characters in type composition. See also *kerning (typography)*.

universe, direct-mail   See *mail universe/mailable universe*.

university bookshops   See *college stores (U.K.)*.

university bookstore   See *college store; college store textbook department; leased bookstores*.

university faculty names   See *college faculty lists*.

university library collection   A book collection designed to serve the needs of a university. Acquisitions, while meeting the needs of the school's curriculum, are focused on the needs of research scholars, with emphasis on retrospective scholarly materials and specialized journals. See also *academic library; college library collection*.

university press   A not-for-profit publisher of scholarly books and journals that is owned by or affiliated with a university or group of institutions of higher learning. Its clientele is chiefly academic and the decision to publish or not to publish is made by a committee of university faculty. It will take risks that commercial publishers would avoid. The concern is with books as ideas rather than as products. See also *commercial publisher; professional association book publishing.*

university presses, largest (1) Cambridge University Press (950 titles, 1986); (2) Oxford University Press (800 titles, 1986); (3) University of Chicago Press (256 titles, 1986); (4) University of California Press (225 titles, 1986).

university press publishing mandate The primary mandate of the university press is to make available the best of scholarly knowledge and important results of scholarly research.

university press scholarly book characteristics See *scholarly book characteristics.*

unjustified margin See *ragged right/rag right.*

unmanned display (conventions) See *unstaffed display (conventions).*

unpaid See *controlled circulation.*

unqualified reader A subscriber to a controlled circulation periodical who does not qualify to receive the magazine for free, but is nevertheless interested enough to pay for a subscription to it. See also *controlled circulation; qualified readership.*

unstaffed display (conventions) An exhibit at a meeting or conference at which no publisher personnel are present. The sponsor of the display usually will set up the display in line with exhibitor's instructions and with display materials supplied, usually on a table. Fee basis is typically a set amount per book, journal, or display item (brochure, catalog, etc.).

until forbid (advertising) See *t.f. ad; till forbid (advertisement)*

up See *two-up/three-up/four-up (printing).*

UP See *university press.*

updating of mailing lists See *mailing list maintenance.*

upkeep service (loose-leaf publishing) An updating service offered by loose-leaf publishers, who sell the basic volume and offer buyers periodical or annual updated replacement or supplementary materials on a subscription basis. See also *loose-leaf publishing*.

up-market book A book appealing to sophisticated tastes. See also *down-market book*.

upper and lower case (typography) Capital and small letters.

upper case, all caps (typography) Capital letters of an alphabet. Type set in upper case is more difficult and slower to read than type set in small letters. The word "case" is derived from the multi-departmented tray in which individual letters of handset type were stored, the upper part of the case being reserved for capital letters. See also *caps (typography)*; *lower case (typography)*.

UPS United Parcel Service, a major auxiliary medium for publisher book shipments that provides tracing capabilities.

usage agreement See *mailing list usage agreement*.

U.S. currency requirement (journals) A requirement by a U.S. publisher that international orders must be paid in U.S. currency.

used book dealer A dealer working out of a traditional-type bookstore who sells used books, usually at low prices. See also *antiquarian book dealer*; *out-of-print dealer*; *rare book dealer*.

used books, descriptive terms for See *antiquarian bookselling terms*.

U.S. Government Printing Office (GPO) Official printer and sales agent for publications of the Federal Government. Established March 4, 1861. GPO-sponsored publications include *GPO Style Manual*, *Word Division*, the *GPO Annual Report*, and customer service materials. GPO also operates 23 bookstores and disseminates its publications through 1,400 depository libraries.

USP See *unique selling proposition*.

USPS delivery standards for third-class mail Up to 150 miles, 4 days; 150-300 miles, 5 days; 300-600 miles, 6 days; 600-1,000 miles, 8 days; 1,000-1,800 miles, 9 days; over 1,800 miles, 10 days. (Note: The Third Class Mail Association, in *DM News*, February 15, 1987, reported that these standards were not met in 1986 studies.)

USPS Form 3602   A postal receipt issued by the U.S. Postal Service as proof of a bulk third-class mailing. Includes such information as weight per piece mailed, total number of pieces in mailing, the rate charged, and the name of the postal permit holder.

USPS mail forwarding regulations   See *mail forwarding (USPS regulations)*.

USPS mail size surcharge   See *mail size surcharge, USPS*.

USPS regulations   See *address line, USPS regulation for*.

USSR copyright agency   See *VAAP*.

USSR export and import agency for books and journals   See *Mezhdunzrodnya Kniga*.

uv coating   A resin coating, uv clear can be applied by roller coating or screen printing to protect a sheet of paper or to improve its appearance. An alternative to varnish and film lamination. See also *film lamination; varnish*.

V

VAAP 1. Copyright Agency of the USSR. Created shortly after the Soviet Union joined the International Copyright Convention in 1973. 2. Acronym for governmental association for USSR authors rights. 3. Transliteration (BGN) of VAAP: Vsesoyuznoye po Avtorskim Pravam. Address: 6a, B. Bronnaya U1., 103670, Moscow, USSR.

value pricing The price of a book based on what the publisher considers the value of its use. "You charge what you think the traffic will bear," according to Frank L Greenagel, former president of Arete Publishing Co. See also *pricing what the traffic will bear*.

Van Dyke See *blue (blueprint or blueline)*.

vanity publisher A firm that exists to produce books, whatever their subject matter or literary value, at the author's risk and expense. Sometimes referred to as a subsidy publisher, but not to be confused with a publisher funded in part by institutional grants or subsidies for scholarly purposes. See also *sponsored book*.

varnish A protective coating (sealer) applied to a printed sheet (such as a catalog cover) for protection and appearance. See also *film lamination; uv coating*.

VDT (video display terminal) Any type of input/output equipment that displays information on a screen. Usually a CRT (cathode ray tube), but also may be a LED (light-emitting diode) or plasma display.

vellum finish (paper) See *vellum paper*.

vellum overlay   A sheet of semitransparent paper, used mainly for protection or for color separations. See also *overlay (artwork)*.

vellum paper   A high-grade, cream-tinted ledger paper, with a dull, smooth finish, made to imitate parchment or vellum.

Velox   1. A photographic contact print made from a screened halftone negative. It can be pasted on a mechanical and used as line copy. Velox is universally used as the term for screen print since most screen prints are on Velox, a Kodak photographic printing paper. 2. Also a term used in some trade publishing houses or departments for co-op ads sent to booksellers in reproducible form, so-called because they contain a Velox or screened print of a book illustration. See also *PMT*.

vendor, library   A term of reference for either a library supplier or a periodical subscription agent.

verso   The left-hand or even numbered pages of a printed publication. See also *recto*.

vertical half page   Periodical half-page advertisement in which the longer dimension is vertical.

vertical mailing list   A list containing names of individuals within a single trade, industry, business, profession, or special interest. See also *horizontal mailing list*.

vertical publication   A publication that covers the interests or activities of a single business, industry, or profession. Periodicals serving a vertical market would circulate to individuals involved in various capacities within the field served. See also *horizontal publication; industry magazine*.

very fine (antiquarian bookselling)   An older book that appears almost brand new, but lacking the freshness of brand new. See also *antiquarian bookselling terms*.

video display terminal.   See *VDT*.

videotape, bookstore   See *promotional video*.

vignette   An illustration in which the edges fade away gradually so as to leave no definite line at the border. In printing production, edge dots in a vignette must have a value of at least 10%.

virgule   A diagonal used to separate alternatives as in and/or. Usually referred to as a "slash."

Vogele eye flow studies (direct mail)   Studies by Professor Siegfried Vogele, Dean of the Institute for Direct Marketing, Munich, West Germany, using eye-camera technology. The camera follows the movement of a subject's eyes as he or she opens and reads a mailing. At the same time, other cameras study body language and hand movements to determine subject's emotional reactions. Results of such studies were reported in the January 1987 issue of the Clark O'Neill *Indicia*. See also *mailing package eye flow studies*.

volume   A single book or one of the books in a set. In a very large scientific work, parts of a single volume may be bound separately—the parts comprising a single volume. In periodicals, a volume is all of the issues printed during a set period, usually one year.

volume discount (bookseller)   See *quantity discount*.

volume discount (space advertising)   A discount given advertisers by a periodical, based, usually, on the amount of space purchased in a single issue. See also *frequency discount*.

volume frequency, journals   See *journal volume frequency*.

volume frequency, magazine   See *magazine volume frequency*.

W

wafers, dots, seals   The pressure-sensitive "circles" or adhesive labels used to seal envelopes and self-mailers.

Walden Journal   A seasonal advertising handout produced by Waldenbooks and listing business books of various publishers in an illustrated newsletter format. Distributed free at 950 Walden bookstores "to customers with business interests." All illustrated listings paid for by the publishers.

wallet-flap envelope   An envelope with a large flap, which can be removed and returned in the envelope as either an order form or response vehicle. The printing is usually on the inside of the flap.

The Wall Street Journal   The most important daily print advertising medium in the U.S. for business, investment, or finance. Over 2 million circulation with numerous regional editions, including Eastern, Midwest, Western, Southwest, and Southern California. Advertising representatives and/or branch offices in numerous large cities from New York to San Francisco. New York address: 420 Lexington Avenue, 10170. Phone: 212-808-6700.

W&F   Work-and-flop. Another name for work-and-tumble. See also *work-and-tumble.*

W&T   See *work-and-turn.*

want (copywriting)   Building into advertising copy a desire on the part of the reader for the product or service offered, even if it is not needed. See also *need (copywriting).*

warehouse clubs   A specialized, growing area of book retailing. These no-frills warehouse sales operations sell popular brand-name items and bestseller books for cash at substantial discounts to consumers and small businesses. While the total number of such outlets is only between 100 and 200, annual book sales are estimated to be in excess of 100 million dollars. The largest warehouse club is the Price Club® operated by the Price Company of San Diego, California. It has 24 branches in California, three each in Arizona, Maryland, and Virginia, and one each in Connecticut, New Jersey, New Mexico, and New York.

warranty (direct mail)   A guarantee that the offering has been represented accurately and that the publisher will back up the product in case of dissatisfaction. People are reluctant to buy books without prior examination. Therefore, a strong warranty is prerequisite to effective mail-order selling. The strongest warranty is a free examination offer. See also *free examination offer.*

war stories, publishing   See *publishing war stories.*

waste circulation   That portion of the circulation of a publication that is not likely to respond to an advertiser's product.

WATS   See *wide area telecommunications service.*

wavy line (typography)   Used to underline a word to indicate to the compositor that it should be set in bold type.

WBIP   See *Whitaker's Books in Print.* See also *British Books in Print (BBIP).*

web-fed offset press   An offset press that prints from rolls of paper. It can be linked to trimming and folding machines for a continuous flow through to the finished piece. Web-fed offset, because of the high-speed capability, is two to four times faster than sheet-fed offset work.

web-fed rotary letterpress   A press widely used for the printing of newspapers or magazines, because of its high speed and capability of folding on the delivery end so that the newspaper is completely ready for the newsstand in a single operation. Book sections printed on a web can be delivered in signatures, ready to bind.

web-fed rotary letterpress, first The first press with continuous roll feed was produced in 1871 by R. Hoe and Company and installed for the *New York Tribune*. It turned out 18,000 newspapers an hour.

web-fed rotary letterpress, first four-color The first such press was made in 1890 by Walter Scott & Co., Plainfield, New Jersey, for the Chicago, Illinois, *Inter-Ocean*. It was placed in operation in 1892.

web offset A high-speed form of offset printing, utilizing paper fed from rolls rather than single sheets. See also *offset printing (offset lithography)*.

web paper A printing paper in a continuous web or roll.

web press A printing press fed from large, continuous rolls (webs) of paper. See also *web-fed offset press; web-fed rotary letterpress*.

weight The basis on which paper is sold; 60-lb. (or 60 substance) means a ream of paper in a certain size (usually 25″ × 38″) that weighs 60 pounds. See also *basis weight (paper)*.

wf Proofreader's mark for wrong font.

what the traffic will bear (pricing) See *pricing what the traffic will bear*.

Whitaker's Books in Print From 1988 the new title for *British Books in Print*. See *British Books in Print (BBIP)*.

white mail Orders not traceable to any promotional effort or source. The term is derived from the fact that such orders are frequently received on plain white sheets of paper. However, white mail may also include untraceable purchase orders or orders by telephone.

white page A blank or unprinted page in a book, catalog, or printed promotion.

white pages The alphabetical name-and-address listings in a telephone directory, as contrasted with the classified business-directory section, or yellow pages.

white sale, publisher's See *pre-remainder sale*.

white space   The blank space around text matter or illustrations in advertising.

Who Distributes What and Where: An International Directory of Publishers, Imprints and Distributors   A directory that lists over 6,500 publishers and their imprints, agents, and representatives worldwide in alphabetical sequence by company. Each entry provides: complete name and address, sales address, telephone and telex, cable address, the names of representatives and their territories, and names of publishers and imprints represented. A separate Geographic Index lists names of each publisher, imprint, agent, representative, and distributor according to country. A useful guide when seeking foreign distribution sources. Published by R.R. Bowker Co., 245 W. 17th Street, New York, NY 10011.

wholesale account   A publisher's book wholesaler account. Because of the sales volume involved, wholesale accounts are almost never handled by commission reps, but are served either by the publisher's sales manager or by an experienced salaried rep.

wholesaler (book)/jobber   One who buys books from publishers, often in large quantities and at favorable or maximum discounts, and resells them to bookstores, libraries, and other volume buyers of books at lesser discounts. The wholesaler also offers a variety of other services such as approval plans, continuation orders, reporting of unavailable books, cataloging and processing services, and more. Most wholesalers specialize in either bookstores or libraries, not both. When given the choice of being referred to as distributor, jobber, or wholesaler, the choice made was "wholesaler." This choice was made at a meeting of wholesalers during the May 1981 ABA meeting in Atlanta.

wholesaler, library   See *library wholesaler.*

wholesaler, medical book   See *medical book distributor.*

wholesaler, specialty   See *specialty wholesaler.*

wholesaler, trade book   See *trade book wholesaler.*

wholesaler electronic order systems   See *FIRSTcall; LaserSearch; One Touch.*

wholesaler preview programs   See *library wholesaler preview program.*

wide area telecommunications service (WATS)   A service offered by telephone companies in the U.S. that permits customers to make or receive calls in a specific area at a special rate. See also *800 number (telephone); inbound telemarketing.*

wide type   See *expanded type.*

widow (typography)   In typography a word or short line of less than (typography) a third of the line length at the end of a paragraph. See also *orphan (typography).*

Wilson indexes   The H.W. Wilson Company produces more than 20 indexes in various areas including the sciences, humanities, education, law, business, and publishing. Most are also available online and on CD-ROM as well as in print. Details from H.W. Wilson Co., 950 University Avenue, Bronx, NY 10452. Phone: 212-588-8400.

Wilson Library Bulletin   A monthly publication (except July and August) dealing with various aspects of librarianship. Reviews and evaluates reference books suitable for most libraries. The approximately 18,000 circulation reaches some 900 elementary school libraries, 6,500 junior high and high school libraries, 2,450 college and university libraries, 5,300 public libraries and branches, and 1,200 special libraries. Publisher: H.W. Wilson Co., 950 University Avenue, Bronx, NY 10452. Phone: 212-588-8400.

window display   A display in a retail bookstore in windows facing outside to attract customers into the store. Studies have shown that a percentage of browsers who come into a bookstore leave with a book purchase. One such study in the U.K. indicated a purchase rate of 1 in 15.

window display kit   An assortment of related display items for a major trade book, to be used for window or other display purposes. May include such items as window banner, cover reproduction or blow-up, counter card, and poster. Such kits are sometimes offered at no charge to booksellers who order a minimum number of copies.

window envelope   An envelope with a die-cut opening, usually glassine covered, through which the mailing address shows. It is a useful device for personalized letters, since the address on the letter, folded so as to show through the opening, eliminates the need for envelope addressing. See also *closed-face envelope*.

window envelope, open-face   Envelope with a plain die-cut opening.

window envelope, two-piece   Envelope with a piece of glassine, cellophane, or some other type of transparent material affixed over the die-cut opening.

wing mailer   A machine that applies certain types of mailing labels to envelopes, cartons, or directly on a book.

WIPO   World Intellectual Property Organization.

wire stitching   Stapling. See also *booklet; saddle stitching*.

WISP   See *Women in Scholarly Publishing*.

Women in Scholarly Publishing (WISP)   An organization of approximately 250 members, formed in 1980. Membership is mainly of women employed at university presses. Write c/o Stanford University Press, Stanford, CA 94305.

word of mouth publicity   See *publicity, word of mouth*.

word processing   The entry, manipulation, editing, and storage of text using a computer.

word processor/word processing machine   An electronic machine with a memory that stores text entered via a keyboard and has programs that assist the operator in locating and recalling any particular items and in making insertions and deletions. Today, stand alone word processors are being replaced in many settings by microcomputers running powerful word processing programs.

word processor letter   A letter prepared through a word processing machine. Process uses two disks—one containing the addresses to be used for mailing, and the other containing the letter. The letter is produced automatically by combining text with address information, giving the appearance of individually-typed letters. Letters and envelopes are produced on continuous forms, or feeding mechanisms, which are added to the equipment to permit insertion of individual personalized sheets and envelopes. Such letters are similar in appearance to a typed letter and can be printed in seconds, using laser techniques, jet-press, or impact printing. (Each has its unique qualities.) See also *personal letter; personalized letter.*

wordspacing The distance between words in a line of typeset matter.

work-and-flop (W&F) See *work-and-tumble.*

work-and-tumble To print both the front and back of a sheet from a single plate. When the sheet is turned to print the second side, the paper is inverted, and the opposite end becomes the gripper edge, which is used to pull the sheet through the press.

work-and-turn To print both the front and back of a sheet from a single plate. When the sheet is turned to print the other side, the same gripper edge is used as was used for pulling through the first side.

workbook An applications book to be used in conjunction with a textbook in a course of study. May include charts, review questions, forms, worksheets, self-evaluation sections, and grading rules.

work-for-hire In publishing, work contracted out to freelancers who are not compensated for such work as regular employees of the publisher. Copyright law requires that the commissioning party of work-for-hire be the owner of the finished work.

working the backlist A concentrated effort to increase backlist sales. In some publishing establishments, sales reps' bonus arrangements are tied to backlist sales, or to increase in backlist sales over the previous year. See also *backlist; backlist incentive programs (bookseller).*

working title A title supplied by an author with a manuscript and used by the publisher during the editorial and production phases of the book. Subsequently, the work may be published under a different title, usually for reasons of greater clarity, or for marketing considerations.

"World's largest subscription agent" A claim by the Faxon Company, Inc., a multidivisional, international periodical subscription agent.

wove envelope   Envelope made of a smooth, white paper some-what softer and bulkier than bond paper, but not as strong.

wove paper   Paper with a uniform unlined surface and a smooth finish. See also *laid paper*.

w.p.m.   Words per minute. In broadcast advertising, the recom-mended rate for greatest effectiveness is 80 to 130 w.p.m., with the rule-of-thumb being two words per second.

wrap-around   1. A wrapper bearing an advertising message and placed over a catalog or periodical. See also *jacket band*. 2. A cover design that continues from the front of a book around to the back.

wrapper   See *jacket*.

wrong font (wf)   Type set in a different size or font from that called for in the place where it appears. See also *font; wf*.

X

X-acto knife A cutting tool useful in graphics and design. Blades are available in various shapes, but the triangular pointed #11 works best in promotion applications.

xerographic edition See *on-demand edition*.

xerography A type of printing technology in which a negative image, formed by an electrically charged plate, is transferred and thermally affixed to a paper as a positive. The printing method was perfected and commercially developed by the Xerox Corporation. The invention is credited to Chester Carlson in 1937.

x-height (typography) The height of the lowercase x in any typeface. The height of x more closely exemplifies type size than does point size since x-heights may vary from one typeface to another. Typefaces with a large x-height have greater legibility than those with smaller ones. See also *baseline (typography)*.

x-line (typography) The top of x-height.

Y

YA Short for "young adult." An abbreviation used to refer to librarians serving and material published for young people between the ages of 11 and 18. Many YA librarians are members of the Young Adult Services Division of ALA.

YA book A book aimed at young adult children, or children in their teenage years. In make-up, some YA books are set in larger type and/or may have more spacing between lines of text. See also *young adult book.*

yardsticks for pricing and promotion The yardsticks for book pricing and promotion are "need to know" and "nice to know." See also *"need to know" (book pricing and promotion); "nice to know" (book pricing and promotion).*

year book 1. An annual reference publication giving facts, statistics, and general information on a particular subject; sometimes updating a previously published larger work such as an encyclopedia. 2. An annual volume devoted to a single discipline or area which digests the most significant and relevant literature of the preceding year. See also *annual.*

year-end bulge A tendency in some publishing establishments of crowding publication of a large number of books into the last month or weeks of a fiscal year to meet annual production quotas and fulfill fiscal budgetary commitments, or for other fiscal reasons.

yearly address change rate of college faculty (mailing lists) See *mobility of college faculty.*

yearly address change rate of professionals See *mobility of professionals.*

yearly price increases   See *price increases for inflation.*

yearly subscription cycle   The annual publication cycle on which a subscription is based. See also *journal subscription cycle; magazine subscription cycle; subscription year.*

year of licensure   An option on medical and dental lists of the American Medical Association and American Dental Association. For certain types of promotions, this information is often useful. For example, it is sometimes helpful when a mailer wants to reach physicians in their early years of practice.

year of publication (directories and annuals)   The year in which a directory, catalog, or annual publication is issued. It is important to ascertain year of publication when ordering mailing lists compiled from a directory, since such compiled lists are partially out of date by the time the catalog is issued, and they lose effectiveness with the passage of time.

yellowing   1. A defect that develops gradually in paper made with groundwood or unbleached pulps. 2. A gradual change in the appearance of paper resulting from the environment or aging.

yield   The overall anticipated return from a promotion. In journals promotion, for example, promotion yield is often estimated on the basis of five-year income from a subscription rather than the one-year value of a paid subscription. Factored into this yield is renewal rate. For a journal subscription with a $100 subscription price and a 75% renewal rate, the five-year yield would be $205.

you (in sales letter copy)   The second person pronoun "you" is one of the most important words in a sales letter. It should be used liberally in copy, not only to involve the reader, but also to point up the benefits to the reader of the work being offered. Examination of any successful sales letter will invariably show that it contains an abundance of the word "you."

you approach (in advertising copy)   Copy appealing to the self-interest of the reader. Considered the most effective type of advertising and promotion copy. In most successful advertising copy, and in direct-mail copy in particular, "you" is used frequently.

young adult book   Essentially any adult book deemed suitable for children in secondary schools (grades 6-12).

Z

z-fold, zig-zag fold   See *accordion fold; fan fold.*

ZIP   See *Zoning Improvement Plan.*

ZIP code   A five-digit numerical code that identifies one of 36,000 specific mailable areas in the United States. The first digit divides the country into 10 major areas, starting in the East with zero for New England and ending with nine for the West Coast. The first three ZIP digits identify a smaller area within a single state. The last two digits represent either (1) a postal zone within the limits of a major city or (2) a small city or town in which all addresses have the same ZIP code.

ZIP code, unique   See *unique ZIP code.*

ZIP code analysis   Evaluation of a mail campaign return by ZIP code to ascertain the most responsive areas.

ZIP codes, international   See *postal code.*

ZIP + 4   A bulk subclass of first-class mail under which a rate reduction is allowed for 500 or more first-class letters mailed at one time bearing the nine-digit ZIP + 4 code that can be read by optical character reader equipment. The code utilizes the standard five-digit ZIP code followed by a hyphen and an additional four digits. See also *first-class voluntary presort.*

ZIP + 4 state directories   A series of state directories, each listing all nine-digit ZIP code numbers for the particular state. In a few instances, adjacent smaller states may be grouped, for example, Delaware, District of Columbia, and Maryland. Price $9 each from St. Louis Postal Data Center, St. Louis, MO 63180-9988.

ZIP select   The computerized selection of specific ZIP code areas from a mailing list.

ZIP sequence   Names on a mailing list furnished according to numeric progression, by ZIP code, starting with the lowest numbers and going to the highest. See also *ZIP string*.

ZIP string   The merging of several small lists into one continuous or consecutively numbered string from lowest to highest ZIP codes. This avoids minimum charges on small list rentals, but does not permit tracking of the individual lists involved in the merge.

Zoning Improvement Plan   A five-digit system introduced by the U.S. Postal Service on July 1, 1963 to improve mail sorting and distribution. See also *ZIP code*.

Appendices

Appendix 1
10 Tested Ideas for Increasing Sales of Professional and Reference Books

1. Sell already published volumes in a series as a set at a reduced price.

2. Identify segments of large expensive works that can stand on their own and publish smaller works at low prices.

3. Combine related titles by different authors into sets at reduced prices.

4. Issue updated new editions of strong titles that have declined in sales as they aged.

5. Issue a low-priced paper edition of strong-selling hardbacks.

6. Conduct a seasonal, anniversary, or special occasion sale.

7. Offer discounts for multiple-title book orders.

8. Offer a special (lower) text price for classroom adoptions.

9. Offer a discount on books as a journal subscription incentive.

10. Offer a prepublication discount or a lower prepublication price.

Appendix 2
20 Mistakes that Diminish Effectiveness of Professional and Scholarly Book Advertising

1. Do not advertise a book as "new" if it is not of the current season.

2. Do not advertise a book without including the year of publication (and, if recent, also the month).

3. Do not advertise a book without showing a price or, at least, a tentative price.

4. Do not advertise a sci-tech or scholarly book without including its full subtitle.

5. Do not advertise an edition about to be superceded without giving some indication of the availability date of the new edition.

6. Do not advertise a symposium proceeding without identifying it as such.

7. Do not advertise a book at the existing price at a time when book prices are about to be increased without a cutoff date or disclaimer about prices being subject to increase.

8. Do not advertise a new edition of a book using an illustration of the old edition unless the covers of the two are similar.

9. Do not advertise a book with a mock-up illustration that does not reflect the true size or thickness of the actual book.

10. Do not include a book in an advertisement without including an ordering provision for it in an accompanying order form or coupon.

11. Do not advertise a book for which the copy is highly technical until it has been cleared with author, editor, or supporting data that ensures its accuracy.

12. Do not advertise a previously published book if there is unlikely to be inventory on hand at the time the advertisement appears.

13. Do not advertise an old book of little potential to please an author when newer titles on your list in the same subject area can do better.

14. Do not advertise a book without giving the exact page count or, if not possible, at least some idea of the page count.

15. Do not advertise a book in a series repeatedly when its sales have reached the levels of earlier titles in the series.

16. Do not advertise only one edition of a book when it is available in both cloth and paper editions.

17. Do not advertise a book during the summer months to academics or to professionals known to be doing field work or on vacation during that period.

18. Do not advertise a book as being available at local bookstores unless you know that it is actually stocked in bookstores.

19. Do not advertise a book in a professional society journal when the sponsoring society is already offering the book to members in the journal under a cooperative sales agreement.

20. Do not advertise a book in periodicals with a readership that has no interest in the subject of the book.

Appendix 3
Comparing Book and Nonbook Advertising Results

Consistently, in studies of readership made by scientific and engineering periodicals, book advertising has scored substantially higher for readership than other nonbook advertising in the same issues. In the example below, *C&E News* made a study of the five advertisers of black-and-white ad pages in a 1983 issue. Four of the five ads were from industrial firms; the fifth advertisement was that of a book publisher, Wiley-Interscience. Here are the study results:

Company	Noted Ad	Began to Read	Read Half or More	Information Useful*
"P" Chemical Co.	54.0%	15.9%	4.6%	25.0%
Wiley-Interscience	51.7%	31.1%	19.9%	51.1%
"V" Chemical Co.	41.7%	11.9%	4.6%	27.8%
"I" Metals Co.	39.1%	16.6%	6.6%	40.9%
"J" Corporation	39.1%	13.2%	6.0%	35.0%
Average for all 5 ads	45.3%	17.7%	8.3%	35.8%

* Based on those who "Began to Read."

Appendix 4

Recommended Format for Publicity Information Sheet

PUBLICITY INFORMATION SHEET

Name _____

Title of Book _____

Position _____ School/Firm _____

Home Address _____

Business Address _____

Date you joined present association _____

Active professional memberships _____

Community activities or area memberships _____

Name/Address of hometown/local newspaper(s) _____

Degrees obtained: _____

List each separately giving year, degree, school and location, and subject _____

Honorary degrees (with details) _____

Other books published _____

List title, year of publication, publisher. _____

Honors/Awards received _____

Date Completed _____

Appendix 5
15 Ways that Complimentary Copies Can Be Used as Aids to Marketing

1. To influential persons in the field as suggested by author.
2. To influential persons in the field as suggested by sponsoring editor.
3. To list of potential academic adopters compiled by marketing department.
4. To academic inquirers who request copies for adoption consideration.
5. To mail-order accounts for consideration toward a catalog listing.
6. To industrial training directors for possible use in training programs.
7. To appropriate book review media for book review consideration.
8. To columnists, feature writers, editors for possible story consideration.
9. To premium buyers for possible premium use.
10. To abstracting and indexing services for inclusion of contents.
11. To book clubs for selection consideration.
12. To foreign publishers for translation or copublishing consideration.
13. To book selection committees of library networks.
14. To specialist bookbuyers for large chains and wholesalers.
15. To buying offices of armed forces library services.

Appendix 6
10 Places Where Review Excerpts Can Be Used to Increase Sales

1. Advertising
2. Fliers and brochures
3. Book inserts
4. Book jackets
5. Correspondence
6. Sales letters
7. Sales presentations
8. Catalogs (sale, seasonal, general)
9. Convention and exhibit posters
10. News releases (especially in announcing a new edition)

Appendix 7

13 More Ways to Make Book Reviews Work for You

Copies of favorable book reviews should be routed to the following places to ensure maximum benefits from the review:

1. Publisher
2. Sponsoring editor
3. Marketing manager
4. Author
5. Advertising copywriter
6. Outlet managers—trade sales, library, special sales
7. Sales reps
8. Catalog accounts in field of book
9. International affiliates or copublishers
10. Booksellers/Standing order agency accounts in subject area
11. Librarians/Standing order accounts in subject area
12. Institutional news bureaus of college-affiliated authors
13. Potential new reviewers

Appendix 8

10 Ways that Library Approval-Plan Jobbers Learn of New Books*

1. Publishers' announcements/Mailed prepublication information
2. Publisher's catalog
3. Review galleys
4. Advance reading copies
5. Publishers' standing order plans
6. Ordering from publishers' reps who visit regularly
7. Publishers' production schedules
8. Monitoring of traditional review media
9. Monthly printouts of forthcoming titles from R.R. Bowker
10. CIP (Library of Congress Cataloging-in-Publication Program)

---

* From a 1982 study by two university acquisitions librarians that was based on responses from eight major domestic approval-plan jobbers.

Appendix 9
Directory of Major General Library Approval-Plan Jobbers

Academic Book Center
5600 N.E. Hassalo Street
Portland, OR 97213
503-287-6657, 800-547-7704

Ambassador Book Service
International
42 Chasner Street
Hempstead, NY 11550
516-489-4011

Baker & Taylor
501 S. Gladiolus Street
Momence, IL 60954
815-472-2444

Ballen Booksellers
International Inc.
66 Austin Boulevard
Commack, NY 11725
516-543-5600, 800-645-5237

Blackwell North America
6024 S.W. Jean Road,
Building G

Lake Oswego, OR 97034
503-684-1140, 800-547-6426

Coutts Library Service Inc.
736 Cayuga Street
Lewiston, NY 14092
716-754-4304

Midwest Library Service
11443 St. Charles Rock
Road
Bridgeton, MO 63044
314-739-3100

Scholarly Book Center
451 Greenwich Street
New York, NY 10013
212-226-0707, 800-223-4442

Yankee Book Peddler Inc.
P.O. Box 307
Contoocook, NH 03229
603-746-3102, 800-258-3774

Appendix 10
6 Ways to Publicize a Convention Exhibit

1. Add a box or several lines to your advertising in pre-convention or pre-show issues of appropriate publications inviting readers to visit your exhibit.

2. Include mention of your exhibit in your direct-mail advertising.

3. Send a publicity release on the highlights of your exhibit to the journal of the sponsoring society. Sometimes the pre-convention issue solicits publicity from exhibitors.

4. Mention the exhibit in outgoing mail to appropriate individuals.

5. Convention television: At some conventions, exhibitors may advertise on closed-circuit television beamed to all hotels in which convention registrants are housed. This may be useful under special circumstances.

6. Leave specially prepared news releases or other material in the press room, center for all contact with the working press at some of the larger shows. At smaller shows, the offices of the sponsoring association or society will sometimes serve the same purpose.

Appendix 11
27 Benefits of Booth Exhibits at Meetings and Conventions

1. To provide hands-on exposure of publisher's appropriate titles.
2. To introduce major new titles.
3. To take orders (and sell books at the booth where permitted).
4. To discuss potential textbook adoptions (and write up exam requests).
5. To enhance the publisher's image in the field.
6. To provide a "home base" for editorial and sales personnel.
7. To attract new authors by demonstrating marketing intent in their field.
8. To meet with and/or impress existing authors by having their books on display.
9. To demonstrate publisher interest and support of the sponsoring society or organization.
10. To obtain names for mailing lists.
11. To provide immediate answers to inquiries about your list, and about forthcoming titles.
12. To field and possibly solve customer service problems.
13. To provide training for in-house personnel.
14. To display encyclopedic and other expensive sets which would not normally be sent through the mails for examination.

15. To scout potential employees (or discuss new job opportunities).

16. To have opportunities to meet with and/or examine the competition.

17. To get away from the office for a fresh perspective.

18. To meet with field sales representatives in a central location.

19. To provide a convenient meeting place for reference work or journal board members.

20. To pick up exhibiting ideas and techniques for future consideration.

21. To prospect for leads and establish contacts with potential cooperative, catalog, and other special sale accounts among the exhibitors.

22. To demonstrate to friends of the authors that you are doing right by their books.

23. To enable authors to show friends and colleagues their book in your display and to tout it.

24. To elicit from authors additional marketing ideas or adoptions suggestions for their works.

25. To engage in dialog with attendees and direct their attention to specific books in your display that may be to their interest.

26. To provide an on-the-spot comparison for attendees of your books with competing works simultaneously displayed at the meeting.

27. To elicit international sales and ideas for marketing to international markets.

Appendix 12
19 Ideas for Attracting Attention to a Special Book at an Exhibit

1. Face-out display on elevated table on the aisle.
2. Special poster on book in booth or on aisle table.
3. Photo enlargement of jacket mounted on back wall of booth.
4. Pressure-sensitive sticker affixed to jacket with such words "New!", "New Edition," etc.
5. Bookmark or souvenir handout advertising the book.
6. Protruding book insert with message about special feature in book.
7. Display a giant replica of the book.
8. Special printed flier on the book.
9. News release handout on the book.
10. Have author present in the booth.
11. If author is at convention, have him or her refer contacts to exhibited book.
12. Display book in several different places in the booth.
13. Have flier on book distributed to attendees at pertinent sessions of meeting.
14. For certain types of textbooks, have a stacked floor display and be prepared to give free exam copies to interested inquirers.
15. Arrange for presenter of a related paper (if not the author) to mention the book and its availability during his or her presentation.
16. Advertise the book in the convention program.
17. Offer free copies of the book for a door prize or drawing.
18. Hand out reprints of a special illustration in the book.
19. Closed-circuit television advertisement to convention hotel rooms.

Appendix 13
Special Sales Questionnaire
(Model Form for Authors)

To enhance activity in its growing special sales department, a leading publisher of business and professional books now adds, with selected author contracts, a "Special Sales Questionnaire" that authors are requested to complete and return with their Author Questionnaire.

The questions are designed to produce information and leads that the special sales department may choose to follow up to cultivate cooperative or bulk sale arrangements for the author's book.

SPECIAL SALES QUESTIONNAIRE

_____ Is there someone in your company/organization who might be interested in a bulk purchase of your book?

☐ No ☐ Yes If "Yes" supply details and possible use.

_____ Is your book useful in conjunction with a specific product?

☐ No ☐ Yes If "Yes" supply name of product, name and address of manufacturer and/or distributor/dealer.

_____ Is there a mail-order catalog from which you buy books that you think might be interested in including your book?

☐ No ☐ Yes If "Yes" can you supply catalog name; name and address of issuer.

_____ Is there a professional association or society you know of that offers books for sale to its members and that might include your book?

☐ No ☐ Yes If "Yes" supply name and address of society.

_____ Do you see your book as having potential as a premium?

☐ No ☐ Yes If "Yes" provide name of potential user and reason; also contact name.

_____ Do you speak before special groups that might have an interest in your book?

☐ No ☐ Yes If "Yes" supply additional details.

_____ Do you teach a special course where your book may be used as a text?

☐ No ☐ Yes If "Yes" supply additional details.

_____ Do you write articles for special publications that might be potential bulk buyers of your book?

☐ No ☐ Yes If "Yes" supply additional details.

Title of Book _____

Prepared by (Author) _____ Date _____

City/State/Zip _____

Phone No. where reachable during business hours _____

Appendix 14
AAP Code of Ethics for College Sales Representatives*

1. Avoid making any improper inducement to any actual or potential customer, directly or indirectly, that can be described as a bribe, kickback or excessive commission, or fee in connection with sales activities on college campuses.

2. Avoid methods of payment that could appear to represent improper inducement to college faculty or administrative personnel. For example, payments made to a professor or college department, depending on the circumstances, may appear to be or may in fact be improper.

3. Refer to your individual company's code of ethics when determining proper conduct and response to any other questionable sales situation.

4. College sales representatives should abide by the highest ethical standards and act with complete integrity when dealing with customers and all college personnel.

---

*Voluntary guidelines prepared by the AAP Higher Education Division.

Appendix 15
Information Needs of Periodical Subscription Agents: International Study Results

In many parts of the world most subscriptions for scientific and scholarly periodicals and journals are placed through subscription agents. In September 1984, the STM* Committee on Scientific Journals issued a report, based on a worldwide study of subscription agents. Following are the STM recommendations to publishers based on that study:

Subscription agents want at the publishers' earliest convenience, but at least three to four months before expiration, the following information on renewals and new subscriptions:

- Rate per year or volume (or group of years or volumes)
- Currency to remit in
- Postal air/surface charges
- Trade discount
- Credit term

Other useful data desired:

- ISSN
- Subject classification
- On new orders, time required to begin the subscription
- Claims and cancellation procedures
- Use of UNESCO coupons

The desired format is an information sheet per journal or group of journals, or as part of the regular renewal notice.

---

*STM is the International Group of Scientific, Technical and Medical Publishers, based in Amsterdam, The Netherlands.

Appendix 16
Fundamentals of UNESCO Coupons: How to Understand, Use, and Redeem Them

Purpose

In many countries the shortage of foreign currency hinders importation of books and publications. In some of these countries, UNESCO Coupons, which express value in U.S. dollars, are sold for national currency to individuals who use them for foreign purchases.

Denominations

UNESCO Coupons are issued in the following values: $1, $3, $10, $39, $100, and $1000. "Blank" coupons held by the distributing body can be made available to buyers in amounts from 1¢ to 99¢.

What Products Qualify

Generally, all publications and materials intended for educational, scientific, or cultural purposes can be bought with UNESCO Coupons.

How UNESCO Coupons Are Used

Purchasers pay for coupons in their national currency. They are charged at the official United Nations rate of exchange on the date they make the purchase. Many publishers, booksellers, and other producers of educational and scientific materials accept UNESCO Coupons as payment.

Where Coupons Can Be Redeemed

Publishers accepting UNESCO Coupons may redeem them at the UNESCO Coupon Office, 7 Place de Fontenoy, 75700, Paris, France. A number of organizations are authorized to redeem coupons under the same conditions as the UNESCO Coupon Office. U.S. Redemption Office: Send to Bankers Trust Company, P.O. Box 2579, Church Street Station, New York, NY 10008.

Redemption Requirements

For purchases of books and minor school supplies no special documentation is required for purchases up to $1000. Over $1000, redemptions require a copy of the invoice.

Redemption Conditions

Although value of the Coupons is expressed in dollars, redemption is in the supplier's national currency at the official United Nations rate of exchange on the day of presentation.

Redemption Charges

UNESCO deducts a handling fee which must be absorbed by the supplier and cannot be charged back to the purchaser. The fee:

5% on amounts up to $100
4% on amounts from $100 to $1000
4% on amounts from $1000 up

Appendix 17
Journal Advertising Rate Card: Essential Ingredients

1. Name of journal.
2. General description.
3. Editors and affiliations.
4. Subscription price.
5. Frequency.
6. Circulation.
7. Rates for full and fractional pages and frequency discounts if applicable.
8. Mechanical requirements (if pubset ads are accepted, mention charges if any).
9. Closing dates.
10. Additional charges, if any for bleed ads.
11. Rates and availability of two- and four-color advertisements.
12. General conditions related to types of acceptable advertising and disclaimers for acceptable advertising.
13. Statement on advertising agency commission and cash discounts.
14. Name and address of advertising representative and phone number.
15. Name and address of production department and contact person with phone number.

Appendix 18
Tips for Improving Periodical Pay-Up Performance*

1. When renting subscriber lists of other periodicals, always ask for current paid or qualified subscribers only.
2. Motivate the debtor to pay by including a reminder about the value of having good credit.
3. When making a trial offer, back it up with a strong billing effort.
4. Make collection letters polite but firm; never attempt to antagonize.
5. Avoid using the same letter in a collection series more than twice.
6. Avoid a form letter appearance; typewriter typefaces give letters a more personal look.
7. Give the debtor a face-saving way out, for example: "Perhaps my earlier letters escaped your attention."
8. Use signatures on your collection letters that signify importance. Perhaps the editor or publisher first, then the circulation director, then the accounts receivable manager.
9. Adding a "Return Requested" to your mailing envelope can sometimes let the debtor know there is no place to hide—you now the letter was received.
10. Continue collection efforts only so long as income exceeds cost expended.

---

* Based on article by Rick Friedman in September 1987 issue of *Circulation Management*.

Index of Names, Titles, Companies, and Organizations

NAT BODIAN is an independent publishing consultant. Until recently, he was for 12 years a marketing head for various professional and reference product lines and encyclopedias in the Sci-Tech Division of John Wiley & Sons. His nearly 30 years in book marketing and bookselling includes management positions with various publishing establishments and as former head of sales for The Baker & Taylor Company. He also enjoys an international reputation as the author of a number of book industry references including the classic two-volume *Book Marketing Handbook*, *The Publisher's Direct Mail Handbook*, and *Copywriter's Handbook* (for advertising and promotion of books and journals).